OLD ENGLISH PORCELAIN

OLD ENGLISH PORCELAIN

A Handbook for Collectors

by

W. B. HONEY

*Lately Keeper of the Department of Ceramics
Victoria and Albert Museum*

Revised by

Franklin A. Barrett

FABER AND FABER
3 Queen Square
London

*First published in 1928
by G. Bell and Sons Limited
Second edition published in 1948 and
Third edition, revised, expanded and reset,
published in 1977
by Faber and Faber Limited
3 Queen Square London WC1
Printed in Great Britain by
BAS Printers Limited, Over Wallop, Hampshire
All rights reserved*

British Library Cataloguing in Publication Data

Honey, William Bowyer
  Old English porcelain.—3rd ed
  1. Porcelain, English—History
  I. Title II. Barrett, Franklin Allen
  738.2'0942   NK4485

  ISBN 0-571-04902-8

Taste must be informed and cultivated
as well as sensitive and discriminating

William Bowyer Honey in
The Art of the Potter

Foreword
to Third Edition
by R. J. *Charleston*

For almost fifty years now the late W. B. Honey's *Old English Porcelain* has held the field as the only satisfactory book by a single author to cover the whole subject of English porcelain of the eighteenth century and the early years of the nineteenth century. Some thirty years ago, when the present writer was first confronted with the necessity of learning something about English porcelain, the 1948 edition had just appeared, and was an obvious godsend to one so situated. In a rapidly changing world, here (it seemed) was one area of knowledge about which everything was known, and here was the book which uniquely put one in a position to master it. Since then, how much has changed! Mr. Barrett, in his Preface, has touched on some of these changes. Yet despite them, this book continued to have a value which rendered it irreplaceable in its field, and was constantly referred to with confidence by those who knew the limitations imposed by these latter-day discoveries. Its method was impeccable, the views propounded being always buttressed by references to the necessary literature; and the judgments expressed deserve the utmost respect even fifty years on.

These merits of the book (on which W. B. Honey's predecessor, Bernard Rackham, put his finger so accurately and aptly in his Foreword to the 1928 edition, reprinted here) have seemed to furnish ample justification for reprinting it now, with the corrections and additions necessitated by thirty years of subsequent research, ably supplied by Mr. Barrett, a friend of W. B.

Honey's and himself the author of three works on English porcelain. With these necessary adjustments, the book should look forward to a fresh long lease of useful life.

Contents

Illustrations

―――――――

xiii

BOW

xiv

DERBY

LONGTON HALL

LOWESTOFT

BRISTOL OR EARLY WORCESTER

WORCESTER

CAUGHLEY

LIVERPOOL

PINXTON

NANTGARW, SWANSEA AND COALPORT

PLYMOUTH AND BRISTOL

STAFFORDSHIRE

SWINTON (ROCKINGHAM)

Foreword
to 1928 Edition
by Bernard Rackham

The art of the porcelain potter—as practised in Europe, at all events—is frankly a minor art, but it is an art of which the products are very readily accessible to all who care to turn their attention to it. Even if all have not the good fortune to possess, or the means to acquire, specimens of old china, museums both national and municipal are so well endowed with them that a desire to enjoy their qualities is not difficult to gratify. But complete enjoyment even of specimens in a museum is not to be had merely by looking at them; even aesthetic appreciation can hardly be attained in this way, whilst to stop short at seeing and to ask no questions as to how or when or by whom these things were made is to miss a genuine intellectual pleasure. A work of art can only be enjoyed to the full if the circumstances of its creation are known and understood.

The handbook which it is my pleasure to introduce has just this straightforward and simple intention of enhancing appreciation of a very delightful if humble branch of English applied art. The devotees of old English porcelain, whether as collectors or merely as admiring visitors to museums, form a steadily growing body, and their first need is a manual which will give them reliable help in a study not altogether easy to the beginner. Just such help as they require will be found in the following pages. With constant reference to examples easily accessible in public collections the author explains the characteristics, technical and artistic, which distinguish the works of one factory from those of another. No statement is made that cannot be substantiated with good written or other evidence. Where plausible surmise must needs make good the lack of such evidence, the reasons for conjecture are clearly set forth and flaws in the argument are honestly taken into account—a noteworthy merit in a book upon a subject in the treatment of which sheer guesses have all too often slipped into the ranks of established facts and passed thenceforward unchallenged from author to author.

It is perhaps allowable here to draw attention to some of the features which should commend this book to collectors and students. The large volume of new facts which more scientific methods of investigation have lately established is here clearly detailed. Those who have been accustomed to turn for information to the older works on the subject will find here gathered together and summarized a quantity of new material—hitherto accessible only in recent volumes of several periodicals—from the study of which they will turn with fresh interest to their specimens, probably to discover that the classification of these will call for revision in many important particulars. Many of the suggestions put forward by the author are in the nature of pioneer work, as for instance with regard to the earliest wares of Bow, the dating of a certain much-debated class of Chelsea figures, the inscriptions on the 'Chelsea toys', the relation of the enameller Giles to the Worcester factory, and the classification of the various Liverpool porcelains. Recent discoveries relating to early Derby and Bristol are also discussed. Perhaps only those familiar with earlier books will fully realize the extent of the material newly published in these pages. Further, the author has confronted the difficult task of indicating the peculiarities of paste and glaze, the subtleties of shape and of painters' mannerisms, which need to be grasped and understood if the great number of unmarked pieces are to be assigned correctly to their places of origin. Even marks are shown to be untrustworthy guides, and the author draws attention to all those other questions which must be taken into consideration before marks can be accepted at their face value.

If the reader, when he reaches the end of this book, lays it aside with a feeling of perplexity, amounting almost to dismay, let him take heart in the reflection that the new methods of study advocated by the author are a challenge to himself to join in the excitements of exploration and discovery. He will have learned that there are more secrets lurking among the specimens in his cabinets than he had been aware of. It may be his lot, by attentive examination and comparison, to make his own contribution to the recovery of the lost history of this branch of English applied art. If his faith in marks is shaken by the disclosure that a red anchor does not always mean Chelsea or a blue crescent Worcester— parenthetically it may here be pointed out that the tables of marks at the end of the book include a number that have never been published before—he may continue undismayed his favourite pursuit; for his sporting instincts will be aroused afresh when he becomes aware that the task of selection and classification is not so easy as he thought. On the other hand, with this new work at his disposal, he cannot justly complain of the lack of competent and trustworthy help.

Author's Preface
to 1928 Edition

The earlier history of English china is still very obscure. Official records such as are to be found in the princely archives of many Continental factories are lacking, account-books have vanished, and local chronicles are usually silent, with the result that unsupported conjecture has frequently been accepted in the place of ascertained fact. New evidence has, however, been brought to light in recent years, and the useful test of chemical analysis has been more extensively applied. With this in view it has been my intention to supply a concise and up-to-date account of the first fifty years or so of English porcelain. With a few exceptions, nineteenth-century wares have been more briefly treated. In spite of technical excellence, the lack of variety in bodies and glazes and (as it still seems to us today) of artistic merit, make the later bone-porcelains comparatively unattractive to the collector who has any familiarity at all with the productions of the eighteenth century.

I have given the fullest references to the available documents, and it is important, now as ever, to bear these constantly in mind. Much is talked, and even written, of the *flair* of the expert, by which the make of a specimen may be recognized though no account could be given of the process of recognition. It is true that a sense of the whole quality and touch of a factory's work can be developed. But that power can only be acquired by familiarity with documentary pieces, and the evidence regarding these cannot be re-examined too often. For instance, the incised triangle was formerly accepted as a Bow mark, and the red and gold anchors were held to indicate quality and not date. Moreover, the anchor occurs also on Derby and Worcester china, and the expert's sense of dates and makes may have been derived from 'documents' as misleading as these. Again in Derby, figures of the 1760s were until quite recently mistaken for gold-anchor Chelsea, whilst those of the previous ten years were generally miscalled Bow or Longton Hall, and many false attributions have been made in consequence of these and other initial errors.

I have endeavoured to assist the student by descriptions of typical specimens, by pointing out distinctive features of paste, glaze, form[1] and decoration, and by references to important pieces which may be seen by everyone in the national collections. Of these, the series at the British Museum, by the inclusion of the Franks Collection, is especially rich in documentary pieces, whilst the Schreiber Collection at South Kensington is unrivalled for quality. Mr. Herbert Allen's collection, on loan at South Kensington, is remarkably complete, particularly as regards that later porcelain which is scarcely represented at all in the others. The student should constantly refer to these collections. It is of course not easy to give in words a really adequate notion of the peculiarities of pastes and glazes, or of a painter's touch. Actual pieces must be seen and if possible handled.

The illustrations to this handbook necessarily include types that will be familiar to the experienced collector; the rare and exceptional would have failed to give a true impression of the work of the several factories. And where subjects and models are so largely common to all, photographs can convey but a small part of the quality of a factory's style.[2] I have therefore not attempted the impossible task of giving an illustration of every type, preferring rather to reproduce a smaller number of pieces which seem to me most characteristic, or admirable as works of art, giving them on a scale sufficient to show something of their charm. For it is by aesthetic virtues in the quarry that the collector's pursuit is finally

1 In the index I have gathered together under some headings (e.g. 'teapots' and 'handles') all the references to peculiarities of form found in the different manufactures.
2 For a similar reason a list of the figure-models used at each factory would be useless for the purpose of identification.

justified, though delight in these may well be kept cleaner and fresher if it comes unsought in the intervals of another task, and for this last there can be nothing better than the difficult one of classification.

The importance of a study and comparison of the actual porcelain cannot be too greatly stressed. Collectors are apt to concentrate their attention on marks, though nothing is more likely to mislead. A mark may be copied, or even added to a piece long after its making, and can never be more than one of several items of evidence in favour of an attribution. The enquiries and disputes about the numbers said to have been used by the Bristol painters provide an excellent instance of the attractions and dangers of the short-cuts offered by marks. The study of the painters' styles is alone likely to be profitable. A painter's work should have as much character as handwriting, and no more rewarding task awaits the collector than the training of the eye to recognise a personal touch.

I wish to offer here my thanks to the collectors who have generously allowed me to reproduce specimens from their cabinets, and to the officers of the British Museum and the London Museum for facilities so readily granted for examination and photography. My wife has given me valuable help in the tabulation of the marks and in the preparation of the unusually long index. To Mr. Bernard Rackham I am particularly indebted. It was his enthusiasm and unequalled knowledge of the subject that first led me to study it seriously, and he has given me invaluable advice and encouragement whilst this book has been in preparation.

Author's Preface
to Second Edition of 1948

Since the publication of the first edition of this book in 1928, much careful research has been made into various aspects of English porcelain, chiefly recorded in papers read to the English Porcelain Circle, which had been formed in the previous year. The present edition has been revised to take account of these researches, and the fullest references have been given to the *Transactions* of the Circle and to other publications in which new discoveries have been published.

No major changes in attribution have been necessitated, but in a number of directions a new light has been thrown on the obscure places in the history of English porcelain. Among these may be mentioned the origin and early uses of transfer-printing, the earliest Staffordshire and the latest Longton Hall and, above all, the activities of the enamellers William Duesbury and James Giles. It has in fact become increasingly clear that a large and virtually unsuspected part was played by the independent decorators, not only in the earliest period, but in the late eighteenth and early nineteenth centuries, when a large part of the productions of the combined Caughley and Coalport factories was sold 'in the white' to decorators and London dealers.

In several directions too a new emphasis has been given, as with the recognition that only a very small part of the porcelain called 'Lowdin's[1] or early Worcester' could have been made at the former

---

1 Now known as 'Lund's Bristol' (F.A.B.).

factory. The attributions to Longton Hall and Liverpool are still uncomfortably conjectural, while the identification of the Worcester figures is still apparently incomplete. The existence of factories at Lambeth, Limehouse and Kentish Town has now beeen established, but nothing is known as yet of their productions.

As originally planned the book dealt but briefly with nineteenth-century wares, and no attempt has been made to alter this; the art of porcelain was essentially an eighteenth-century art, and the limitation of scope implied by the title has been interpreted accordingly. Nor has it been thought desirable to expand the book to deal more fully with the aesthetic values of the wares or their place in ceramic history. The book was, and is, an attempt to provide the collector with a guide to the classification and identification of the various makes of English porcelain, with the fullest references to the documents and to trustworthy literature.

All the original illustrations have been retained; and sixteen further pages of plates, figuring some twenty-four objects, have been added.

W. B. HONEY
Victoria and Albert Museum
South Kensington

September 1946

Preface
to Third Edition

by Franklin A. Barrett

William Bowyer Honey's *Old English Porcelain* has been the foremost standard work on the subject since its first appearance in 1928. Combining scholarship with a deep aesthetic sense, it not only provides a comprehensive account of the eighteenth- and early nineteenth-century English porcelain factories and their products but, in a masterly introduction, describes their work and achievements within the context of European ceramics as a whole.

In his preface to the 1948 edition, Mr. Honey made no apology for largely confining his account to the period up to about 1860: the art of porcelain, he said, was essentially an eighteenth-century art, and his title implied this limitation. In revising the text, I saw no reason to depart materially from the plan laid down by Mr. Honey, nor substantially to extend the period covered by the book. It is true that at the present time, partly due to the increasing scarcity of early examples of English porcelain, and partly to a greater appreciation of ceramics after that date, much attention is being paid to the work of our Victorian forebears in this and other fields. It is also true, however, that the whole approach to ceramic manufacture, as well as to its social and industrial context, changed with the rapid development of large-scale industry and commerce during the nineteenth century. And the general imposition of current fashions, through the Great Exhibition and in other ways, combined with the almost universal adoption of the English bone-china body, robbed these later productions of the distinctiveness and variety attained by English porcelain during the first hundred years of its manufacture. This is not to say that the later porcelains are without significance. On the contrary, there is to be found in their study a valuable commentary upon the development of art and industry, as well as upon the social scene during the latter half of the century. But such a study is essentially different from that essayed so successfully by Mr. Honey—a study that has already attracted the attention of a number of specialists whose works are available for reference.

In introducing his bibliography, Mr. Honey remarked upon the lack of trustworthy books on the subject. The situation is vastly different today. Interest in old English pottery and porcelain is no longer the hobby of the few and the business of museums only. Through the agency of the latter and the works of numerous authorities, of whom W. B. Honey was one of the most distinguished, a wide public has been educated and has become knowledgeable about our ceramic heritage. The English Ceramic Circle, of which he was himself a prominent member, has done much to encourage investigation and research into the history and problems of English ceramics, and the pages of its *Transactions* are a mine of information for all who write upon the subject. Each in their own particular field, specialists have in recent years imparted the results of their work in book form. One thinks of Dr. Bernard Watney's remarkable discovery of the documents relating to Longton Hall that has so satisfactorily filled the gap in our knowledge of that factory; or of the many contributions to our knowledge that flowed from the indefatigable investigation of old wills and other documents by the late Aubrey Toppin, among them the disclosure of the names of the Bristol proprietors and the facts of the Bristol-Worcester relationship, which dispelled the speculation of years. There are many other instances one could name. The museums, too, have continued to advance our knowledge, perhaps the most noteworthy event being the exhibition of documentary Bow china at the British Museum in 1959, which focussed attention on this factory and brought to light a great deal of new information concerning its early proprietors and history. Prior to this, Mr. Honey's observation that 'the materials for a history of Bow are indeed of the scantiest' was only too accurate.

In a different field we may recall the collaboration of the late Arthur Lane and Robert Charleston that did so much to clarify our minds over the 'Girl-in-a-Swing' factory. The bicentenary of the Worcester factory in 1951 was the occasion for an important exhibition of its early polychrome wares. It provided a unique opportunity to view in one place almost the whole range of Dr. Wall-period coloured porcelain. It is of particular interest that two private collections which contributed largely to this exhibition, those of the late C. W. Dyson Perrins and of the late H. Rissik Marshall, are now on permanent exhibition, the former at the Worcester China Works' Dyson Perrins Museum, and the latter at the Ashmolean Museum in Oxford. Together they provide an unequalled opportunity for the intimate study of the wares both of Worcester and of its predecessor at Bristol.

Since the 1939–45 war, museums throughout the country have increased the scope of their ceramic collections, partly through the benefactions of collectors and other donors, and partly with the financial aid of the National Art-Collections Fund. The latter has been of special value to some provincial museums. The Derby Museum and Art Gallery collection of china made in that town, which was formerly lacking in the early Derby wares and can now be counted as one of the most representative in the country, is but one example.

The understanding and appreciation of old English porcelain has, therefore, been greatly enlarged in recent years for a variety of reasons, and a new edition of this standard work was clearly desirable. In preparing the new edition my aim has been to retain as much as possible of the original text, and to preserve the individual character of the book, whilst at the same time incorporating newly discovered facts and fresh viewpoints to bring it up to date. Obviously, in a comprehensive work of this character, the amount of detail that can be included has to be restricted, but readers desiring further information will find full reference in the text to such sources as may provide it.

Our knowledge of the history and work of the English china factories may be expected to continue to grow, and certainly the field open to future researchers is a wide one. It is noticeable that, although much progress has been made with regard to the major factories, the information available to us concerning, for instance, most of the factories included by Mr. Honey in chapter 17 (Miscellaneous Factories, etc.) has increased hardly at all. In the case of Limehouse, for example, whilst the approximate site of the factory has been located and some names have been suggested as possible proprietors, we appear to be little nearer to identifying its products. Perhaps the future will lift the veil of obscurity that surrounds these factories. The discoveries on the 'Pomona' site at Newcastle-under-Lyme are encouraging in this respect. Meanwhile, as regards the major factories, the attribution to particular potteries of the productions of the Liverpool group has been much advanced by Dr. Knowles Boney, Mr. Alan Smith and Dr. Bernard Watney, and the latter's promised monograph on these factories is eagerly awaited. The crediting of the early Derby figures to Andrew Planché, though not disputed, is, to be honest, supported by slender and circumstantial evidence and more concrete facts concerning Planché's share in the Derby factory's activities would be welcome. The virtual absence of recognised pre-Duesbury table wares remains to be satisfactorily explained. The Bow factory is now, thanks to the 1959 exhibition and to the work of Dr. Ainslie, Mr. Hugh Tait and others, much better documented and understood. Mr. Henry Sandon's excavations at Worcester on the site of Warmstry House have yielded a rich harvest of wasters that have yet to be fully classified and examined—work that is still proceeding. They have been well described by him in his book on the subject. Confirmation of Mr. Geoffrey Godden's earlier inspired hypothesis that certain blue-printed wares long thought to be from the Salopian factory at Caughley were in fact made at Worcester, was furnished by sherds disinterred on the Warmstry House site. It is hoped that further light may be thrown upon the earliest Worcester productions, at present confused with those of Benjamin Lund at Bristol, by the results of this excavation or subsequent ones.

A new and perhaps surprising source of information concerning the early pottery and porcelain factories is that of contemporary insurance policies, and Mrs. Elizabeth Adam's work in this field is likely to result in the reassessment of some aspects of ceramic history.

All these developments, together with many others, are dealt with in the new text. It has been my privilege to assemble from these and many other sources the material for this revision, and to marry this wealth of new information to the original text; and I gratefully acknowledge the contribution of all those whose labours and interest have, in various ways, enabled the results of their work to be made public. Without them this new edition could not have appeared.

References in the original text to certain private collections then extant have posed something of a problem. Some have been dispersed, some have found permanent homes in various public collections. Where possible, an indication is given on page 412 of the location of these collections at the present time.

The publishers have arranged for a considerable number of new and additional illustrations to illustrate the text, including four in colour, and in selecting the subjects for these regard has been had to pieces which Mr. Honey considered to be of particular interest or sufficient importance to mention specifically in the text. The unity of text and illustrations apparent in the earlier editions has thereby been maintained.

The thanks of all lovers of English porcelain are due to Mr. Honey's widow for agreeing so willingly to this revision of her late husband's work. To the publishers, and to Mr. Giles de la Mare in particular, I am more than grateful for their encouragement in the carrying through of this project, and I acknowledge especially the patience and helpfulness of Mr. Robert Charleston and his staff at the Victoria and Albert Museum in dealing with my numerous queries and providing much valuable advice and information.

My thanks are also due to the owners of the pieces now illustrated that come from private collections, and to the museum authorities who have taken so much trouble to provide excellent photographs for illustrations: their names are included in the captions to the plates.

Finally, may I say that the work involved in the preparation of this revision has to no little extent been a labour of love, enabling me to repay in some small degree the debt which I owe to one who, in my early days as a collector and author, gave unstinted encouragement in the midst of a busy life, besides bequeathing to all of us his own unique contribution to the literature of English ceramics.

FRANKLIN A. BARRETT
Church Stretton, Salop

February 1977

Chapter 1

Introduction

The history of the earliest English porcelain[1] belongs to that of the numerous attempts made in Europe, from the sixteenth century onwards, to discover a secret for long known only to the Chinese. Attempts of this kind are believed to have been made at one of the Venetian glass-works at least as early as the end of the fifteenth century, but the first European factory to achieve any considerable measure of success was that established at Florence in 1568 by Francesco de' Medici. The material produced there was the first example of the type now known as artificial or soft-paste[2] porcelain, obtaining the quality of translucency from the presence of a substance of the character of an actual glass or frit,[3] and not

1 The word porcelain is apparently derived from the Italian *porcellana*, a cowrie-shell, literally, a little pig. Marco Polo, who reported porcelain in China in the fourteenth century, used the word for both porcelain and shell.

2 The name soft-paste is sometimes held to refer to the relative fusibility of the porcelain, distinguishing it from the highly refractory body of hard-paste, which requires a 'hard fire' to vitrify it. But its softness in material is equally characteristic, and the name has passed into common usage in this sense.

3 In the early manufactures the ingredients forming the glass, sometimes with actual broken glass (cullet), were subjected to a preliminary fusing or 'fritting' (the root of the word is the same as in *frying* and *fritter*), and the resulting substance was powdered before the admixture of the clay or chalk which gave the paste its 'body' and the resulting china its whiteness. The purpose of this was to 'fix' the alkali in the mixture, which would otherwise have crystallised on the drying of the piece and caused it to crumble: see the articles by Donald A. MacAlister in *The Burlington Magazine*, LI (1927), pp. 134–77, LIII (1928), p. 140, and LIV (1929), p. 192, which give a very full account of the materials used in soft-paste manufacture and their chemical properties. The Handbook to the Jermyn Street Collection (1893) also gives much useful information on the subject.

from the use of the fusible natural silicate of alumina (*petuntse* or china-stone, or feldspar) which combines with china-clay (*kaolin*) to form true porcelain of Chinese type. The characteristic hardness of the latter is such that any ordinary steel file will not readily scratch it. Soft-paste, on the contrary, is easily cut or filed; it has usually but not invariably a sugary fracture, unlike the conchoidal or flinty fracture of true porcelain.[1] Soft-paste is relatively porous and may absorb liquids and so become stained; hard-paste is impervious. In true porcelain the feldspathic glaze material is akin to the body[2] and may be fired with it; in soft-paste a lead glaze is added at a second firing in a 'glost' kiln, at a lower temperature. The glaze of the early soft-paste made at Chantilly in France contained a considerable quantity of oxide of tin, the characteristic ingredient which gave whiteness as well as opacity to the glaze of *maiolica*, Delft earthenware and other *faïence*, which is called on this account *tin-enamelled* (or familiarly, *enamelled*). It is probable that varying small quantities of tin-oxide were used also in many English soft-paste glazes: the formula for the Worcester glaze offered to Derby by Richard Holdship[3] in fact included 'tin-ashes', and the early Chelsea glaze often has a milkiness suggesting its use.[4] The hard-paste glaze specified by Richard Champion of Bristol also included it.

The importation of tea by the East India Companies in the seventeenth century, with teapots and cups of Chinese porcelain, gave a new impetus to the search for the secret of the Chinese manufacture, but it was not until 1709 that it was re-discovered in Europe by Johann Friedrich Böttger at Meissen, near Dresden in Saxony, and in the course of the next sixty or seventy years the method was passed on to many other factories in Germany. Meanwhile, in France, soft-paste porcelain is said to have been

1 In his evidence before the House of Commons, Richard Champion, speaking of his hard-paste porcelain, is quoted by Owen (p. 117) as saying 'the *Seve* and several other kinds [of soft-paste] . . . when they are broke seem as dry as a Tobacco Pipe, that is the case with all the *English* China; but the *Dresden*, the *Bristol* and the *Asiatic*, China, have when broken a moist and lucid appearance.'

2 It is, in fact, found in association with it, and is the same material a stage removed in the process of decay.

3 See p. 248.

4 Since confirmed by analysis: J. V. G. Mallet, 'A Chelsea Talk', in *Transactions E.C.C.*, vol. 6, part I, p. 15.

made for a short time by Edme and Louis Poterat at Rouen about
1673, and in the first half of the following century factories were in
existence at Chantilly, Mennecy, Saint-Cloud and Vincennes. The
last-named was in 1756 transferred to Sèvres, having become the
Royal factory, protected by high customs duties and the rights of
monopoly. Soft-paste remained the characteristic French porcelain
of the eighteenth century, and though true porcelain began to be
made at Sèvres from 1769, the manufacture of the *pâte tendre* was
not entirely discontinued until 1804.

In England, John Dwight of Fulham claimed in 1671 to have
discovered 'the mistery of transparent earthenware, commonly
knowne by the names of porcelaine or china'; but the material
made by him was almost certainly a thin stoneware,[1] and no
porcelain of English manufacture can be ascribed to a date earlier
than 1744.[2] A patent for the manufacture of porcelain was in fact
taken out in that year by Edward Heylyn and Thomas Frye (who
later, in 1748, became the manager of the factory at Bow), but no
specimens made as early as this have been certainly identified
amongst those surviving. The earliest date recorded in a mark or
inscription (1745) occurs on specimens of the 'goat-and-bee' jugs
from the Chelsea factory.[3] By the middle of the century the Bow
and Chelsea factories appear to have been well established, and

---

1 Certain white porcelain mugs of a form common in Fulham stoneware were
formerly ascribed to Dwight's manufacture. Similarly, an English origin has been
claimed for some white porcelain cups of the same *form* as a stoneware specimen
made by Francis Place (d. 1728) at York. This specimen, at South Kensington, is
accompanied by a certificate in Horace Walpole's handwriting declaring it to be of
'Mr. Francis Place's china': clear evidence of the loose way in which this word was
used. See also Aubrey Toppin, 'Francis Place', in *Transactions E.C.C.,* vol. 3, part
I, pp. 65–8 and Richard E. G. Tyler, 'Francis Place's Pottery', *loc. cit.,* vol. 8, part
2, pp. 203–12, where three authenticated Place salt-glazed stoneware mugs are
identified at the Patrick Allan-Fraser Art College, Arbroath. These white cups
and mugs, however, are all of Chinese origin, of the so-called *blanc-de-Chine,* from
Têhua in the province of Fukien, made to order in European shapes. Chinese
specimens in both these forms may be seen in the Museum at South Kensington.
The 'glass-house clay' mentioned in 1686 by Dr. Plot, Dwight's friend and
contemporary (see D. A. MacAlister, LI, p. 139), was not used in the making of
artificial porcelain in glass-works, but for the crucibles or pots in which glass was
melted. Opaque white glass normally owes its opacity to oxide of tin or arsenic
and not to the presence of white clay.
2 The date 1742, erroneously stated by Church (p. 30) to be inscribed on an inkstand of Bow porcelain in the Willett Collection at Brighton, is actually '*1752*'.
3 See p. 16.

others, also making soft-paste porcelain, were soon in existence at Bristol, Worcester, Derby, Longton Hall, Liverpool and Lowestoft. These were all conducted by private enterprise, unlike those of the Continent, which were usually subsidized by royal or princely households.

Soft-paste porcelain is of a fragile nature. Not only is the finished product liable to crack at the touch of hot liquids, but it was prone to collapse or lose shape in the kiln, even at the comparatively low temperature required for its firing. Its manufacture was therefore unlikely to prove commercially profitable, and the efforts of English potters were directed to the production of a material less unstable in the kiln and more durable in use. At Bow, a novel ingredient in the ash of calcined bones was used with the effect of strengthening the porcelain, and the productions of that factory and of its offshoot Lowestoft were more largely of the character of 'useful wares'. The risk of breakage from sudden changes of temperature was also considerably reduced by the inclusion in the paste of soapstone (steatite), a substance first employed in England[1] at a Bristol factory, and later the distinctive ingredient of the porcelain made at Worcester, where useful wares always formed a large part of the total output. Soapstone porcelain, which at times approaches true feldspathic porcelain in hardness to the file, was also made for a time at Liverpool and at Caughley, both offshoots of the Worcester factory.

The Chinese method of making hard-paste porcelain was independently re-discovered in England before 1768 and patented in that year by William Cookworthy of Plymouth, whose establishment was transferred in 1770 to Bristol, and three years later purchased by Richard Champion. This manufacture was a precarious one commercially, and unable without subsidy or protection or fashionable patronage to withstand the competition of the cream-coloured earthenware made in Staffordshire in the flourishing industry led by Josiah Wedgwood. In 1781 the patent

---

1 In China, a 'slippery stone' (*hua shih*) was used in the manufacture of the so-called 'Chinese soft-paste' porcelain, which is a decidedly hard feldspathic material, quite distinct from European soft-paste; but this 'slippery stone' has lately been declared to be pegmatite, not steatite: compare E. Morton Nance, 'Soaprock Licences', in *Transactions E.C.C.*, III (1935), p. 73.

rights in hard-paste and its materials were sold to a company of Staffordshire potters. The manufacture was gradually discontinued, and by the second decade of the nineteenth century true hard-paste had virtually ceased to be manufactured in England.

Experiments had meanwhile been made, towards the end of the eighteenth century, by the second Josiah Spode of Stoke-on-Trent, by which the essential ingredients of hard-paste were combined in a certain proportion with bone-ash, the same material that had first been used, as already stated, nearly fifty years before as a strengthening ingredient in the soft porcelain of Bow, as well as later in those of Lowestoft, Liverpool, Chelsea and Derby.[1] Spode's hybrid composition, which proved a manageable one, was soon generally adopted, and during the nineteenth century Staffordshire bone-porcelain[2] followed Staffordshire cream-coloured earthenware in supplying a world-wide market.

Though Spode's hybrid bone-porcelain remained the English standard, a glassy soft-paste of very beautiful quality but exceedingly unstable in the kiln was made between 1813 and 1817 at Nantgarw and Swansea in Wales, and to some extent at Coalport in Shropshire, from the recipe of its inventor, William Billingsley. Amongst the few unusual bodies, introduced for special purposes, may be mentioned the unglazed 'Parian porcelain', so called from its resemblance to the Parian marble of antiquity, introduced in about 1845 by the Staffordshire firm of Copeland, Spode's successors at Stoke-on-Trent, and soon adopted by several others. 'Parian' was composed of the ingredients of true porcelain in slightly altered proportions. Like the earlier 'biscuit' of the Derby factory, which it imitated, it was used principally for figures and plastic work. The 'stone china' and 'ironstone china', respectively introduced in 1805 by Spode and patented by the Masons of Lane

1 Appendix B shows clearly the gradual but unfailing supersession of the various eighteenth-century pastes by a composition containing bone-ash.

2 The distinction between china (bone-porcelain) and porcelain proper (hard-paste), though customary in Staffordshire and the English pottery-trade, is less familiar elsewhere in England. The word 'china' has been in use as a familiar name for porcelain of all kinds, including the 'Dresden', since the early eighteenth century. Unfortunately, the word china seems to have been used also, in the seventeenth and eighteenth centuries, for white earthenware painted in Chinese style, and this sometimes makes the contemporary advertisements rather misleading.

Delph in 1813, were varieties of hard earthenware having some of the characteristics of porcelain.

The usual mode of decorating English porcelain was by painting, most often in fusible enamels over the glaze. In the best artificial porcelains the customary lead glazes melted at a comparatively low temperature and allowed the colours to sink into them with pleasantly soft effect, unlike the refractory feldspathic glazes on which the enamels rest like a superficial incrustation. Of true underglaze colours, cobalt-blue alone was in general use, though rare instances of the use of manganese-purple occur on early Bristol and Longton Hall porcelain.[1] As a ground colour cobalt-blue was extensively employed, both as a coloured glaze and as a 'powdered' surface, the latter generally produced by blowing the dry pigment through a tube closed with gauze over the moistened surface of the piece.

Painting in unfired pigments seems to have been used, in imitation of enamelling, to a much greater extent than was formerly believed. The independent decorator Duesbury in his work-book seems to have made a distinction between 'painting' and 'enamelling', while at a somewhat earlier date the Worcester factory thought it necessary to advertise its wares as 'warranted true enamel'. It is very rare to find specimens with unfired colouring surviving in good condition; in most cases it has been cleaned away. But the great number of figures now uncoloured may perhaps be explained by supposing that they once bore unfired painting.

Printing began to be used on porcelain about 1756. In this process, designs were reproduced by transferring to the surface of the porcelain an impression from an engraved metal plate taken in enamel pigment on paper. At first the colours were applied over the glaze, but the process was before long adopted for designs in

1 Cobalt-blue and copper-red, alone of the colours known to the eighteenth century will withstand without alteration the high temperature needed for the running of most glazes. Nineteenth-century chemistry, however, brought other underglaze colours, and these are in common use today.

underglaze blue.[1] The invention of printing has been claimed for various English and Continental factories; it now seems certain that it was first used at the Battersea enamel-factory between 1753 and 1756,[2] where the engravers Brooks, Ravenet and Hancock were employed;[3] it was in use at Worcester[4] before 1757; and at Liverpool, where John Sadler and Guy Green established printing works about 1756 for printing on delftware tiles.[5] Printing was also used on Bow china probably dating from 1756.[6] Extensive use was eventually made of the process at Worcester, where the well-known engraver Robert Hancock executed many designs. By a later method, adopted towards the close of the century, the copperplate was oiled instead of being inked, and the design transferred to the procelain by means of a flexible glue sheet or 'bat'. The powdered colour was then dusted on, adhering to the design thus printed in oil.[7] Stipples in the style especially associated with Bartolozzi and Angelica Kauffmann were well-suited to this method, which is still in occasional use, though the general practice has been to revert to the use of paper-transfers.

Gilding was of course much used on the more ambitious pieces. At some early factories (Longton Hall, for instance) the gold was fixed, without firing, merely with oil or japanner's size: this gilding is especially liable to be rubbed away. On the best soft-pastes—at Sèvres and at Chelsea and Worcester in the 1760s and 1770s— gold leaf was ground up with honey and painted on the ware, and then fixed by a gentle firing; this gold had a rich and slightly dull appearance and could be applied thickly and chased with an agate

1 At least as early as 1759. See p. 254.

2 The process is referred to, as practised at Battersea, by Rouquet in *L'État des Arts en Angleterre* (p. 143), a book published in 1755 from notes made two years earlier. Horace Walpole in a well-known letter, dated September 1755, mentioned a printed Battersea enamel snuff-box. The invention of printing at Battersea, apparently by John Brooks, is discussed in an article by W. B. Honey, 'New Light on Battersea Enamels', in the *Connoisseur*, LXXXIX (1932), p. 82.

3 Research by Dr. Bernard Watney and R. J. Charleston has since shown that attempts to patent a process for printing on enamels and china were made by John Brooks in Birmingham in 1751, i.e. before he went to Battersea. Birmingham and Bilston were centres for the manufacture of enamels during the eighteenth century. *Transactions E.C.C.*, vol. 6, part 2 (1966), pp. 61–123.

4 See pp. 222, 246.

5 See p. 295. Also Anthony Ray, *English Delftware Tiles*.

6 See p. 116.

7 This method was in use in Birmingham for printing on paper *c.* 1760.

or metal point. Later on the cheaper method of mercury-gilding replaced this; an amalgam was applied and the mercury was driven off in a vapour by firing. The resulting dull surface then required burnishing, and an excessive brassy polish is the note of this later gilding.

The fragile character of some of the early English soft-pastes to a large extent forbade their employment in objects of daily use, and their makers were generally content to produce decorative pieces which should compete in charm with the imported Chinese and Japanese wares. These last (particularly the contemporary Chinese *famille rose*, and the 'Kakiemon' and 'brocaded Imari' porcelains of Japan) were not only copied and adapted directly, but also at second hand from the productions of the older European factories, in particular those of Meissen, themselves often inspired by or copied from Far Eastern models.

But the chief amongst the inventions of the Meissen factory in the second quarter of the eighteenth century was the porcelain figure. Figures in enamelled earthenware had been made in Italy in Renaissance times, and later in Holland, sometimes after Chinese models. In China, porcelain had of course for long been employed for this purpose, and statuettes were included in the earliest specimens of the hard brown stoneware made by Böttger in his first attempts towards the discovery of porcelain. But the distinction of first employing glazed porcelain in Europe for small original works of sculpture belongs to the Meissen factory, and in particular to the modeller Johann Joachim Kaendler (1706–75), to whom can be traced most of the styles seen in mid-eighteenth-century china figures. Kaendler was a modeller of genius, and quick to understand the part which glaze and colour may play in the total effect of a porcelain model. Porcelain became the medium of a branch of *Kleinplastik* bearing the same relation to monumental sculpture as an etching or engraving bears to mural decoration. In Kaendler's hands, it was seldom, as in later times it tended to be, merely a means of reproducing marble or stone sculpture on a small scale. Kaendler's original genius, too, was responsible for the innovation by which porcelain figures came to be used as a satiric commentary on contemporary life. The many novel forms of table-wares with plastic decoration were also due to Kaendler's fertile powers of invention.

Suggestions for models may well have been obtained from the German school of ivory-carvers, and some examples may in fact be traced to originals in this material.[1] But in the part they played at first in the social life of the time porcelain figures appear to have been the successors of those in wax, or in sugar (*Schauessen*), which had long been in use for table-decoration at German court festivals. Such figures were often grouped on the tables at the conclusion of a banquet to form connected scenes, mythological or pastoral, with palaces and temples and accessories of various kinds.[2] Figures were also mounted in ormolu to serve as candelabra, and these were often decorated with porcelain flowers. The German fashion was soon brought to England, and Horace Walpole, writing in 1753, remarked that '. . . jellies, biscuits, sugar plumbs and creams have long given way to harlequins, gondoliers, Turks, Chinese and shepherdesses of Saxon china'.[3] And these 'symbolic, domestic and rustic statuettes' (as Church gravely called them) are the most charming and the most characteristically trivial of all English china of the century. The sale catalogues of English porcelain of this time make frequent mention of objects 'for desart', and many figures carrying baskets or receptacles may have been used singly as sweetmeat dishes, rather than as part of a connected scene. Figures of animals and birds were commonly used in this way, and as tureens, in the Meissen style. A little later it

1 See B. Rackham in *The Burlington Magazine*, vol. XXX (1917), p. 168. Kaendler was a pupil of Permoser, and J. C. Ludwig Lücke, another Meissen modeller, had been an ivory carver. See also Arthur Lane, *English Porcelain Figures of the 18th Century*.

2 In a Dresden inventory of 1753 a 'Temple of Honour in 264 parts' is mentioned. In *The Public Advertiser*, 1 March 1756, were advertised 'several very curious desarts used at the most elegant and great entertainments and now divided into proper lots: consisting of Domes, Temples, Triumphal Arches, Epargnes, etc., embellished with Trees, Arbors, Flowers, China Figures, Vauses, Girandols, Candlesticks, Branches, and other ornaments used at Desarts, with several sets of China Dishes, Plates and Tureens'. See also King, p. 7, and Adolf Brüning, *Schauessen und Porzellan-plastik*, in *Kunst und Kunsthandwerk*, vol. VII (1906), p. 130.

3 Quoted by Mrs. Arundell Esdaile in *The Observer*, 22 June 1924.

became the fashion to use porcelain figures as mantelpiece ornaments, often in sets. To this class belong the numerous examples, most of them no earlier than 1760, with elaborate backgrounds of foliage and flowers (*bocages*), as a rule summarily finished at the back and thus obviously unsuited for table use.

In style, the vivacious *rococo* of the 1750s and 1760s, which affected the forms of vases and ornamental pieces as well as of figures, gave place in the last quarter of the century to the sentimental groups, Classical figures and personifications associated with the *Louis Seize* and Neo-Classical styles. In conformity with the revived fashion for antique marble sculpture, unglazed white porcelain ('biscuit')[1] was often used for figures and groups, for which in England the Derby factory was especially famous. Useful and decorative objects assumed those 'Classical' forms which, like all too many of their Greek and Roman examples, suggest metal or stone rather than plastic clay. At first these were simple and graceful and sometimes beautiful, but pompousness was the note of their early nineteenth-century successors. When these in turn gave way before the 'Brighton Pavilion *chinoiseries*' of the Regency and a revived *rococo*, ill-proportioned forms and tasteless extravagances in modelling became the rule; and for the next fifteen or twenty years, lavish decoration of applied flowers in full relief too often accompanied the ostentatious painting and gilding which were fashionable on all but the humblest wares in the second quarter of the nineteenth century.

In painted decoration, Kaendler's contemporary at Meissen, Johann Gregor Herold, had by 1740[2] created a distinctive European style in porcelain-painting. Not only were the characteristic 'German' (as distinguished from the Chinese and Japanese, called 'Indian') flowers an invention of Herold, but the

1 The name 'biscuit' is inexplicably given to porcelain of which the body has been fired (once) but not glazed. The fashion for biscuit was led by Sèvres where Bachelier had introduced the material in 1751.
2 Herold went to Meissen in 1720.

fantastic *chinoiserie*, of pseudo-Chinese figures, was invented, or at least first employed, as porcelain decoration during his period of directorship at Meissen.[1]

In England the Meissen flowers were at first frankly copied, though in various highly individual manners, but distinctive English styles of flower-painting were quickly developed, at first at Chelsea and Bow, and afterwards at Worcester and Derby. Many designs, besides those copied from Chinese or Japanese examples, were adapted from engravings, particularly those after Boucher and Watteau, and by the decorative designers (*ornemanistes*) of the period, such as Jean Pillement. Collections of engraved designs of the last-named class were published in England under such titles as *The Artist's Vade-Mecum*, *The Draughtsman's Assistant* and *The Ladies' Amusement or the Whole Art of Japanning*. In these are conspicuous the fashionable pastoral subjects as well as the *chinoiseries* already mentioned. Designs after Rubens, Teniers, Wouwerman and Berghem, and engravings from drawings of animals and birds by Francis Barlow, amongst others, were employed, and it is known that illustrations from botanical treatises were copied for a distinctive series of designs which appear on Chelsea[2] and Bow porcelain.

In the last three decades of the eighteenth century the influence of Sèvres largely superseded that of Meissen. Many designs, such as the 'exotic birds', as well as the use of coloured grounds—*gros bleu*, *bleu de roi*, green, turquoise and crimson—and the use of 'biscuit' porcelain for figures, are directly traceable to the Sèvres fashions, though the credit for the actual innovation in most cases lies with the Meissen factory.

The 'Japan patterns' which were particularly favoured from about 1760 onwards at Worcester, and to a slighter extent at Derby and elsewhere, were very free adaptations of Far Eastern originals, both Chinese and Japanese. In feeling they were of course far removed from their examples, but often fanciful and accomplished

1 It was in any case fully developed long before the publication of Sir William Chambers's *Chinese Architecture* in 1757, to which event it has sometimes been ascribed. See E. Zimmermann, *Meissner Porzellan*, pp. 66–73 for a full discussion of *chinoiseries* on porcelain.

2 See p. 44.

in execution. Soon after 1800, however, many coarse 'Japan patterns' made their appearance on Spode's porcelain and 'ironstone china', as well as on Chamberlain's Worcester and at Derby. The credit (if credit it be) for these patterns is often given to Bloor of the last-named factory, but these loud designs seem to have first appeared in Staffordshire. The phenomenon is sometimes unconvincingly explained by the cutting off of civilising Continental influences during the Napoleonic Wars.

Contemporary with the so-called 'return to Nature' in English literature of the late eighteenth and early part of the nineteenth centuries, there appeared a naturalistic style of flower-painting, often associated with the name of William Billingsley. This flower-painting soon developed into a rather mannered style, which was carried to Coalport and Rockingham by the Steeles of Derby and imitated in the Staffordshire factories. This hardened into lifeless formality, and rather after the middle of the century a lax naturalistic style again appeared. About the time of the great Exhibition of 1851, ambitious attempts were made to rival the finest work of Sèvres, and careful and highly finished painting is found on the best Coalport and Staffordshire porcelain. The subsequent history of English china lies beyond the scope of this book, but I may note here the potter's growing consciousness of 'Art' in the period after 1850, the influence of Renaissance styles shown in motives drawn from *maiolica* and Limoges enamels, and the vogue of designs in the style of the Turkish and Syrian pottery called at that time Rhodian and Persian. The influence of Japanese naturalism and asymmetry is also noticeable in the second half of the century.

The classification of English porcelain of the eighteenth century is made difficult by the common absence of factory marks such as were generally used on Continental china, and even where marks occur, they cannot be accepted as proof of origin without confirmation by other evidence. The marks of the larger factories were often employed by their minor rivals. For instance, the anchor of Chelsea was freely used at Derby and Coalport; the

Worcester crescent at Bow, Lowestoft and Caughley; whilst even the most respectable establishments imitated the marks of Continental factories when making 'replacers' to complete defective services. Further, the addition of a mark at any time after the manufacture of a piece presents no great technical difficulty, and this possibility sometimes adds a further element of doubt. Another element of confusion arises from the practice of several of the earlier factories of selling undecorated porcelain to enamellers working independently.[1] Similarity of painting, therefore, can only be regarded as a reason for grouping a number of specimens if supported by other evidence. Of these enamellers, William Duesbury, afterwards proprietor of the Derby factory, is known from a published work-book for dates between 1751 and 1753 to have painted porcelain from Bow, Chelsea, Derby and Staffordshire factories. Reference will be made[2] to examples believed to have been decorated by him. Duesbury apparently worked for several dealers who purchased china 'in the white'.[3] Receipted bills from 'Richard Dyer, at Mr. Bolton's, enameller, near the church, Lambeth', are among the papers of John Bowcocke, clerk to the Bow factory, but nothing further is known of him.[4] Another London enameller, James Giles, of Kentish Town and Cockspur Street, is known from advertisements to have decorated Worcester and probably other porcelain to the order of his customers, between 1760 and about 1780. Two miniature-painters, John Donaldson and Jeffrey Hamet O'Neale, also decorated Worcester porcelain in this way, probably in London.[5] At a later date, white or slightly decorated porcelain from Nantgarw and Swansea was painted in London for the firm of Mortlock by Richard Robins and T. M. Randall and the painters in their employment, who also decorated white porcelain from Sèvres in the same way.[6] A similar establishment at Poolbeg Street,

1 Migrant painters cause a similar difficulty.

2 P. 96.

3 A portion of the stock of Thomas Turner, who was among the employers named in Duesbury's work-book, was sold at Christie's in 1767, and included a large proportion of pieces described as 'white Chelsea figures'. See Nightingale, p. xxxviii, and Bemrose, *Bow, Chelsea and Derby Porcelain*, pp. 7–17.

4 But see also p. 86.

5 See pp. 268, 270

6 See p. 383.

Dublin, was carried on about the same time by James Donovan and his son; their productions, however, were usually marked with their name.[1]

The English porcelain bodies were of widely varied composition, and chemical analysis is sometimes helpful in confirming attributions made on grounds of style; several instances of this will be mentioned in the course of this guide. The use of one particular ingredient, bone-ash, is readily ascertained from the presence of phosphoric acid,[2] and since it is known to have been adopted at certain factories at certain dates, its presence revealed on analysis often provides a last and convincing link in a chain of argument. The value of bone-ash in a porcelain body is sufficiently proved by the later history of English china.[3] We may be sure that once adopted at a factory it would never be abandoned.

Excavations on factory sites can provide evidence of the utmost value; but it must always be remembered that nothing short of an undoubted 'waster'[4] can prove conclusively that a particular type was made on the factory site in question. Moulds may have been taken from pieces brought to be copied; and finished pieces, unless of a single type and found in great quantity, may perhaps have been made elsewhere.

In spite of the foreign origin of most of the models employed for figures, and of so many of the usual decorative themes, the earlier English porcelain shows unquestionable originality in interpretation if not in invention. Borrowed styles of painting quickly acquired an individual and English quality, and the scope allowed by the process of moulding and assembling of the parts of a figure and by its painting in many cases resulted in an entire

---

1 A cup and saucer in the British Museum (No. XIV. 10) so marked has the Minton mark also. A vase in the Herbert Allen Collection (No. 588) is a pretentious example of Donovan's painting.

2 Dr. H. J. Plenderleith has published in *The Burlington Magazine*, vol. LI (Sept. 1927), a simple method of testing for phosphoric acid. More sophisticated methods, e.g. spectroscopic analysis, are also utilised nowadays. The use of ultra-violet light to examine fluorescence, has a limited value (F.A.B.).

3 See Appendix B, p. 410.

4 That is to say, a piece obviously not finished or fit to be sold.

recreation of the subject, which assumed a fresh and novel character. This, with a beauty of material and colour, is the chief source of the delight we experience before the best Chelsea and Bow china figures. Even if we do not know the Meissen or other examples from which they were derived, there is probably in most cases an original either in porcelain or some other material waiting to be found. We may, however, ascribe to Nicholas Sprimont and his modellers the whole invention of the exquisite Chelsea 'toys',[1] and of many of the figures, 'red anchor' and 'gold anchor' alike. In fact the Chelsea factory was pre-eminent in most respects. For the rest, one may note here the *naïveté* and rich colour of the early Bow, and the freshness and individuality of the best Longton Hall figures. And if Duesbury's Derby china was the product of industry rather than art (and this is especially true of the figures) the factory has the credit of creating many beautiful things in the table-wares of the last thirty years of the eighteenth century. Worcester of the 'Dr. Wall period' stands a little apart; its earliest and best work has something of the Bow simplicity, its later has much of the Chelsea splendour, and in all there is an unmistakably English quality.

1 It now seems likely that the Chelsea toys originated at a short-lived nearby rival factory, and that their manufacture was continued by Sprimont. See pp. 32, 76.

Chapter 2

Chelsea

———————

The earliest specimens of porcelain presumed to have been made at Chelsea are the famous 'goat-and-bee' jugs, incised with the word '*Chelsea*', the date 1745 and a triangle.[1] A specimen with these marks is in the British Museum (No. II. 16A); another coloured example is at Luton Hoo[2]. Others, lacking the date and name and marked only with the triangle, are at South Kensington, in the Schreiber Collection, No. 117 (plain white, Plate 1F), and in the Museum Collection, painted in colours. These jugs are usually in the form of a vessel supported on the back of two reclining goats, with a twig handle and a bee in relief under the lip, though the bee is sometimes absent. The form is copied from a silver model, of which an example existing in 1912[3] was stated to bear the hall-mark for 1724. We have, however, no sure information regarding the name of their maker and the date of foundation of his factory.

No earlier reference to the Chelsea factory has yet been found than that contained in the *London Tradesman* of 1747,[4] speaking of

1 See Appendix A, p. 384, No. 1. An example with date, name and triangle (formerly in the collection of Mr. William Russell) was first described by Sir A. W. Franks in *The Archaeological Journal*, vol. XIX (1862), p. 340; illustrated by Jewitt, vol. I, p. 193. The model was reproduced in Staffordshire earthenware and salt glaze as well as in Liverpool and Coalport porcelains.

2 *English Porcelain, 1745–1850* (ed. Charleston), Plate 1A.

3 Chaffers, 13th edition (1912), p. 947. An example stated to bear the London hall-mark for 1737, and the initials 'EW' (for Edward Wood), was illustrated in *The Cheyne Book*, No. 14. The genuineness of the silver specimens (or their hall-marks) has been questioned.

4 Nightingale, p. viii.

attempts to make 'Porcelain or China-ware' at Greenwich[1] and Chelsea. More definite evidence is contained in newspaper advertisements of the china of 1749 and 1750[2] in the last of which N. Sprimont, speaking for the 'Chelsea Porcelaine Manufacture', disclaimed connection with a 'Chelsea China Warehouse'; to which S. Stables, writing from the latter, replied that he was supplied by no other than Charles Gouyn, 'late Proprietor and Chief Manager of the Chelsea-House'. A map reproduced in the *Cheyne Book of Chelsea China* indicated that Sprimont's factory was situated at the corner of Justice Walk, extending northwards up the east side of Lawrence Street. More recent investigations by John Mallet and Dorothy Griffiths, however, show that from about 1747 to 1764 the factory was on the site of Monmouth House which at that time closed off the northern end of Lawrence Street. During various periods between 1750 and 1769 the factory occupied sites southward from Monmouth House down the west side of Lawrence Street and on the east side of the parallel Church Street, onto which the Lawrence Street premises backed.[3]

Nicholas Sprimont (*b.* 1716, *d.* 1771[4]) was a silversmith of Compton Street, Soho, originally of Liège, whose name had been entered at Goldsmiths' Hall in 1742 as that of a plateworker. A pair of oval silver-gilt dishes made by him, dated 1743–4, with scalloped edges and shells and coral in high relief, is now in the collection at Buckingham Palace and was exhibited at the Special Loan Exhibition at South Kensington, 1862, Catalogue Nos. 5941–2. A pair of sauce-boats made by Sprimont, bearing the hall-mark for 1746, were exhibited at Chelsea in 1924 (*Cheyne Book,* No. 11): they are not unlike the triangle-marked sauce-boats mentioned below. In view of the early use of silver models, it seems likely that Sprimont was connected with the work almost from the first, and that the advertisements of 1749 were issued on the occasion of his assuming the management of a factory in which he

1 Greenwich porcelain has not yet been identified.
2 *The Daily Advertiser*, February and March 1749, 15 May 1750, and *The General Advertiser*, 29 January 1750. See Nightingale, p. v., and H. Bellamy Gardner in *Transactions E.P.C.*, I (1928), p. 16.
3 *Transactions E.C.C.*, vol. 9, part 1, pp. 115–31: J. V. G. Mallet, 'The Site of the Chelsea Porcelain Factory'.
4 He was buried in Petersham Churchyard, Richmond, Surrey. See an article by Dr. H. Bellamy Gardner in *The Connoisseur*, vol. LXV (1923), p. 159.

had been previously employed as modeller or designer. On the other hand it has been found that Sprimont was paying rates for premises in Lawrence Street, where the factory was situated, as early as 1747.[1] Gouyn was also a silversmith, of Soho and elsewhere in London.[2] He was apparently a Frenchman[3] and an analysis of the paste of the earlier Chelsea porcelain shows a high percentage of lime (probably derived from chalk), a characteristic also of French soft-pastes. It may thus perhaps be conjectured that Gouyn was concerned with the technical part of the manufacture; he was possibly the chemist referred to in an unsigned and undated document (evidently written by Sprimont) in the British Museum, entitled *The Case of the Undertaker of the Chelsea Manufacture of Porcelain Ware*.[4] Appealing for heavier import duties on 'Dresden' (Meissen) china, the writer speaks of himself as a silversmith by profession who had begun to make porcelain after 'a casual acquaintance with a chymist who had some knowledge that way'. That Gouyn or someone connected with Chelsea had been employed at the French factory at Saint-Cloud is suggested by a resemblance not only in the paste but in the style of modelling of some grotesque figures, such as a teapot in the British Museum in the form of a seated Chinaman.[5] A similar teapot, delightfully modelled, with the spout in the form of a parrot, from Mr. Wallace Elliot's collection, is figured in Plate 1E. On the other hand, it is noteworthy that virtually nothing resembling the characteristic Saint-Cloud painting in underglaze blue is found on Chelsea porcelain. The 'chymist' may have been a technician only. A Thomas Briand, who showed some specimens of what was

---

1 Bellamy Gardner, *Transactions E.P.C.*, I (1928), p. 18.

2 *Transactions E.P.C.*, I (1928), p. 19, II (1929), p. 24.

3 See Church (*English Porcelain*, p. 18), who asserted that both Sprimont and Gouyn are Flemish names. Horace Walpole (*Letters*, ed. Mrs. Toynbee, vol. V, p. 291), writing in 1763 (see below, p. 68), spoke of Sprimont as a Frenchman; and Rouquet in *L'État des Arts en Angeleterre*, a book published in 1755, but based on notes of a visit two years earlier, spoke of 'un habile artiste françois' as director of the factory.

4 Lansdowne MSS. No. 829, fol. 21. Quoted in full by Marryat, *History of Pottery and Porcelain* (3rd edition), p. 373, and Jewitt, vol. I, p. 171. See also King, p. 33.

5 *Catalogue*, No. II. 12. Both Saint-Cloud and Chelsea pieces may, however, have a parallel derivation from Meissen models. Also Mackenna, *Chelsea Porcelain, The Triangle and Raised Anchor Wares*, fig. 12.

A. DISH Ht. 2¼in (5.7cm); W. 4¾in (12cm). About
1745–50. No mark. *Victoria and Albert Museum*
(305-1869)

B. SAUCER Dia. 4⅝in (11.7cm). About
1745–50. Triangle mark. *Schreiber*
Collection (118)

C. CUP Ht. 1¾in (4.4cm); Dia. 2⅞in
(7.3cm). About 1745–50. Triangle
mark. *Schreiber Collection (118)*

D. CUP Ht. 2⅞in (7.3cm); Dia. 2⅝in (6.6cm). About 1745–50. No mark.
Schreiber Collection (119)

E. TEAPOT Ht. 6¾in (17.1cm). About 1745–50. Triangle mark. *Victoria and*
Albert Museum (C.46-1938)

F. JUG Ht. 4⅜in (11.1cm). About 1745–50. Triangle mark. *Schreiber Collection (117)*

See pages 18, 20   Plate 1 CHELSEA (*White porcelain*)

apparently a soft-paste of French type before the Royal Society in 1742–3, has also been conjectured to have been the pottery-chemist concerned; but there is no proof of this. A document now at the City Museum, Stoke-on-Trent, sets out Articles of Partnership between Thomas Briand of Lane Delph etc., 'Painter', and Jos. Farmer, in which is recited that Briand 'had found out ye art of making a beautiful Earthenware Little inferior to Porcelain or China Ware'. This Thomas Briand appears to have died in February 1747.[1]

The early Chelsea porcelain of the type marked with a triangle is a very translucent material, resembling milk-white glass.[2] Transmitted light reveals small flecks which show a greater translucency than the surrounding paste. Comparatively few models are recorded.[3] In addition to the 'goat-and-bee' jugs, we may single out as especially fine and characteristic the teapots and cups and saucers in the form of overlapping strawberry leaves (Plate 1C), of which there are examples at South Kensington and Bloomsbury. The saucer figured in Plate 1B is a rare piece, also found with the raised-anchor mark of the following period. Sauce-boats with festoons and masks in relief (such as Schr. No. 129), and fluted dishes (Plate 1A) are all in forms obviously derived from silver, as is a fine triangle-marked cream jug, painted in underglaze blue, at the Cecil Higgins Museum, Bedford (Plate 3A). The well-known pattern of 'raised flowers', sometimes called 'tea plant', is clearly of the same origin: examples are in the British Museum and Schreiber Collections (Plate 1D). Where painting has been added to these early pieces, it is generally of a rather artless but not unattractive quality, the small detached flower-sprays and insects often serving to conceal blemishes in the material. Rather laboured Meissen 'botanical flowers' are more rarely seen on triangle-marked pieces,

1 *Transactions E.C.C.*, vol. 7, part 2, pp. 87–99; Arnold Mountford, 'Thomas Briand—A Stranger'.
2 A marked strawberry-leaf jug in the Trapnell Collection was actually catalogued as Bristol glass.
3 A full account of the early history of the Chelsea factory and a list of examples of the period are given in a paper by O. Glendenning and Mrs. Donald MacAlister, 'Chelsea: the Triangle Period', in *Transactions E.C.C.*, 3 (1935), p. 20.

A. Bird on a Branch Ht. 4¼in (10.8cm). About 1750. No mark. 'Girl in a swing' class. *Ex. Alfred E. Hutton Collection*

B. Girl with a Basket Ht. 2½in (6.3cm). About 1750. No mark. 'Girl in a Swing' class. *Boston Museum of Fine Arts*

C. Taperstick Ht. 3⅘in (9.6cm). About 1750. No mark. 'Girl in a Swing' class. *Museum of London*

D. Bust of the Duke of Cumberland Ht. 4½in (11.4cm). About 1750. No mark. *Schreiber Collection (127)*

E. Cup and Saucer Cup ht. 2⅜in (6cm); Saucer dia. 5¹³⁄₁₆in (14.7cm). About 1750. Raised Anchor mark. *Boston Museum of Fine Arts*

F. Figure of a Hound Ht. 4⅝in (11.7cm). About 1750. No mark. *Boston Museum of Fine Arts*

G. Europa and the Bull. About 1750. No mark. 'Girl in a Swing' class. *Ex Owen Glendenning Collection*

See pages 26, 30, 32   Plate 2 CHELSEA (*White porcelain*)

as on a pair of cups in the Museum of London. Painting in precisely the same style occurs on two dishes in the Schreiber Collection (No. 180), marked with the raised anchor, and supplies evidence of continuity between the earliest and the later periods.[1] A triangle-marked teapot in the Schreiber Collection (No. 130) is painted with a Japanese design in the style of Kakiemon,[2] but this decoration was perhaps added some years after the manufacture of the porcelain. That stock was kept in this way is shown by the occurrence in the catalogue of the sale of 1756 of two 'beautiful crawfish salts'. These are not uncommon (a pair is in the British Museum, No. II. 18), but are generally marked with the triangle. Horace Walpole in his description of Strawberry Hill made an often-quoted reference to a pair. Of figures belonging to this period we know very few, apart from the *Chinaman* teapots. But a group of *Lovers* in the British Museum (No. II. 6A)[3] may be put down to this time by the evidence of its mark, a trident intersecting a crown, in underglaze blue, which occurs also on a cup with 'raised flowers' in Mr. Frank Hurlbutt's collection, on a strawberry-leaf cream-jug in Dr. J. W. L. Glaisher's collection, and on a *Greyhound* at the Victoria and Albert Museum.[4] Other figures are sometimes conjecturally given to the factory for this period on the evidence of a paste showing pinholes by transmitted light, a feature of many triangle-marked pieces, but the evidence cannot be considered conclusive, since pieces apparently of different origin show a similar appearance.[5] A white glazed figure

1 Another style of painting in a style derived from Meissen is seen on two vases in Mr. Alfred Hutton's collection figured in an article by Dr. Bellamy Gardner in *The Connoisseur*, vol. LXXVI (1926), p. 232, where several other interesting early painted specimens are reproduced. And in Mackenna, *op. cit.*, fig. 33.

2 The potter Kakiemon, who worked at Arita in the mid-seventeenth century, gave his name to a type of decoration of which the characteristic productions have slight painting mainly in red, blue, turquoise and green. Arita porcelain is usually known as 'Imari', from its place of export. Many copies of the Kakiemon designs will be referred to in this book.

3 Lane, *English Porcelain Figures of the 18th Century*, Plate 4.

4 See an article by Dr. Bellamy Gardner in *The Connoisseur*, vol. LXIV (October, 1922). Chaffers (*Marks and Monograms*, 8th edition, 1897) also asserts that the mark occurs in combination with the incised triangle. Illustrated in fig. 20, Mackenna, *op. cit.*

5 The *Waterman with Doggett's Badge* and the *Fortune-telling Group* conjecturally ascribed to this period in Mr. King's *Chelsea Porcelain* (p. 22) would now be classed as Bow (see p. 108); for another series discussed by Mr. King, and ascribed to the factory in this period, see below, p. 28.

A. CREAM JUG Ht. 4¾in (12cm). Painted in underglaze blue. About 1745–50. Triangle mark. *Cecil Higgins Museum, Bedford*

B. ITALIAN COMEDY FIGURE Ht. 7¾in (19.6cm). About 1755. Red Anchor mark. *Victoria and Albert Museum (C.1327-1924)*

C. FIGURE OF A CARPENTER Ht. 7¾in (19.6cm). About 1755. Red Anchor mark. *Victoria and Albert Museum (2923-1901)*

See pages 20, 38, 48, 50

Plate 3 CHELSEA

of a sleeping naked child, thought to be Chelsea, at the British Museum[1] has the date 'June ye 26th 1746'.

It is probable that the incised triangle was used only on pieces made before 1750, when Sprimont is presumed to have become manager, though the milk-white porcelain of the dated jugs apparently gave place to a harder and rather colder-looking material before the models of the early period ceased to be employed. A coffee-pot from Mr. Alfred Hutton's collection,[2] marked with a triangle, with 'raised flowers' of the kind just mentioned, is from the same mould as another (unmarked) at South Kensington, which is of a colder white approaching the colour of the 'raised-anchor' paste of the next period. A fragment of a similar coffee-pot was found on the site of Sprimont's factory in Justice Walk,[3] thus tending to prove the continuity of the triangle-marking factory and that using the anchor. A salt-cellar in the Museum of London has the triangle and incised date '1746'.[4] It is possible that the later cool white body was introduced, in preference to the earlier, more glassy porcelain, as more manageable, and in particular as more suitable for use in the thicker masses required for the figures which now began to be made in some quantity; and that the mark of an anchor in relief on an applied oval medallion was introduced to distinguish this paste as soon as it was proved. It is likely that the marks employed at Chelsea at first indicated different pastes. Since a glaze needs to be suited to the composition of a body, it would obviously be desirable for a factory to record the latter, for its own information, by a mark in the paste, especially when pieces of several varieties of body were stocked in biscuit condition over a long period. Two instances have already been mentioned suggesting that stock was held in this way at Chelsea. The introduction of the mark of the gold anchor in the last period, though coinciding with a change of paste, could not of course have the same significance, since it was painted over the glaze. It should be remembered that marks on early English porcelain were never registered officially or openly adopted as in Germany and France.

1 Lane, *op. cit.*, Plate 2.
2 *Cheyne Book*, No. 30, also Mackenna, *op. cit.*, fig. 9.
3 A. J. Toppin, in *Transactions E.P.C.*, 3 (1931), p. 69.
4 *English Porcelain* (ed. Charleston), Plate 1C.

VASE IN IMARI STYLE Ht. 12½in (31.7cm). About 1755. Red Anchor mark. *Schreiber Collection (156)*

The 'raised anchor' was sometimes outlined in red. This has been thought to indicate a piece made late in the 'raised anchor period' but decorated at a time when the red anchor was the usual mark. More doubtfully it has been thought to indicate decoration outside the factory by William Duesbury.[1]

Some Chelsea porcelain of this second period, however, seems to have been left unmarked, and its identification therefore depends upon resemblances in style to the marked pieces. I may mention as typical of the latter some pieces painted in the Kakiemon manner (for example, the pair of bottles in the British Museum No. II. 20), and some examples of the famous *Nurse and Child* copied from a late sixteenth-century earthenware model made at Avon, near Fontainebleau, and ascribed to Barthélemy de Blémont (or Bertélémy de Blénod), but sometimes erroneously attributed to Palissy.[2] A plain white example of the last is in the Schreiber Collection (No. 122).[3] The *Nurse* was popular for a long time, and many examples date from the red-anchor period. The raised-anchor mark occurs also on some copies of the *blanc-de-Chine* of Fukien province: a plate in the British Museum (No. II. 10)[4] is decorated with the applied sprays of plum-blossom more familiar on the rival Bow porcelain, as are the fine substantial cup and saucer in Mr. Alfred Hutton's collection, figured in Plate 2E. (Raised anchor was often thick but seldom clumsy.) In Mrs. Radford's collection is a figure of Kuan-yin, obviously moulded from a Chinese specimen in the same material. The raised anchor also occurs on the exceedingly rare transfer-printed Chelsea porcelain, of which there is a specimen with a very unusual print in the British Museum (a typical octagonal saucer, No. II. 244).[5] It is

1 Compare *William Duesbury's London Account Book 1751–53* (E.P.C. Monograph), 1931.
2 See M. L. Solon, *History and Description of Old French Fayence*, p. 35, where a copy signed 'BB' is mentioned; and M. J. Ballot, *Musée du Louvre: La Céramique française—Bernard Palissy et les fabriques du XVIe siècle*, p. 31, Plate 47.
3 Another is figured in Mackenna, *op. cit.*, figs. 81–2.
4 Mackenna, *op. cit.*, fig. 38.
5 Figured in W. Turner, *Transfer Printing on Enamels, Porcelain and Pottery* (1907), fig. A7.

A. CUP AND SAUCER Cup ht. 2in
(5.1cm); Saucer dia. 4⅝in
(11.7cm). About 1755. No mark.
*Victoria and Albert Museum
(1067 and A-1924)*

B. CUP AND SAUCER Cup ht. 1⅞in
(4.7cm); Saucer dia. 4⅜in
(11.1cm). About 1750–55. No
mark. *Schreiber Collection (163)*

C. PLATE Dia. 9¼in (23.5cm). About 1755. Red Anchor mark. *Victoria and
Albert Museum (C.1331-1924)*

See page 36   Plate 5 CHELSEA (*'Kakiemon' patterns*)

not certain that this mode of decoration was ever actually employed at Chelsea, though at the neighbouring Battersea enamel factory it was much in favour, and the existing specimens may well have been decorated there. An advertisement in the *Liverpool Advertiser* for 11 February 1757, quoted by Mr. Hobson,[1] mentions 'printing . . . upon porclane, enamel and earthenware . . . as lately practised at Chelsea, Birmingham, etc.'. But probably Chelsea and Battersea were confused. The raised anchor also occurs on many pieces belonging by their decoration rather to the next period. In fact, it is scarcely possible to define a style of 'raised-anchor' painting. A certain artlessness is perhaps more noticeable on these than on the red-anchor-marked specimens, and the colours used are often thicker and more opaque, with a warm rich brown usually prominent. But otherwise the styles are alike and will be covered later.

A much-discussed class of pieces,[2] closely related to Chelsea, contemporary with the Chelsea raised anchor figures, may be conveniently described here. A *Girl in a Swing*[3] which gives its name to the class, a *Boy playing a Hurdy-gurdy*, and his dancing companion,[4] all at South Kensington, are typical examples, left unpainted as are most of the class.[5] A specimen of the *Boy* has been analysed[6] and proved to contain an unusual quantity of lead (20%), suggesting the use of flint glass cullet in place of the usual mixture of sand, lime and alkali. Many examples are defective (one of *Ganymede* formerly in Mr. Glendenning's possession has even received its glaze-firing, though the legs of the figure were damaged before it was fired to the biscuit state); some have partially collapsed in the kiln, and others show considerable firing cracks in the paste. The whole question of the 'Girl-in-a-Swing' porcelain is fully examined by Arthur Lane and R. J. Charleston in

1 *Catalogue*, p. 61.

2 See *Transactions E.C.C.*, VIII (1942), p. 153, and *Transactions E.C.C.*, vol. 5, part 3, pp. 111–44.

3 An example is reproduced in W. King, *English Porcelain Figures*, fig. 16, and *op. cit.*, Plate 30.

4 Figured in W. King, *Chelsea Porcelain*, Plate 11.

5 A coloured pair of the Hurdy-gurdy Boy and his Dancing Companion is in the British Museum and is illustrated in *Transactions E.C.C.*, vol. 5, part 3, Plate 128b I and II.

6 See *Transactions E.C.C.*, vol. 5, part, 3, p. 136.

A. PLATE Dia. 9in (22.8cm). Painted in underglaze blue. About 1755. Blue Anchor mark. *Schreiber Collection (128)*

B. PLATE Dia. 9in (22.8cm). About 1755. Red Anchor mark. *Victoria and Albert Museum (C.1421-1924)*

See page 38   Plate 6 CHELSEA (*Blue and white and 'Kakiemon' patterns*)

Transactions E.C.C., vol. 5, part 3, pages 111 to 143. The evidence adduced supports the view that the 'Girl-in-a-Swing' porcelain was made by workmen seceding from Sprimont's factory, as recorded by Simeon Shaw,[1] and, perhaps under the supervision of Charles Gouyn, setting up a manufactory nearby in about 1749, which ended in 1754.

For dating 'Girl-in-a-Swing' porcelain, we have a figure of *Britannia mourning the death of Frederick, Prince of Wales*,[2] who died on 20 March 1751. The modelling of the head and slender limbs of this *Britannia* is exactly that of many others, and one can cite here a rare and unusually fine example of the class in Mr. Glendenning's *Europa* (Plate 2G). The fine *Hercules and Omphale* in the Schreiber Collection (No. 120) shows similar features in the head of *Omphale*. It has been conjectured by Mr. William King that the hollow tops of the tree-stumps in the *Girl-in-a-Swing* were intended to hold porcelain flowers, such as were made at Vincennes. We have no evidence that these were made at Chelsea before 1755[3] (when they are mentioned in a sale catalogue), though they may have been, and a date later than 1751 rather than earlier would be suggested by this feature. Coloured examples of this class are relatively rare. A figure of the *Dancing Girl* in Col. and Mrs. Dickson's collection[4] shows colouring decidedly late in style. It is more than likely, however, that this is the work of an outside decorator, such as James Giles, added to a figure of an earlier date.

Closely akin to the pieces just described are some others, re-presented here by a taper-stick from the Museum of London (Plate 2C)[5] and by Mr. Hutton's white *Bird* (Plate 2A) and *Girl with a Basket* (Plate 2B). A hexagonal base with bevelled edges and alternate convex and concave lobes seems peculiar to the 'Girl-in-a-Swing' factory; it may be compared with the simply chamfered

1 *History of the Staffordshire Potteries* (1829, reprinted 1971). Much of Simeon Shaw's record has been discredited from time to time, but Lane and Charleston provide good circumstantial evidence for accepting Shaw at least in this instance.

2 In King, *op. cit.*, Plate 8, and Lane, *op. cit.*, Plate 32.

3 There are examples probably of Chelsea manufacture at the British Museum.

4 Figured in Mackenna, op. cit., fig. 102, and *Transactions E.C.C.*, vol. 5, part 3, fig. 128(b), 111.

5 An example of the bird figured in Plate 2C, once in the Martin Koblitz Collection, bears an incised mark resembling the Chelsea triangle with one side scarcely visible, or perhaps an incised 'V'.

A. Plate Dia. 9½in (24.1cm). About 1755. Red Anchor mark.
Victoria and Albert Museum (3833-1853)

B. Plate Dia. 9in (22.8cm). About 1755. Red Anchor mark.
Boston Museum of Fine Arts

See pages 40, 42   Plate 7 CHELSEA

square bases of, for instance, the *Dancing Girl* and the *Boy with a Hurdy-gurdy*.[1] The modelling of the figures shows the same slenderness. Besides the flat leaves, their supports are decorated with flowers of a peculiar convex form resembling, but not identical with, those on a large white figure of a *Gardener's Companion*[2] once in Dr. and Mrs. Bellamy Gardner's collection, which is marked with the raised anchor. The glaze of all these is even closer to that of 'raised-anchor' Chelsea than in the case of the *Girl in a Swing* family; and the painting on the examples here reproduced is in addition not far removed from the more primitive styles found on some 'raised-' and 'red-anchor' pieces. The finely modelled *Hound*, also figured in Plate 2F, may be linked with the others on the showing of its paste and glaze, and similar hounds were made at Bow.

The 'Girl-in-a-Swing' factory is likely also to have been the place of origin of the famous Chelsea 'Toys', manufacture of which was later continued at Chelsea under Sprimont and, after 1769, by Duesbury of Derby.[3] Some few domestic wares have in addition been ascribed to the 'Girl-in-a-Swing' factory.

A series of important white pieces apparently dating from this time, and in their modelling standing apart from the others, includes busts of *King George II* (Schreiber No. 126), of *George III as Prince of Wales*,[4] and of the *Duke of Cumberland* (Plate 2D). Whilst there is reason to regard the two latter figures as Chelsea on the grounds of paste and glaze, the bust of George II has long presented a problem and has been variously attributed to Plymouth, Chelsea, Bow, Longton Hall and Derby. More recently two such busts have been shown, on analysis, to contain soapstone as a major ingredient, and as a result of this and other arguments, Chaffers' Liverpool factory has been tentatively thought of as a possible source.[5] Other possible places of origin are Worcester or,

---

1 Figured in Lane, op. cit., Plate 31B.

2 Figured in King, *English Porcelain Figures*, fig. 17, and in the *Cheyne Book*, No. 215, Plate I.

3 See p. 148.

4 *Cheyne Book*, No. 212 (Plate I), and King, Plate 15. Also Lane, op. cit., Plate 9.

5 Bernard Watney, 'The King, the Nun and other Figures', *Transactions E.C.C.*. vol. 7, part 1, p. 48ff.

A. JUG Ht. 3¼in (8.2cm); W. 3⅝in (9.2cm). About 1755. No mark. *Schreiber Collection (191)*
B. MUG Ht. 4¾in (12cm). About 1755. Red Anchor mark. *Victoria and Albert Museum (C.945-1924)*
C. BOWL Dia. 4⅛in (10.5cm); ht. 2⅜in (6cm). About 1755. Red Anchor mark. *Schreiber Collection (187)*

D. PLATE Dia. 8½in (21.6cm). About 1755. Red Anchor mark. *Boston Museum of Fine Arts*

See pages 38, 40, 42, 44, 46 Plate 8 CHELSEA

perhaps, Crisp and Saunders' factory at Lambeth.[1]

The tradition that associated the French sculptor Louis-François Roubiliac[2] with the Chelsea factory has been discovered to have a foundation in fact, since Nicholas Sprimont is known to have stood as godfather to a daughter of the sculptor,[3] and an impressed 'R' often found on certain later Chelsea models[4] was formerly believed to indicate Roubiliac's work. But marks of this kind are more probably those of 'repairers', or workmen responsible for assembling the parts, rather than of the artist responsible for the original model of a figure. It is quite likely, however, that the *Prince of Wales* portrait was modelled by Roubiliac, to whose work it shows a distinct resemblance.[5] Some examples of these Royal busts were stated by Franks[6] to bear the raised-anchor mark (though I have never seen one so marked); it is, however, found on the *Sphinxes* (such as Schreiber No. 125), which are usually of a similar cool white porcelain.[7] A bust of a *Boy* in Dr. and Mrs. Bellamy Gardner's collection also seems to belong to this series but was probably moulded from a French bronze.

Most of the Chelsea productions of the fine middle period of the factory may be readily identified by the customary mark of a small anchor in red enamel.[8] We may assume that the raised anchor ceased to be used when it was no longer necessary to distinguish the reformed paste from that of the first period and those tried experimentally. Surviving catalogues of the second and third

---

1 *The Connoisseur*, June 1970: Patrick Synge-Hutchinson, 'Some Rare White English Porcelain in the Dudley Delevingne Collection'.

2 Roubiliac was born in 1695, came to England about 1738 and died in 1762.

3 Mrs. Arundell Esdaile had kindly pointed out a passage relating to this in the *Publications of the Huguenot Society*, vol. XXVI. Further particulars are given in her *Life of Roubiliac*.

4 See p. 60.

5 This opinion is not accepted by Lane, op. cit., p. 30.

6 Loc. cit., p. 345.

7 Triangle-marked *Sphinxes* are also known (*Apollo*, June 1960, p. 184).

8 The inexperienced collector may overlook the tiny anchor mark of Chelsea—raised, red or gold—which is often tucked away in the most unexpected places, and rarely appears under the base of a figure.

B. 'HANS SLOANE' PLATE Dia. 9¾in (24.7cm). About 1755. Red Anchor mark. *Victoria and Albert Museum (2953-1901)*

A. PLATE Dia. 7in (17.7cm). Painted in crimson monochrome. About 1755. Red Anchor mark. *Victoria and Albert Museum (C.244-1935)*

See page 44

Plate 9 CHELSEA

annual sales of the factory's productions, held in 1755[1] and 1756[2], afford a pleasant opportunity for identifying many surviving pieces. Sales were advertised in 1754,[3] but no copies of the catalogues are known to survive.

The exceptionally beautiful porcelain of the early red-anchor period has a very soft paste of fine grain, often showing by transmitted light the round spots of higher translucency known to collectors as 'moons'[4] and due to the presence of air bubbles in the paste.[5] The glaze is smooth and even, of a cool white, seldom crazed, and free from the black specks which sometimes disfigure the raised-anchor-marked pieces. The raised- and early red-anchor pastes and glazes, however, appear to have been essentially the same, but by about 1754 both paste and glaze were modified, moons largely disappearing and the glaze becoming clearer and liable to craze. An almost constant feature of red-anchor pieces is the appearance of three or four small round 'spur marks' on the base. These very distinctive features greatly assist the identification of the relatively few unmarked Chelsea pieces of this period.

Chelsea painting in this period was almost always of great distinction, though many of the designs were of Japanese or German origin. Free copies of the Japanese 'Imari' designs in the so-called Kakiemon style (Plates 4 and 5) were especially popular and were designated in the Catalogues of 1755 and 1756 as 'wheatsheaf and pheasant', 'tyger and wheatsheaf', 'tyger and rock', 'nurl'd partridge pattern', and 'octogon plate, Hob in the Well'. The last was apparently the name of a popular play of the time, misapplied to a Japanese design illustrating the story of a boy who saved the life of a companion by breaking a water-jar into which he had fallen. A Chelsea example of the design is at South Kensington.

1 Reprinted in W. King, *Chelsea Porcelain* (1922), pp. 69–130.

2 Reprinted in R. W. Read, *The original Catalogue of One Year's Curious Production of the Chelsea Porcelain Manufactory*, Salisbury, 1880. Some extracts from both the 1755 and 1756 catalogues are given in Mackenna, *Chelsea Porcelain; The Red Anchor Wares.*

3 See Nightingale, pp. ix and x.

4 These were first observed by the famous collector Dr. H. W. Diamond.

5 Formerly thought to be due to aggregations of frit.

A. Bowl Dia. 6in (15.2cm); Ht. 3⅛in (7.9cm). Painted in
crimson monochrome. About 1755. No mark. *Schreiber
Collection (168)*

B. Bowl Dia. 3¾in (8.2cm); Ht.
2⅝in (6.6cm). About 1755. No
mark. *Schreiber Collection (190)*

C. Saucer Dia. 4¾in (12cm). About
1755. Red Anchor mark. *Schreiber
Collection (194)*

See page 42   Plate 10 CHELSEA

The large hexagonal vases (Plate 4), the bowls (Schr. No. 161), and the cups and saucers (Plate 5A, B) show the Chelsea treatment of these designs, which were all most probably copied at second hand, through versions made at Meissen.[1] The form of the bowls with outturned rim (as in the Schreiber Collection, Nos. 167 and 187: Plate 8C) was also exactly copied from Japanese porcelain of this type. Why one of the Kakiemon designs was called the 'old pattern' in the Catalogue is not clear. Another Japanese (Imari) type, copied in a single recorded instance,[2] has much underglaze blue as well as the red and green of the Kakiemons. The type was also copied at Worcester.[3] Chinese designs were more rarely used: a saucer-dish in the Allen Collection (No. 88: Plate 11A) is a charming original composition only slightly resembling the *famille rose* design by which it was inspired. The decoration on a basin of Japanese form in the Schreiber Collection (No. 167) is a version of Chinese painting of the *famille verte*. Blue-and-white porcelain, which inspired so much of the decoration at other factories, seems to have enjoyed little favour at Chelsea. The only known specimens in this mode are certain plates (examples are in both the National collections[4]), marked with an underglaze blue anchor and painted with a bird and plants in the Chinese style (Plate 6A), an octagonal saucer in the F. C. Dykes Collection[5], a fluted tall cup at the Victoria and Albert Museum,[6] and a cream jug at Bedford (Plate 3A). They are of an extremely rare and pleasant quality in both colour and glaze. The 'India plants' of the Chelsea catalogues were perhaps the '*indianische Blumen*' of early Meissen, adapted from the Chinese. Like most Eastern things at this time, Chinese and Japanese were alike 'Indian', from the name of the importing 'East India Companies'. The familiar brown edge of the Chinese 'export porcelain' was frequently copied, with a totally different effect, on Chelsea china of this period. Gilt edges are seldom seen, and gilding is in fact generally absent.

1 Compare E. Zimmermann, *Meissner Porzellan* (1926), Plate 5. See M. Shono, *Japanisches Aritaporzellan als Vorbild für die Meissener Porzellanmanufaktor*, Munich, 1973.

2 Frank Tilley, in *The Antique Collector*, vol. 18 (1947), p. 65.

3 Frank Lloyd No. 57.

4 Schr. no. 128 and B.M. II. 56.

5 *Transactions E.P.C.*, I (1928), p. 26.

6 Bernard Watney, *English Blue and White Porcelain of the 18th Century* (1963), Pl. IA.

A. DISH IN 'FAMILLE ROSE' STYLE Dia. 7in (17.7cm).
About 1755. Red Anchor mark. *Victoria and Albert
Museum (C.247-1935)*

B. DISH IN 'BROCADED IMARI' STYLE Dia. 9¼in (23.5cm).
About 1755. No mark. *Victoria and Albert Museum (C.245-
1935)*

39

See pages 36, 38, 68   Plate 11 CHELSEA

Meissen designs were at first quite frankly imitated.[1] It is known from a letter dated 1751[2] that pieces of Meissen porcelain, the property of Sir Charles Hanbury Williams, were lent for copying at Chelsea to Sir Everard Fawkener, who was stated in a letter to be 'concerned in the manufacture of China at Chelsea . . .' The writer added, '. . . I find that the Duke is a great encourager of the Chelsea China'. This is a reference to the Duke of Cumberland, whose secretary Fawkener became in 1744. It was stated by Mason, a workman at the factory (in an account quoted by Chaffers, third edition, 1870, p. 701) that the manufacture was at first carried on by the Duke of Cumberland and Sir Everard Fawkener, who employed 'a foreigner of the name of Sprimont . . . at a salary of a guinea per day'.[3] Scattered bunches of half-naturalistic flowers were directly copied from the '*deutsche Blumen*' of the Saxon factory, which also furnished the models for some of the moulded patterns of the rims, the 'nurl'd [or gnarled] borders' of the catalogues, many of which, however, were original in design though following the Meissen manner. (It is noteworthy that silversmiths' terms were often employed in descriptions in the Catalogue of

1 It has been argued by Mrs. Arundell Esdaile ('Some Eighteenth-Century Literary Allusions to Chelsea China', in the *Burlington Magazine*, vol. XLVI, Jan. 1925), that Meissen examples were copied as early as 1744. The specimen cited, a 'tankard' with a harbour scene, is of a type one would expect to find marked with a raised or red anchor, and we have no other evidence that pieces so marked can be ascribed to so early a date—a year earlier, it should be noted, than the 'goat-and-bee' jugs. Crude versions of Meissen flowers on triangle-marked pieces have already been mentioned. Mrs. Esdaile further quotes a letter from Lord Chesterfield dated 9 August 1750, referring to a 'little snuff-box', apparently of Chelsea china but perhaps from the 'Girl-in-a-Swing' factory, and saying 'how well we imitate the Dresden china, and for less than a quarter the price'. About a year later, Lord Chesterfield sent 'two china baubles', unspecified, to the same correspondent in Paris, who sent in return a present of china, apparently of French make, which the 'manager' of 'our manufacture' (presumably Nicholas Sprimont) begged to be allowed to borrow 'for a pattern'. One may guess that this was Mennecy or Saint-Cloud porcelain. Nothing of Vincennes origin of this date seems to have been copied at Chelsea, except perhaps porcelain flowers. See also T. H. Clarke, 'French Influences at Chelsea', in *Transactions E.C.C.*, vol. 4, part 5, pp. 45–57.

2 See a letter from the Earl of Ilchester to the *Burlington Magazine*, vol. XX (1911–12), p. 361.

3 The Duke's concern was probably limited to patronage only. Rouquet (op. cit., p. 143) said of the factory '. . . un riche particulier en soutient la dépense'. At a later date (1764) Sprimont, in an advertisement, contradicted the statement that the Duke of Cumberland proposed 'to purchase the secret', 'that so matchless an art should not be lost.'

B. CUP Ht. 2⅜in (6cm).
Painted in crimson. About
1752. Raised Anchor mark.
*Victoria and Albert Museum
(C.558-1920)*

A. SAUCER Dia. 4¾in (12cm). Fable
painting. About 1750–55. No mark.
Schreiber Collection (175)

. PLATE Dia. 5½in (14cm). About
752. Raised Anchor mark. *Victoria and
Albert Museum (C.558-1920)*

D. SAUCER Dia. 4⅝in (11.7cm). About
1750–55. No mark. *Schreiber Collection (174)*

ee pages 42, 44

Plate 12 CHELSEA

1755, even for pieces apparently not specifically of silver shape. 'Chas'd', 'wro't', 'scollop't' and 'nurl'd' constantly occur in the descriptions.) But before long the Chelsea painters developed several highly individual styles. On a seemingly early bottle of Chinese form which belonged to Jewitt, and is now in the Schreiber Collection (No. 155), the rather childish painting of a landscape already shows an original touch. A bowl (Schr. No. 187) figured in Plate 8C shows a scarcely modified Meissen style, whilst the plate of silver form in Plate 7A shows the typical Meissen-Chelsea flowers of this period. In *The Case of the Undertaker of the Chelsea Manufacture*, already quoted, the writer speaks of the employment of '. . . a nursery of thirty lads . . . bred to designing and painting', and the Chelsea painting may perhaps be indebted to these for its freshness, as much as to Fawkener and Sprimont for their taste in the direction of the work.

A gifted painter[1] with a manner all his own is associated in particular with a number of pieces with delightful designs illustrating Aesop's Fables (Plate 12A and Colour Plate A). Dr. Bellamy Gardner has shown[2] that some of these designs seem to have been suggested by an edition of the fables illustrated by Francis Barlow. The pattern of some splendid large dishes (Schreiber No. 182), which combines the scattered Meissen flowers with border-panels of figures and landscapes by this 'Fable Painter', is known as the 'Warren Hastings pattern', from a set with this design having formed part of his effects at a sale at Daylesford House in 1818. Plate 7B shows a smaller example with charming groups of figures. The same hand is seen in the attractive painting in crimson monochrome, the 'purple landskips' of the catalogues, very well represented by a bowl (Plate 10A) and a cup (Plate 12B) in the Schreiber Collection (Nos. 168 and 169), and Mr.

1 The names of the earlier Chelsea painters have never been discovered. The gossiping and inaccurate J. T. Smith in his *Nollekens and his Times* mentions one Paul Ferg, apparently the son of an artist of the same name; but we have no means of identifying his work. It has been argued from a cryptic 'signature' and from the style of some signed prints that the Chelsea Fable Painter was J. H. O'Neale (compare p. 268), whose signed work occurs on Worcester porcelain. But while red-anchor Chelsea pieces with fable subjects by O'Neale undoubtedly exist, it is strange that the gifted Fable Painter here in question should have so far lost his skill as to be capable of the crude work on the signed Worcester specimens.

2 *The Connoisseur*, vol. LXIV (Oct. 1922).

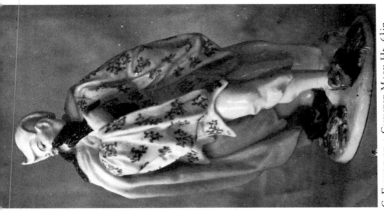

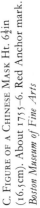

A. Figure of a Nun Ht. 5 7/16 in (13.8cm). About 1755–6. Red Anchor mark. *Boston Museum of Fine Arts*

B. Figure of a Chinaman Ht. 5 3/16 in (13.1cm). About 1755–6. Red Anchor mark. *Boston Museum of Fine Arts*

C. Figure of a Chinese Mask Ht. 6 1/2 in (16.5cm). About 1755–6. Red Anchor mark. *Boston Museum of Fine Arts*

See pages 48, 50

Plate 13 CHELSEA

Allen's dish figured in Plate 9A. This manner was a Meissen invention, and landscape styles from the same source, translated into English, are seen on another dish (Allen No. 84) and a charming cream-jug (Schr. 191 : Plate 8A), all probably by the hand of the same 'Fable Painter'. The river-scene on the pretty saucer shown in Plate 12D depicts a church which it is tempting to identify with that at Chelsea. A similar picture of Battersea Church occurs in a gold-anchor piece painted in black and green.[1] A rare style of figure-painting, one of the most attractive of all, is represented by a bowl in Mr. Bunford's collection[2] painted with cupids bearing a basket of grapes, in light brick-red; a cup and saucer is in Mr. Wallace Elliot's bequest to the Victoria and Albert Museum (Plate 31A). The charming piece figured in Plate 8D, with figures of children framed in a *rococo* scroll, shows the red-anchor style of painting at its most gracious.

A novel manner of flower-painting, found on Chelsea porcelain of this period, was apparently inspired by the earliest '*deutsche Blumen*' of Meissen, but many examples have been traced to drawings by Philip Miller of the Chelsea Physic Garden.[3] These 'botanical flowers' were doubtless those referred to as 'Sir Hans Sloane's' in a contemporary advertisement and perhaps the 'India plants' of the catalogues. This kind of decoration became common, and rather dull, on later English porcelain—at Derby and Swansea, for instance : but at Chelsea the freedom and feeling with which the painter interpreted his subjects entitle such examples as the plate at South Kensington and the cups and saucers in the Schreiber Collection (Plates 9B and 10C) to rank among the finest achievements of the factory, beautiful alike in drawing and colour. Of the same high quality are the cups, tureens and sauce-boats of a very distinctive class (again suggested by Meissen), in which applied leaves and flowers and twig handles, beautifully painted in by no means natural colours, play an important part. A masterpiece of this class is a large tureen in the collection at South Kensington with forget-me-nots in relief, well described in the

---

1 See p. 66.

2 *Cheyne Book*, No. 24, Plate 3.

3 H. Bellamy Gardner, 'Sir Hans Sloane's plants on Chelsea porcelain', in *Transactions E.P.C.*, IV (1932), p. 22; also Patrick Synge-Hutchinson, 'G. D. Ehret's Botanical Designs on Chelsea Porcelain' in *The Connoisseur*, October 1958.

A. GROUP OF 'DUTCH DANCERS' Ht. 7in (17.7cm).
About 1755. Red Anchor mark. *Schreiber Collection*
(137)

B. FRUIT SELLER Ht. 8¾in (22.2cm).
About 1755. Red Anchor mark.
Fitzwilliam Museum (Lord and Lady Fisher Collection)

C. FRUIT SELLER Ht. 8¼in (20.9cm).
About 1755. Red Anchor mark.
Fitzwilliam Museum (Lord and Lady Fisher Collection)

See pages 48, 50   Plate 14 CHELSEA

1755 Catalogue as 'a beautiful round tureen and cover, sprig handles, and a dish to ditto enamell'd with blue flowers'. The monochrome-blue flowers are of an exquisitely soft colour, essentially *rococo* and far more beautiful than the colour of their Meissen original. The characteristic applied leaves are seen by the handle of the beautifully painted mug figured in Plate 8B. The painting on two finger-bowls in the Schreiber Collection (No. 190: Plate 10B) was also suggested by Meissen. Of the fine tureens and dishes in the form of vegetables, fishes, animals and birds, all suggested by Meissen, the rabbit (Schr. No. 151: Plate 21D) 'big as the life', as the 1755 Catalogue described it, the rare swan (Plate 19B), the richly coloured fantastic hen and chickens (Plate 18B), the plaice, and the beautiful asparagus and cauliflower dishes (Plate 16A)—all represented at South Kensington—may be specially mentioned. A large assemblage of tureens in the form of birds is in the Cecil Higgins Collection at Bedford.[1] A problem in classification is presented by an unmarked dish given to the Victoria and Albert Museum by Dr. and Mrs. H. Bellamy Gardner, decorated with ears of corn in relief and painted with feathers. An unglazed fragment apparently from the same mould was found on the site of the Bow factory;[2] but a similar dish in Dr. Gardner's collection[3] is marked with the red anchor, and the model is almost certainly that sold in 1755 to accompany a tureen in the form of a partridge, such as that in the Allen Collection (No. 65), marked with the red anchor, which matches it in colour and painting. The Catalogue of 1755 mentions 'Two fine partridges in a beautiful dish with corn etc.' The Bow fragment must therefore be regarded as a piece of a copy of the Chelsea dish.[4]

The Chelsea porcelain figures of this period are by general consent among the finest ever made and the modeller Joseph Willems (b. 1716, d. 1766) was responsible for many of them.[5]

1 Mackenna, op. cit., figs. 73–87.
2 See *The Burlington Magazine*, vol. XL (1922), p. 224.
3 See his article in *The Connoisseur*, vol. LXV (1923), p. 150.
4 Tureens in the form of partridges of a different model were, however, made at Bow and Derby. See p. 110.
5 Arthur Lane, op. cit., pp. 63–4.

A. Finch with Cherries Ht. 8⅛in (20.6cm). About 1755. Red Anchor mark.
Schreiber Collection (146)

See page 52   Plate 15 CHELSEA

The rare raised-anchor figures differ from the red-anchor chiefly in colouring. There is, for instance, the characteristic way of tinting the cheeks bright red. Most of the raised-anchor figures are grotesque 'Callot figures' or characters from the Italian Comedy (Plate 3B), apart from the figures of birds, which are one of the chief glories of raised-anchor.

Meissen models were again a source of inspiration (though it is rare to find such exact copies as at Bow). But many examples were based on engravings, as in the case of the beautiful red-anchor *Leda and the Swan* (Schr. No. 134),[1] adapted from a composition of Boucher; and a group of a Chinese lady and boy formerly in Mr. Alfred Hutton's collection, which exactly reproduces an engraving by J. J. Baléchou after the same painter.[2] Some of them, such as the fine *Carpenter with his Tools*, of which there is an unsurpassed example at South Kensington (Plate 3C), appear to have been entirely original creations, but all have the freshness that can come with the spirited rendering of a borrowed theme. The Chelsea pair of *Masked ('Dutch') Dancers* (Schr. No. 137: Plate 14A) far surpasses its model, and all have a clear soft colouring with a sparing use of gold that is peculiar to the factory. In some instances (such as the *Beggars* in Plate 17A) the colouring is virtually limited to touches of a fine black. This slight colouring of the red-anchor figures gives special value to the delicious white material, which one is tempted to describe as the most beautiful porcelain ever made. The *Nurse* already mentioned occurs in various colourings of most distinguished quality. The three figures reproduced on Plate 13 well illustrate the delicate and significant modelling of the best red-anchor specimens.

A well-known model of a flower-holder in the form of two boys struggling with a large fish (Plate 19A) bears a close resemblance in style to certain Sèvres groups by La Rue, modelled about 1757.[3] It is unlikely, however, that La Rue worked for Chelsea, and all the models probably have a common origin in engravings after

1 R. J. Charleston (ed.), *English Porcelain 1745–1850*, Colour Plate 1.

2 See King, p. 38 and Plates 2 and 18. Though a similar model was made at Meissen, the closer correspondence of the Chelsea version with the engraving suggests that both were independently copied from it.

3 Two of these are in the Jones Collection at South Kensington (Nos. 138 and A).

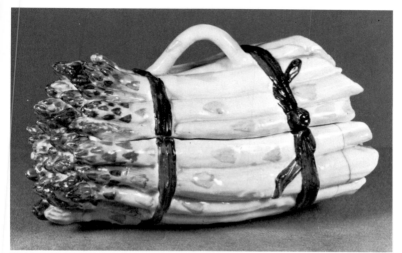

A. Asparagus Tureen L. 7in (17.7cm). About 1755. No mark. *Victoria and Albert Museum (C.176 and A-1940)*

B. Pair of 'Callot Dwarfs' Ht. 6⅛in (15.5cm) and 5⅛in (13cm). About 1750 and 1755. Male figure has the Red Raised Anchor mark; the female a Red Anchor mark. *Schreiber Collection (131)*

See pages 46, 48, 50   Plate 16 CHELSEA

Boucher. Bronzes in the same style are also known. A 'fine white group of boys and fish' was included in the sale of the stock of Thomas Turner[1] (one of Duesbury's employers).[2] Perhaps the finest of all the red-anchor figures are the wonderful *Man and Woman seated beside Baskets*, of which examples from Lord and Lady Fisher's fine collection are illustrated in Plate 14B and C. The *Madonna and Child*[3] is a unique instance of the treatment of this subject in English porcelain in the eighteenth century, whilst the *River God* and *Goddess*[4] in Mr. Alfred Hutton's collection and the big *Ceres* in Lord Fisher's collection[5] are noteworthy among the rare representations of the nude figure. The laughing head of a young girl, in Mr. Cyril Andrade's collection,[6] has been called Sophie Roubiliac, but is more probably an adaptation from a French bronze or marble original.

The *Pantaloon* and *Doctor* and others are specimens of the very popular figures after the Italian *Commedia dell' Arte*, adapted at Meissen from designs (some of them by Jacques Callot) in Riccoboni's *Histoire du Théâtre Italien*, first published in 1728.[7] The catalogue of 1755 speaks of 'Figures of the Italian Theatre' (Plates 3B and 13C). The *Carter* is probably adapted from Teniers; several figures are so described in the Catalogue of 1755. Of the 'Cupids for Desart' or 'Love in Disguise', which appear so often in the lists, one may mention such amusing creations as the *Cupid frying hearts*, and another with a heart in each hand. These are apparently original, though such figures were among Kaendler's numerous inventions. The figures of *Dwarfs* in the Schreiber Collection (No. 131) are of a type made at Meissen in the early years of the factory; these were adapted from the illustrations in a Dutch book *Il Calotto resuscitato*, and are consequently known as 'Callot figures' (Plate 16B). The male Chelsea figure (the earlier of the two at South Kensington) is actually derived from an etching of Jacques Callot

1 Nightingale, p. xxxviii.

2 Bemrose, *Bow, Chelsea and Derby Porcelain*, p. 8.

3 King, Plate 39. Lane, op. cit., plate 13. The 1755 Sale Catalogue included the item: 'An exceeding fine figure of a Madonna and Child with a cross in its hand'.

4 *Cheyne Book*, No. 137, Plate 9, and King, plates 35 and 36. Also Mackenna, op. cit., figs. 103 and 104.

5 Lane, op. cit., Plate 11.

6 *Transactions E.C.C.*, vol. 4, part 5, 1959, Plates 28d and e. Now in the Fitzwilliam Museum, Cambridge.

7 Mackenna, op. cit., fig. 130.

A. PAIR OF BEGGARS Ht. 7¾in (19.7cm). About 1755. Red Anchor
mark. *Victoria and Albert Museum (C.84 and A-1938)*

B. FIGURE REPRESENTING 'TOUCH' Ht. 11in
(27.9cm). About 1755. Red Anchor mark.
Fitzwilliam Museum (Lord and Lady Fisher Collection)

See pages 48, 52　　　　　　　　　　　　　　　　Plate 17 CHELSEA

in a series executed at Florence in 1616,[1] and was perhaps done directly from the print: no Meissen version is known. The woman is apparently an original creation, unless both were derived from examples in bronze or another material; there is a specimen of the male dwarf in silver-gilt in the Jones Collection at South Kensington (No. 295).

Three unusually large (11 in. high) figures, representing *Sight*,[2] *Smell*[3] and *Touch* (Plate 17B) from a set of the *Senses*[4] have an almost turbulent sweep that goes beyond the usual movement of the red-anchor style, but it is questionable whether the quality of a porcelain figure—essentially a toy—is not lost in a model on so large a scale.

A set of Meissen figures by Kaendler, doubtfully declared to be a caricature of the Saxon Court Orchestra and known as the '*Affenkapelle*'[5] served as models for the three monkeys (No. 136)in the Schreiber Collection ('*Monkies in different attitudes* playing on musick' is an entry in the Catalogue of 1756). These provide a rare instance of the exact copying of Meissen models.

The figures of birds, again suggested by Meissen examples and dating from the earlier part of this period, were copied with some fidelity from a text-book of natural history, shown by the late Dr. Bellamy Gardner to be *The Natural History of Uncommon Birds* by George Edwards (1743).[6] The charming *Blue Tits* in the British Museum (II. 52), the *Whip-poor-will* in the Fitzwilliam Museum at Cambridge (Plate 18A) and the *Barn Owls*, *Ptarmigan* and *Ducks* in the Schreiber Collection (Nos. 149, 143 and 142), are all fairly exact renderings of natural species, but the brightly coloured *Finch with Cherries* (Schr. No. 146, Plate 15) is apparently a fancy of the

---

1 Published at Nancy six years later under the title *Varie Gobbi figure di Jacopo Callot* (Meaume, No. 752). These figures were also much done at Derby and appear in the price list as 'pair grotesque punches'. See p. 147.

2 Figured as *Ganymede and the Eagle* in *The Cheyne Book*, No. 221, Plate 1.

3 King, *English Porcelain Figures*, fig. 18.

4 They are probably the 'large and beautiful' figure of *Smelling*, etc., of the 1755 Catalogue. *Hearing*, in white, is in the British Museum.

5 'Monkey Orchestra', not 'Ape's Chapel' as in one English book. Lane, op. cit., Plate 22A'

6 'The Chelsea Birds', in *Transactions E.P.C.*, III (1931), p. 55. Almost all the Chelsea figures of birds are of the raised-anchor period. Very few birds were made in the succeeding red-anchor period.

A. A 'WHIP-POOR-WILL' Ht. 6¼in
(15.8cm). About 1750. Raised
Anchor mark. *Fitzwilliam Museum*

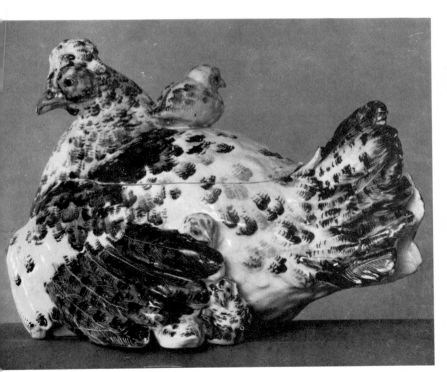

B. HEN AND CHICKEN TUREEN Ht. 9⅞in (25cm); L. 13¾in (34.9cm). About 1755. Red
Anchor mark. *Victoria and Albert Museum (C.75—b-1946)*

ee page 52

Plate 18 CHELSEA

painter's, and later in date. The three spirited birds figured in Plate 21 are all from the Schreiber Collection and show the characteristic treatment of the bases. The 'moss' on these is apparently peculiar to the 'raised-anchor' decoration; it distinguishes the earlier from the later of the two *Dwarfs* mentioned on the previous page. A charming use of the miniature Chelsea birds appears in the pigeon-houses, of which there is an example at South Kensington, evidently the 'magnificent perfume pot in the form of a Pidgeon House with pidgeons, a fox, etc.', of the Catalogue of 1755.[1] A similar piece with a dog and chickens, forming a clock-case, is at the British Museum (No. II. 32). A characteristic of the applied flowers on the bases of Chelsea figures of both the raised- and red-anchor periods is the ring of dots marking the centre and the distinct painting of the veins of the leaves in fine lines. Bases in this period were generally simple mounds.

No sale of Chelsea productions was held between 1756 and 1759, and Sprimont's illness, mentioned in an advertisement of 1757, may well have been the cause of inactivity, though another explanation is suggested by the financial difficulties of Sir Everard Fawkener, who died in 1758.[2] After this date Sprimont seems to have obtained complete control of the factory and sales began to be held again.

A change in the composition of the paste apparently dates from 1758 or the following year, when bone-ash began to be used at Chelsea.[3] This ingredient had already been in use at Bow for the previous ten years, and it is probably no coincidence that in 1758 the use of calcined bones in porcelain manufacture had been described in an anonymous work attributed to Robert Dossie, entitled *The Handmaid to the Arts*. It is also possible, of course, that the

1 Mackenna, op. cit., fig. 92. Reproduced in slightly different form by William Duesbury in the Chelsea-Derby period (1770–84).

2 See the account of Mason, previously mentioned, in Chaffers, op. cit., 3rd edition (1870), p. 701. Fawkener's family are said to have been left in poor circumstances (King, p. 32).

3 See analysis in Church, p. 25, and *Analysed Specimens*, pp. 13 and 30. It is stated in Groseley's *Tour to London* (1772) that Cornish clay was used at Chelsea in 1763; see Donald A. MacAlister, loc. cit., p. 139.

A. FLOWER HOLDER Ht. 8½in (21.6cm). About
1755. No mark. *Victoria and Albert Museum
(C.196-1926)*

B. SWAN TUREEN L. 21in (53.3cm). About 1752–6. Red Anchor mark. *Cecil
Higgins Museum, Bedford*

See pages 46, 48   Plate 19 CHELSEA

use of this ingredient was suggested by a workman who had been employed at Bow during the period just before this date.[1] Sprimont was no doubt much concerned to make his manufacture as little hazardous as possible, and would readily have adopted the strengthening ingredient. The glaze of this period was as a rule thick and glassy ('juicy' is the collector's word), and especially liable to craze, collecting in pools and hollows and there showing a greenish tone. It was, however, no less soft than before, and the colours sank into it with equally rich effect. The practice of grinding the foot level, common in the red-anchor period, now became the rule, and the paste thus exposed is so smooth as to seem almost greasy to the touch.

Sales of the Chelsea china were held in 1759 (when a different auctioneer—Burnsall—was for the first time employed in place of Ford), in 1760 and in 1761.[2] In 1761 it was advertised that no further sales would be held, owing to Sprimont's 'indisposition', and no sale was in fact held in 1762, though certain pieces may be quite definitely assigned to that year.[3] The seventh sale was held in 1763, when the moulds and premises and Sprimont's household furniture were also offered, as he proposed to 'retire farther into the country'. Some items have been found in auctioneers' catalogues for 1764 and the following years, but no further sale was held until 1769. The workman Mason declared that by this time Sprimont had amassed a fortune, and that little work was done at the factory after 1763. The reduction of the manufacture is implied in a dealer's advertisement of 1768, speaking of porcelain 'even still brought from that noble manufactory'. In advertising the sale in 1769, Burnsall spoke of the china as the work of 'Mr. Nicholas Sprimont, the Proprietor of the Chelsea Porcelain Manufactory, he having entirely left off making the same . . .'. The models and materials were again offered, and in August of the same year Sprimont actually sold the factory to James Cox, by whom it was in February 1770 re-sold to William Duesbury and John Heath, of Derby. The last sale of the Chelsea porcelain was held by Christie,

1 Mason, the workman previously mentioned, had been so employed. See p. 82 for an account of the introduction of bone-ash at Bow.

2 For the catalogue of this sale, see W. H. Tapp, in *Apollo*, 1941, xxxiii, p. 140 and xxxiv, p. 15.

3 See below, p. 62.

REAPER Ht. 12½in (31.7cm). About 1760. No mark. *Schreiber Collection (196)*

See page 60

Plate 20 CHELSEA

beginning on 14 February 1770. The catalogue of this sale survives and was published by Nightingale.[1] An inventory has been preserved[2] of certain porcelain disputed between Duesbury and Heath and the executors of the factory foreman Francis Thomas (*d.* 1770), who was accused of having embezzled it in 1769. The advertisements of the earlier sales, however, help us to date the introduction of the coloured grounds which rank among the fine achievements of the period. The general use of the mark of a gold anchor assists in the identification of Chelsea porcelain of the last period, though it is sometimes doubtful whether a late piece was made at Chelsea or at Derby after the sale of the factory. Duesbury appears to have used the anchor mark freely, even before his purchase of the Chelsea concern.[3] The gold anchor, it should also be remembered, has often been added on Coalport, Tournay and modern French and German imitations of Chelsea and Derby models.

Accompanying the change in composition of the paste is to be noted a marked change of style, which may have been due to Sprimont's unshared management of the factory in this last period. A similar development is, however, to be noted in the productions of the German factories in the same period. The inspiration was shared by all. At Meissen, Kaendler had created before 1760 such models as the *Shepherdess with a Birdcage*;[4] at Frankenthal, Konrad Link modelled his *Thetis* and *Oceanus*;[5] and these amongst many others, show the same largeness of style with sumptuous colouring and profuse gilding such as are characteristic also of the best 'gold-anchor' figures of Chelsea. The bases broke into a riot of scrollwork, and this last and most splendid expression of the *rococo* spirit produced in the porcelain which is its fittest embodiment, works which may perhaps be considered the most important plastic sculpture of their time. The modelling of some of the large

1 Nightingale, p. 1

2 Bemrose, *Bow, Chelsea and Derby Porcelain*, p. 45.

3 Compare the Derby *Lord Chatham* in the Schreiber Collection, No. 306. See p. 140.

4 See M. Sauerlandt, *Deutsche Porzellan-Figuren*, Plate 18. This figure, as it happens, was copied at Chelsea late in the red-anchor period, within a short time of its appearance at Meissen. But in this it merely anticipates the 'grand manner' of the later style.

5 Sauerlandt, op. cit., Plates 76 and 77.

A   C

A. Crested Bird Ht. 8¼in (20.9cm). About 1750. Raised Red Anchor mark.
Schreiber Collection (139)
B. Crested Bird Ht. 6½in (16.5cm). About 1750. Raised Anchor mark.
Schreiber Collection (144)
C. Hen Harrier Ht. 6¾in (17.1cm). About 1750. Raised Anchor mark.
Schreiber Collection (140)

D. Rabbit Tureen Ht. 8⅞in (22.5cm); L. 14½in (36.8cm). About 1755. Red
Anchor mark. *Schreiber Collection (151)*

See pages 46, 54   Plate 21 CHELSEA

vases (such as those in the Jones Collection: Plate 28) is remarkable for its wanton extravagance, but truly fascinating to one who has fallen under its spell. The forms of 'useful wares' (if the term may be used of such things) show the same extravagant fancy (Plate 29A).

Some of the best examples in the national museums are those in the Schreiber Collection, and there are very fine pieces in Mrs. Salting's Bequest at the Museum of London. Typical of the period in their grand manner are the *Shepherd and Shepherdess* (Schr. No. 199) and the *Actor in Turkish Costume* (No. 201: Plate 30), and, above all, the *Reaper* (Plate 20), all of them apparently original work by the same gifted modeller. The *Music Lesson* (Schr. No. 197), the pair of groups symbolising the *Seasons* (Schr. No. 198) and the *Fable Candlesticks* (Schr. No. 222: Plate 25B) show the extravagant development of the *bocage* at this time. These all bear the 'repairer's' mark of an impressed 'R', mentioned above in connection with the sculptor Roubiliac, to whom they were formerly ascribed. The *Music Lesson* was evidently based on an engraving, probably by R. Gaillard,[1] after Boucher's painting *L'Agréable Leçon*. Another version of the same subject, widely different in treatment, occurs also in Frankenthal[2] porcelain. The specimen in the Schreiber Collection is in astonishingly good preservation, and it is interesting to note that an example was sold in 1770 for £8. The Catalogue entry reads: 'A very large and curious group of a shepherd teaching a shepherdess to play on the flute'. A characteristic breadth of style distinguishes the superb *Apollo* and *Muses* (from which is reproduced in Plate 27 the stately *Melpomene*), the *Una and the Lion* and the *Bacchus*. The curious *Roman Charity*, adapted from an engraving after Rubens, is no less splendid, and was evidently popular, since it was singled out for special mention in the advertisements of the sale in 1769. The model of the great *Pietà*[3] was also used at Tournay,[4] and may have been adapted from

1 Prints were engraved by R. Gaillard and J. E. Nilson after this painting; and an impression of one by the latter is exhibited as part of the Schreiber Collection (No. 1818). It is known that an engraving by Gaillard, *Le Berger Récompensé* after Boucher, was reproduced on the Chelsea vase given to the Foundling Hospital, mentioned below, p. 74.

2 See Hofmann, *Frankenthaler Porzellan*, vol. I, Plate 35.

3 Figured in King, Plate 64. Also Lane, op. cit., Plate 28.

4 Compare Soil de Moriamé, *Les Porcelaines de Tournai*, Plate 11 (No. 691).

A. Plate Dia. 8½in (21.6cm). About 1760–5. Gold Anchor
mark. *Schreiber Collection (211)*

B. Plate Dia. 8¾in (22.2cm). About 1760–5. Gold Anchor
mark. *Victoria and Albert Museum (2948-1901)*

See page 68   Plate 22 CHELSEA

a painting by Van Dyck or one of his school.[1] It was almost certainly the work of Joseph Willems, to whom may be attributed many of the finest Chelsea models produced between 1750 and 1766, in which year he went to Tournay, where he died.[2]

Another new type first seen apparently in the early part of this period is represented by the *Family Groups*, of which one is figured in Plate 25A. Usually marked with the gold anchor, they have a somewhat Bow-ish simplicity and charm though often falling between the delicacy of red-anchor and the magnificence of the more usual later style. The *Fortune Tellers* and the groups and candlesticks on large flat bases with scrolled feet also belong to this transitional class. The *Hawker with Lantern* and his companion at South Kensington are smaller but not less attractive pieces, again to some extent following the Meissen style of the preceding period.

Meissen styles had been by this time largely superseded by those of Sèvres, and the coloured grounds, brought to perfection by the latter though in most cases invented in Germany, apparently began to be imitated at Chelsea as early as 1755 when 'an exceeding rich blue enamel' is mentioned in the Catalogue. This may have been the so-called 'Mazareen' or 'Mazarin'[3] blue, one of the chief splendours of the gold-anchor period. A blue described by this name is in fact mentioned in the catalogue of the following year (1756), but most of the characteristic pieces surviving are evidently of later date. Evidence as to this is furnished by two large vases presented to the British Museum[4] in 1763 by an anonymous donor who stated that they had been made at Chelsea in the previous year. The Chelsea advertisement of 1763 specially mentions 'the most

1 Compare E. Schaeffer, *Van Dyck* (*Klassiker der Kunst*), p. 447, where a painting in the Hofmuseum at Vienna is reproduced; another painting, apparently a copy of the last, is in the Prado at Madrid, and is there ascribed to Rubens or one of his school. See Adolf Rosenberg, *P. P. Rubens* (in the series just cited), p. 391.

2 W. B. Honey, 'The relations between English and Continental porcelain', in *Transactions E.C.C.*, VII (1939), p. 88. Also Arthur Lane, *English Porcelain Figures of the 18th Century*, p. 81.

3 There is no evidence to connect the name with Cardinal Mazarin, and its origin remains a mystery. It is sometimes used for a 'powdered blue' ground, but in the Chelsea catalogues a dark-blue glaze or underglaze blue is meant—the *gros bleu* of Sèvres. The term is discussed by J. V. G. Mallet in *Transactions E.C.C.*, vol. 6, part I, pp. 19–20.

4 *Catalogue*, No. II, 28, Plate 8.

VASE, mazarine-blue and gold. Ht. 12¼in (31.1cm). About
1765. Gold Anchor mark. *Schreiber Collection (207)*

rare and truly inimitable Mazarine Blue and Gold'. Among the finest of all the specimens justly so described are a pair of vases formerly in Mr. R. W. M. Walker's collection. From the time of its manufacture, this type has always been especially prized, and it is indeed a wonderful fancy. Specimens described as 'Satyr bottles of the mazarin blue, embellish'd with burnished gold grapes, highly finish'd with gold birds, most curiously chas'd' were sold in 1770 for £10 5s and £13; and another of the same pattern was sold to 'Esdail' for £38 17s at the sale of Queen Charlotte's effects in 1819. In *A Book for a Rainy Day* (London, 1845), J. T. Smith said these vases with raised gilding and mazarine blue are in the Schreiber collection, seen by him in 1829. Mr. Walker's vases may well be the same pair. The vases in the Jones Collection (Plate 28) are superb examples of *rococo* modelling, and their painting in gold shows a remarkable combination of refinement and vitality. Three fine vases with raised gilding and mazarine blue are in the Schreiber Collection (No. 207: Plate 23), as well as a mirror-stand (No. 208), which may be mentioned as showing especially original and successful application of the mazarine colour. The model of the last, with its amusing scroll-work, is repeated in a complete mirror and stand in the Herbert Allen Collection (No. 54). The pea-green ground made its first appearance in 1759, and in 1760 the sale advertisement announced the production of 'some new Colours which have been found this year by Mr. Sprimont, the proprietor, at very large expence, incredible Labour, and close Application': these were probably the turquoise-blue and the so-called claret-colour, the 'crimson' of the contemporary catalogues. The last, though probably intended as an imitation of the very different pink or *rose Pompadour*[1] of Sèvres, has never been equalled as a sumptuous ground. Its unevenness adds a vibrating quality to a very rich colour. Perhaps the finest of all surviving examples are in the bequest of Miss Emily Thomson at South Kensington (Plate 29A). The service to which this beautiful group of pieces belonged may well have been the '*very curious and matchless tea and coffee*

---

1 Often miscalled *rose du Barry*. Madame du Barry did not come to Court until 1769, by which time this colour had fallen into disfavour at Sèvres. The Chelsea ground now called 'claret-colour' was at first called 'crimson' in contemporary references, but an advertisement of 1768, cited by Nightingale (p. xxvi), speaks of 'Mazareen and Pompadour Sets for Deserts'.

A. PLATE Dia. 8½in (21.6cm). About 1760–5. Gold Anchor mark.
Ex. A. H. S. Bunford Collection

B. PLATE Dia. 6¼in (15.8cm). About 1760–5. Red Anchor mark.
Victoria and Albert Museum (C.669-1938)

See pages 68, 70   Plate 24 CHELSEA

equipage, crimson and gold, most inimitably enamell'd in figures from the designs of Watteau', sold for £43 at Christie's in 1770. Other good specimens are the dishes at the British Museum No. II. 70, and in the Schreiber Collection No. 215. The pea-green and the turquoise are not so often seen as ground colours on Chelsea, the vase in Plate 29B being an example of the latter. A yellow ground, one of the first to be introduced at Meissen, is seen surrounding some beautifully painted flowers on a fine chocolate-cup and saucer and on a pair of dishes, of the favourite heart-shape, with the rare mark of an anchor in blue enamel (Schr. Nos. 184 and 216). The yellow ground with panelled decoration is rare in Chelsea porcelain, but occurs on a tea-service in Mr. Alfred Hutton's collection, exhibited at Chelsea in 1924.[1] As these are all decorated in the style of the German factory, they are possibly earlier specimens on which the ground colour was copied from Meissen rather than from the *jaune jonquille* of Sèvres. But Meissen styles were rarely used in this period, and Vincennes inspiration probably accounts for an attractive style of painting in black washed over with green, as on a group of pieces in the Schreiber Collection, including a plate (No. 204 with a view of Battersea Church), and charming sets of heart- and fan-shaped toilet-boxes. This decoration may have been done in the workshop of James Giles,[2] outside the factory; the specimen shown here (Plate 31B) is apparently the work of the painter of the dishevelled birds whose hand is recognisable on Bow and Worcester porcelain.[3] The green-and-black style is also found on Worcester.

A famous service of later Chelsea porcelain[4] was given in 1763 by George III and Queen Charlotte to the latter's brother, the Duke of Mecklenburg-Strelitz. It was mentioned by Horace Walpole in a letter of 4 March 1763: '. . . I saw yesterday a magnificent service of Chelsea China, which the King and Queen are sending to the Duke of Mecklenburg. There are dishes and plates without number, an épergne, candlesticks, salt-sellers, sauce-boats, tea and coffee equipages, in short, it is complete, and

1 *Cheyne Book*, No. 52, Plate 21.
2 Compare p. 268.
3 Or perhaps more a 'style' than the work of a particular artist.
4 Now in the Royal Collection. Ref. J. V. E. Mallet in *English Porcelain, 1745–1850* (ed. Charleston), p. 37 and Plate 5A.

A. FAMILY GROUP Ht. 7in (17.7cm). About 1760.
Gold Anchor mark. *Ex. Alfred E. Hutton Collection*

B. FABLE CANDLESTICK Ht. 10¼in (26cm). About
1765–70. No mark. *Schreiber Collection (222)*

See pages 60, 62   Plate 25 CHELSEA

costs twelve hundred pounds! I cannot boast of our taste; the forms are neither new, beautiful, nor various. Yet Sprimont the manufacturer is a Frenchman. It seems their taste will not bear transplanting.' The Schreiber Collection includes a specimen of this service in a pair of branch candelabra (No. 210), sold as damaged by the steward of the ducal household. A plate with a similar pattern (Schr. No. 211: Plate 22A) is probably part of the service advertised in 1763 and 1764[1] as 'the same as the Royal Pattern which was sold for 1150 Pounds'.

A favourite decoration in this period took the form of scale pattern (sometimes applied in gilding over the coloured grounds) resembling peacock's feathers, as on a plate and a cup and saucer in the Allen Collection (Nos. 70 and 93: Plate 26A), and the fine chocolate-cup and saucer in the Schreiber Collection (No. 218). The cups of 'artichoke pattern' of the 1770 Catalogue were probably of a similar pattern moulded in slight relief, which is often seen. This moulded scale pattern is shown on the plate at South Kensington figured in Plate 24B, which also shows the characteristic flowers of the gold-anchor period. It is interesting to note that this plate, though of the later body and glaze and decorated in the later style, bears a *red*-anchor mark. A singular style, totally different in effect from anything in English porcelain of the time, is seen in some pieces painted with crowded flowers on an entirely gilt ground. A covered bowl and stand at the British Museum is an example (II.95); whilst a plate at South Kensington (Plate 22B) is a rare instance of flowers by the same hand on a ground left white.

Far-Eastern models were seldom copied in this period, but an exception is found in the versions of the 'brocaded' Japanese porcelain made at Arita and so largely exported from Imari. These greatly surpass in beauty their dull originals. The brocaded design is common to earlier and later periods, and two specimens in Mr. Herbert Allen's collection (Nos. 86 and 87: Plate 11B) are of red-anchor paste; similar plates are sometimes marked with the anchor in underglaze blue,[2] like the blue-and-white plates already mentioned. The soft tone of blue is similar on all these. But two

1 Nightingale, pp. xxiv and xxv.

2 Mackenna, op. cit., figs. 3 and 4; other Far-Eastern designs shown in figs. 5–17.

A. PLATE Dia. 8⅜in (21.9cm). About 1760–5. Gold Anchor mark. *Victoria and Albert Museum (C.252-1935)*

B. PLATE Dia. 8½in (21.6cm). About 1760–5. Gold Anchor mark. *Victoria and Albert Museum (2945-1901)*

See pages 68, 70

Plate 26 CHELSEA

examples in the Schreiber Collection (No. 221), with a stronger blue, have the gold anchor, and this is more usually found. The pattern doubtless continued to be used in the 'Chelsea-Derby' period.

In general, the painting of the later Chelsea porcelain, though more extravagant than in the preceding period, is not less accomplished, and the same hands may sometimes be recognised. The so-called exotic birds[1] which frequently appear were soon to become a characteristic feature of the more ambitious English porcelain. One bird-painter of ability is proved to be no other than the artist of the fable-subjects of the earlier pieces by the occurrence of these subjects, treated with somewhat greater assurance than before, on a large gold-anchor-marked tureen in the Allen Collection (No. 61), while its fellow (No. 63) is painted with the very distinctive birds (including one in red monochrome) often seen on pieces marked with the gold anchor. The same touch may be recognised in the handling of trees and ground. This painter's work is seen again on two beautiful flower-holders in Mr. Allen's collection (No. 53) and on a pear-shaped vase in the Schreiber Collection (No. 220). Another sort of exotic bird (Plate 26B) shows the bold touch of a painter who also painted Worcester porcelain,[2] and associated with these are the no less sumptuously rendered fruit (again inspired by Meissen), which became, like the birds, a favourite subject for porcelain-painting. They are rendered with the most magnificent effect in the set of dishes in the Thomson Bequest at South Kensington, in which the fruit-painting is combined with the finest mazarine blue and the richest gilding. The dusky richness of colour of these dishes represents perhaps the highest pitch of splendour ever reached in English porcelain. More naturalistic bird-painting is seen on the charming plate from Mr. Bunford's collection figured in Plate 24A and on a plate with 'peacock's eye' ground and beautiful gilding in Mr. Allen's collection (No. 93: Plate 26A). The birds in crimson monochrome, represented by a bowl and stand in the British Museum (Barwell Bequest), should also be mentioned here.

1 The 'Fantasievögel' invented at Meissen.
2 Perhaps a James Giles artist. See p. 264 for his Worcester work. His style was closely copied in the nineteenth century at Derby. There is a dish in this manner at South Kensington, with the red Crown-Derby mark.

THE MUSE MELPOMENE Ht. 15in (38.1cm) (including detachable base). About
1765. Gold Anchor mark and 'R' impressed. *Ex. R. W. M. Walker Collection*

Sèvres porcelain was the medium through which were derived the delightful *chinoiseries* on the claret-ground tea-service in the Thomson Bequest (Plate 29A). These were described in the catalogue quoted above as 'from the design of *Watteau*', but Watteau actually did little work in this style, which is more justly ascribed to Pillement. The *chinoiserie* is an interesting phenomenon. As porcelain-decoration it may be traced to J. G. Herold, and Meissen examples can be dated as early as 1725. The name 'Chippendale Chinese' sometimes given to these figures records the phase when the vogue spread to English furniture. Two hands may be recognised in these 'Chinese' figures on Chelsea porcelain. One of these, the painter of the tea-service just mentioned, perhaps went to Worcester.[1] Another, who painted larger figures, was perhaps an 'outside decorator', since the fine octagonal vases with his work[2] seem rarely to be marked, though a set of three apparently from his hand, formerly in Lt.-Col. Croft-Lyons' collection,[3] has the gold-anchor. Two other vases with this painting, in the Barwell Bequest at the British Museum, have an unusually light blue ground. They also are unmarked. This style is sometimes attributed to John Donaldson (*b.* 1737, *d.* 1801), a miniature-painter who by tradition is said to have worked for the factory. A charmingly direct style of figure-painting is seen in some other subjects, such as that after Teniers on the vase with turquoise-ground figured in Plate 29B. The 'Watteau subjects' by this hand on a fine vase in the British Museum (Barwell Bequest) have also been ascribed to Donaldson, but this style is seen on toys which are not likely to have been painted by him, and it is very unlike his signed work on Worcester porcelain.[4]

If Donaldson did in fact decorate Chelsea porcelain he is far more likely to have been the painter of some of the elaborate figure-subjects in the style of Boucher and Rubens, or the naturalistic birds after Hondekoeter, which decorate the imposing vases in the Sèvres manner made in this period. These are commonly modelled in the most riotous *rococo* style, and the

1 See p. 270.
2 Such as one at South Kensington, or that in Mr. Hutton's collection (*Cheyne Book*, No. 83, Plate 24), closely imitated from Meissen.
3 King, *Chelsea Porcelain*, Plate 54.
4 See p. 270.

Vase, mazarine-blue and gold. Ht. 14¼in (36.2cm). About 1765. Gold Anchor mark. *Jones Collection, Victoria and Albert Museum (827-1882)*

See pages 60, 64   Plate 28 CHELSEA

painting in panels reserved on the coloured grounds is remarkable for its directness and freedom. The classics of this style are of course the seven 'Dudley vases' said to have been made for presentation by George III to Lady Liverpool, subsequently in the possession of Lord Dudley and now in Lord Bearsted's collection.[1] Typical figure-painting is seen on the fantastic vase in Plate 34. Most of those pieces were evidently made to order for presentation, and could never have been articles of commerce. Two such vases in the British Museum with mazarine-blue ground (No. II. 28) are recorded as 'made in the year 1762, under the direction of Mr. Sprimont'. The anonymous donor is supposed to have been a Dr. George Garnier, who presented to the Foundling Hospital at about the same time a somewhat similar vase with a subject after Boucher; its companion was in the possession of Lord Chesterfield. Both are illustrated in M. L. Solon, *Old English Porcelain*, Nos. 21 and 22.[2] In the British Museum, too, are a great vase and stand, and a large covered jar with a figure of Diana (Nos. II. 27 and 29), which represent this elaborate manner at its best; and a group of fantastically modelled vases in this style is in the Jones Collection at South Kensington.[3] On one of these last is a careful landscape which is apparently an early work by Zachariah Boreman, who afterwards created a broader style familiar on Derby porcelain. Askew, who also went to Derby, was perhaps the painter of figure-subjects on some of these vases. Their styles were continued into the Chelsea-Derby period, when Classical symmetry began to replace the caprice of the *rococo*,[4] and a further account of the work of these painters will be found on a later page.

1 Three of them are illustrated in King, Plates 57 and 58.

2 Both the 'Foundling' and 'Chesterfield' vases are now in the Victoria and Albert Museum collection (C.52 and 53—1964). These vases, and their history, together with the similar pair in the Judge Untermyer Collection (New York), and that in the British Museum, are described and illustrated by J. V. G. Mallet in the *V. & A. Bulletin*, I (Jan. 1965), pp. 29–36.

3 Nos. 172 and 172A.

4 It has been remarked by Mr. William King that the *Louis Seize* style made its appearance some years before the death of Louis XV; and three stately vases in Mr. Herbert Allen's collection (Nos. 47 and 48, Plate 57B), obviously made in imitation of Sèvres porcelain, might be regarded as Chelsea from the quality of their claret ground, though the symmetry of their forms decidedly suggests the later period. See also pp. 148, 150.

A. TEA SERVICE WITH CLARET GROUND WITH 'CHINESE' FIGURES Teapot ht. 5⅜in (13.6cm); W. 4¼in (10.8cm); Cups ht. 2¾in (7cm); Saucers dia. 5⅜in (13.6cm). About 1760–5. Gold Anchor marks. *Victoria and Albert Museum (517-523-1902)*

B. VASE WITH TURQUOISE GROUND WITH TENIERS SUBJECTS Ht. 6¾in (17.1cm). About 1760–5. Gold Anchor mark. *Victoria and Albert Museum (477-1902)*

See pages 60, 64, 72   Plate 29 CHELSEA

If these great vases represent Sprimont's most ambitious performances, the unique and tiny objects for long known as 'Chelsea toys' are more rightly regarded as among the most highly prized of all Chelsea productions (Plates 32 and 33). These scent-bottles, *bonbonnières*, needle-cases, thimbles, seals, knife-handles, miniature figures and the like, were for long mistaken for Sèvres productions but this can only have been in England! They seem to have originated, not at Sprimont's factory, but at the 'Girl-in-a-Swing' factory. Most of Sprimont's examples were produced in the gold-anchor period and their manufacture in quantity continued after the factory had passed into the control of Duesbury of Derby in 1769. They were even much exported to the Continent: specimens in the Schreiber Collection were bought at Valencia and Granada,[1] and an advertisement of 1756 includes 'Chelsea China Knives and Forks' and 'Smelling Bottles' in the sale of the 'intire stock of Laumas and Rolyat, late of Lisbon'. A reference to 'flacons de sel d'Angleterre' occurs in Beaumarchais' *Mariage de Figaro*[2] and Chelsea scent-bottles may have been meant. A sale devoted solely to these objects was advertised in 1754, 'By Order of the Proprietors of the Chelsea Porcelain Manufactory', as follows: '. . . All the entire stock of Porcelain Toys . . . consisting of Snuff-boxes, Smelling Bottles, Etwees and Trinkets for Watches (mounted in gold and unmounted) in various beautiful shapes, of an elegant design and curiously painted in enamel. . . . A large parcel of Porcelain Hafts for table and Dessert Knives and Forks.' It has now been shown[3] that the contents of this sale were not likely to have been made by Sprimont at all, but were almost certainly acquired from the then defunct 'Girl-in-a-Swing' factory.

Though some of the 'Chelsea' toys were inspired by Kaendler, most of them show the characteristic English sentiment of the time, surprising in the work of a foreigner. That the delicious mottoes in mis-spelt French were copied from script is proved by

---

1 Nos. 250 and 273.

2 Quoted by Max Sauerlandt in the *Kunstsammlerjahrbuch* for 1924–5, in an essay on 'Chelsea Toys', which is an admirable study of eighteenth-century sentiment as well as a tribute to Sprimont's genius.

3 Lane, op. cit., pp. 77–84, and *Transactions E.C.C.*, vol. 5, part 3, pp. 111–43, and see pp. 49–51.

ACTOR IN TURKISH COSTUME Ht. 12¾in (32.4cm). About 1760. Gold
Anchor mark. *Schreiber Collection (201)*

See page 60

Plate 30 CHELSEA

such mistakes as 'L'ESPERANU' for 'L'ESPÉRANCE'.[1] Such an error would be unlikely to occur in copying from another model bearing the inscription in capitals, but is easy to understand if the legend were provided for the English painter in the form of a manuscript copy.

The Schreiber Collection is rich in toys of the finest quality. The patch-box in the form of a woman's head (No. 231 : Plate 33A), and the even finer man's head (No. 274), the *bonbonnière* with a lady caressing a dog (No. 271), and the charmingly indefinite group of a rabbit with its young (No. 229) may be specially mentioned. All these and many others have lids of enamel-painting on copper, presumably made in the London or Midlands enamel factories. Some of the models are found also entirely in enamel,[2] as, for instance, the scent-bottles in the form of a *Boy as a gardener* (No. 279 : Plate 33I). Many Kaendlerish small figures represent Cupid in various employments. Among the tiny figures mounted as seals (Plate 33B) he is seen holding a heart in each hand; the *bonbonnière* (No. 270 : Plate 32B) in the form of a Cupid playing upon a pair of kettledrums in the form of a woman's breasts, with the inscription 'POUR LES CAVALIERS DE CITHERE'; Cupid with a woman, standing beside a clock (No. 242) inscribed 'L'HEURE DU BERGER FIDELLE', and No. 243, Cupid at a furnace distilling a potion ('MON FEU DURERA TOUJOURS') are typical of these. Soft colouring and a purposeful indefiniteness mark such models as the *étui* with Daphne turning into a laurel (No. 227 : Plate 32I), and that with Cupid and a pair of doves on a column (No. 266 : Plate 32G), inscribed 'IMITEZ NOUS'. The same quality distinguishes a fine *bonbonnière* in the Museum collection at South Kensington (Plate 33H), in the form of a fantastic crouching camel, with panniers containing hay and lambs over its back. Some beautiful painting distinguishes the *rococo* scent-bottle (Schr. No. 234 : Plate 33C), and an *étui* in the British Museum (Plate 32E). A charming fancy of Sprimont's took the form of a group of nautical instruments, a set of hunting implements (inscribed '[LA] CHAS[SE] DES BELLES), or a table laid for a meal. The inscriptions with their almost invariably

---

1 'JE VOUS COFFRE' (for L'OFFRE) and 'JE VOUS CHARMEIAY' contain similar errors.

2 Almost certainly South Staffordshire.

A. Cup and Saucer Cup ht. 1¾in (4.4cm); Saucer dia.
5in (12.7cm). About 1755. Red Anchor mark. *Victoria
and Albert Museum (C.18 and a-1938)*

B. Plate Painted in Black and Green Dia. 8¼in (20.9cm).
About 1770. No mark. *Schreiber Collection (205)*

See pages 44, 66 Plate 31 CHELSEA

amorous suggestions are a study in themselves: Cupid triumphant, with a net or holding a bag of hearts ('AUCUN NE L'ECHAPERAS' or 'AQUIS PAR MON COURAGE'), holding up a globe ('JE SOUTIENS LE MONDE'), or in a lawyer's wig ('JE PLAIS POUR MA BELLE'); the boy trying to rouse a pig ('PEINE PERDU') or Europa garlanding the bull ('TROMPERIE D'AMOUR'); the cat ('JE BRILLE DANS L'OBSCURITE') and the toy dog ('CHIEN SAVANT'). 'JE VIS EN ESPERANCE' is significantly written on a scent-bottle with a boy snaring birds (Plate 33G). But the parrot is 'DISCRET EN AMOUR'; the soldier, 'MUNI POUR VOUS RESISTER'; and among the exquisite fruits and bunches of flowers we find 'POINT DE ROSES SANS EPINES'. A snuff-box with the British lion devouring the Gallic cock, with the inscription 'MALGRE TA FIERTE TU PERIS' (B.M. No. II. 165), is a rare instance of a political reference, revealing Sprimont the Huguenot as no lover of France. Many of these can be seen in the British Museum as well as in the Schreiber Collection, and a complete repertory is contained in Mr. Bryant's monograph on these very charming objects. Of the toy figures, the delightful gardeners may be mentioned. One of these and two other specimens from Lord and Lady Fisher's collection are figured in Plate 33D, E and F. The little man with a wheelbarrow is represented at South Kensington, where there is also a specimen, in the form of strawberries and leaves, of the 'matchless knives and forks of the Chelsea china' advertised in 1759.

Chapter 3

Bow

The materials for a history of Bow china were until recently of the scantiest; however, largely as a result of the special exhibition of documentary material relating to the Bow China Factory held at the British Museum in 1959–60, stimulus was given to research and valuable documentary evidence concerning the date of commencement and place of manufacture in particular has been brought to light.

Bow (properly Stratford-le-Bow) is in East London. But the manufactory with whose products we are concerned was actually established at Stratford Langhorne, in the nearby parish of West Ham on the east or Essex side of Bow Bridge over the River Lea.[1] The factory has generally been regarded as having been founded in 1744 when a patent[2] for a 'new method of manufacturing porcelain' was taken out by Edward Heylyn,[3] merchant (1695–1765), and Thomas Frye (1710–62), an artist best known as a mezzotint engraver.[4] Under the patent a clay '. . . the product of

---

1 Hugh Tait, 'Some Consequences of the Bow Exhibition', *Apollo*, April 1960, pp. 93–4. Also Watney, *English Blue and White Porcelain*, pp. 10–11.

2 Jewitt, vol. I, p. 112.

3 See Pountney, *Old Bristol Potteries*, pp. 195–200, for details of his family history. See also p. 212 for a possible connection with Lund's Bristol factory.

4 He studied engraving under John Brooks of the Battersea enamel-factory (see p. 7), and his works in mezzotint include his own portrait, of which there is an impression in the Schreiber Collection (No. 1814); he also painted in oils, and a portrait of Jeremy Bentham by him is in the National Portrait Gallery.

the Chirokee nation in America,[1] called by the natives *unaker'*, was to be mixed with a frit made of 'pott ash, fern ash, pearl ash, kelp, or any other vegetable lixiviall salt', and 'sands, flints, pebbles or any other stones of the vitrifying kind'. Mr. William Burton has asserted,[2] on technical grounds, that a paste so made would lack plasticity and that little, if any, porcelain could have been made under this patent. The *unaker* (or china clay) was imported from America in 1743–4, doubtfully through the agency of one Andrew Duché, a potter from Savannah, in Georgia.[3] No specimens of Bow china as early as 1744 can be identified, the earliest dated examples being of 1750, and it is doubtful whether anything was produced on a commercial scale at so early a date.

A second patent was granted to Frye alone on 17 November 1749, and enrolled on 17 March the following year (1749 by the old calendar, 1750 by the modern calendar).[4] The doubtless intentionally vague specification mentions a material called 'Virgin Earth', to be produced by 'calcining all animal substances, all Fossils of the Calcarious kind such as Chalk, Lime Stone, etc.' Bone is the only animal substance which yields by calcining a white, abundant and insoluble material such as Frye described, and the phosphoric acid in the paste, due to this ingredient, is now generally recognised as a characteristic of all Bow porcelain. It was suggested by Professor Church that Frye became acquainted with the whiteness of calcined bones through his knowledge of the bone-black used by engravers.[5]

1 In 1745 William Cookworthy of Plymouth mentioned the discovery of this china-clay. Both Heylyn and Cookworthy had Bristol connections, and the introduction of this American clay at Bow may have been due to Cookworthy's report of it. See pp. 211–12 and 332.

2 *English Porcelain*, p. 59.

3 For details of Andrew Duché and his activities see Graham Hood, 'The Career of Andrew Duché' in the *Art Quarterly XXXI* (1968), pp. 168–85. Whilst there exists no doubt that Bow obtained from America a quantity of clay (*unaker*) as specified in its first Patent, the presumed association with Duché is shown by Mr. Hood to be based on circumstantial evidence, and he concludes that 'Duché appears to have had no significant connection with Bow'.

4 The date of the second patent was erroneously quoted as 17 November 1748 by Jewitt and others who failed to take into account that under the old style of calendar the year ran from 25 March to 24 March.

5 But oyster-shells and burnt bones were given in a porcelain recipe published in Germany in 1649: see E. Zimmermann, *Erfindung . . . des Meissner Porzellans*, p. 37.

H. SCENT BOTTLE About 1760. No mark. 'Girl in a Swing' class. *Ex. A. H. S. Bunford Collection*
I. BODKIN CASE Ht. 5¼in (13.3cm). About 1750. No mark. 'Girl-in-a-Swing' class. *Schreiber Collection (227)*

A. Scent Bottle Ht. 2¾in (7cm). About 1750. No mark. 'Girl in a Swing' class
B. Patch Box Ht. 2⅞in (7.3cm). About 1760. No mark
C. Scent Bottle Ht. 3½in (8.9cm). About 1760. No mark. 'Girl in a Swing' class.
Schreiber Collection (239, 270 and 240)
D. Scent Bottle Ht. 3½in (8.9cm). About 1760. No mark
E. Etui Ht. 3¾in (9.6cm). About 1760. No mark
F. Scent Bottle Ht. 3½in (8.9cm). About 1760. No mark. *British Museum*
G. Bodkin Case Ht. 5⅛in (13cm). About 1760. No mark. *Schreiber Collection (266)*

See pages 76, 78   Plate 32 CHELSEA (*Chelsea 'Toys'*)

One of the early proprietors of the Bow factory was Alderman George Arnold. The firm is described in the Overseer's Account for West Ham, in 1749–50, as 'Alderman Arnold and Company', and it is known that, in association with Edward Heylyn, Alderman Arnold also acquired some property in Stepney (Bow), Middlesex where, perhaps, the early experiments were carried out. Arnold, however, appears to have withdrawn from the firm some time in 1750,[1] the name being recorded in March of that year as 'Messrs. Porcelain and Company', and from Michaelmas in the same year as 'Frye and Company'. Hugh Tait[2] has also brought to notice the account of the Bow China Manufactory in Samuel Richardson's fourth edition of Daniel Defoe's *Tour of Great Britain* published in 1748–9, which states that the Bow works had, at that time, 'lately been set up' and 'had already made large quantities of *Tea cups, saucers &c*'. No doubt the wares were made under the November 1749 patent referred to above, of the bone-ash body.

Much of the information we have about the factory has been obtained from a collection of memoranda and account-books and other papers left by John Bowcocke, clerk to the factory,[3] who died in 1765. In the Account Book for August 1752, there are recorded sales to the firm of Weatherby and Crowther,[4] who became proprietors of the Bow China Warehouse in Cornhill from February 1753,[5] and of the Bow factory itself.[6] In October 1762 the *London Chronicle* announced the death of Mr. Weatherby, 'one of the proprietors of the Bow China Warehouse in Cornhill'. John

1 In fact, an insurance policy does not include Alderman Arnold among the proprietors named. Elizabeth Adams in 'The Bow Insurances and Related Matters', *Transactions E.C.C.*, vol. 9, part 1.

2 *Apollo*, June 1960, p. 181.

3 Extracts from these were first published by Chaffers (3rd edition) in 1870. Some of them are preserved at the British Museum, but others, once in the possession of Lady Charlotte Schreiber, have been lost. Bowcocke was formerly a purser in the Royal Navy.

4 Described as 'Potters, St. Catherine's', in *Kent's Directory of London*, 1753–63; Hugh Tait, loc. cit., p. 44.

5 *General Evening Post*, 8 February 1753.

6 The partners in 1756 were named as John Crowther, Edward Heylyn, John Weatherby and Thomas Frye: Public Record Office, B1 31 (Watney, op. cit., p. 24). An insurance policy taken out with the Sun Insurance Company on 7 July, 1749, names the partners as 'Edward Heylyn Thomas Fry John Weatherby and John Crowther'. Elizabeth Adams in 'The Bow Insurances and Related Matters', *Transactions E.C.C.*, vol. 9, part 1, p. 69.

A B C

D E F

G H I

A. PATCH BOX Ht. 1⅜in (3.5cm). About 1750. No mark. 'Girl in a Swing'
Class. *Schreiber Collection (231)*
B. SEALS Ht. 1in (2.5cm) (top three) and 3¼in (8.2cm) (bottom three). About
1755–70. No mark. *Schreiber Collection (l. to r. 426b, 253, 260, 426c, 262, 426e)*
C. SCENT BOTTLE Ht. 3¼in (8.2cm). About 1760. No mark. *Schreiber Collection
(234)*
D. E and F. MINIATURE FIGURES Ht. 3in (7.6cm) and 3¼in (8.2cm). About
1755–60. No mark. *Fitzwilliam Museum (Lord and Lady Fisher Collection)*
G. SCENT BOTTLE Ht. 3¼in (8.2cm). About 1765. No mark. *Schreiber Collection
(276)*
H. BONBONNIERE Ht. 1⅛in (2.8cm). About 1755–60. No mark. *Victoria and
Albert Museum (C.1332-1924)*
I. SCENT BOTTLE Ht. 3¼in (8.2cm). About 1765. No mark. *Schreiber Collection
(279)*

See page 78   Plate 33 CHELSEA (*Chelsea 'Toys'*)

Crowther became bankrupt in 1763 but apparently was able to continue as a proprietor of the factory, but the Warehouse was closed in the following year. Thomas Frye managed the factory from its commencement until his retirement in 1759, and on his death in 1762 was described in his epitaph as 'the inventor and first manufacturer of porcelain in England'. He was in part the inventor of the bone-porcelain which was later to win universal adoption in England, and the pious tribute may well be allowed to stand.

It was stated in the Catalogue of the Jermyn Street Collection,[1] issued in 1855, that when the Bow factory was discontinued all the moulds and models were purchased and removed to the Derby works. No date was given for the event, and no authority was quoted for the statement, which has often been repeated. In Chaffers[2] (3rd edition, 1870, page 691) '1775 or 1776' is given, without any authority or reference, as the date of the purchase, but in the recollections of Samuel Keys, a Derby workman, reported in the same work (page 595), the purchase or part-purchase of Bow models is again mentioned.[3] It has been suggested,[4] with some probability, that after Crowther's bankruptcy in 1763 the factory was continued with the aid of loans from William Duesbury of Derby, who similarly assisted the Kentish Town enameller Giles.[5] This connection would explain the surprising fact that Craft, a Bow hand, took his bowl (now in the British Museum) to Giles for its enamel firing.

This curious fact and the circumstance that in Bowcocke's papers mention is made of Bow porcelain enamelled in 1760 by 'Richard Dyer, at Mr. Bolton's, enameller, near the Church, Lambeth', raises a doubt as to how much of the china was enamelled outside the factory. Bowcocke in his memoranda speaks of 'bisket ware made at New Canton', as if the glazing and enamelling were done elsewhere.

Lambeth is again brought into the question by some references to the employment in a china-factory of John Bacon, R.A.

1 London Museum of Practical Geology. Transferred to the Victoria and Albert Museum in 1901.
2 *Marks and Monograms.*
3 Compare also p. 175.
4 F. Hurlbutt, *Bow Porcelain*, p. 20.
5 Jewitt, vol. I, pp. 214–18. See also p. 264.

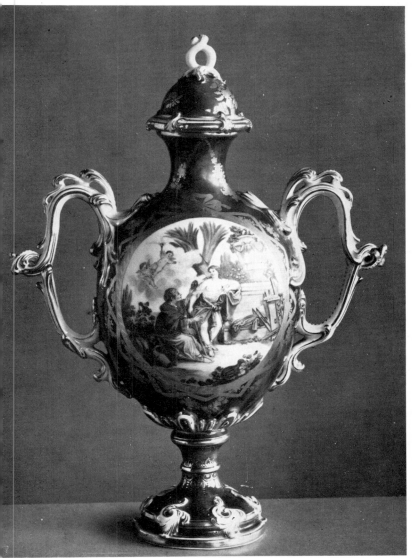

ᴀsᴇ Ht. 15in (38.1cm). About 1756. Gold Anchor mark. *Victoria and Albert Museum llidge Loan No. 9)*

ee page 74   Plate 34 CHELSEA

(1740–99). In Alan Cunningham's *Lives of the Most Eminent British Painters, Sculptors and Architects* (1830), vol. III, p. 201, Bacon is stated to have been apprenticed in 1755 at the age of fourteen, 'to one Crispe of Bow Churchyard, an eminent maker of porcelain, who taught him the art of modelling the deer and holly tree, the bird and the bush, the shepherd and the shepherdess, and birds and beasts of every kind such as are yet made for show or for use in our manufactories. That these early attempts contained the rudiments of his future excellence has been asserted by some and denied by others. . . . It ought to be mentioned that he was frequently employed in painting on plates and dishes: these were probably a repetition of his models with the addition of the duck in the pond, the angler and his rod, and the hunter with his hounds.' This shamelessly padded passage is probably based on R. Cecil's *Memoirs of John Bacon* (1801), where it is further stated that 'Mr. Crispe' had a manufactory of china at Lambeth (actually Vauxhall, in Lambeth Parish) at which Bacon occasionally attended. Bacon is also known to have worked for Coade's 'Artificial-Stone Works' at Narrow Wall in Pedlar's Acre, at Lambeth,[1] and Jewitt states that in addition to purchasing the Bow factory, Duesbury also 'owned the pottery at Pedlar's Acre at Lambeth, the rents of which he assigned in 1781'.[2] It has therefore been supposed that there was a Lambeth branch of the Bow factory; but there is confusion in this between Bow in east London and Bow Churchyard in the City. Crisp had a warehouse in the City, but his china-factory was at Vauxhall.[3] Its productions have not been identified but presumably included some figures.

The theory that much of the Bow porcelain was enamelled outside the factory gives special interest to William Duesbury in the early period, to Dyer about 1760, and later still to James Giles, as possible decorators of Bow porcelain.

---

1 Jewitt, vol. I, p. 139.
2 Vol. II, p. 74.
3 See a paper by A. J. Toppin, 'Nicholas Crisp, Jeweller and Potter', in *Transactions E.C.C.*, I (1933), p. 38. Also R. J. Charleston and J. V. G. Mallet in *Transactions E.C.C.*, vol. 8, part 1, pp. 105–13, where we find, *inter alia*, that Crisp subsequently attempted the manufacture of porcelain at Bovey Tracey, in Devon, where he died and was buried in 1774.

A. and B. INKWELL Dia. 3$\frac{3}{10}$in (8.4cm). Dated
1750. Inscribed '*Made at New Canton 1750*'. *British
Museum (Franks Collection I.61)*

C. PLATE Dia. 7$\frac{4}{5}$in (19.8cm). Transfer printed in blue. About
1760. No mark. *British Museum (1942-12-9, 2)*

See pages 92, 121   Plate 35 BOW

It is clear that the Bow factory output largely consisted of table-ware. *The Case of the Undertaker of the Chelsea Manufacture*[1] mentioned that 'the chief endeavours at Bow have been towards making a more ordinary sort of ware for common uses', and this is borne out by the advertisements. 'All sorts of China' were offered in advertisements in Birmingham and Derby newspapers in 1753. Public sales were announced in 1757 and 1758, but the catalogues of these do not seem to have survived. The earlier announcement mentioned 'Epargnes, Branch Candlesticks, Services for Deserts, etc. etc. exquisitely painted in enamel and Blue and White. Also a large assortment of the most useful China in Lots, for the Use of Gentlemen's Kitchens, Private Families, Taverns, etc.' At a later sale were offered 'beautiful groups of Figures', essence and perfume pots, jars, beakers, bottles, 'Services of Dishes, Plates, Sauce-boats, compleat Tea and Coffee Equipages, a large Assortment of fine Enamel and fine partridge Sets which are most beautifully painted by several of the finest Masters from Dresden'. This advertiser's reference to painters 'from Dresden' is not to be accepted literally. In 1753 the factory had advertised in Birmingham for enamellers and 'Painters in the Blue and White Potting Way'; and for a 'Person who can model small figures in Clay neatly'. We know from the advertisements of 1753 that the firm had a retail shop in Cornhill, near the Royal Exchange. This was closed after Crowther's bankruptcy, in 1764. Later, from 1770 to 1775, the warehouse was in St. Paul's Churchyard.

The identification of the Bow china depends (apart from the evidence of chemical analysis[2]) upon the following documents:

(i) The papers of John Bowcocke mentioned above, relating to the period between 1750 and 1758.

(ii) A bowl in the British Museum, decorated in underglaze blue with, externally, *rococo* panels on a powder blue ground, enclosing

1 See p. 18.
2 This cannot itself be conclusive, as bone-ash was also used at Lowestoft, and at a rather later date at Chelsea.

A. HENRY WOODWARD AS *THE FINE GENTLEMAN* FROM GARRICK'S *LETHE* Ht. 10¾in (27.3cm). About 1750. No mark. *Schreiber Collection (1)*

B. THE MARQUIS OF GRANBY Ht. 14⅛in (35.9cm). About 1760. Mark 'T' impressed. *Schreiber Collection (54a)*

C. PAIR OF TAWNY OWLS Ht. 7⅞in (20cm) and 7¾in (19.7cm). About 1760. No mark. *Schreiber Collection (61)*

See pages 94, 108, 110   Plate 36 BOW

scenes in the Chinese manner. The interior has a scene of sailors with staves in their hands and a fourth figure of a man holding a punch bowl. Inscribed on the base 'John & Ann Bowcock, 1759', and having the monogram 'I.B.' incised in the blue ground.

(iii) A bowl in the British Museum accompanied by a note dated 1790 stating that it was made at 'Stratford-le-Bow in the County of Essex' in 1760 and painted by Thomas Craft.[1] In the course of a wordy account, Craft states that he took the bowl to be burnt at Mr. Gyles' kiln in Kentish Town, that the Manufactory was carried on for many years by Crowther and Weatherby (but Weatherby had been dead many years), that about three hundred persons, including ninety painters, were at one time employed at the factory.[2]

(iv) Some inkstands dated 1750 and 1751 and inscribed '*Made at New Canton*' (Plates 35A and B). Bowcocke spoke of the factory by this name, and Craft described the factory as modelled on one 'at Canton'.

(v) Some blue-and-white plates in the British Museum[3] and elsewhere dated January 1770 and inscribed '*Robert Crowther*', presumed to be the name of a relative of the Bow proprietor.

(vi) Wasters and fragments of porcelain found on the site of the works in 1867[4] and 1922.[5] Several pieces from the earlier find, as well as those from the 1922 excavation, are at South Kensington.[6]

It is now fairly well established that the ware made at Bow was, from its beginnings as a commercial venture, phosphatic, and certain non-phosphatic figures, notably one of *Kitty Clive* as the Fine Lady in Garrick's farce *Lethe* (an example in the Schreiber Collection at South Kensington), hitherto thought to be of Bow manufacture prior to the second patent, must now be excluded

---

1 Hobson, *Catalogue*, No. I. 62.

2 Thomas Craft's statement is reproduced in full in the 1959–60 Bow Exhibition Catalogue, p. 43.

3 *Catalogue*, No. I. 36.

4 Described in Jewitt, vol. I, 203–6 (reprinted from *The Art Journal* of 1869), and in Chaffers, op. cit., pp. 694–9.

5 See an article by Aubrey J. Toppin in *The Burlington Magazine*, vol. XL (1922), p. 224.

6 Altogether twenty-six documentary specimens were included in the 1959 Bow Exhibition at the British Museum, of which ten are in the British Museum collection.

A. LION Ht. 3½in (8.9cm). About 1750. No mark. Probably Derby. *Schreiber Collection (8)*

B. TEAPOT Ht. 4¾in (12cm). About 1750. No mark. Derby. *Schreiber Collection (36)*

C. PIGGIN AND SPOON Ht. 2¾in (7cm). About 1750. No mark. Bow. *Schreiber Collection (15)*

D. PLATE Dia. 9½in (24.1cm). About 1750–5. No mark. *Victoria and Albert Museum (C.1005-1924)*

See pages 100, 116, 134 Plate 37 BOW AND DERBY

from this factory's productions.[1] Other somewhat larger models of *Kitty Clive* are phosphatic. These are undoubted Bow figures,[2] as is the companion figure of *Henry Woodward* as *The Fine Gentleman* (Plate 36A), also a figure of *Falstaff* from an engraving of 1743 by C. Grignion after Francis Hayman,[3] formerly believed to be of James Quin in the part. Both the latter have been proved to be phosphatic on analysis. Describing a visit to Hampton Court in 1829 in his *A Book for a Rainy Day* (1845),[4] J. T. Smith refers to these three as Chelsea figures; but the same author elsewhere[5] mentions *Quin* as a Bow model. White figures of *Woodward* and *Kitty Clive* were also offered as Chelsea at a sale in 1767 of the property of Thomas Turner, a china-dealer who had employed Duesbury as an enameller.[6] But as the pieces would have been without marks in the paste, and the Bow factory was in disrepute whilst that of Chelsea was at the height of its fame, it is probable that the name of the latter would have been unscrupulously used wherever possible. The surviving specimens of these models, moreover, bear no resemblance whatever to admitted Chelsea porcelain. Examples of the pair in Mr. E. S. McEuen's collection[7] are painted with small sprigs of flowers, obviously by the same hand as those on two other specimens in the Schreiber Collection—the *Charity* (Plate 41) and the large figures of *Boys with Baskets* (No. 32), and on the *Lovers with a Birdcage* also at South Kensington (Plate 43B). All these have a phosphatic paste; they belong in fact to a very distinctive class of figures grouped round some *Muses*, to be attributed to Bow on other grounds.

At one time certain characteristics seemed to point to a Bow origin for a well-defined class marked by an exceptionally thick greenish-toned glaze made opaque with minute bubbles, which

1 See p. 128.

2 An example with incised date 1750 is at the Fitzwilliam Museum, Cambridge. It has been shown (Hugh Tait, loc. cit., p. 98) that the characters of the *Fine Lady* and *Fine Gentleman* were not introduced into the play *Lethe* until 1749, and that the first engraving from which these Bow figures were taken was published in 1750.

3 Lane, op. cit., p. 86 (footnote).

4 pp. 266–7.

5 *Nollekens and his Times* (1829), vol. I, p. 191.

6 See p. 13 (footnote).

7 Probably the pair now at Upton House, Warwickshire.

A. VASE AND COVER Ht. 9⅜in
(23.8cm). About 1755. No mark.
Victoria and Albert Museum (C.33 and
a-1926)

B. CUP AND SAUCER Cup ht. 2½in
(6.3cm); Saucer dia. 5in (12.7cm). About
1760. No mark. Schreiber Collection (80)

C. TANKARD AND COVER Ht. 8¼in (20.9cm).
About 1760. No mark. Schreiber Collection
(79)

See page 116

Plate 38 BOW ('*Kakiemon*' patterns)

obscures the modelling of the figures. A pair of cows, a crane and some horses (Plate 65) in the Museum Collection at South Kensington may be taken as typical. A clumsy applied flower, like a single, formal rose, is often found on the bases. Mr. Wallace Elliot had a pair of bagpipers so smothered in this glaze that they might be 'snow-men'.[1] It now appears, however, that these are Staffordshire figures, made at Longton Hall in its earliest period.[2]

The fact that Duesbury painted 'Bogh', including figures described as 'Mrs. Clive' and 'Mr. Woodward', as well as other makes of china, suggests the need for caution in arguing from similarity of painting. But I think we may probably detect Duesbury's hand in the painting of certain early Bow models. Some of these belong to a class which is sometimes marked with the sign for Mercury incised.[3] The *Man and Woman in Turkish Costume* (Schreiber No. 33) are typical. The male model is one frequently repeated in later Bow porcelain.[4] Now the painting on the *Turk* and his companion, which includes a smudgy use of bright green and brown, a strong uneven red, and some rather crude pink and green flowers, is obviously by the same hand as a *Lady with a Basket*, of non-phosphatic paste, which for various reasons may be regarded as a Derby production.[5] This painting must therefore be regarded as either that of a migrant workman, or done in an independent enameller's workshop such as William Duesbury's.[6]

The important class of early Bow figures already mentioned, which we may ascribe to the period shortly after 1750, has been proved

1 Mr. Bernard Rackham tells me that this term was actually used long ago to describe some ancient Cypriote figurines.

2 Compare p. 180.

3 See Appendix, p. 385, for this 'planet-mark'.

4 There is a specimen marked with the anchor and dagger in the Schreiber Collection (No. 87).

5 See p. 133.

6 The published Duesbury account-book covers the period 1751-3; but it is probable that he was at work as an enameller before this.

A. TEAPOT Ht. 4in (10.1cm). Painted in *famille rose* style. About 1755. No mark. *Schreiber Collection (41)*

B. MUG Ht. 3½in (8.9cm). Painted in *famille rose* style. About 1755. No mark. *Victoria and Albert Museum (C.970–1924)*

C. VASE Ht. 7⅞in (20cm). Painted with 'Bow flowers'. About 1755. Mark 'B' in blue. *Victoria and Albert Museum (C.975-1924)*

See pages 112, 114

Plate 39 BOW

phosphatic by chemical analysis,[1] and is brought together by a distinctive manner of modelling the heads. A damaged figure of a woman, in plain white, at South Kensington, of this class came from the Jermyn Street Collection in company with many wasters and fragments from the Bow factory site, and may itself be a waster. There is no record, however, of the provenance of this figure, which shows the characteristic, somewhat receding chin and brow and heavy eyelids of this class. The charming *Lovers with a Birdcage* (Plate 43B)[2] and the group allegorical of *Charity* (Plate 41), already mentioned for their painting of small sprigs, are also good examples of this modelling. The *Boys with Baskets* on their heads (Schr. No. 32), which have similar painting and the same rather dull white glaze, are of the same model as certain pieces of Delft earthenware, a circumstance not uncommon in Bow porcelain. To this group belong also the delightful *Muses*,[3] represented at South Kensington by the *Polyhymnia and Erato* (Plate 44A), inscribed 'Polimnie' and 'Eraton for the Love',[4] suggesting a French 'repairer'.[5] The name 'the *Muses* family' has in fact been familiarly given to this easily recognised class of early Bow figures; they include many naïvely charming compositions (Plate 44B). Many specimens of the class are painted with characteristic small sprigs, seen also on the *Kitty Clive* and *Woodward* which are mentioned in Duesbury's work-book, as well as the strong yellow and uneven painty red of the palette already described.[6] The frequent occurrence of plain white glazed unpainted figures from

1 We may safely assume that once bone-ash was established as an ingredient in Bow china, it would never be abandoned. This is proved by the firm adoption successively at Chelsea (1758), Derby (1770), and eventually throughout England of a bone-porcelain body. See also Appendix B.

2 Analysed by Dr. H. J. Plenderleith with the following result:

Silica	-	-	-	- 47·8
Oxide of lead	-	-	-	- 0·5
Alumina	-	-	-	- 8·1
Lime	-	-	-	- 24·6
Phosphoric acid	-	-	-	- 17·6
				98·6

3 Compare an article by A. J. Toppin, 'Some early Bow Muses', in the *Burlington Magazine*, LIV (1928), p. 188.

4 The inscriptions incised on the bases.

5 Perhaps 'Mr. Tebo': see pp. 102 and 106.

6 p. 96.

A. A Cockerel Ht. 4⅛in (10.5cm). About 1755. No mark. *Schreiber Collection (60)*
B. Vase Ht. 8¾in (22.2cm). About 1755. No mark. *Schreiber Collection (70)*
C. A Hen Ht. 4⅛in (10.5cm). About 1755. No mark. *Schreiber Collection (60)*

D. Plate Dia. 8in (20.3cm). Painted with 'Bow flowers'.
About 1755. No mark. *Victoria and Albert Museum*
(C.652-1925)

See pages 110, 112   Plate 40 BOW

the Bow and other factories of the early 1750s may be explained by the practice of decorating porcelain with unfired colour, which would eventually be cleaned away. Duesbury's work-book mentions figures 'painted' as distinct from 'enhamild'.

It is impossible to generalise about the colour of the early Bow paste; a greenish-toned material is characteristic of much of the early useful ware,[1] but the colour varied widely. Many pieces bear decoration of sprays of plum-blossom in applied relief,[2] copied from Fukien porcelain, and many wasters with this decoration were found on the factory site. Examples of these wasters, and many fine pieces in the same style, are in the collection at South Kensington (Plate 37C). A pair of sauce-boats moulded with festoons (Schr. No. 35) are of similar material; formerly believed to be Bristol (from an error in W. Moore Binns' book *The First Century of English Porcelain*, where a marked specimen was said to exist),[3] they have been analysed and proved phosphatic. A sauce-boat and a vase at South Kensington, marked with an incised 'CT' and 'R' respectively, both reveal on analysis a highly phosphatic body; both are linked with a vase in the Schreiber Collection (No. 38) by some rather crude, stringy painting with leaves outlined in brown, and we may regard this style as one of the earliest of those seen on the useful wares. The 'R' mark identifies as Bow some vases painted in Chinese style in red and blue, of which there are examples at South Kensington. The ink-stands inscribed '*New Canton*' (those at the British Museum and South Kensington are dated 1750 and 1751 respectively) show that enamelled porcelain of excellent quality was made by the Bow factory, even in this early period; they are of a fine ivory-like material, decorated with enamels of the *famille rose*.

The blue-and-white sauce-boat, on three lion-mask feet, figured in Plate 42B, has an incised planet-mark. A similar mark is found on the sweetmeat-dish also mentioned above, and both are painted

1 Also described as 'mushroom-grey' and 'creamy-white'. Watney, op. cit., p. 44.

2 Doubtless the 'sprigged' patterns of Bowcocke's notes. 'Sprigging' is the Staffordshire name for the process of applying these reliefs.

3 Sauce-boats of a somewhat similar shape were indeed made at Lund's Bristol factory, and a few have the embossed mark 'Bristoll'. See p. 218. Also at Liverpool, especially William Ball's factory. See p. 300.

FIGURE OF CHARITY Ht. 11¼in (28.6cm). About 1750–5. Mark 'T' impressed. *Schreiber Collection (31)*

See pages 94, 98

Plate 41 BOW

in an especially bright blue. The distinctive colour of these two specimens helps us to identify other early Bow blue-and-white. The painting has a certain fantastic quality, and a script '*G*' of varying form is sufficiently common to be a useful guide. A white shell-salt from Dr. Bellamy Gardner's collection, incised '1750', provides us with a date.[1] The form of these salt-cellars and sweetmeat dishes suggests that they were moulded from actual shells, and the notion was probably taken from place to place by a repairer, perhaps the 'Mr. Tebo'[2] to be mentioned presently. The larger Bow shells often have a transverse ribbing underneath, not found on those made elsewhere: a powdered-blue dish in the Schreiber Collection (No. 25) also shows this feature.

The fine Bow productions of the second period, dating from about 1754 to 1760, include some of the most attractive porcelain ever made in England. The paste was of a warm creamy-yellow tone, often showing brighter flecks by transmitted light. These flecks are due to 'tearings' in the paste which are sometimes visible on the surface, resembling the 'parting' of uncooked dough, or of dry non-plastic clay. The glaze is rather waxen-looking, so soft as to be easily scratched, but of an ivory tone and smoothness. The pure and rich enamel colours used include a very distinctive opaque light blue, a strong rose-purple, a soft rose-pink and a bright translucent green. The clean strength of the colours and their juxtaposition in bold discords give the best Bow china much of its charm. The gilding in this as in other periods of the factory was not of high quality technically, but has the soft and rather dull appearance that is so much pleasanter than the brassy gilding of modern times. In this period it was used very sparingly with good effect. This middle-period enamelling is as distinctive as the earlier work seen on the 'Muses family', and the references to the enameller Dyer, dated 1760, may be recalled. But there is no proof that Dyer was responsible for the new style.

1 There is also the '*Edward Vernon* 1752' blue-painted inkstand in the Willett Collection at Brighton Museum, Bow Exhibition Catalogue figs. 11 and 12, and 16 and 17.

2 Plymouth specimens, such as that figured in Plate 125, often bear his mark.

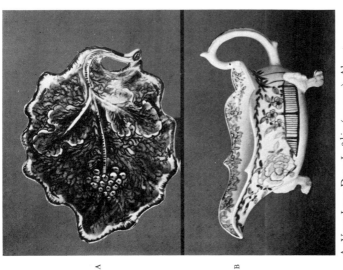

C. PLATE WITH POWDER-BLUE DECORATION Dia. 9⅜in (23.8cm). About 1755–65. Mark—simulated Chinese characters. *Schreiber Collection (24)*

A. VINE LEAF DISH L. 8¼in (20.9cm). About 1755–65. Mark—simulated Chinese characters. *Victoria and Albert Museum (C.822-1925)*

B. SAUCEBOAT L. 7½in (19cm). About 1755–65. Planet mark incised and 'G' in blue. *Victoria and Albert Museum (C.759-1924)*

See pages 100, 121, 122, 218   Plate 42 BOW (*Blue and white porcelain*)

Many attractive figures were made, most of them closely copied from Meissen models,[1] but with a remarkable vivacity and delicacy of execution. Bases for the figures were at first of simple mounded or rectangular form, but latterly a characteristic four-footed pedestal was invented, its scroll-work outlined in the strong crimson-purple enamel which is peculiar to Bow. A square hole at the back of many of the figures was intended to receive a metal mount, and is almost a mark of Bow manufacture.[2] The holes commonly found in the bases however were vents for the escape of air and steam during the firing; they occur in porcelain from other factories. Bow figures are usually heavy in the hand, a feature which distinguishes them from the contemporary Derby. Many of the models bear an impressed mark, 'T' or 'T°', which is found at a later period on Worcester, Plymouth and Bristol porcelain.[3] This has been regarded as the mark of a modeller employed by Josiah Wedgwood in 1775, called 'Mr. Tebo' in his correspondence.[4] He was probably a Frenchman who altered his name Thibaud to its phonetic form in English spelling.[5] Whilst there is in fact no evidence to connect this Tebo with the person who used the mark in question, the incompetence as a modeller[6] of the 'Mr. Tebo' so scathingly referred to by Wedgwood is not inconsistent with a high degree of skill as a 'repairer', such as is shown in some of the Bow and Bristol pieces with this mark. It is not always accepted that the mark is that of a 'repairer' or other workman, and it has been

1 Models from other factories may seem to have been copied: the *Gallant* and his companion holding a fan at South Kensington are of the same models as figures found in Frankenthal porcelain figures (compare F. H. Hofmann, *Frankenthaler Porzellan*, Nos. 210 and 211), and this circumstance might account for their unusual colouring, which includes a dull green. Two charming white figures in the same collection, of a fiddler and his companion, are of a model known to occur in Höchst faïence. But all were probably copied from Meissen originals.

2 A similarly placed *round* hole is found on some early Derby figures.

3 See pp. 272, 340 and 345.

4 *Letters of Wedgwood*, II, pp. 119, 121, 130; *Owen*, p. 242. For a discussion of this question see *The Burlington Magazine*, vol. XXV (1914), p. 108. Owen seems to have made the suggestion that 'T°' stood for Tebo.

5 Such anglicising occurs also in the spelling 'Busha' for Boucher, quoted on p. 154.

6 This incompetence would be quite consistent with my suggestion that 'Mr. Tebo' was the inventor of shell-salts. The notion would have appealed to a 'repairer' with limited powers of invention.

B. Lovers with a Birdcage Ht. 7½in (19cm). About 1750–5. No mark. *Victoria and Albert Museum (C.1320–1924)*

A. Woman and Children Group Ht. 5½in (14cm). About 1750–5. No mark. *Museum of London*

suggested (F. Rathbone, *Old Wedgwood*, 1898, p. 16) that the letters indicate 'top of oven'; the mark 'TBO' on certain experimental slips of Wedgwood jasper ware is definitely stated to mean 'top of biscuit oven'. The abbreviation in this instance certainly implies a technical usage (though at the same time a perfect abbreviation for the name!), but such purpose hardly fits the numerous occurrences of the 'To' initials on the products of several factories in a haphazard manner inconsistent with an instruction as to firing. 'Mr. Tebo', fable or fact, must yet remain unresolved. An impressed 'B' found on a pair of figures of a *Man and Woman carrying dishes*, usually known as the *Cooks* (Colour Plate B), was formerly regarded as the mark of John Bacon. These figures, which rank amongst the very best produced at Bow, may well be the 'Cooks' mentioned in a memorandum of Bowcocke's of 1756, when sixteen of them were ordered by a dealer named Fogg. Bacon was only sixteen years old at this date, and it is unlikely that he was then responsible for such figures as these, either as 'repairer' or modeller. The fine *Flora* (Plate 48), from the antique statue at the Farnese Palace at Rome, is traditionally associated with Bacon, and is much more likely to be the work of an apprentice-sculptor such as he was about this time.[1] The untrustworthy J. T. Smith, in his *Nollekens and his Times*, declared that Moser, afterwards Keeper of the Royal Academy, also modelled for Bow porcelain.

The Bow figures continue to show a fairly close sequence in the modelling of the heads in a style quite distinct from those of other factories. This is a useful criterion. The head of the little boy in the early *Charity* already mentioned is almost identical with that of another *Boy seated on a mound* (Schr. No. 49), and is similar, again, to that of the characteristically coloured *Boy and Girl selling Fish* (Schr. No. 51). The rare group of a *Woman and Children* in the London Museum (Plate 43A) also corresponds in this respect. This feature alone almost identifies many Bow figures of about 1755. Rather later models show increasingly delicate rendering of the faces, as in the group figured in Plate 45B, though these are still recognisably akin to those in the earlier style. Among the models closely copied

1 Arguments more recently adduced tend to discredit the tradition. See Lane, op. cit., pp. 93–5; also *Apollo*, LXIII, 1956, pp. 125–7; R. J. Charleston and Geoffrey Wills, *The Bow Flora and Michael Rysbrack*.

A. FIGURE OF POLYHYMNIA Ht. 6⅜in (16.2cm). About 1750–5. Incised 'Polimnie'. *Victoria and Albert Museum (C.63-1927)*

B. WOMAN AND CHILD WITH FRUIT Ht. 6in (15.2cm). About 1750–5. No mark. *Victoria and Albert Museum (C.98-1938)*

See page 98 Plate 44 BOW

from Meissen, but nevertheless ranking with the best English figures, may be mentioned the delightful *Pierrot* in yellow and the lively *Harlequin* and *Columbine* (Bowcocke speaks of 'Harliquin' and 'Pero'); the *Negro and Negress*; the *Woman in Turkish Costume holding a shell*, and the *Gallant kissing his hand*. All of these are represented in the Schreiber Collection. A *Boy holding a bunch of grapes* is represented at South Kensington in two copies, differing slightly in colour. One is marked with a script 'D' and so has been thought to be an early Derby figure, but analysis has revealed a bone-ash paste. And the other is marked 'AF'![1] The *Waterman wearing Doggett's badge*, in the British Museum (No. II. 3), is often thought to be Chelsea, but is proved as Bow by the colouring of a characteristic Bow base on a specimen in the Willett Collection at Brighton.[2]

In the Museum collection at South Kensington is a case filled with figures of the finest quality, most of them part of Mr. Broderip's magnificent gift. The delicate poise and balance of the modelling and the directness and simplicity of the colouring of their smooth ivory surface could not be better studied than in the *Apollo*, the *Air* (from a set of *Elements*), the *Bagpiper* (Plate 45A) and the *Sportsman* and his companion. The last-named have a rare mark in an incised '*W*' on the upper surface of the base. Another pair of models, rather similar to the last but apparently later (about 1760), shows the more delicate modelling of heads of the later figures of this period; the male figure has a curious impressed mark like a ladder.[3] One of these pairs is presumably the 'sporters' mentioned by Bowcocke. The group figured in Plate 45B is of about the same date as the last-mentioned pair, and has the 'T°' mark.

The most ambitious Bow figures were the famous *General Wolfe* and *Marquis of Granby* (Plate 36B), large models over a foot high, represented both at the British Museum and in the Schreiber Collection.[4] These were probably made to celebrate victories over

1 See Appendix, p. 385, Nos. 8 and 9, for both these marks.
2 The British Museum specimen has lately been tested and found to have a phosphatic paste: see *British Museum Quarterly*, vol. II, No. 1, p. 31. But Chelsea versions may also have been made.
3 Appendix, p. 386, No. 10.
4 Schr. No. 54 and A, and B.M. No. I, 19.

A. BAGPIPER Ht. 5⅞in (14.9cm).
About 1750–5. No mark. *Victoria and
Albert Museum (C.1408-1924)*

B. BOY AND GIRL Ht. 7¾in (19.7cm).
About 1760. Mark 'To' impressed.
Schreiber Collection (57)

C. A LADY Ht. 8 1/16in (20.5cm). About 1765.
No mark. *Museum of London*

See pages 106, 108, 123, 124

Plate 45 BOW

the French in 1759–60 at Quebec, Minden and Warburg, battles in which these generals were engaged. They seem to have been modelled after engravings by Richard Houston,[1] who was, like Frye, a pupil of John Brooks. Fragments identical with parts of these figures were found on the site of the works,[2] and the distinctive opaque light blue, used on the uniforms, confirms a Bow origin, or at least an association with Bow figures of this period.

Two charming figures of a 'Fluter and Companion' at the British Museum (I. 23) also belong to the latter part of this middle period.[3] Sketches slightly resembling them, with this title and the prices '3s. and 4s. 6d.' are among the Bowcocke papers. Like other drawings included in the papers they are apparently the work of a child or amateur, and not in the least likely to be designs for the figures.

Figures of birds and animals follow the Meissen and Chelsea fashion. But most of the Bow birds are wholly fanciful in their clear, bold colouring. The plumage of the *Tawny Owls* in the Schreiber Collection (Plate 36C), for example, is beautifully rendered by a pure convention, in purple and rich brown; and the applied leaves, here and on many other pieces belonging to this period, are enamelled in the characteristic Bow rich emerald-green, with an admirable disregard of natural appearance. On the other hand, the tureens in the form of sitting *Partridges* are decidedly closer to nature than those made at Chelsea. A note in Bowcocke's papers reads 'to buy a partridge alive or dead', and it is perhaps not fanciful to see in this a reference to the exactness in the rendering of these birds. The dishes on which the tureens stand are quite different from those with the Chelsea partridges, though a fragment from one of the latter was found on the Bow site.[4] The *Cock* and *Hen* (Schr. No. 60), figured in Plate 40, are in modelling typical of the birds made at Bow.

1 The engraving used for *Wolfe* is based on a sketch by Captain Hervey Smyth (discussed in *The Century Magazine*, New Series, XXXIII, p. 327). The portrait of Granby, published in 1760, was engraved after a painting by Sir Joshua Reynolds, and shows the General bare-headed—referring to an incident in the battle of Warburg.

2 *The Burlington Magazine*, vol. XL (1922), p. 224, Plate K.

3 A pair in the Schreiber Collection (No. 83), representing *Spring* and *Winter*, are of the same models slightly altered.

4 See p. 46.

A. Mug Ht. *c.*4½in (11.4cm). Transfer-printed in red. About 1755. No mark. *Ex. Dr. S. W. Woodhouse's Collection*

B. Plate Dia. 8in (20.3cm). Transfer-printed in red, border painted with enamelled flowers. About 1755. No mark. *Victoria and Albert Museum (2908-1901)*

See pages 118, 120   Plate 46 BOW

We may associate with the figures some fine decorative pieces. The frilled *rococo* vases (Plate 40B), sometimes with applied masks, seem to have been a favourite with 'Mr. Tebo'; we find them with his mark also at Bristol and Worcester. One may, I think, assume that models of this kind would have been the inventions of repairers, like the shell-salts previously mentioned. There are good specimens in both collections at South Kensington. The similar flower-holders in the form of cornucopias, and such things as the four-sided pedestals in the Schreiber Collection (Nos. 71 and 72), with their ivory-like glaze and rich colours, rank among the best work of the factory. A pot-pourri vase (Schr. No. 68) marked 'T°', of bronze or silver form, with gadroonings picked out in that characteristic and delightful Bow crimson which Mr. William Burton found 'barely tolerable', has on the lid a figure of a seated bagpiper identical with one found in Delftware, but ultimately to be traced to a bronze by Giovanni Bologna.

A remarkably soft and delicate style of flower-painting is quite peculiar to Bow amongst the English factories, though so like that on some Mennecy porcelain as to suggest the hand of a migrant Frenchman.[1] Two vases mounted in ormolu in the Schreiber Collection (No. 73) are painted by this hand, and a mug in Mr. Broderip's gift is inscribed in crimson '*William Taylor 1759*'.[2] The vase painted with these flowers figured in Plate 39C is marked with a '*B*' in underglaze blue, which some would regard as a Bow factory mark. But as other letters, as well as numerals, occur at least as frequently it is probably no more than a workman's mark. An octagonal plate (Plate 40D) also shows the Bow flowers at their best.

Much Bow 'useful ware' was painted in a rather summary style

1 A vase in the Victoria and Albert Museum is a Bow piece on which the incised 'DV' mark of Mennecy has been added; it was acquired as authentic Mennecy porcelain by the donor, J. H. Fitzhenry. A Mennecy figure of a boy with a shell, in the same collection, shows a kinship in modelling as well as in flower-painting.

2 Victoria and Albert Museum Cat. No. 103. A William Taylor was employed as a painter at Derby, but more than thirty years later. Another was apprenticed at Worcester in 1763.

B. PLATE Dia. 8½in (21.6cm). About 1760. No mark. *Schreiber Collection (75)*

A. BOTTLE Ht. 7⅞in (20cm). About 1755–60. No mark. *Victoria and Albert Museum (C.86-1938)*

See page 116

Plate 47 BOW

copied from the Chinese *famille rose* (Plate 39A and B). This painting is distinguished by clean fresh colouring, and is proved as Bow not only by paste and glaze, but by certain peculiarities of form. An inkstand at South Kensington so painted is of nearly the same shape as those inscribed '*New Canton*'. Mr. Wallace Elliot had a document for this style in a large tureen, with applied sprigs of *prunus* and painting in *famille rose* style, dated 1753. Many plates with this decoration are of the favourite Bow octagonal form, with a rather deep well having thick walls rounded towards a hollowed base, which is without the usual foot-ring. This form is not, I believe, found on other English eighteenth-century china, but is common in Chinese 'export porcelain' and is seen also in Delft pottery. This is perhaps another instance of the Dutch influence previously mentioned. A plate in the British Museum, of this form, is inscribed 'P TB DARBY' in incised script letters, and has on that account been claimed for Derby.[1] It is painted in the *famille rose* style here referred to, has been proved phosphatic, and was almost certainly made at Bow, but the significance of the inscription remains obscure.

Amongst other typical Bow shapes of this and the earlier period I may mention here the cup or cylindrical mug with a loop handle that joins the body almost horizontally at the bottom, instead of, as usual, descending to join it below at a more or less acute angle. Another type of mug with nearly cylindrical body slightly spreading to the base was made at several factories, the heart-shaped lower termination of the handle helping to distinguish those made at Bow (though a heart-shaped terminal was sometimes used elsewhere[2]).

The so-called Kakiemon designs, mainly in red, blue and gold, must have been even more popular here than at Chelsea, and, as we have seen, Bow specialised in 'useful wares'. We meet the 'parteridge octogon plates' in Bowcocke's papers (1756) as well as in the advertisements. There is a whole shelf of pieces painted in this style—shell-salts, plates, cups and saucers—in Mr. Broderip's

1 *Transactions E.P.C.*, No. II, Plate XIV.

2 On porcelain attributed to William Ball's Liverpool factory (Watney, *English Blue and White Porcelain*, p. 89); and occasionally on Derby (op. cit., p. 92) and Champion's Bristol porcelain (op. cit., p. 132).

FIGURE OF FLORA Ht. 18¼in (46.3cm). About 1760. No mark.
Victoria and Albert Museum (533-1868)

See page 106   Plate 48 BOW

gift at South Kensington. An immense Bow service with the 'parteridge pattern' in the possession of the Duke of Northumberland bears the mark of a bow and arrow; this is rare on Bow porcelain and is often regarded as apocryphal. To distinguish Bow, Chelsea and Worcester 'Kakiemons' by painting alone is a simple matter, once the differences have been observed; Bow partridge patterns tend to a rather careless freedom, soft and rich in total effect (Plate 37D). The garrulous Craft spoke of his bowl as painted in 'what we used to call the old Japan Taste, a taste much esteemed by the then Duke of Argyle'; but the colouring alone recalls the Japanese designs. The garlanded flowers of the bowl[1] appear also with phoenixes on a plate in the Schreiber Collection (Plate 47B), which we may attribute to Craft's hand. Another class closely imitating the Kakiemons has the 'banded hedge', the bursting pomegranates and other motives of the Japanese porcelain executed with great delicacy. A cup and saucer in the Schreiber Collection (Plate 38B) is a good example; a mug (Schr. No. 79) figured in Plate 38C shows a delightfully rendered piece of heraldry boldly combined with Japanese motives, the whole surmounted by a typical Bow figure of a pug dog. Such combinations of motives are entirely characteristic of the factory. A beautiful square dish at South Kensington has Chinese plum-blossom in relief, finely painted Meissen flowers in colours, and a red Kakiemon border. A bottle in the Wallace Elliot Bequest at South Kensington (Plate 47A) with its fresh vivid green, red and amethyst colour, was apparently inspired by some Meissen versions of the Kakiemon decoration. Another fine Kakiemon piece is figured in Plate 38A; it is of an elongated egg-shape which is almost peculiar to Bow among the English factories, and the form serves to confirm as Bow a class with Chinese subjects faintly printed in outline and enamelled over in colours. A characteristic Bow freshness of colour is the chief merit in these.

Printed decoration seems to have been used at Bow quite early in this period, but no document is available to give a precise date for its introduction. Bowcocke wrote in 1756 of 'printed teas', but it would be rash to assume that this is a reference to printed wares as

---

[1] Craft's monogram is also inscribed in garlands of flowers in the interior of the bowl.

A. STAND FOR TUREEN L. 13in (33cm). About 1765. Anchor and Dagger mark.
Victoria and Albert Museum (C.307-1927)

B. DISH L. 9⅝in (24.4cm). About 1770. No mark. *Schreiber Collection (103)*

See page 124   Plate 49 BOW

we understand the word.[1] A print in brick-red on a plate in the Schreiber Collection (No. 111) with the subject of Æneas and Anchises, with its long, fluent lines and distinctive use of cross-hatching once attributed to Simon-François Ravenet at Battersea,[2] is now recognised as having been engraved by Robert Hancock after Gravelot.[3] A similar style is seen in the engraving copied from a print by J. P. Le Bas after Chardin, entitled *Le Négligé, ou La Toilette de Matin*, of which examples are known on unquestionable Bow porcelain.

Some very attractive plates of children playing games (Plate 46A) are also early work of Hancock engraved under the influence of Ravenet. That some of these prints occur also on Worcester[4] is confirmation of the view that they are Hancock's work. Rouquet,[5] the French traveller previously quoted, reported a china-factory at Battersea where decoration was carried out by a kind of printing. The suggestion has been made that this was Bow or Chelsea ware brought to Battersea for printing; but it is more probable that the 'china' seen by Rouquet was in fact of enamelled copper, which in the best Battersea work is remarkably like porcelain.

The common belief in Hancock-at-Battersea was shown by Mr. Rackham[6] to be based entirely upon the mistaken attribution to Battersea of a Staffordshire enamel. But the evidence of Hancock's work at or for Bow exists in the form of a signed print on an unmistakable Bow plate at the British Museum (No. I. 65) printed

1 Bowcocke's notes were of course never intended to be understood by others, and the tantalisingly brief descriptions can but seldom be identified with existing pieces. The 'fine landskip pattern', 'image pattern', 'Newark pattern', and 'Dresden sprig' leave us altogether in doubt as to the particular designs in question. And 'Paris Cries', 'Dutch Dancers', 'Nuns and Fryers', 'Fostinas', 'Swan', and 'Woman with Chicken', etc., are models well-known also in porcelain from other factories, and we are thus not helped in the task of identifying those made at Bow.

2 See *Catalogue of the Schreiber Collection*, vol. III, p. 7.

3 *Burlington Magazine*, December 1972: Watney, 'Origins of Designs for English Ceramics of the Eighteenth Century'.

4 See an article by Frank Tilley, 'Robert Hancock at Bow', in the *Antique Collector*, April 1939, p. 80. Also Cyril Cook, *The Life and Work of Robert Hancock*, Ch. 3.

5 Op. cit., p. 143. This passage and the probably mythical china-factory are discussed on p. 378.

6 In *The Burlington Magazine*, vol. XXVI (1915), p. 155; the assertion that he learnt mezzotint engraving from Thomas Frye and line-engraving from Ravenet, is based on nothing better than surmise.

A. MUG Ht. 5¾in (14.6cm). About 1765–70.
Anchor and Dagger mark. *Victoria and Albert
Museum (3272-1853)*

B. DISH L. 8⅞in (22.5cm). About 1765–70. Anchor and Dagger mark. *Schreiber
Collection (104)*

See page 125 Plate 50 BOW

in red with the 'Tea Party' subject.[1] (That figured in Plate 46B is similar.) As stated above there are other Hancock prints on porcelain attributed to Bow, but the ascription either to the factory or the engraver has been open to question. Here there can be no doubt: the specimen shows all the characteristics of Bow porcelain of about 1755. The partings in the paste, the bright flecks and warm cream-colour by transmitted light, and the soft glaze, no less than the Kakiemon border naïvely combined with a brick-red transfer-print, speak clearly of a Bow origin. I think we may confidently assign this plate to a date before 1757, the year of the earliest dated Hancock prints on Worcester porcelain. If the primitive style of engraving on the early Worcester china to be described on a later page[2] is by Hancock, we must conjecture, either an interval spent in London by the engraver, that he sold some plates to the Bow or Battersea proprietors, or that Bow china was sent away to be printed, perhaps in the Midlands.[3]

But printing on Bow china was never well-established as a mode of decoration. The Bow glaze was evidently too soft and fusible, and prints, especially those in the purplish or brownish black which was favoured, were apt to be blurred or fuzzy. The beautiful warm brick-red of many of the prints seems to have made for success, and such examples as those figured in Plate 46 are surpassed by none in delicacy of line and charm of effect. The groups of sheep and poultry and the Italian landscapes (Schr. Nos. 113 and 114) should also be noted as typical Bow prints quite different in effect from those of other factories. The naïve mixture of motives so characteristic of Bow is well seen again in a teapot in the Schreiber Collection (No. 110), printed with a portrait of Frederick the Great, and having a twig handle with brilliant green leaves attached and a spout painted with flowers in Chinese style!

---

1 This evidence was for long overlooked; the latest historian of the Battersea factory, who was much concerned with the matter, did not mention it.

2 See p. 222.

3 Compare an article by W. B. Honey, 'New light on Battersea enamels' in *The Connoisseur*, LXXXIX (1932), p. 82, and a very important paper by H. W. Hughes, in *Transactions E.C.C.*, III (1935), p. 85. Also Watney and Charleston, 'Petitions for Patents concerning Porcelain, Glass and Enamels etc.', in *Transactions E.C.C.*, vol. 6, part 2, pp. 57–123, where evidence seems to show that Hancock, far from working at Battersea or Bow, spent his working life in the Midlands.

The portraits of Frederick the Great, common on English porcelain of this time, commemorate his successes in the Seven Years War and his convention with England in 1756 against France and her allies. The date of these again points to the period of the Bow printing.

For long there existed no known evidence in favour of underglaze-blue printing at Bow, but a number of examples have since been recognised dating from about 1760, including a fragment of a waster from the factory site.[1] Six subjects are recorded by Bernard Watney.[2] One such, attributed to Hancock, is the well-known 'La Dame Chinoise' (Plate 35C).

Porcelain painted in blue undoubtedly formed a large part of the Bow productions in this period and later, but its identification continues to be the subject of some dispute, as between Bow and Lowestoft and even Liverpool. One can, however, describe some characteristics which identify certain well-defined types. The earliest specimens attributed to the factory, painted in a very bright blue, have already been mentioned. An apparently later specimen, a dish of the familiar type in the form of a leaf painted with vines and grapes (Plate 42A), and bearing a common and distinctively written mark of four simulated Chinese characters,[3] has been analysed[4] and found to contain phosphoric acid; and fragments were found on the site of the factory[5] with part of the design of a Chinaman with a staff and a boy attendant, seen on a sauce-boat, a large dish and a plate in the Museum collection at South Kensington. The characteristics of these, together with the marks on the leaf dish, supply evidence for the attribution to Bow of certain other specimens of blue-and-white. Letters and numerals in blue on the base (not on the foot-ring as in Lowestoft) are common on Bow blue-and-white; the 'B' which sometimes occurs is more likely to be a workman's mark than to stand for Bow. A mark resembling 'T' and 'F'[6] conjoined was for long believed to be a

1 Dr. John Ainslie, 'Underglaze-blue printing on Bow porcelain', *The Antique Collector*, April 1957.
2 Watney, op. cit., pp. 21–3.
3 See Appendix, p. 386, No. 17.
4 *Analysed Specimens*, No. 13.
5 *The Burlington Magazine*, vol. XL (1922), p. 229. Plate F.
6 See p. 240, and Appendix, p. 392, No. 5.

Bow mark, standing for Thomas Frye; the oviform vases and other examples so marked are now known to be of Worcester porcelain. This mark is an imperfect copy of the Chinese character *yü* (jade), commonly found on Chinese blue-and-white. Another form of the same letters is, however, sometimes seen on Bow porcelain,[1] but is easily distinguished from the Worcester mark. The 'alchemists'' marks on porcelain formerly ascribed to Bow but now known to be early Worcester[2] do occur on blue-and-white from the London factory, but much more rarely; paste and glaze should distinguish the Bow examples.

Amongst the later Bow blue-and-white are certain dishes and plates with Chinese subjects painted in fan-shaped and circular panels reserved on a powdered-blue ground.[3] The Bow glaze and strong blue are usually sufficient proof of the origin of these.[4] And two plates with this decoration in the Schreiber Collection (Plate 42C) bear marks not dissimilar to those on the analysed dish and are also of the distinctive Bow shape, a form found also in the '*Robert Crowther*' plate, dated 1770, in the British Museum.[5] A punch-bowl in the Schreiber Collection (No. 29), painted in blue with masonic emblems, is noteworthy for the date it bears (1768). Apart from the evidence of style, the Bow blue-and-white may often be distinguished from the similar ware made at Lowestoft (which also contained bone-ash) by the quality of its glaze. An unusual quantity of lead was apparently used, giving a markedly yellowish tone to the enamel-painted pieces, and rendering it liable to decomposition, especially at the foot. The faint iridescence of surface, also due to excess of lead, is more marked on Bow than on any other English china. A liability to blackish specks is also noticeable in the commoner wares. The blue-painted pieces rarely

1 As an early blue-and-white bowl at South Kensington. See Appendix, p. 386, No. 11.

2 See p. 391.

3 Some of these are also attributed to Lowestoft (Spelman, *Lowestoft Porcelain*, Plate 25) and to Worcester and Caughley (Hobson, *Worcester Porcelain*, pp. 58, 189), but in the Lowestoft examples the reserves are of a different shape, unlike those from Worcester and Caughley in which they are also fan-shaped and circular. See pp. 202, 240 and 290.

4 Bow coloured enamels, including a 'stale-mustard' yellow and a slaty blue, on a powdered-blue plate in Mr. Herbert Allen's collection (No. 24), prove this specimen to belong to the factory.

5 See pp. 92 and 112.

have the ivory colour of the others, and one may suppose that the glaze for these was deliberately 'blued' with a minute quantity of cobalt, or the blue-colour used for the painting has perhaps 'flown' in the kiln. At Bow the colour was always inclined to run, from the softness of the glaze. An occasional feature of Bow bowls and plates is the trace of the second firing in spur-marks on the *rims*.

The later productions of the factory show a great falling-away from the standard of originality and charm previously reached. The porcelain itself was no longer of fine quality; the paste was often nearly opaque, showing a dusky brownish translucency, and the uneven-surfaced glaze, now much disfigured by black specks, was strongly tinged with blue, apparently to counteract the former yellowish or ivory tone, which was evidently regarded as a shortcoming. (The admired Chinese export porcelain was bluish or greyish.) For the greater part, the designs and styles were frankly imitated from those of contemporary 'gold anchor' Chelsea. In this, Bow was perhaps aided by the migration of Chelsea workmen; Mason[1] stated that he worked at Bow when the other factory was closed on account of Sprimont's illness. Figures were more clumsily modelled, the costumes extravagantly but crudely decorated with diaper-patterns in colours dull and lifeless in comparison with those of the earlier period. The beautiful opaque blue enamel was replaced by a dark translucent blue, and pink and watery green colours were much employed. The Schreiber Collection is again representative. The *Dancing Peasants* (No. 90), and the well-dressed *Gardener*, symbolical of Autumn (No. 85), are perhaps the best modelled of the later figures. The last-named is adapted from the famous Chelsea gardener in the gold-anchor *Autumn* (as in the Schreiber Collection, No. 198). The *Man in Turkish Costume* (No. 87) is interesting as a version of a model made in the earlier periods. The droll *Dancing Girl*, adapted from a Meissen model, figured in Plate 45C, is typical and charming; it shows the Bow version of the 'gold-anchor style'. The four-footed

1 See p. 40.

pedestal of this figure belongs to a rather earlier phase, and was now often replaced by a moulded base decorated with *rococo* scroll-work (again in imitation of Chelsea), sometimes picked out in underglaze blue, as in the *Bishop* in the Schreiber Collection (No. 91), and the candlestick with a *Woman holding a Boy* (No. 93). The heads of many of these late Bow figures are quite distinctive: the *Drummers* (Schr. No. 84), as well as the *Dancing Peasants* mentioned above and the *Girl* figured in Plate 45C, should be noticed as typical.

The decoration on table-wares and vases also largely followed Chelsea models. The 'exotic birds' were copied, as on the panels of a plate in the Schreiber Collection (No. 105), on which the ground colour is probably intended to imitate the 'mazarine' blue: the fantastic and ugly large *rococo* vases are also painted with birds in this style, in panels on a powdered-blue ground. Worcester scale-blue was copied, and a specimen of this kind in Mr. Wallace Elliot's collection had the square-mark of the Worcester factory as well as the Bow anchor and dagger in red. The scale-blue of the Worcester factory was also copied on a plate in the British Museum (No. I. 40). The 'dishevelled birds', best known on Worcester porcelain, are seen on a late Bow plate in the Schreiber Collection (No. 107). The occurrence of painting by this hand on porcelain from several factories confirms the suggestion already made that some Bow porcelain of this, as of earlier periods, was painted by an outside decorator, who may have been James Giles or one of his employees.[1] The fact or presumption that Duesbury was assisting both the Bow factory and the enameller Giles makes this seem not improbable. The 'Watteau figures' of Chelsea were imitated, perhaps by the same hand, on a 'frill vase' in the Herbert Allen Collection (No. 11), and on a fine tureen at South Kensington, the stand for which is figured in Plate 49A. The painting of flowers and fruit (as on Schr. Nos. 76 and 103: Plate 49B), though obviously inspired by the rival London factory, is often very successful in its bold drawing and full-toned colour. A Chelsea plate in the Museum collection at South Kensington is painted with fruit

---

[1] Compare p. 264 and a paper by W. B. Honey, 'The work of James Giles', in *Transactions E.C.C.*, V (1937), p. 7. Also H. R. Marshall, 'James Giles Enameller' in *Transactions E.C.C.*, vol. 3, part I, 1951, p. 1ff.

apparently by the same hand as these Bow pieces; we may wonder whether this is perhaps the work of the migrant painter Mason. This plate should be compared with a fine mug in the Schreiber Collection (No. 102), from which a mark (presumably a dagger) has been ground away to leave an anchor only. A previous owner evidently felt that it was worthy to be regarded as Chelsea!

Some painting in red-brown, green and purple of lake-scenes with trees and foliage, as on a pair of dishes in the Schreiber Collection (No. 104) and on a mug in the Museum collection at South Kensington (Plate 50A), has a peculiar artless charm, and may well be by the hand of the painter O'Neale,[1] who seems to have worked, at least occasionally, for Giles.

Many pieces attributable to Bow in its last period are marked with an anchor and a dagger, in red or brown, often accompanied by letters, dots or symbols in underglaze blue. These last were of course necessarily added, like the underglaze blue in the decoration, in the factory itself; but the red enamel anchor and dagger may well have been added in Giles' workshop. The obvious difficulty of keeping this anchor and dagger mark for Bow porcelain alone might account for the occasional occurrence of the anchor only, sometimes found on unquestionable Bow porcelain. The anchor may have been first used by a migrant Chelsea workman. The dagger of the mark is sometimes said to have been drawn from the arms of the city of London. It is found also in underglaze blue, sometimes with the red dagger as well. The letter 'I' and an 'A' of archaic form[2] in underglaze blue are common. These are doubtless workmen's marks, and the cursive 'B' in blue, also found, is no more likely to stand for Bow than the similar letter sometimes found on earlier pieces, as already mentioned. The recurrence of a rather clumsy blue crescent has led to the mistaken attribution to Worcester of figures with this mark. Analysis has, however, proved a crescent-marked figure to contain bone-ash, whilst a similar test has shown that the few figures believed to have been made at Worcester contain magnesia due to soapstone, the

---

1 Or possibly Fidéle Duvivier. For his work on Worcester porcelain, see Barrett, *Lund's Bristol and Worcester Porcelain*, p. 54.

2 See Appendix, p. 386, Nos. 23 and 24. The 'A' is erroneously stated by Chaffers to be a Longton Hall mark.

characteristic Worcester ingredient.[1] Moreover, the blue crescent sometimes occurs on figures in combination with the characteristic Bow red anchor and dagger.

1 See pp. 274 and 386, Nos. 22 and 27.

Chapter 4

Derby

According to a vague tradition preserved by the older workmen at the factory, porcelain was made at Derby as early as 1745. William Locker, clerk to the factory towards the end of its existence, reported a statement by Samuel Keys, a workman who had been apprenticed in 1785, to the effect that a foreigner in poor circumstances, living in Lodge Lane, had 'about 1745' modelled 'small articles in china, such as birds, cats, dogs, sheep and small ornamental toys', and fired them at a kiln in the neighbourhood, belonging to Woodward, a pipe-maker.[1] Mr. F. Williamson has shown[2] that the only pipe-maker's kiln that could be in question was built as late as 1795, and that this part of the tradition at least must be mistaken.

That porcelain was in fact made in Derby as early as 1750 seems to be proved by certain white porcelain cream-jugs, decorated with strawberries and leaves in applied relief. One of these, in the possession of Mr. Egerton Leigh, is inscribed under the base with the word '*Derby*'[3] incised; another, in the Victoria and Albert Museum, has the inscription '*D 1750*'[4]; a third, in the British Museum, is marked with the initial '*D*' alone. All are of porcelain of

---

1 Quoted by Chaffers, op. cit., 13th edition (1912), p. 818.
2 *The Connoisseur*, vol. LXXVII (1927), p. 228.
3 This jug is erroneously stated by Chaffers (op. cit., p. 829) to be painted. The jug is reproduced in an article by W. B. Honey, Bernard Rackham and Herbert Read in *The Burlington Magazine*, vol. XLIX (1926), p. 292, where the question of the earliest Derby china is fully discussed.
4 Barrett and Thorpe, *Derby Porcelain*, Plate I.

poor quality; they bear little resemblance to most other existing specimens, and their use, as a means of identifying the remainder of the earliest Derby productions which may be presumed to survive, is, therefore, limited. However, a white figure of the actress Kitty Clive, in the character of the *Fine Lady* in Garrick's *Lethe*, in the Schreiber Collection (No. 1a), previously thought to be non-phosphatic Bow, is possibly a Derby production of 1750 or slightly later (Plate 52A). She stands upon a star-shaped base which has a spray of prunus in relief corresponding closely to those on the 1750 cream jugs. Two such versions are known, one in the S. J. Katz Collection (now in the Boston Museum of Fine Arts) being smaller in size than the others and apparently modelled directly from the well-known Bow example,[1] and both versions are slip-cast, as were all Derby figures, in contrast to the press-moulded Bow pieces.

From entries in the work-books of William Duesbury relating to his employment in London as an enameller, we know that figures were in fact made at Derby soon after 1750. Frequent entries for dates between 1751 and 1753 mention 'Darbey' and 'Darbishire figars' of dancers, 'sesons' and the like. No dated specimen is available for dates between 1750 and 1756. Evidence does, however, exist concerning an actual porcelain factory at Derby before 1756 in a report in the *Derby Mercury* of 26 January 1753, recording the drowning of a workman 'from the China Works near Mary Bridge' on Christmas Eve, 1752.

As has been pointed out,[2] it is inconceivable that the china works referred to could have meant the Potworks at Cockpit Hill (to which place the earliest Derby porcelain has sometimes been attributed), which is a considerable distance from St. Mary's Bridge, and on the other side of the River Derwent.

There is also an entry dated June 1754, in the register of a Derby church, recording the marriage of William Whitehall, 'labourer at the China House'.[3] A workman of the same name was a fireman at the Nottingham Road, Derby, china-works eighteen years later.

1 See p. 92.
2 Barrett and Thorpe, op. cit., p. 6.
3 See an article by F. Williamson in the *Museums Journal*, vol. XXII, p. 141. No earlier entry of this kind can be quoted, as occupations began to be entered in the registers only in 1754.

For 1756, however, we have an important document in a famous draft agreement dated 1 January in that year published by Jewitt,[1] which in fact was never executed. 'John Heath of Derby . . . Gentleman . . . Andrew Planché of the same place, China Maker . . . and Wm. Duesbury of Longton, Enamellor', were named as partners 'in the Art of making English China'. Heath, a Derby banker, was to find a thousand pounds and take a third share of the profits; he was already a proprietor of the pottery at Cockpit Hill in the town of Derby. Duesbury had in 1755[2] made an arrangement with his father, a currier of Cannock, by which he agreed to support him for the rest of his life in return for the transference of his possessions. It seems highly probable that this arrangement was made to provide the younger Duesbury with capital with which to start a china-factory. Of Andrew Planché little is known. He is said to have been in Saxony and 'there learnt the art of making porcelain in Dresden', but this family tradition would merely imply that he had been abroad and there acquired some knowledge of china-making. He is generally assumed to have been the 'foreigner' referred to by Keys, though he would have been only seventeen years old at the date given (1745). He was apparently living in Derby in 1751, as in that year he had a son baptised at St. Alkmund's church.[3] It is likely enough that the figures enamelled by Duesbury in London were the work of Planché.[4]

No place is named in the 1756 agreement. There is evidence,[5] however, that it referred to an existing china factory in Nottingham Road, near St. Mary's Bridge, Derby, which the new partners at once set about enlarging. The premises at which this china manufactory was being carried on were, on 30 July 1756, offered for sale by the then owner, one Charles Shepherdson, and they were described as 'occupied by Mr. Heath and Company in the China Manufactory', and later, in the following November,

---

1 Vol. II, p. 64. Now in the Victoria and Albert Museum Library.
2 He was, at this time, working at Longton Hall, Staffordshire.
3 Jewitt, vol. II, p. 65.
4 Mrs. Donald MacAlister, 'The early work of Planché and Duesbury', in *Transactions E.P.C.*, II (1929), p. 45.
5 *Transactions E.C.C.*, vol. 4, pp. 29–36, where the evidence is fully set out. Also Barrett and Thorpe, op. cit., pp. 5–7.

'Mr. Heath and Company' purchased the property as sitting tenants. But prior to this, in April 1756, Heath and Company had already purchased the adjoining properties in order to extend the Works.

John Heath became bankrupt in 1780 and on 1 August in that year the whole of the properties comprising the manufactory passed into the ownership of William Duesbury. We hear no more of Planché in connection with Derby porcelain. He was presumably still living in Derby in 1756, since he had an illegitimate son baptised there in March of that year and a lawful son four months later, but we can scarcely accept the suggestion of Bemrose and others that the low moral standard implied by this led to his exclusion from the partnership. He is said to have been living in Bath at the 'ripe age of 76 in 1804 and died soon afterwards'.[1]

The first undoubted contemporary reference to Derby porcelain is contained in announcements in the *Public Advertiser* of December 1756 of an auction sale to be held in London 'by order of the Proprietors of the DERBY PORCELAIN Manufactory', offering 'A Curious Collection of fine *Figures, Jars, Sauceboats, Services for Deserts*, and Great *Variety* of other useful and ornamental Porcelain, after the finest Dresden models'. In May 1757 an advertisement in the same paper announced '. . . the largest variety of the Derby or second Dresden', and a paragraph also spoke of 'the Perfection the Derby figures in particular are arrived to'. In 1758 another advertisement announced the sale of 'great variety of Figures, the nearest the Dresden. . . . As with great Care and Expence, this Factory is allowed by all Judges to exceed any Thing of the kind made in England, and the great demand there is for them, has encouraged the Proprietors to enlarge their Manufactory, and have engaged double the Number of Hands they used to employ'. In 1770 the Chelsea factory was bought, and for fourteen years carried on in combination with that at Derby. It is commonly said that about 1776 the Bow works were also purchased, the evidence for this has already been discussed under the heading of Bow.[2]

1 Mrs. Donald MacAlister, loc. cit.
2 See p. 86.

A. CHINESE FIGURE Ht. 9¼in (23.5cm). About 1750–5. No mark. 'Dry edge' class. *Schreiber Collection (284)*

B. FIGURE REPRESENTING TASTING Ht. 6⅝in (16.8cm). About 1750–5. No mark. 'Dry edge' class. *Schreiber Collection (286)*

C. PLUTO AND CERBERUS Ht. 6⅛in (15.5cm). About 1750–5. No mark. 'Dry edge' class. *Schreiber Collection (285)*

Plate 51 DERBY *Early White (figures attributed to Andrew Planché)*

Relatively little is known at present of the very earliest Derby porcelain, contemporary with or rather later than the dated cream-jugs, particularly as to table-wares. A process of elimination and the common feature of a band at the foot bare of glaze have led to the identification of the Planché figures with a group loosely named 'the dry-edge class', represented by a pair of *Goats* in the Schreiber Collection (No. 307) and several other pieces at South Kensington.[1] The 'dry-edge' is perhaps no more than the evidence of timidity or a lack of skill on the part of the workman dipping the piece in the glaze, such as might occur anywhere. But in point of fact the peculiar appearance of shrinkage is rarely found on pieces more certainly attributable to other factories. Another peculiarity seen on a number of these pieces (including the *Lady with a Basket* to be mentioned presently) is a funnel-shaped hole in the base, different from the straight-sided hole of the Bow figures.[2] Moreover there is a decidedly un-English look about Mr. Herbert Allen's *Florentine Boars* (No. 1) that suggests the work of a 'foreigner'; and they do not resemble anything we know as Chelsea. Similarly, a fine little series of Chinese groups was for long assigned to Chelsea, but cannot be linked with any other ascertained productions of that factory. These are represented at South Kensington by the *Chinaman and Boy* (Schreiber Collection No. 284: Plate 51A) and at the British Museum by two other groups, a man and woman, and a woman and child (Nos. II. 4 and 5). Coloured versions exist, their painting the presumed work of William Duesbury. All are most beautifully modelled and of milk-white porcelain with a 'solid' glaze suggesting the use of more than the usual small quantity of tin-oxide. The 'dry-edge' is apparent on most of them, and a variety of the funnel-shaped hole is seen on their bases; in this case it proceeds from a cup-shaped depression. The funnel-shaped hole appears on a pair of white figures of *Bagpipers* in Mr. Wallace Elliot's collection[3] of a model often found in Bow. The glaze and the treatment of the ribbons suggest that these are early Derby specimens.

1 See *The Burlington Magazine*, loc. cit.
2 The form of the hole recalls the conical head and top of the shank of a wood-screw.
3 Figured in *The Connoisseur*, vol. LXXIX (Sept. 1927), p. 7.

The ascription of these pieces to Derby is supported by some links with the later and better-proved productions of the factory. One specimen of this 'dry-edge' class, the *Lady with a Basket*, at South Kensington (Schr. No. 286; Plate 51B) is of the same model and perhaps from the same mould as a rather later *Lady playing a lute*, also in the Museum collection, which can be shown with fair probability to be Derby. The former of these two figures has already been mentioned in connection with certain Bow pieces,[1] apparently painted by the same hand. The *Lady* is, however, of a non-phosphatic paste, and we may regard her as one of the earliest Derby figures, made soon after 1750. A solidly milk-white glaze is a feature, but it is scarcely distinctive enough to identify others of a like origin. A figure of a *Dancing Man* at South Kensington in plain white, with rather dirty white but somewhat opaque glaze, has the funnel-shaped hole in the base, mentioned above, and is of the same model as a coloured figure in Mr. A. H. S. Bunford's collection bearing the incised mark '*N 318*' and quite certainly Derby.[2] The white group of *Pluto and Cerberus* (Plate 51C), for long ascribed to Bow, has been proved non-phosphatic and is certainly a Derby piece: it was probably intended for *Earth* in a set of *Elements*.[3] A 'dry-edge' and a similar rather dirty-coloured and opaque glaze distinguishes two interesting pieces that bear a curious mark resembling a 'Y' within a triangle enclosed by a circle. A *Dancing Youth* at South Kensington[4] and a defective group of a dog barking at a cat in a tree, belonging to Mr. F. E. Sidney, both bear this mark.[5] The painting on the first-named bears a slight resemblance to the pale-coloured family of Derby figures ascribed below to the period about 1755; but a smeared surface-quality

---

1 See p. 96.

2 No. 318 in the Derby price-list is '*Pair of Dancing Figures*'. Another example of this model at Derby Museum dates from 1756–60; Barrett and Thorpe, op. cit., Plate 51.

3 Mr. Wallace Elliot had others from the same set (figured in *The Connoisseur*, vol. LXXIX, Sept. 1927, p. 7). See p. 344 for a connection with the Bristol *Elements*, which resemble these and were said to be the work of a Derby modeller. Later Derby examples are also known, including a 'pale-period' one (see p. 137) at Derby Museum; Barrett and Thorpe, op. cit., Plate 47.

4 Illustrated in *The Burlington Magazine*, loc. cit.

5 See p. 387. Lane, op. cit., p. 100, regards these and others similar as 'transitional' between Planché and the first Duesbury, a view also supported by Barrett and Thorpe, op. cit.

distinguishes it, and we may conjecturally regard these pieces as coloured specimens of the 'Planché period', enamelled, it may be, in Duesbury's London workshop. It will be remembered that 'Darby' pieces are mentioned in his account-book. The white recumbent *Lion* (Plate 37A) is also now regarded as likely to be early Derby.

It may be argued that a resemblance in model is of little account where one factory so commonly moulded its figures from those of another; and that Planché may well have removed his stock of moulds on his exclusion from the new partnership if, indeed, he was so excluded. But links of some kind between later and earlier are generally to be found in the work of a factory with an unbroken tradition. It was in fact by this means that the Derby pieces of the period from about 1755 to 1770 were eventually identified. These had remained for many years unrecognised amongst the Bow and unmarked Chelsea until Mr. Bernard Rackham found a clue in their similarity in certain respects to later and well-authenticated Derby porcelain. An almost constant feature of the figures is the presence on the base (which is commonly flat) of three or four dark unglazed patches left by the pads of clay upon which the pieces rested during their second or glaze firing. These patches do occur also, but much more rarely, on pieces known to have been made elsewhere; for example, on the red-anchor *Leda* in the Schreiber Collection and on a gold-anchor vase also at South Kensington. They occur constantly, however, not only on these early pieces in question but also on the later figures which bear the incised serial numbers of the Derby price-list and are therefore unquestionably of Derby manufacture. The 'patches' clearly indicate a continuous factory practice, or perhaps even the custom of a single workman. A further proof of the origin of the class is furnished by the recurrence of the same models in later Derby. The *Falstaff* is one of these, and a remarkable confirmation of Mr. Rackham's conjecture was furnished by the occurrence of a mark on a figure of a *Bagpiper* of this class, in Mr. Wallace Elliot's collection.[1] This model is

1 Illustrated in *The Burlington Magazine*, loc. cit.

A. THE ACTRESS, KITTY CLIVE, AS *THE FINE LADY* FROM GARRICK's *LETHE* Ht. 9¾in (24.7cm). About 1750. No mark. *Schreiber Collection (1a)*

B. LOVERS AND A CLOWN Ht. 6⅛in (15.5cm). About 1756. No mark. 'Pale-coloured family'. *Schreiber Collection*

C. MANSION HOUSE DWARF Ht. 6⅛in (15.5cm). About 1770–80. No mark. *Victoria and Albert Museum (C.1132-1924)*

See pages *128, 137, 147*

Plate 52 DERBY

repeatedly found in all sorts of sizes and dates down to the closing of the factory,[1] and Mr. Elliot's specimen, which from its style seems to date from about 1760, bears the faintly incised mark '*WD-Co*', reasonably regarded as an abbreviation of 'William Duesbury and Company'.

The figures belonging to this 'patch family' form a coherent class with many other common characteristics. The colouring includes a very easily recognised turquoise-green with a tendency to become discoloured to a dirty brownish tone. Modelling of heads (and in particular noses) and the flesh-painting (with bright patches on the cheeks) are also distinctive; a 'family likeness' is easily perceived. By style these figures seem to date from the period *c.* 1760–70, and confirmation of this is provided by a figure formerly in the Leverhulme Collection, marked '*George Holmes did this figer 1765*'.[2] Holmes was probably a 'repairer' and perhaps the G. Holmes named in a list of hands working at the factory in 1787, quoted by Jewitt.[3] The class formed by far the greater part of the unmarked figures previously assigned to Chelsea, but it seems difficult now to understand how they could have ever been so confused. Not only do they vary in style, but their material is quite different. The soft greenish-toned glaze is absent; the paste has been proved non-phosphatic,[4] whilst Chelsea from 1758 contained bone-ash. But their owners hotly disputed (and perhaps still dispute) any attribution other than Chelsea![5]

1 There are two examples of different sizes in Mr. Herbert Allen's collection (Nos. 38 and 40), and two others, of nineteenth-century date, in the Museum collection at South Kensington.

2 *Sale Catalogue*, part 3 (New York, 20 February 1926), No. 113 (described as Chelsea); illustrated on p. 39.

3 Op. cit., vol. II, p. 102.

4 Analysis by Dr. Plenderleith of the *Man carrying a keg* in the Victoria and Albert Museum (No. C768—1917) shows no phosphoric acid. The full analysis is as follows:

Silica	-	-	-	- 68·5
Oxide of lead	-	-	-	- 4·5
Alumina	-	-	-	- 5·5
Lime	-	-	-	- 17·6
Magnesia	-	-	-	- 2·5

98·6

The magnesia may be due to soapstone, but obviously in much smaller quantity than at Worcester, q.v.

5 It is surprising that the partisans of particular factories should so constantly

If these lavishly gilded figures represent the Derby work imitating, and contemporary with, the later figures of Chelsea, what were the productions of the preceding years? The argument by a 'throw-back' again helps. We find such a model as Kaendler's well-known *Lovers with a Clown*, familiar in the 'patch' family,[1] occurring on a smaller scale and with different colouring in typical specimens of another class.[2] A smaller version of the model just mentioned is in the Schreiber Collection (Plate 52B). This earlier class of figures evidently aped the red-anchor Chelsea; their pale colouring, usually without gold, was the Derby version of the delicate tones of the London productions. A body of noticeably light weight and a strongly blued glaze are characteristic but not invariable features. Many of these figures were for long mistaken for Bow, but analysis again shows a non-phosphatic paste.[3] The same argument also helps to disprove the Derby origin claimed for the figure of a boy, marked with a script 'D', already mentioned under the heading of Bow.[4] In both this and the subsequent period the applied flowers on the bases of the figures sometimes show centres in the form of a bun cut with a cross. This may be detected in the figures shown in Plate 53.[5]

It is by no means certain that figures of this 'pale-coloured family' only began to be made in 1756 when Duesbury came to

prefer quantity to quality. The average of excellence reached by the remaining authenticated Chelsea productions is raised by the withdrawal of those impostors 'the patch-family'!

1 An example from Mr. F. E. Sidney's collection is illustrated in W. King, *English Porcelain Figures*, fig. 43. Also Barrett and Thorpe, op. cit., Plate 57.

2 Most of them formerly ascribed to Bow, and, occasionally, to Longton Hall.

3 The analyses by Dr. Plenderleith of the *Diana* and the *Lady with a Lute* at South Kensington show:

Diana—				Lady with a Lute—			
Silica -	-	-	- 74·1	Silica -	-	-	- 70·4
Alumina	-	-	- 4·8	Oxide of lead	-	-	- 2·1
Lime -	-	-	- 22·8	Alumina	-	-	- 5·4
				Lime -	-	-	- 20·6
				Magnesia	-	-	- 1·3

101·7   99·8

4 See p. 108, and E. E. Hyam, *The Early Period of Derby Porcelain* (1926), p. 18, where this figure is claimed for Derby.

5 This form of flower-centre does, of course, occur elsewhere, and is not by itself conclusive evidence. Staffordshire salt-glaze and Worcester porcelain figures show the same feature.

Derby[1] and the Nottingham Road factory was opened. Even after allowance has been made for the 'lag' in the provincial imitation of a metropolitan fashion, the red-anchor style might well have been copied by Planché for several years before this date. Such figures as those offered in the sale of 1756 are unlikely to have been the productions of a year-old factory; a tradition covering a longer period must be inferred.

Sufficient has been said to enable the collector to identify the Derby figures of these two periods. As works of art their merit is decidedly a matter of opinion. Meissen models were copied no less constantly (as indeed the advertisements indicate) than at the other factories. The earlier 'pale-coloured' family has occasionally the toy-like quality that helps to make a porcelain figure a delightful thing, but the chalky-looking paste and blued glaze are distinctly unpleasant. A pair of *Turkish Dancers* (Plates 53A and C) and the *Musicians*—the *Lady playing a Lute* and a *Flute-player* (Plate 53B), all at South Kensington, are perhaps the best in the public collections. The later 'patch' figures have a stiff doll-like quality that is not unattractive, but a growing tendency to increase the scale of the models accentuates their clumsiness. The well-known group after Vanloo in the Schreiber Collection (No. 299) of a *Youth and a Girl with a Performing Dog* and the popular *Minuet Dancers* (Schr. No. 297)[2] are characteristic and well-finished examples. Exact copies of Meissen models, such as the charming pair of a *Man carrying a cock* and a *Woman carrying a hen* at South Kensington and the *Mapsellers* and *Pedlars*, are among the best of the class. Pastoral figures with elaborate *bocages* were often fitted as candlesticks, and the applied flowers on these are sometimes very large and of a button-like form which occasionally helps to identify the rare pieces without other distinguishing marks. The three figures shown in Plate 54 (all from Mr. Herbert Allen's collection) are typical specimens of these Derby figures of the 1760s. The birds and animals cannot be compared for quick vitality with those of Chelsea, and evidently soon became a 'stock line' for the provincial market. Some of them, however, may date from the 'Planché period': a group of two birds on a clumsy base in Mr. Herbert Allen's collection (No.

1 We know that Duesbury was still 'of Longton' in 1755.
2 Figured in many books on English porcelain as Chelsea.

B. FLUTE PLAYER Ht. 7in (17.7cm). About 1755–60. No mark. 'Pale-coloured family'. *Victoria and Albert Museum (678-1925)*

C. TURKISH DANCER Ht. 5⅜in (13.6cm). About 1755–60. No mark. 'Pale-coloured family'. *Victoria and Albert Museum (C.697-1925)*

A. TURKISH DANCER Ht. 6¾in (17.1cm). About 1755–60. No mark. 'Pale-coloured family'. *Victoria and Albert Museum (C.696-1925)*

See pages 137, 138

Plate 53 DERBY

5) is an example, evidently early. *Miltons* and *Shakespeares* and *Britannias*, afterwards so popular, were already being made in this period.

The useful wares and decorative vases of these two periods show a link with the figures in the painting of flowers with stalks having a peculiar thread-like appearance (Plate 55A): these are found quite early on the costumes of the figures, as on the pale-coloured *Diana* at South Kensington, already mentioned, and are very common later; Mr. Wallace Elliot's marked *Bagpiper* is painted with them. Another painter's hand is seen in the very large moths, beetles and other insects, copied of course from Meissen but treated in an individual and distinctive manner. The 'moth-painter's' hand is also seen in the sketchily drawn birds (Plate 55B) and landscapes common on these pieces: there is a group of coffee-pots and jugs with this painting in the Schreiber Collection (Nos. 317 to 328, etc.). Characteristic miniature landscapes are seen on an inkstand at South Kensington. The moths, with the typical applied flowers and 'dirty turquoise' serve to identify as Derby the well-known pierced frill vases or perfume-pots for long regarded as Chelsea, of which there are specimens at the British Museum (No. II. 25), South Kensington, and in Mr. Allen's collection (No. 45). A set of vases in the British Museum (Nos. IV. 1 and 2), with moths and birds by this painter and figure-subjects in Watteau style in panels reserved on a dark *gros bleu* ground, has been usually regarded as Longton Hall on account of the tone of blue, but they are unquestionably of Derby origin, as the applied flowers and painting alone would show. Curiously enough the 'patches' on the base of these vases were remarked upon by Nightingale, who did not, however, appreciate their significance. A plate in Mr. Allen's collection (No. 89), painted by the 'moth-painter' and marked with a red anchor, should be mentioned here as an example seeming to support the former Chelsea attribution for this group. But the mark counts for little against the evidence of paste and glaze and painting, and it is probably a case of a pirated mark, as is another instance, the thoroughly Derbyish *Chatham* in the Schreiber

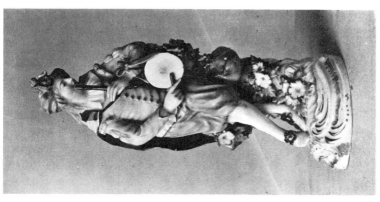

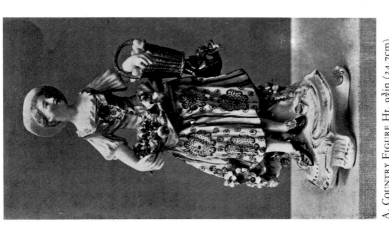

A. COUNTRY FIGURE Ht. 9¾in (24.7cm).
About 1760–5. Patch marks. *Victoria and
Albert Museum (C.196-1921)*

B. MUSICIAN Ht. 9¾in (24.7cm). About
1760–5. Patch marks. *Victoria and
Albert Museum (C.195-1921)*

C. COUNTRY FIGURE Ht. 9¾in (24.7cm).
About 1760–5. Patch marks. *Victoria and
Albert Museum (C.196-1921)*

See page 138

Plate 54 DERBY

Collection (No. 306), which has a gold anchor though it dates from about 1766 or later.

It seems that Richard Holdship, who left Worcester in 1759, went to Derby and in 1764 offered Duesbury, among other things,[1] to teach printing in 'Enamell and Blew'; but printing on existing examples of acknowledged Derby porcelain is exceedingly rare. Jewitt stated that he had in his possession letters from Holdship to his employer complaining that no work was given him for his presses, but showing an engagement that lasted at least until 1769. Jewitt further published an account for engraving plates for 'small china' and other articles, done in 1771 by John Lodge for William Duesbury. It is evident, therefore, that some printed decoration was done on Derby china, though the glaze was probably too soft to be suitable for it. At present the chief examples described are a mug formerly in the Bemrose Collection, now in the British Museum, printed in underglaze blue and marked under the handle with the word 'DERBY', an anchor and a sun;[2] and a mug with a black print of George III and Queen Charlotte, inscribed '*Crowned March 1761*' and marked with the anchor and '*Derby*'.[3] Jewitt declared[4] that this mark occurred on an engraved copper plate from Caughley, but it seems possible that both these pieces were printed by or for Holdship, if not at Derby, then at some other factory, for the purpose of providing specimens to be shown to the Derby proprietors. Printed cream-coloured ware with the same mark is also recorded, presumed to have been made at the Cockpit Hill Potworks.[5]

---

1 He had acquired the soapstone rights from Benjamin Lund of Bristol (see p. 229), and offered to the Derby proprietors the porcelain recipes including this ingredient. A small quantity of magnesia to be observed in the analysis of a Derby figure, given on p. 137, is perhaps to be accounted for by the use of soapstone at Holdship's instance, and if so the figure would be of a date subsequent to 1764. It is known that Duesbury was owner in 1776 of a lead mine in Derbyshire that also produced a form of soapstone ('Halloysite'), which could, alternatively, have provided a source of this material. Barrett and Thorpe, op. cit., p. 138.

2 Bemrose, p. 140.

3 Binns (2nd edition), p. 69. Some five or six subjects are known.

4 Vol. I, p. 273.

5 For an account of the Cockpit Hill Potworks see F. Williamson's 'Derby Pot Manufactory Known as Cockpit Hill Pottery', *Derbyshire Archaeological Society* publication, 1930; also Donald Towner, 'The Cockpit Hill Pottery, Derby', *Transactions E.C.C.*, vol. 6, part 3, pp. 254ff.

C. PLATE Dia. 8⅝in (21.9cm). Perforated rim. Painted in underglaze blue. About 1760. No mark. *Victoria and Albert Museum (C.711-1924)*

B. DISH L. 8¼in (20.9cm). About 1760. No mark. *Schreiber Collection (322)*

A. DISH L. 11in (27.9cm). Moulded in relief. About 1760. No mark. *Schreiber Collection (330)*

See pages 140, 154

Plate 55 DERBY

The figures of the Chelsea-Derby period (1770–84) represent a continuation of the earlier tradition of Derby rather than that of Chelsea. The use of the gold anchor on figures that are so unmistakably in the style of the former suggests that this mark cannot, as is often supposed, indicate work done at Chelsea in the period. The Chelsea sales were, however, continued. The advertisement of a sale by Christie in 1772 was delightfully announced as 'a Display of Elegance and Taste' that 'reigns almost uninterrupted through the Articles that comprize this Sale. The Ornaments are a continued Variety of antique, select and peculiar Forms and Shapes, ætherial Colours and elaborate Decorations that alternately rise with increasing Beauty, and which distinguish Genius (British) not less conspicuous or meritorious than the Saxon or Gallic. Human Actions lively and naturally represented in many expressive and agreeable Characters; the Figures graceful, the Attitudes just, the Drapery loose and flowing, and finished with a nicety incredible; nor does the Table want its Requisites and Embellishments in all its various Occasions; the several Apparatus are contrived and adapted with much Skill, and painted and adorned with a luxuriant Fancy. Emulous to excell and happy to please, no Labour, no Expence have been spared; a chearful and vigorous Perseverance in the arduous Task, has, it is humbly presumed, brought this Porcelain to a Degree of Perfection that merits public Attention'.[1]

The mark of a 'D' intersected by an anchor, in gold, or more rarely in red,[2] belongs to this period, but was added as a rule only on tablewares. Rare exceptions are the figure of *George III* in the British Museum (No. II. 300) and the pair of figures of so-called *Vauxhall Singers*[3] of which Mr. A. H. S. Bunford has a marked specimen. An anchor and a 'D' side by side is also known on a table-service with hop-trellis pattern (Plate 58A).[4] An anchor in red occurs on a dish at South Kensington in a Derby style too late

1 Sale Catalogues of this and later dates (1773–85) are published in Jewitt, vol. I, pp. 75–83, and Nightingale, pp. 15–92. See also Barrett and Thorpe, op. cit., pp. 159–77.

2 As on a basin at South Kensington (No. C266—1922).

3 An unmarked pair is in Mr. Herbert Allen's collection, No. 95.

4 An example is in the Victoria and Albert Museum (No. C1272—1919).

A. Group Representing Commerce Ht. 7in
(17.7cm). Companion group dated 1773. No mark.
Schreiber Collection (345b)

B. Group Ht. 6½in (16.5cm). About 1770–80. No mark.
Victoria and Albert Museum (1315-1871)

See pages 146, 147   Plate 56 DERBY (*'Chelsea-Derby' period*)

to be ascribed to a date before 1770. The only mark usually found on the figures is a script 'N', or 'No' followed by a numeral referring to the Derby price-list, and occasionally a reference to the size (such as '*small*'). A useful extract from this list was published by Haslem.[1] The biscuit statuettes for which the factory was afterwards famous began to be made in this period,[2] and were similarly marked. Early specimens of these are in the Schreiber Collection (Nos. 422, 423 and 424), which is especially rich in Chelsea-Derby.

In general, the figures of this time show rather insignificant modelling and an affected grace and sentiment in the fashion set by the Sèvres factory, but copied also by Meissen at this time. The *Boy and Girl dancing* (Schr. No. 384) are actually adapted from Sèvres models by Falconet, as are the two pastoral groups, the famous *Bergère des Alpes* and *L'Oracle* or *Le Nœud de Cravate* (Schr. No. 352) based on designs by François Boucher.[3] Another popular group (Schr. No. 355) is adapted from an engraving by Jacques Philippe Le Bas, after a painting by Boucher, entitled *Pensent-ils au Raisin?*, now in the National Museum, Stockholm. The Schreiber Collection includes an impression of this print (No. 1820) as well as of that (dated 1772) of *Time clipping the Wings of Love* (Schr. Nos. 343 and 1819) engraved by Charles Phillips after Van Dyck. The Cupids and allegorical figures of the contemporary *Louis Seize* style were in fact much in evidence: *Cupid* as *Discretion* and as *Astronomy* (Schr. 344 and 345) and *Commerce* (Plate 56A) are amusing instances. The *Boy with a Dog* and *Girl with a Cat* (Schr. No. 349) are similar to a pair described in the Sale Catalogue for 29 March 1773, as 'Laughing figures enamell'd white and gold dressing a macarony dog and cat'. Rare instances of the earlier Meissen-Chelsea style are the *Cupid in a Wig* (Schr. No. 358), and the *Bacchus* (Schr. No. 341), which is a rather weak and pallid

---

1 pp. 170–81. Haslem included some notes and additions of his own, and the list must be used with caution. Another list is given in Bemrose, *Bow, Chelsea and Derby Porcelain*, p. 67; in this the numbering is different. See also Barrett and Thorpe, op. cit., pp. 180–92.

2 At least as early as 1771: compare Nightingale, p. 19.

3 *Maquettes* of the original groups, known by the names given above, are preserved in the Musée Céramique, Sèvres. See Bourgeois and Lechevallier-Chevignard: *Le Biscuit de Sèvres*, Plate 19, Nos. 110 and 481.

version of a vigorous Meissen figure of about 1745. The group of a *Boy and Girl dancing*, in Mr. Allen's collection (No. 96), is a sentimentalised version of one by Kaendler. The lively group figured in Plate 56B is of rare quality in this period, and was doubtless inspired by the same modeller. The *Dwarfs*, of one of which there is a specimen in Mr. Broderip's gift at South Kensington, were from the same model as the 'Callot figures' made at Chelsea, and appear in the price-list as a 'pair grotesque punches' (Plate 52C).

Many figures of popular personages were made in the style of contemporary monumental sculpture. The *George III* in the British Museum, after Zoffany's picture now at Windsor Castle, painted in 1770 and engraved by Earlom in the same year, is to be dated between this and 1773 or 1774, by an entry in a catalogue of 'Principal Additions' to the stock of the Bedford Street (London) warehouse of the factory: 'Their present majesties the King and Queen, and royal family, in 3 grouped pieces in biscuit—the center piece represents the King in a Vandyck dress'.[1] A complete set of these groups is in the Royal collection at Windsor Castle. The *John Wilkes* and *Marshal Conway* in the Schreiber Collection (No. 362), once called Chelsea, are late copies, of about 1775, of Derby figures made in the previous decade. The *Garrick as Richard III* (Schr. No. 342) is a very feeble work, though attributed in the price-list to 'Bacon', presumably John Bacon, R.A.,[2] who is known to have worked for Duesbury. The Chelsea-Derby figures are as a rule enamelled in insipid weak colours—amongst them unpleasant but distinctive pale 'watery' greens and pinks are noticeable; but a characteristic rich brown is an exception. The 'dirty turquoise' of the earlier times now gives place to a much pleasanter clear colour inclining to blue (evidently from a Chelsea recipe), which provides a useful means of deciding the date of a piece when the model is common to both periods.

1 W. Bemrose, *Bow, Chelsea and Derby Porcelain*, p. 54.
2 See also p. 88. Haslem (p. 43) quotes a letter from Mr. Henry Duesbury dated 27 November 1862, stating that a memorandum of his grandfather's shows a payment to Bacon in 1769 of £75: 7: 2 for models.

The formal flower-painting on the dresses of the Chelsea-Derby figures often shows the greatest delicacy and refinement, and the same quality marks the 'useful wares' of this period, upon which rests the chief claim of Derby to an honourable place amongst the English china-factories. These alone amongst the Derby productions carry on in any degree the fine Chelsea tradition. In fact a doubt as to their place of manufacture is even possible in the case of some earlier specimens, especially when these are marked with the anchor. That the gold anchor was used at Derby is proved by its occurrence on a piece marked also with the incised 'N'.[1] In general, however, the Derby versions of Chelsea themes, like the designs newly created there, are less free in style and at times mechanical in finish. The Neo-Classical style had scarcely appeared in England by 1770 and on this account the pieces with gilt-striped patterns[2] though sometimes marked with the gold anchor must be ascribed to the Chelsea-Derby period. From the weekly accounts of work done at Chelsea between 1771 and 1773, quoted by Jewitt, it would seem that toys were the principal articles made there after Sprimont's retirement. We read, for example, of 'Cupid as a Bacchus', paid for by the three dozen at 3s 6d; the billing doves are 'Double-doves' at 1s. Some workmen's names are given in the accounts but they do not enable us to identify their work. The names of Barton, Boyer, Wollams (or Wolliams), Jenks (or Jinks) and Boarman (Boreman) are mentioned;[3] the name of Gauron also occurs. Claret and turquoise ground-colours on Derby pieces did not always reach the level of quality obtained under Chelsea management. Nevertheless the factory was not always unsuccessful in this field and some important *rococo* as well as classical style vases with coloured grounds are included in the Derby sales catalogues of 1771 and 1773; also in the Derby *London Warehouse Catalogue* of 1774. Mr. J. V. G. Mallet has noted a crimson-ground *rococo* vase painted with the subject of *Vertumnus and Pomona* from

---

1 A cup and saucer (Allen Collection No. 67). Derby cannot, in fact, be distinguished from Chelsea in this period.

2 First used on porcelain at Frankenthal. Derby copies of pieces in this style sometimes bear the Frankenthal mark.

3 Jewitt, vol. I, pp. 179–86, and vol. II, pp. 71 and 72.

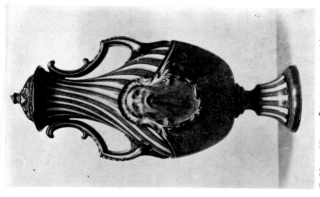

A. EWER Ht. 10⅞in (27.6cm). About 1770–80. Mark Crowned 'D' in gold, incised No. '892'. *Victoria and Albert Museum* (C.264-1935)

B. VASE Ht. 13¾in (34.9cm). About 1770–5. Mark Anchor in gold. *Victoria and Albert Museum* (C.208 and a-1935)

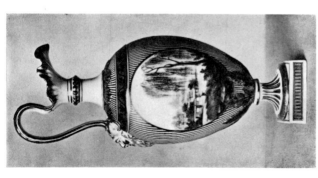

C. VASE Ht. 12⁷⁄₁₀in (32.2cm). About 1770–5. No mark. *British Museum*

See pages 74, 150, 152, 168

Plate 57 DERBY

an engraving published in 1771,[1] whilst one of classical form is figured in Plate 57B. A Derby origin for some at least of these important productions is not, therefore, to be ruled out. The dark mazarine blue gave place to a large extent, towards the end of the Chelsea-Derby period, to an opaque enamel of a much brighter lapis-lazuli colour, imitated from the *bleu-de-roi* of Sèvres, but distinctive enough to be known as 'the Derby blue'.[2] A border of this colour is seen on an important large bowl in the Schreiber Collection (No. 387) marked with a gold anchor and dated 1779, and painted with the arms of the Coopers' Company and with coopers at work. A bowl in similar style in Mr. R. W. M. Walker's collection is painted with views of Chelsea and Battersea Churches before the rebuilding of the latter in 1776, and we may therefore with some probability regard these as belated Chelsea productions, made under Duesbury's management. The vase in the British Museum figured on Plate 57C is a rare Derby production, its hybrid style combining the *rococo* with the Neo-Classical.

Though the Sèvres influence is unmistakable, the Derby table-ware of the Chelsea-Derby period (Plates 58 and 59), included some highly creditable work, employing a fine and sympathetic but practical material,[3] decorated in excellent taste. The Derby patterns of this and the succeeding periods created a quite distinct style which was not without influence on the other English factories. The swags and festoons, small detached sprigs of flowers, wavy lines and the often very charming monochrome painting of urns, vases and classical figures in grey or crimson monochrome are well represented at South Kensington in the Schreiber Collection, and more especially in the large collection bequeathed to the Museum by Mr. Sydney Erwood. Green monochrome painting of flowers was beautifully done; the work of a fruit and flower-painter of great ability is seen on a teapot and a

---

1 *English Porcelain 1745–1850* (ed. Charleston), p. 38 and Plate 7B.
2 Or 'Smith's blue', from the name of the Derby colour-man, Constantine Smith.
3 The soft and very pleasant glaze, however, was especially liable to craze. The paste from the time of the amalgamation with Chelsea contained bone-ash. An entry in the weekly accounts in Jewitt, already mentioned, refers to 'bone-ashes to Derby £4: 5: 6'.

A. CUP AND SAUCER Cup ht. 1⅞in (4.7cm); Saucer dia. 7⅞in (20cm). About 1770–80. Mark Anchor and 'D' (side by side) in gold. *Victoria and Albert Museum (C.1272 and a-1919)*

B. COVERED CUP AND SAUCER Cup ht. 3¼in (8.2cm); Saucer dia. 4¾in (12cm). About 1770–5. Mark Intersected Anchor and 'D' in gold. *Schreiber Collection (399)*

C. CUP AND SAUCER Cup ht. 2½in (6.3cm); Saucer dia. 5¼in (13.3cm). About 1770–5. Mark an Anchor in gold. *Schreiber Collection (379)*

D. JUG Ht. 7¼in (18.4cm). About 1770–5. No mark. *Schreiber Collection (406)*

See pages 144, 150, 154　　　　　Plate 58 DERBY (*'Chelsea-Derby' period*)

sugar-basin, as well as on the custard-cup figured in Plate 59F. The striped and wavy patterns resembling those of contemporary brocades are noteworthy. One of the most beautiful of all the patterns is the simple black and grey husk (Plate 59G). It should be mentioned here that some Worcester patterns were closely imitated at Derby. The well-known Worcester pattern with panels alternately containing pseudo-Japanese dragons and plants, and white rosettes reserved on a blue ground,[1] is sometimes found with the Chelsea-Derby mark. The other imitations are usually unmarked. The Derby 'Queen's' or whorl pattern[2] has a dark mazarine blue instead of the Worcester indigo, but in general these copies can only be distinguished by their glaze-quality and by the Derby gilding which seems to have been applied in a thicker condition, making fine brush-strokes difficult.

The earliest of the Derby painters whose names and work are known to us[3] is Edward Withers, and the painting on a dish and plate at South Kensington is traditionally his. This so-called Withers style is marked by a still slightly conventionalised manner of outlining the petals of a flower. The little jug figured in Plate 59H is in this style. By the same hand are the flowers on a so-called Rodney jug (Schr. No. 408 and B.M. III. 18) made to commemorate that admiral's victory over the French under de Grasse in the West Indies on 12 April 1782.[4] This date is inscribed under the spout, which is in the form of the head of Lord Rodney in a cocked hat.[5] A form of the familiar 'Crown-Derby' mark, the crowned 'D', here in purple enamel, appears on this jug and seems to have been used at times on Derby productions quite soon after the amalgamation. A set of urn-shaped vases and a ewer in the Allen Collection (Nos. 104 and 105: Plate 57A) bear the same mark in gold; their classical forms indicate a date about 1775 and the painting on medallions reserved on a gilt-striped ground may well

1 Frank Lloyd No. 75 and Schreiber No. 575 are examples. Also Barrett and Thorpe, op. cit., Plate 113.

2 See p. 258.

3 See below, p. 162, for a discussion of the evidence for this and other attributions.

4 A jug of this pattern, used by Derby workmen, is described by Haslem, p. 202. Also Barrett and Thorpe, op. cit., Plate 112.

5 The type of spout, however, was evidently suggested by a Meissen coffee-pot. See *Festive Publication of the Meissen Factory* (Dresden, 1911), fig. 97.

A. Trembleuse Cup and Saucer Cup ht. 2⅞in (7.3cm); Saucer dia. 5½in (14cm). About 1770–80. Mark Anchor in gold. *Victoria and Albert Museum (2932-1901)*

B. Covered Cup and Saucer Cup ht. 4⅛in (10.5cm); Saucer dia. 5½in (14cm). About 1770–80. Mark Intersected Anchor and 'D' in gold. *Victoria and Albert Museum (C.280-1922)*

C. Cup and Saucer Cup ht. 2¾in (7cm); Saucer dia. 5⅝in (14.3cm). About 1770–80. Mark Anchor in gold. *Victoria and Albert Museum (C.283-1922)*

D. Custard Cup Ht. 3¼in (8.2cm). About 1780–1800. Crown and crossed batons mark in purple. *Schreiber Collection (417)*

E. Plate Dia. 7⅝in (19.4cm). About 1780. Mark Anchor in gold and incised 'N'. *Victoria and Albert Museum (469-1905)*

F. Custard Cup Ht. 3⅜in (8.5cm). About 1775–80. Mark Intersected Anchor and 'D' in gold. *Victoria and Albert Museum (C.331-1922)*

G. Cup and Saucer Cup ht. 2½in (6.3cm); Saucer dia. 5½in (14cm). About 1770–80. Mark Intersected Anchor and 'D' in gold. *Victoria and Albert Museum (C.298-1922)*

H. Mug Ht. 4in (10.1cm). About 1780. Mark Crowned 'D' in purple. *Schreiber Collection (392)*

I. Cup and Saucer Cup ht. 2in (5.1cm); Saucer dia. 5½in (14cm). About 1780. Chinese seal mark. *Victoria and Albert Museum (C.327-1922)*

See pages 150, 152, 155, 161   Plate 59 DERBY (*'Chelsea-Derby' period*)

be the work of Zachariah Boreman (*b.* 1737, *d.* 1810), a landscape painter, and of Richard Askew, both of whom came to Derby from Chelsea.[1] The latter's earlier style is also seen in the figure subjects in Boucher's manner on a vase with a claret ground of poor quality, also in Mr. Allen's collection (No. 49). The charming grey and crimson *camaieu* painting of cupids (Plate 58B),[2] already mentioned, is attributed to Askew by a tradition attached to a plate at South Kensington (formerly in the Jermyn Street Collection); this presumably represents Askew's second style.[3] A third manner is suggested by the traditional ascription of a plate at South Kensington with an elaborate painting of children and sheep sheltering under a tree (after an engraving published in 1790), but this is so different in handling that another artist seems perhaps more probable. Askew (Richard) had a son Robert, also a painter employed at Derby, and this work may be his. A fine covered cup in the British Museum (Plate 62B) is in this style.

Blue-and-white porcelain such as was produced in quantity elsewhere seems to have been less favoured at Derby. The number of examples that have survived, however, is now recognised as evidence that the output of such ware was considerably larger than was at one time thought to be the case. Most of it is unmarked and largely passed as Bow, but patch marks are usual on pieces decorated in a strong violet blue that date from about 1760. Examples include some plates (Plate 55C) with applied rosettes, and perforated baskets similarly ornamented, distinguished from the Worcester and Caughley baskets by double-looped handles and reeded foot. Shell centre-pieces, some of large size,[4] were also

1 See p. 74 for their work at Chelsea. Askew is recorded to have gone to Derby in 1772 (but may have returned to London), Boreman in 1783 (Jewitt, vol. II, p. 98). For their later work, see pp. 164 and 168.

2 As early as 1771 the sale catalogue of the joint factories included an item, 'enamell'd in Cupids, after Busha'.

3 Jewitt, vol. II, p. 99, gives a list of work done in Birmingham by Richard Askew in 1794 and 1795 for William Duesbury the Second. The items were principally 'coffee-cans' (cylindrical mugs) painted with 'Cupeds' and classical subjects.

4 Barrett and Thorpe, op. cit., Plate 84.

painted in this inky blue. Blue and white ware of the Chelsea-Derby period is painted in a much softer blue. A few examples are marked with a script 'N' incised in the paste, and a teacup and saucer formerly in the Hurlbutt and Foden Collections had the Crowned 'D' in blue.

Some printing in underglaze blue was also carried out, presumably under Richard Holdship, who, having left Worcester, went to Derby in 1764.[1] Most of this printed decoration is of poor quality, and ill-defined, a notable exception being the fine jug in the Derby Museum with the town's arms of a Stag at Lodge.[2] A few subjects transferred in black enamel are known but are of little consequence.

The 'Derby Japan' patterns now made their first appearance and were as a rule in this period much more attractive than the Japanese export porcelain, known as the 'brocaded Imari', from which they were very freely adapted. I illustrate a specimen (Plate 59I), of a pattern most frequently found, from the Erwood Bequest at South Kensington. This pattern was usually marked with an imitation Chinese seal-character, and was 'No. 3' in the Derby pattern-book to be mentioned presently.

William Duesbury died in 1786 and was succeeded by a son of the same name, who was manager until his death in 1796, having in 1795 taken into partnership a miniature-painter named Michael Kean. The latter carried on the factory until 1811, when he sold it to Robert Bloor, previously clerk to the firm. In 1826 Bloor became insane and the factory was managed by James Thomason and Thomas Clarke in succession until its closing in 1848. The productions of these two periods, 1786 to 1811 and 1811 to 1848 respectively, are commonly known as 'Crown-Derby' and 'Bloor-Derby' china, from the marks in general use. The former, as we have seen, was introduced some years before the elder Duesbury's death; about 1782 it was modified by the addition of crossed batons and six dots. It was painted at first in blue, lilac or crimson-

1 See p. 142.
2 Barrett and Thorpe, op. cit., Plate 81.

purple (puce); a similar mark was incised on biscuit figures, and the incised script 'N', already mentioned, continued in use until about 1800. The monogram 'DK', for Duesbury and Kean, is rarely found,[1] and porcelain so marked can be dated very precisely to the period of a few months between the date of Kean's admission to the partnership and that of the second Duesbury's death. A rare and unexplained mark 'DUESBURY LONDON' written in a rectangle in crimson-purple, occurs on a service with the arms of the eighth Duke of Hamilton (about 1786–99); other pieces of the service bear the usual Crown-Derby mark in puce. In the 'Bloor period' (from 1811) the Crown-Derby mark was painted in red, often very carelessly.[2] But after about 1820 various printed marks (such as 'BLOOR DERBY') were general,[3] and the crossed 'L's' of Sèvres and the Meissen swords were quite frequently imitated.

The soft biscuit-porcelain made at the factory from about 1773 at latest onwards[4] was employed for a noteworthy series of groups and statuettes, generally in the classical taste. Of the Derby modellers it must be re-asserted that we know very little indeed. Many of their names and dates were discovered by the industry of Jewitt, but nothing of their work. The price-lists of models already mentioned give in only a few cases the names of modellers. John Haslem (nephew of James Thomason and a painter in the factory in its last period) recorded some traditions regarding their personal characters and their best-remembered works; but the attributions in more recent books on the subject are little more than guess-work based on these scanty and untrustworthy materials. Among the best of the modellers was evidently the temperamental John James Spängler or Spengler, a Swiss, son of Adam Spängler, director of the Zürich porcelain-factory. Spängler worked intermittently at Derby in the last ten years or so of the eighteenth century and

1 A large mug in the Victoria and Albert Museum appears to be the only recorded example.

2 It should be clearly understood that the red 'Crown-Derby' mark belongs only to the Bloor period or at the earliest from about 1805.

3 See Appendix for particulars and dates of these. That printed marks were in use as early as 1818 or 1819 is proved by the Persian ambassador's service, of which a specimen in the British Museum bears the Mohammedan date corresponding to this year with the mark '*Bloor Derby*' in a ring surrounding a crown.

4 See p. 147.

GRACES DISTRESSING CUPID (Biscuit group) Ht. 14in (35.5cm). About 1780.
Incised number 235. *Victoria and Albert Museum (C.59-1924)*

See page 158   Plate 60 DERBY

Jewitt[1] prints two agreements between him and Duesbury, dated 1790 and 1795. Bemrose's list, which dates from 1819, is supposed to cover the models in stock in 1795, and includes as Spangler's a group of *Belisarius and his Daughter* (No. 370), which Mr. Stuart G. Davis has shown to be copied from an original in *terre de Lorraine* modelled by Cefflé.[2] The Zürich porcelain was made from *kaolin* from Lorraine, and this and other models perhaps came into Spangler's hands by the same channel. The same vigorous style is seen in the *Russian Shepherd* group (No. 387). Other models attributed to Spangler in Bemrose's list are No. 363, 'Two pair female figures with dead bird', Nos. 11, 371, 373 and 381 (figures unnamed), and Nos. 123, 124 and 126 (vases). The *Diana* (No. 3012—1901, at South Kensington), after the *Diane Chasseresse* in the Louvre, and the set of three comprising '*Bacchantes adorning Pan*' (Herbert Allen, No. 114), the '*Graces distressing Cupid*' (Plate 60), and the '*Virgins awaking Cupid*'[3] (Herbert Allen, No. 115) are delicately modelled pieces, declared by Haslem to be Spangler's work. The presence of groups with these or similar titles in sale catalogues for 1778 and 1782,[4] however, suggests that he may have been mistaken; Pierre Stephan (see below) is more likely to have been responsible for these models. It is significant that an illegitimate daughter of Spangler's was baptised at Zürich in 1783, and difficult to believe that he spent an interval there between periods of employment at Derby both before and after that date. The incident mentioned was apparently the occasion of his leaving Zürich; on the death of this daughter in 1801 Spangler was described in the register as a 'vagabond' and his whereabouts were unknown. The set of three groups just mentioned was based on paintings by Angelica Kauffmann, the first two engraved by Bartolozzi, the other by W. Wynne Rylands in a print published in 1776, and the models may well have made their first appearance soon after this date. Others of the same series, enamelled in colours, are at South Kensington and at the British Museum. Certain incised marks sometimes found on these figures were

1 Vol. II, pp. 94–7.

2 'Some English Pottery and Porcelain Figures connected with Alsace and Lorraine', in *The Burlington Magazine*, vol. LI (Nov. 1927), p. 221.

3 These are the titles in the sale catalogues and price-list.

4 Nightingale, pp. 52, 53 and 68.

stated by Haslem[1] to be those of 'repairers'. Amongst these, Isaac Farnsworth is said to have used an incised star and Joseph Hill a triangle.

Another modeller was Pierre Stephan, who came in 1770 and continued to work for the factory as late as 1795. He is said to have modelled a series of figures of English admirals and generals, and some of these are recorded as bearing his name, incised on the base. One, said to represent General Drinkwater and formerly in the Waldo-Sibthorp Collection, is in biscuit; another in dark grey clay and apparently an original model, was formerly in the possession of Mr. J. B. Robinson of Derby, and later in the Alcock Collection. The *Lord Howe* is in the British Museum (III. 1).[2] A set of *Elements* is ascribed to Stephan in the price-list. *Earth* and *Water*, in biscuit, are in the Allen Collection (No. 119), and *Fire*, enamelled in colours of the Chelsea-Derby period, is in the Museum collection at South Kensington. William Coffee had been a fireman at Coade's Artificial-stone Works at Lambeth, and after leaving the Derby factory is said to have manufactured porcelain on his own account for a short time, and later made terra-cottas and architectural pottery. The well-known *Shepherd*, of which there is an example in biscuit at South Kensington, is usually said to be his. It was adapted, by the addition of clothing, from an antique figure of Adonis in the collection of the painter Wright of Derby, sold after his death in 1797.[3] The companion *Shepherdess* is said to have been by Spängler, and the pair bore the number 396, not included in Haslem's list. Coffee's name is also attached in the price-list to several figures of animals and to a 'Scotchman and his lass'.

The finest kind of Derby biscuit was made towards the end of the century, especially during Kean's time. Haslem repeats a tradition that biscuit porcelain at Derby was actually Kean's invention, but unglazed porcelain was of course already being made in the Chelsea-Derby period. At its best, it was of ivory smoothness, with a slight film of glaze (technically, a 'smear'), due

1 Op. cit., p. 150.

2 Jewitt (vol. II, p. 94), however, declared that the *Lord Howe* was modelled by Coffee, for whom see below.

3 Haslem, p. 157. Wright is also said to have advised the factory on occasion in his lifetime. The clay-model for this *Shepherd* is in the Nottingham Castle Museum.

to the intentional presence of volatile glaze-material in the kiln. The biscuit of the Bloor period was of inferior quality, tending to dryness. Associated with this, but not strictly Derby china, may be mentioned the porcelain made by George Cocker (*b.* 1794, *d.* 1868), a modeller who was trained at Derby but left about 1817, working for a time at Coalport and Worcester. He returned to the Derby factory for a short period,[1] and finally left to begin the making of china figures, animals, baskets of flowers, etc., on his own account, at first at Derby (between 1825 and 1840) and later in London. In 1853 he moved to Staffordshire and was for a time employed by Minton's. His biscuit has a dry and chalky surface, and is sometimes signed with his name, incised, but more commonly with a cross.[2]

The glazed and enamelled figures of the last fifty years of the factory were to a large extent repetitions of those of the previous periods, apparently supplying a large provincial market. Instances have already been given of figures repeated over as long a period as sixty years. The popular *Tailor on a Goat* and his companion (the 'Welch Taylor and Family' of the price-list)[3] may be mentioned as examples of models made in large quantities and several sizes. After the turn of the century, the modelling became more and more insignificant and the decoration tasteless and showy, with excessive use of hard, brassy gilding. The enamels of the later time often have a thick paint-like appearance probably due to a harder glaze. This unpleasantness of surface was further increased by the free use of such meretricious ornament as porcelain lace-work,[4] of which there are examples at South Kensington and at the British

1 His work for Bloor includes a pair of kneeling figures, of which Haslem (*Catalogue of a Collection of China*, 1879, p. 29) cites the girl (with the title 'Goodnight, Mother') as one of the last figures issued at Derby. A pair of these figures is in the Herbert Allen Collection, No. 129. These execrable models were used again at Minton's.

2 Similar biscuit figures were also made for a short time by one Robert Blore at Bridge Gate, Derby.

3 Copied from Meissen models very doubtfully said to caricature the Saxon court tailor. See *Herbert Allen Catalogue*, No. 124. Barrett and Thorpe, op. cit., Plates 123 and 124.

4 Produced by dipping actual lace in a mixture of porcelain paste and water: the

Museum. In general, the later Derby figures are rarely worth the attention of collectors who are concerned with aesthetic merit alone.

Edward and Samuel Keys (sons of the Samuel Keys who had been apprenticed in 1785) were the chief modellers whose work is known; some of their pieces are in the price-list given by Haslem ('Keys' Fancy Figures'). In particular, Edward Keys was responsible for the *Dr. Syntax* series, after Thomas Rowlandson's illustrations. There is a specimen at South Kensington. The forms of decorative vases shared the general taste. The elaborately modelled and applied flowers so popular at Coalport and elsewhere were also made at Derby in the Bloor period. A 'Peacock among Flowers' of this kind is named by Haslem as a work of John Whittaker, who was foreman modeller at the factory between 1830 and 1847. A specimen in Mr. Herbert Allen's collection (No. 130) is probably identical with this.

The table-wares of the Crown-Derby period maintained the fine tradition of their predecessors (Plates 61 and 62). The material remained of excellent quality but for the tendency to crazing. In addition to the sprays and garlands of the preceding period, sprig patterns (such as the familiar 'cornflower' design of Paris porcelain) were especially popular (Plate 59D).[1] This last was known as 'No. 129',[2] from its number in the still-extant pattern-book; it was sometimes called the Angoulême sprig, since it is believed to have been first used at the Paris factory of the Duc d'Angoulême in the rue de Bondy. It was favoured also at

thread is burnt away in the kiln, and a reproduction of the lace in porcelain is left. It was introduced at Meissen in 1763, and used at Derby, occasionally, as early as the Chelsea-Derby period: in the catalogue of the first sale (1771) a piece is described as 'most curiously ornamented with lace'. A pair of figures in the Allen Collection (No. 127) may be quoted as an example.

1 A datable specimen, apparently rather late, is the jug in the Schreiber Collection (No. 418) with the initials of Daniel Parker Coke formed of these flowers, and apparently made to commemorate his re-election as member of Parliament for Derby in 1802.

2 See Haslem, Plate 3 and p. 190.

Lowestoft, Pinxton and Worcester, in England. The gilt 'sea-weed' and certain foliate and scrolled patterns only faintly recalling the Classical style were characteristic Derby adaptations from Sèvres in the late eighteenth and early nineteenth centuries.[1] The fawn and pale red grounds were also of excellent quality and distinct from those of other factories if not actually earlier in date. Pale pink and yellow grounds of distinctive colour were also used. The wares were almost always marked, and there can seldom be any doubt about their attribution to Derby.

Much has been written about the styles of the Derby painters of this period. However, their work was very rarely signed, and our only real evidence is contained in two lists of patterns which have survived,[2] together with the ascriptions of certain pieces formerly in the collection at the Museum of Practical Geology in Jermyn Street, and now at South Kensington. These in some instances embody traditions handed down by Haslem and other workmen in the factory. But it should be remembered that in many cases Haslem had no personal knowledge of the workmen in question. Jewitt gives a list of the names of the painters.[3] The rest is inference from very ill-established premises, or else sheer conjecture.

The pattern-books are undated but apparently relate to a period towards the end of the eighteenth century. It should be borne in mind that even the names attached to certain subjects painted in the reserves by no means prove that all pieces painted with those subjects were the work of the artists named. Pattern pieces by the latter may well have been kept at the works and copied by the others. The numbers have no reference at all to the subjects in the panels, but relate merely to the formal borders or diapering of the ground; the painting in the panels might be the work of any one of several hands. An undated document published by Jewitt[4] showed that at one time the Derby painters were instructed to add identification numbers to their work: this would scarcely have been needed had not several workmen painted the same pattern.

1 Samuel Keys the elder was an accomplished gilder, and one may conjecture that these patterns were his work.

2 Published in part of Haslem, p. 185, and by W. Moore Binns, *The First Century of English Porcelain* (London, 1906), p. 138.

3 Vol. II, pp. 94–114. See also Barrett and Thorpe, op. cit., pp. 71–109.

4 Vol. II, p. 103.

A. COFFEE CAN AND SAUCER
Probably painted by Banford. Can ht.
½in (6.3cm); Saucer dia. 5¼in
13.3cm). About 1790. Mark
Crowned 'D' and batons in mauve
H' impressed. Pattern No. '239'.
Victoria and Albert Museum (3000 and
-1901)

B. PLATE BY BREWER Dia. 5⅝in (14.3cm).
About 1800. Mark Crowned 'D' and batons
in puce. Pattern No. 447. *Victoria and Albert
Museum (C.323-1935)*

C. PLATE BY BOREMAN Dia. 9⅝in (24.4cm). About 1790. Mark
Crowned 'D' and batons in blue. *Schreiber Collection (413)*

See pages 161, 166, 168, 169

Plate 61 DERBY

Further, as the painters left, their numbers would have been taken up by others, and without the date of the Jewitt instruction and the exact date of a piece it would be impossible to ascertain a painter's name from the number on it.

In spite of this uncertainty, the collector will find pleasure in classifying the interesting painting on the later Derby china, even if names cannot be attached to the several hands recognisable. Many pieces were evidently intended from the first to be 'cabinet specimens'; the little cylindrical mugs known as 'coffee cans' are often painted with miniature-like delicacy and care. Of the artists mentioned in the pattern-books Edward Withers belonged to an earlier generation, and his style has been described on a previous page. Askew's work, too, is prominent on some of the most charming Chelsea-Derby porcelain and has already been discussed. The name of Billingsley (or 'Billensley') occurs several times in the pattern-book and his work is in fact of great importance. If not the creator of the naturalistic style of flower-painting, he was at least one of its first exponents. Instead of the simple direct brushwork of his predecessors he employed a style in which the lights were wiped out of washes of colour. Thus the whole treatment of shadows and details became softer and more 'faithful to nature', though perhaps less appropriate as porcelain decoration.

William Billingsley was born in 1758, apprenticed for five years on 26 September 1774, and left the factory for Pinxton in 1796.[1] His work was evidently in favour with the firm's customers, since the London agent, Joseph Lygo, wrote at the time of his leaving that '. . . his going into another factory will put them into the way of doing flowers in the same way, which they are at present ignorant of'. A dish from the Jermyn Street Collection, at South Kensington (Plate 63A), 'authenticated' by Haslem as Billingsley's, is a document for his style, which can be readily recognised if its peculiarities are once fully grasped. Another dish (No. 3046—1901) bears the pattern number '53', which is given in the pattern-book as 'by Billingsley'. A plate (Plate 62D) and a jug, also at South Kensington, and a ewer, a pair of vases and a flowerpot in Mr. Herbert Allen's collection (Nos. 166, 135 and

1 His later work is described under that heading and that of Nantgarw on pp. 309–317.

A. CUP AND SAUCER Cup ht. 2 7/10in (6.8cm); Saucer dia. 5½in (14cm). Probably painted by Boreman. About 1790. Mark Crowned 'D' and batons in puce. *British Museum*
B. COVERED CUP AND SAUCER Cup ht. 5in (12.7cm); Saucer dia. 6⅘in (17.3cm). Probably painted by Askew. About 1795. Mark Crowned 'D' and batons in puce. *British Museum*
C. CUP AND SAUCER Cup ht. 3 7/10in (9.4cm); Saucer dia. 7in (17.7cm). About 1800. Mark Crowned 'D' and batons in red. *British Museum*

D. PLATE Dia. 8in (20.3cm). Probably painted by Billingsley. About 1790-5. Mark Crowned 'D' and batons in puce. *Victoria and Albert Museum (C.175-1910)*

See pages 154, 161, 164, 166   Plate 62 DERBY

136) are further examples believed to be his work. 'The 'Prentice plate', painted by him and used by the younger painters as a copy, is in the Derby Museum, much worn.[1] Billingsley's 'number' was said to be 7, but pieces with this are variously painted, and rarely in his style. This number does, however, occur on a plate formerly in the Bemrose Collection, similar to that figured in Plate 62D. A ewer and basin formerly in Mr. Frank Hurlbutt's collection and now in the Victoria and Albert Museum,[2] which may reasonably be attributed to Billingsley, actually bear '172', corresponding to an item in the pattern-book said to be by him. The painting on a dish in the Derby Museum,[3] declared by Haslem to be Billingsley's, corresponds with a sketch also believed to be his, published by Bemrose.[4] A successor of Billingsley's, William Pegg, 'the Quaker', was famed for an even closer fidelity to Nature (Plate 63C), and a large tureen at South Kensington, with the Jermyn Street ascription to him, is painted in the now familiar 'botanical' style. He sometimes adopted the practice of adding on the reverse of the piece the name of the flower depicted.[5] A plaque signed by Pegg is illustrated in *The Connoisseur*, vol. X (1904), p. 190. Pegg worked at Derby for two short periods only, from 1796 to 1801 and from 1813 to 1820, twice abandoning china-painting on the ground of conscientious scruples regarding the 'making of a likeness of anything'. His actual work is consequently somewhat rare.

Figure-painting was done by several hands. Askew has already been mentioned. James Banford's name also appears several times in the pattern-lists, and a cup and saucer from Jermyn Street (Plate 61A) with the figure of a girl, are ascribed to him. The number on this cup ('239') is in the pattern-books as 'Hope by Banford', and though the subject on the cup is different, it is customary to regard

1 Barrett and Thorpe, op. cit., Plate 141.
2 Figured from a water-colour drawing in F. Hurlbutt, *Old Derby Porcelain* (1925), Frontispiece. Also Barrett and Thorpe, op. cit., Colour Plate E.
3 F. Hurlbutt, *Old Derby Porcelain*, Plate 54.
4 *Bow, Chelsea and Derby Porcelain*, Plate XVI.
5 There was another, later, William Pegg, who also worked at Nantgarw and subsequently designed for calico prints. But this ascription cannot possibly refer to him, as the tureen has the *blue* mark. Pegg appears always to have used the English, or common, names of the flowers depicted. Those inscribed with Latin, or botanical, names are by another hand, perhaps John Brewer (see below).

A. Dish L. 11¼in (28.6cm). Painted by
Billingsley. About 1790–5. Mark Crowned
'D' and batons in mauve. Pattern No. '127'.
Victoria and Albert Museum (3045-1901)

B. Plate Dia. 9in (22.8cm). Painted by
George Robertson. About 1800. Mark
Crowned 'D' and batons in blue. Pattern
No. 222. *D. A. Hoyte Collection*

C. The 'Thistle' Dish
W. 8½in (21.6cm). Painted by
William Pegg. About 1800.
No mark. *Derby Museum*

See pages 164, 166, 172

Plate 63 DERBY

painting in this style as his. In a letter, however, he spoke of his work in 'any line of painting', and he was evidently more than the figure-painter he is generally represented to have been. The pattern-books describe classical, allegorical and landscape subjects as by him. His wife Bernice seems also to have painted porcelain. The Brewers, John and Robert, were artists of some repute, apart from their painting on porcelain. John Brewer began to work for Duesbury in 1782, but only in 1795 removed to Derby. Some of the accomplished paintings of shipping depicted on the best Derby china are believed to be his, others are by George Robertson;[1] their style being that of a water-colourist. A list of Brewer's work given by Jewitt includes several items of shipping, but many other subjects also! The customary attribution of a single class of decoration to each well-known painter is evidently false. A fine seascape by John Brewer or George Robertson is painted on a cup and saucer in the Allen Collection (No. 162 : Plate 61B); in the same series is a pair of vases (No. 136) with camp scenes presumably of the kind attributed to 'Brewer' in the pattern-books, and perhaps by John or Robert. Many delicate miniature landscapes on cylindrical coffee cups are also probably by Brewer.

Most of the painters seem to have painted birds, and there is no evidence by which to identify Complin's (which figure largely in the pattern-book) or Dodson's, which were rather later, and stated by Haslem to be 'somewhat heavy in colour'. Cuthbert Lawton has repeatedly been said (following a note of Jewitt's) to have painted the hunting-subjects; but these were also painted by others, and in the pattern-books 'a bird on a tree' is alone ascribed to him.

Zachariah Boreman, first of the landscape painters, came from Chelsea[2] in 1783 and continued to work at Derby until 1794. The striped ewer figured in Plate 57A shows his earliest ('Chelsea') style. In his better-known manner (developed only at Derby) details were drawn in monochrome and coloured with low-toned washes, as in the work of Paul Sandby and the early water-colourists. Several pieces in the National collections are plausibly

---

1 See below.

2 See pp. 74, 148 and 154. A signed plaque of uncertain origin, dated 1797, painted by Boreman after leaving Derby, is in the Victoria and Albert Museum. His name is erroneously given by Marryat as Beaumont.

attributed to him. Two plates in the Schreiber Collection (No. 413: Plate 61C) are very charming examples; and a fine cabaret with pink ground in the Herbert Allen Collection (No. 161) is painted with a series of typical Derbyshire landscapes by him. No. 178 in the pattern-book is described as 'Near Crich by Boreman', but a cup at South Kensington is also described 'Near Critch' though it has the number '230'—yet another indication of the need for caution in the use of the pattern-books for purposes of identification. Boreman is also said to have painted birds, which would show the same quiet tones as his landscapes. Haslem states that the landscape-painting of 'Jockey' Hill, a contemporary (whose name, like Boreman's, appears several times in the pattern-books), differed from the latter's only in the use of stronger local colour, 'with greens and yellows rather prominent'. It is probable that their work is often confused. A painter named William Longdon is said to have used the number '8', and a landscape on a cup and saucer in the British Museum (III. 23) is so marked, but according to Haslem (p. 230), William Longdon was chiefly employed in painting the 'Chantilly sprig' pattern. There were, however, two William Longdons, father and son, the latter apprenticed in 1790.

The Bloor period was marked by artistic decline in all respects. Financial difficulties led to the sale of a large accumulation of imperfect pieces (known in the trade as 'seconds'). Latterly, too, the glaze was harder, the body approximating to the normal Staffordshire type. The factory had lost the pre-eminence it may justly be claimed to have held during the last two decades of the eighteenth century. We find Bloor in 1817 advertising in Staffordshire for painters of those 'Japan patterns' which include some of the worst of his productions, at once crowded, showy and tasteless. The flower-painters largely deserted naturalism for a mannered style, adopted also at times at Coalport and Rockingham and in Staffordshire, particularly at Spode's. This was perhaps the invention of the younger Steeles of Derby, and is at all events conveniently associated with them. Thomas Steele (*d.* 1850, aged

79), their father, painted highly coloured fruit with care and skill,[1] and his flowers were still in the Billingsley tradition; but his sons Edwin and Horatio developed a style with hard, facile drawing, associated with a conventional colouring in which a sharp pink, a foxy red and a deep orange are conspicuous. Their work is often minutely finished, but the naturalism of the earlier work has frozen into mannerism. At South Kensington there are well-authenticated examples of Thomas Steele's fruit-painting (a plate and a vase in Mr. Allen's collection, No. 152, Plate 64C), and a vase decorated with flowers by Horatio Steele, as well as a number of other examples in his style. A dessert-service made for Queen Victoria is said to have been painted by Horatio Steele: a specimen from this at South Kensington has panels painted with birds, reserved on a chrome-green enamel ground. Both Edwin Steele and his father worked for a time at the Rockingham factory, and Horatio went to Staffordshire. Leonard Lead (*b.* 1787, *d.* 1869) worked in the same style: two plates in Mr. Allen's collection (Nos. 179 and 194) show his manner, which is marked by smooth-curved flower-stems. Moses Webster (*b.* 1792, *d.* 1870) was a flower-painter with an individual style inclining to the older naturalism. Apprenticed at Derby, he worked for a time for the London enamellers Robins and Randall, decorating much Nantgarw porcelain for them,[2] and returning to Derby about 1820. 'Crushed hat-roses' (a phrase of Mr. Rackham's) well indicates a quality of his painting, which is, however, free in style and shows a sensitive touch. A Derby plate at South Kensington is in an unusual purple monochrome. The arabesques and 'Pompeiian' scrollwork on the cups and saucers figured in Plate 64A and B maintain the excellent tradition of the earlier period.

Of the later landscape-painters George Robertson (*c.* 1796–1820) was probably the painter of a set of vases at South Kensington and a cup and saucer and a dish in Mr. Herbert Allen's collection (Nos. 169 and 185); his landscape style shows a monotonous, coarse stippling and thick colour, but the seascapes

---

1 A famous dessert-service made for the Earl of Shrewsbury was painted with fruit by him. He subsequently went to Davenport's at Longport. His method obviously depended on the use of the finger in smoothing away brush marks.

2 See p. 322.

A. CUP AND SAUCER Cup ht. 2½in
(6.3cm); Saucer dia. 5¼in (13.3cm).
About 1810. Mark Crowned 'D'
and batons in red. *Victoria and
Albert Museum (C.334 and a-1935)*

B. CUP AND SAUCER Cup ht. 2⅛in
(5.4cm); Saucer dia. 5½in (14cm).
About 1820. Mark Crowned 'D'
and batons in red. *Victoria and
Albert Museum (C.332 and a-1935)*

C. VASE Ht. 8¾in (22.2cm). Painted by Thomas Steel. About 1830. Mark
Crowned 'D' and batons in red. *Victoria and Albert Museum (C.312-1935)*

See page 170   Plate 64 DERBY

attributed to him have fine detail (Plate 63B). A large bowl in the Derby Museum depicts a View of Matlock High Tor which corresponds with a watercolour signed by Robertson and dated 1797, also in the Derby Museum and Art Gallery. Jesse Mountford, who left Derby for Longport in 1821, was perhaps the painter of a set of three vases in the Allen Collection (No. 143), with minute stippling and a certain cleanness of style in rendering rocks and buildings. Daniel Lucas, who came from Longport, was the chief landscape painter in the later years of the factory, and is represented at South Kensington by a set of vases formerly in the Joicey Collection: his rendering of foliage with small hard touches and his shaky tree-stems help to distinguish his work, which is very common. But there is little real individuality in this later landscape-painting; the now stronger colours have the thick, paint-like quality already remarked upon.

William Corden (*b.* 1797, *d.* 1868) was among the first of the painters to employ porcelain for decoration in the manner of contemporary oil-paintings. He left the Derby factory about 1820 and began business as a painter of miniature portraits on china, and a little later was engaged at the Rockingham factory to decorate a service ordered by William IV. A painting of his of *The Death of Cleopatra* is on a plate at South Kensington. The proper medium for this branch of art was found in the china plaques used by John Haslem during the last years of the factory; there are two of his works at the Victoria and Albert Museum.

On the closing of the old Derby works in 1848 a few of the hands started a small china-factory in King Street, Derby, under the management of Bloor's clerk, William Locker; their mark was 'Locker & Co. late Bloor' on a band enclosing the word 'Derby', printed in red. Locker was succeeded by Stevenson, Sharp & Co., Stevenson & Hancock, and by Sampson Hancock alone. Many of the earlier Derby figure models were reproduced at King Street. These are generally clearly marked and present no difficulty of identification. The Bloor Japan patterns were much used on table wares and some accomplished miniature-style painters decorated dessert services with local views, flowers and other subjects. In 1876 another, entirely new, company opened a factory in the Osmaston Road with the style of the 'Royal Crown Derby Porcelain Company'; the marks of these companies are given in the Appendix.

Chapter 5

Longton Hall

A porcelain-factory was conducted for a short period in the middle of the eighteenth century at Longton Hall, near Stoke-on-Trent, Staffordshire, by William Littler and others. Littler had previously been successful in the manufacture of salt-glazed stoneware. The direct information we have concerning this factory is contained in brief accounts in William Pitt's *Topographical History of Staffordshire* (1817), Simeon Shaw's *History of the Staffordshire Potteries* (1829) and Ward's *History of Stoke-on-Trent* (1843). Shaw is sometimes an untrustworthy authority, and the date (1765) given for Littler's first attempts towards the manufacture of porcelain is obviously an error, as will be seen from the indentures and advertisements shortly to be quoted. Ward[1] only mentions that Littler succeeded in making china of good quality, although at great financial loss; but Pitt, the earliest authority, gives 1750 as the date of commencement.

The existence of the factory was rediscovered, after many years of obscurity, by J. E. Nightingale,[2] who found advertisements of its productions in contemporary newspapers of dates between 1752 and 1758. The earliest of these, which first appeared in *Aris's Birmingham Gazette* of 27 July 1752 (and was repeated later), does not specify the nature of the 'Porcelain or China Ware' made and offered for sale by 'William Littler and Co. at Longton Hall near

---

1 p. 50.
2 *Contributions*, pp. li–lxvi.

Newcastle'. A dealer's advertisement in the *Manchester Mercury* of 10–17 December 1754, announces 'the first produce of the Factory at Longton near Newcastle in Staffordshire of useful Porcelain or China ware'.[1] As far as is known, no further advertisement appeared before April 1757, when 'new and curious Porcelain or China . . . of the LONGTON HALL MANUFACTORY' was announced in the London *Public Advertiser*, 'consisting of Tureens, Covers and Dishes, large Cups and Covers, Jars and Beakers, with beautiful Sprigs of Flowers, open-work'd Fruit Baskets and Plates, Variety of Services for Deserts, Tea and Coffee Equipages, Sauce Boats, leaf Basons and Plates, Melons, Colliflowers, elegant Epargnes, and other ornamental and useful Porcelain, both white and enamell'd.' An advertisement in *Aris's Birmingham Gazette* two months later speaks also of 'Variety of Services for Deserts with Figures and Flowers of all Sorts, made exactly to Nature'. The latest-known advertisements appeared in the following year; that of June 1758 in the *Birmingham Gazette* specifies 'Services of Dishes and Plates, Tea and Coffee Equipages, and great Variety of Services for Deserts, Beautiful Essence Pots, Images, Flowers, Vases, etc. with fine Blue and White Ribb'd, Fluted and Octagonal Chocolate Cups and Saucers, Tea Sets, etc.' offered for sale by 'William Littler and Co.'. Another advertisement of the 'Longton China-warehouse' appeared in the London *General Evening Post* of September and October, 1758.[2]

It has been suggested[3] that William Duesbury, who was described in the unsigned and presumably Derby agreement of 1756[4] as 'of Longton', was in some way connected with the Longton Hall factory; and a descendant of his, writing in 1865,[5] asserted that Duesbury was proprietor of 'china works at Chelsea, Bow, Longton and Derby'.

Although Duesbury did, in 1769, absorb the Chelsea factory, and is thought to have acquired that of Bow some years later,

---

1 Thanks are due to Mr. Francis Buckley for the discovery of this advertisement.
2 A. J. B. Kiddell, in *Transactions E.P.C.*, III (1931), p. 74.
3 Nightingale, p. lvi.
4 p. 129.
5 *Derby Chronicle*, quoted in Nightingale, p. lv.

recent discoveries (see below) have shown that he was never a proprietor of the Staffordshire factory.[1]

An earlier connection between Duesbury and a Staffordshire factory is established by his London Account Book,[2] in which entries for dates between 1751 and 1753 show him to have enamelled 'Stafartshire figars' and other objects, presumably of pottery or porcelain. The name of 'Littler and Co.' appears in the account book for 1751,[3] and the articles in question may well have been of salt-glazed stoneware, such as we know Littler to have made. Their appearance in lists containing Chelsea and Bow specimens might seem to show that they were of porcelain; yet such decoration as that described as 'swiming swans donn all over' may almost certainly be identified as that on just such surviving salt-glaze figures.

Many of the doubts and conjectures concerning the founding of the Longton Hall China factory and its proprietors were dispelled following the remarkably fruitful researches of Dr. Bernard Watney. With great good fortune, and inspired by Mr. A. J. B. Kiddell's discovery of announcements concerning the dissolution of the Longton Hall partnership which named the then partners, Robert Charlesworth and Samuel Firmin,[4] Dr. Watney was instrumental in discovering two important indentures dated 25 August 1753, and 1 September 1755 respectively. These disclosed the names of the proprietors of the factory at those dates. The 1753 Agreement, reciting an earlier Agreement dated 7 October 1751, also disclosed that the first proprietors were William Jenkinson, who had interests in mining, William Nicklin, a member of the legal profession, and the Willliam Littler mentioned above. In 1753 Jenkinson retired from the partnership and one Nathanial Firmin, described as a water gilder, took his share; he, in turn, was

---

1 In a schedule of debts due to workmen and others appended to an agreement of 1 September 1755, between the then Longton Hall proprietors, the item 'Mr. Duesbury for work' appears: Bernard Watney, *Longton Hall Porcelain*, p. 61. Duesbury was, perhaps, employed at Longton, or may even have been at Derby at this date.

2 *William Duesbury's London Account Book, 1751–1753*, English Porcelain Circle Monograph, 1931.

3 Loc. cit.

4 *Transactions E.C.C.*, No. 1, 1933, p. 60. Quoted from *Aris's Birmingham Gazette*, 9 June, 30 June and 8 September, 1760.

A. FIGURE OF A CRANE Ht. 6in (15.2cm).
About 1750. No mark. 'Snowman' type.
Schreiber Collection (9)

PAIR OF HORSES L. 6⅞in (17.4cm) and 7¼in (18.4cm). About 1750. No mark. *Victoria and Albert Museum (C.104-1938)*

e pages 96, 180

Plate 65 LONGTON HALL

succeeded by his son, Samuel. By the 1755 Agreement the Rev. Robert Charlesworth joined the firm, bringing in fresh capital; throughout, however, it was William Littler, former salt-glaze potter, who was responsible for the practical running of the works.[1]

The Longton Hall partnership was dissolved in 1760[2] and the manufacture came to an end. But two further events remain to be chronicled before Littler's activities as a potter are finally concluded. For some reason so far unascertained the remaining stock, consisting according to the Sale Notice of ninety thousand pieces, was sold at Salisbury in September 1760, apparently by the Rev. Charlesworth's agents (Littler having disappeared from the scene)[3]; but whether it was sold to Baddeley and Fletcher at Shelton, as stated by Simeon Shaw, remains unconfirmed.[4]

What has now been positively established, however, is that by 1764 Littler was at West Pans, near Musselburgh, in Scotland, where he was enrolled as an Honorary Burgess in that year, being described as 'Mr. Wm. Littler China Manufacturer at West Pans'. Billheads from his West Pans manufactory, dated in 1766, have survived. The late Arthur Lane in a paper read to the English Ceramic Circle on 2 March 1960, described researches by himself and others into Littler's activities at West Pans resulting in the conclusion that, so far as porcelain was concerned, it seemed probable that he, with his wife Jane, engaged themselves there in decorating a quantity of early Longton ware which he had, in some way, acquired on the closure of the factory at Longton. Among these West Pans productions are the well-known 'Over Hailes' mugs and other armorial or crested ware.[5] The jug (Plate 67), referred to on page 188, the dish (Plate 72A) and other similar pieces have been ascribed to this phase of Littler's activities.[6] A

1 The manner of these discoveries, and full details of the proprietors, are fully set out in Dr. Watney's *Longton Hall Porcelain*, London 1957, where the content of the Agreements is also set out.

2 Watney, op. cit., p. 18.

3 Ibid., pp. 47–8.

4 The very full documentation of the Shelton factory discloses not a single mention of Littler. John Mallet, 'John Baddeley of Shelton', *Transactions E.C.C.*, vol. 6, part 3, p. 199.

5 *Transactions E.P.C.*, III (1931), p. 75.

6 *Transactions E.C.C.*, vol. 5, part 2, pp. 82–94.

A. Tureen L. 6⅜in (16.2cm). Painted in underglaze-blue and gilding. About 1752. Mark: a 'cross' in blue. *Victoria and Albert Museum (C.733-1924)*

B. Butter Boat Ht. 3⅛in (7.9cm). Painted in underglaze-blue. About 1752. No mark. *Victoria and Albert Museum (C.561-1924)*

C. Sauceboat L. 5in (12.7cm). Painted in underglaze-blue. About 1752. *Victoria and Albert Museum (C.452-1924)*

D. Leaf Moulded Dish L. 7½in (19cm). Painted in underglaze-blue with gilding. About 1752. Mark Crossed 'L's and dots. *Victoria and Albert Museum (C.684-1924)*

See pages 182, 184, 188   Plate 66 LONGTON HALL

trial dig on the presumed site of the West Pans factory in 1964 disclosed a glost kiln, some few cream-ware wasters and a few porcelain wasters 'indistinguishable from Longton'. Since some were unglazed this is evidence of probable manufacture on the site, but further examination is called for.[1]

No recognised mark is positively known to have been used at Longton Hall, and the identification of the porcelain produced there has depended principally upon the occasional similarity which may be presumed to exist between it and Littler's productions in salt-glazed stoneware. The identification of the Longton Hall porcelain is in fact one of the most fascinating exercises in argument by resemblances.[2] However, excavations on the site carried out in recent years have revealed a quantity of wasters which have in some cases confirmed existing attributions, or have enabled fresh ones to be made. Some of these wasters, together with other excavated material, are at the Hanley Museum, Stoke-on-Trent.[3]

Earliest of all are some figures, usually plain white, of birds and animals (Plate 65), formerly ascribed to Bow and referred to under that heading.[4] These generally have a very glassy glaze so thick as to obscure the details of the modelling, and on that account have been called the 'snow-man family'. They were identified as Staffordshire porcelain[5] on account of their similarity in model and in the form of certain rosette-like flowers to well-known types of 'Whieldon ware' and salt-glazed stoneware, and a connection between the factory which made them and Longton Hall was suggested by the appearance on a shell-shaped sweetmeat dish— formerly in the Wallace Elliot Collection and now in the British Museum—of a 'snowman' group of *Ceres and a Child*,[6] together

1 Mavis Bimson, John Ainslie and Bernard Watney, 'West Pans Story—The Scotland Manufactory', *Transactions E.C.C.*, vol. 6, part 2, pp. 167–76.

2 Longton Hall porcelain is perhaps the most difficult of all to identify correctly, and specimens are often found mistakenly classified as Bow or Liverpool or even Chelsea, whilst early Derby pieces were commonly regarded as Longton Hall.

3 Watney, op. cit., pp. 24–5.

4 See pp. 94 and 96.

5 Mrs. Donald MacAlister, 'Early Staffordshire China', in *Transactions E.C.C.*, I (1933), p. 44. Excavated wasters have confirmed this attribution.

6 Watney, op. cit., Plate 10A.

JUG Ht. 7¼in (18.4cm). Blue painted, with white enamel scrolls and coloured decoration, the latter probably added at West Pans, Scotland. About 1764–70. No mark. *Victoria and Albert Museum (C.48-1928)*

See pages 178, 181, 188 Plate 67 LONGTON HALL

with flower-painting by a familiar Longton Hall hand. This connection is confirmed by the occurrence among the factory wasters of 'snowman' sherds. The figures may well be the examples decorated by Duesbury, those now found as plain white having, perhaps, once borne his unfired painting.

For the identification of the main body of Longton Hall porcelain other arguments apply. Thus, it was stated by Shaw[1] that Littler had discovered a method of dipping pieces of stoneware in a glaze of special composition producing a blue colour of exceptional richness and brilliancy, and a very important covered dish and a pair of plates of porcelain in the British Museum are decorated with a colour apparently of the kind described by Shaw. They are, moreover, further painted over the blue in opaque white enamel in a manner unique to this porcelain. This white enamel on blue is in fact not uncommon on Staffordshire salt-glazed wares of this time. These pieces of porcelain also bear a mark resembling crossed L's, one of them reversed, in combination with three dots. The mark is not unlike and may be a copy of that of Vincennes and Sèvres, but may equally well have stood for the initials of 'Littler, Longton'. A somewhat similar 'mark' in the field of blue-painted designs is of fairly frequent occurrence. See Plate 66D and Appendix, p. 390. It is difficult to explain; both forms can scarcely represent crossed L's, since they sometimes occur on the same piece. Two sauce-boats in the Herbert Allen Collection at South Kensington (No. 499) were made in a mould used also for salt-glazed ware,[2] and may on that account be presumed to be of Littler's manufacture. The painting in purple on these is unusual in colour, but by the same hand as a number of pieces to be ascribed to the factory on other grounds, as will be mentioned later. A bunch of broad strap-leaves, some of them turned over at the top, was a favourite motive of this painter; the peculiar, artless but charming landscape with a building[3] on one of these sauce-boats is also repeated on other Longton specimens (compare Plate 68A). Their paste and glaze are also important as

1 Op. cit., pp. 168 and 169.
2 Both a mould or 'block' and a salt-glazed sauce-boat of the pattern are in the Museum collection at South Kensington.
3 Perhaps painted by one John Hayfield. See Watney, op. cit., pp. 36–7.

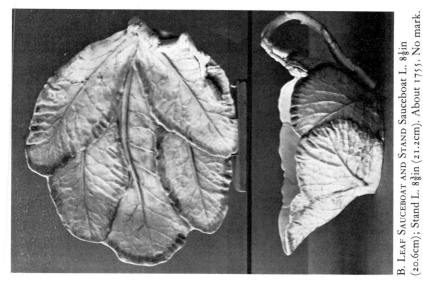

B. LEAF SAUCEBOAT AND STAND Sauceboat L. 8⅛in (20.6cm); Stand L. 8⅜in (21.2cm). About 1755. No mark. *Victoria and Albert Museum (C.1242 and a-1924)*

A. LEAF DISH Dia. 8½in (21.6cm). Painted in colours. About 1755. No mark. *Victoria and Albert Museum (C.710-1921)*

See pages 182, 184, 186

Plate 68 LONGTON HALL

evidence regarding the porcelain produced at the factory. Certain other pieces at South Kensington with not dissimilar paste and glaze, such as the teapot (Schr. No. 443), a sauce-boat (Plate 68B), and a butterboat (Plate 66B), all in the form of folded leaves, resemble in style much earthenware made in Staffordshire in this period. The handle of the Schreiber teapot is in fact of a form quite peculiar to Staffordshire. The sugar-bowls in the form of melons (Schr. No. 444) are further instances, and it is to be noted that 'leaf basons' and 'melons' were in fact mentioned in the Longton advertisements. Such articles were of course made at most European china-factories, but these specimens show distinctive Staffordshire character, and may reasonably be regarded as of Longton Hall manufacture.

In addition to the important pieces at the British Museum already mentioned, there are in the collections at South Kensington several pieces bearing the crossed 'L's' believed to be Littler's mark. In the Schreiber Collection are two plates, moulded in relief with overlapping leaves, the rims painted with a brilliant uneven blue. A similar dish is figured in Plate 66D. The crossed 'L's' in some cases appear on the face of the dishes in the field of the design, as well as on the back. The small tureen figured in Plate 66A shows well the manner of applying this 'Longton blue'.

A mug of Staffordshire shape with indefinite moulding and a bright blue border resembling that on the double-L-marked dish in the British Museum is, like it, painted with bouquets and sprigs of flowers, in which pink roses are prominent, the petals clearly but tremulously outlined in a distinctive manner. Painting by the same hand assists in the identification of many specimens of the manufacture, including at South Kensington a mug (Plate 72B) and a characteristic basin in outline like a fig leaf. The painting on a pair of vases of fantastic form, with handles in the shape of monsters, and two small *rococo* vases is earlier in style than that on the others, but perhaps by the same hand. They are likely to be the 'essence pots' of the advertisement. A *rococo* specimen painted in blue only and figured in Bemrose[1] is said to be marked with the

---

1 *Longton Hall Porcelain*, Plate XLVI, No. 4 (formerly in the Merton Thoms Collection). It should be noted that many of the pieces illustrated in Bemrose's book are wrongly ascribed to Longton Hall.

C. Butter Seller Ht. 5⅞in (14.9cm). About 1756. No mark. *Schreiber Collection* (432)

B. Hercules and the Lion Ht. 6in (15.2cm). About 1756. No mark. *Victoria and Albert Museum* (C.1335-1924)

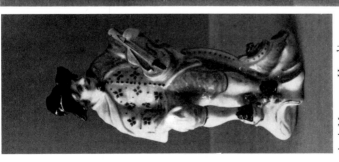

A. A Musician Ht. 5¼in (13.3cm). About 1756. No mark. *Schreiber Collection* (430)

See pages 194, 195

Plate 69 LONGTON HALL

double 'L's'. The form is repeated in an amusing, large and very prickly vase in the Schreiber Collection (No. 445). The decoration consists of applied flowers and, on the cover, a small figure, which provide links with other specimens and more particularly with the figures of the same origin. This vase is also painted with a bird in a landscape by the same hand as similar compositions which appear on a not uncommon class of plates and dishes. Amongst these, in the collection at South Kensington, are several plates moulded in relief with strawberries and leaves (Plate 72C); others of the same pattern are painted with the peculiar roses just described, and this serves to confirm the attribution of the whole of this group of pieces to a single factory.[1]

A further chain of argument may be put together from pieces at South Kensington. The style of landscape-painting seen on the leaf teapot in the Schreiber Collection already mentioned appears again on a dish (Plate 68A), the rim of which is moulded in the form of leaves and painted with a peculiar yellowish-green enamel often seen on pieces attributable to Longton. A pair of plates from the same mould in the Allen Collection (No. 500) show primitive flower-painting, probably by the same hand as the specimens with roses described above. The melon-tureens (Plate 73C) and the 'Staffordshire' leaf-sauce-boats (Plate 68B) provide further instances of this yellowish-green colour.

The blue-painted porcelain, apart from the marked pieces and those exactly resembling them (such as a covered sugar-bowl at South Kensington),[2] may also be identified with the aid of the

1 This bird- and flower-painting should be carefully distinguished from the somewhat similar work, perhaps from the same pattern-books, appearing on Worcester and Liverpool porcelain. See p. 262.

2 Analysed by Dr. H. J. Plenderleith with the following result:

Silica - - - - - - -	65·1
Oxide of lead - - - - -	trace
Alumina - - - - - -	10·7
Lime - - - - - - -	19·3
Phosphorus pentoxide - - - -	2·2
Magnesia - - - - - -	trace
Sodium and potash - - -	not estimated

97·3

The small quantity of phosphoric acid shown in this analysis may have been accidentally introduced with the alkali or some other ingredient, and does not prove the regular use of bone-ash as at Bow and elsewhere.

VASE AND COVER Ht. 10⅞in (27.6cm). About 1755–60. No
mark. *Victoria and Albert Museum (C.88-1938)*

See page 190   Plate 70 LONGTON HALL

coloured flower-painting already described. The unusual handle of a mug with this decoration (Plate 72B) is repeated on another, rather crudely painted with a Chinese landscape in blue, and blue-painting, perhaps by the same hand, is seen on a sauce-boat moulded in relief in imitation of basketwork, a form of decoration found also on a cup painted with the presumed Longton Hall birds. The butterboat in the form of folded leaves (Plate 66B) is of a type peculiar to Staffordshire, as is a plain white teapot also at South Kensington. Another type of leaf-sauce-boat (Plate 66C), of a shape which originated at Meissen,[1] is distinguished in the Longton versions by a transverse ribbing of the handle and the pendent fruit attached to it.

The distinctive handle just mentioned is found also on another mug, in Mr. Wallace Elliot's collection,[2] painted with flowers in *famille rose* style; a teapot at South Kensington, of salt-glaze shape with crabstock handle, was painted by the same hand. A dish (Plate 72A) of characteristic Longton paste and shape is decorated with flowers within a border of *rococo* scroll-work in enamel once white, but now discoloured to a dull brown. A border in white enamel on blue, composed of the same elements, is also known.[3] The shape of this dish is similar to that of many other Longton specimens. A dish in Mr. and Mrs. Donald MacAlister's collection[4] is of a kindred fig-leaf shape and has a green twig handle of a kind much favoured at Longton; it is painted by the hand mentioned above with birds and plants. Among these appears the bunch of strap-like leaves already referred to as occurring on Mr. Allen's sauce-boats painted in purple. The strawberry-and-leaf moulding was an especial favourite at Longton, and was even applied to jugs, as on a charming specimen in the London Museum.[5]

The Longton jugs are of distinctive form. The specimen figured in Plate 67 is remarkable in being decorated with the Longton blue ground with white enamel painting, the Longton flowers, and

1 Compare Adolf Brüning, *Porzellan*, Berlin, 1907, Abb. 47.
2 See *The Connoisseur*, vol. LXXIX (Sept. 1927), p. 15.
3 Bemrose, *Longton Hall Porcelain*, Plate 6.
4 Figured in *Apollo*, Jan. 1927, fig. V.
5 Figured in *Apollo*, Jan. 1927, fig. VIII. A deep bowl of fig-leaf outline decorated with the same moulding was sold as Bow at New York in January 1927 (Tom Cannon Collection, No. 89).

AMERICA FROM A SET OF 'CONTINENTS' Ht. 13⅛in (33.3cm). About 1758–60. No mark. *Schreiber Collection (86)*

See page 196 Plate 71 LONGTON HALL

some quite exceptional figure-painting. The 'Chinese' figures on the artless but extremely characteristic and charming vase and cover in Plate 70 were apparently inspired by Chelsea.

The peculiar handle already pointed out (Plate 72B) again helps in the identification at Longton Hall of a class of mugs for long regarded as Liverpool on account of the printed decoration they bear, which is sometimes signed by Sadler of that city.[1] Such a specimen at South Kensington has a handle almost identical with that illustrated here; and another very similar mug has been analysed[2] and proved to contain a high proportion of lead such as is also present in some figures attributable to Longton, to be mentioned presently. The very small quantity of phosphoric acid present also in other presumed Longton specimens is again found in this analysis in exactly the same quantity. Paste and glaze also agree in appearance (including the 'scum line')[3] with other Longton pieces. This analysed mug is of a shape with grooved foot for long held to be typically Liverpool, and a similar shape certainly does occur in porcelain from that city. But a mug of this very form at South Kensington is painted with birds by the same hand as those on the piece figured in Plate 72C, and the curious bunch of leaves again appears.[4] But though the material of the mugs seems proved as of Longton origin, it may seem difficult to account for the presence of Liverpool prints upon them. We know, however, that Wedgwood, at least as early as 1764, sent wares by road to Liverpool to receive printed decoration, and some Staffordshire salt-glazed plates printed with fable-subjects in brick-red may well belong to the later 1750s. That porcelain made in Staffordshire may also have been sent in the same way is thus by no means impossible, and the links with Longton Hall here detailed make it impossible to resist such a conclusion.[5]

The body of porcelain thus assembled on grounds of style is in general characterized by a heavy but glassy paste, possessing pale-

1 See p. 295.
2 *Analysed Specimens*, No. 9.
3 See below, p. 192.
4 Another mug of the same form at South Kensington has the Longton *famille rose* flowers mentioned above.
5 Sadler may, of course, have bought undecorated Longton stock on the closing of the factory.

A. LEAF DISH Dia. 8⅜in (21.2cm). About 1755.
No mark. *Victoria and Albert Museum (C.233-1915)*

B. TANKARD Ht. 5in (12.7cm). About
1755. No mark. *Victoria and Albert
Museum (C.947-1924)*

C. STRAWBERRY-MOULDED PLATE Dia. 9in
(22.8cm). About 1756. No mark. *Victoria and
Albert Museum (C.260-1940)*

See pages 178, 184, 186, 188, 190   Plate 72 LONGTON HALL

greenish translucency with large irregular 'moons',[1] generally not free from imperfection. The glaze is usually of cold tone, often with a surface quality not unlike that of paraffin-wax or candle-grease. In general character the Longton Hall porcelain resembles that of Chelsea, for which many specimens were formerly mistaken. Flat bases are common, and the paste has sometimes been manipulated in a way suggesting the consistency of dough. Long spur-marks are commonly but not invariably present, and where glaze meets body at the foot there is often a dark line like that left by dirty scum on water. The rich streaky blue and yellowish green may almost be regarded as peculiar to the factory, though not by themselves conclusive evidence of origin. Dull size-gilding of poor quality was sparingly used. These indications, with the moulded leaves and peculiarities of form, the white enamel and the characteristic flower-painting, should enable the collector to recognize specimens of the kinds here ascribed to Longton Hall.

Figures are known from the advertisements to have been made by Littler, but with the exception of some small models of pug-dogs, painted in underglaze manganese-purple, illustrated in Bemrose[2] (similar but unmarked pieces are at South Kensington), no figure bearing the presumed Longton Hall mark is known to exist at the present time. A specimen said to have been so marked (and a very important one if the mark was genuine) was, however, sold at Christie's (Merton Thoms Collection) in February 1910, described as a 'Figure of a Sportsman with Gun, Dog and Dead Bird, 6¾ in. high'.[3] Apart from the evidence of the supposed Longton blue and the character of glaze and paste, the attribution of a certain coherent class of figures to this factory rests upon the evidence (for what it is worth) of the applied flowers and the rather crudely modelled figure with star-diapered skirt, on the large 'prickly' vase already mentioned. These flowers, like those often found on the

---

1 Due to air bubbles in the paste. Compare Chelsea 'moons', p. 36.
2 Bemrose, *Longton Hall Porcelain*, Plate 15.
3 See *The Connoisseur*, vol. XL (March 1910): Auction Sale Prices.

A. and B. EQUESTRIAN FIGURES AFTER MEISSEN Ht. 8in (20.3cm) and 8½in (21.6cm). About 1758. No mark. *Schreiber Collection (441 and a)*

C. MELON TUREEN AND STAND Tureen L. 6¼in (15.8cm); Stand L. 9¾in (24.7cm). About 1755. No mark. *Schreiber Collection (444)*

See pages 186, 195   Plate 73 LONGTON HALL

bases of the figures in question, are of a form quite peculiar in English porcelain, and markedly double, unlike the large flat flowers of early Derby porcelain, or the smaller ones of the Chelsea bases, which often have the centre painted with a ring of dots. Bow flowers are of more various forms, but are, as a rule, quite different from these, which are of very constant occurrence on this class of figures. That the modelling of these applied flowers was left to the individual fancy of the repairer is shown by the appearance of quite different forms on the Plymouth and presumed Longton versions of the same models.[1] It is noteworthy that the Longton flowers are very exact copies of those favoured at Meissen. It must be admitted that the flowers on the bases of the figures are never precisely similar to those on the vase, though sufficiently close to suggest they are the work of the same hand, perhaps at a rather later date.

The group of *Boys feeding a Goat* (B.M. IV. 7) is usually decorated with patches of dark blue not unlike that on the marked dishes. A coloured version of the same model in the Schreiber Collection (No. 435) shows a flesh-painting of peculiar quality, seen also on a pair of figures of a *Girl with a Basket* and a *Boy with Flowers* (Schr. No. 439).[2] The former has been analysed[3] and shows a composition markedly different from that of the sugar-bowl mentioned above. It seems likely, however, that most of the figures of the class here ascribed to Longton Hall represent the later work of the factory for which the earliest receipt may have been considerably modified.[4] The presence of lead, due perhaps to the use of flint-glass cullet in the frit, makes them heavy in the hand, a feature which helps to distinguish them from the contemporary and not altogether dissimilar Derby figures. The chemical composition of a group of *Hercules and the Lion*[5] (No. C1335—1924 and B.M. No. IV 6) is very close to that of the other analysed figures; and a differently coloured specimen of the same model in Mr. Broderip's gift at South Kensington (Plate 69B) shows also patches of the dark

1 See p. 342.

2 From Meissen originals. See Album of the Royal Saxon Porcelain Manufactory, Plate 3, No. 15. See also Watney, op. cit., Plate 64A.

3 *Analysed Specimens*, No. 8.

4 It is possible, too, that a differently composed body would be used for figures to secure plasticity and stability in the kiln.

5 Watney, op. cit., Plate 58A.

streaky 'Longton blue'. The excellent modelling of these figures, which rank amongst the best made in England, is particularly evident in the skilfully rendered heads, of a type quite different from those on any specimens known to have been made elsewhere. These distinctive features are seen again in a large figure of *Britannia* (Schr. No. 436 and B.M. I. 18) for long ascribed to Bow, with a base picked out in dry crimson and decorated with crude transfer-prints roughly coloured.[1] Others of this class in the Schreiber Collection are a *Market Woman selling Butter* (No. 432: Plate 69C), a *Seated Musician* (No. 430: Plate 69A) and a *Boy holding Grapes* (No. 434), all apparently original compositions with a decidedly Staffordshire flavour. Their modeller, who showed a strong preference for seated figures half turned to right or left, was perhaps the 'Dr. Mills, a tolerable modeller' of Shaw's account.[2] Fairly close copies of Meissen models include a *Turk* (Schr. No. 438)[3] and the *Negro and Turk leading Horses* (Plates 73A and B).[4] The modelling of the animals may be compared with that of a group of a *Boy on a Galloping Horse* (Schr. No. 440).[5] The distinctive looped flower-stalks (like the applied flowers, exactly copying the Meissen) on the base of the last recur on a plain white figure of a *Turkish Lady*, companion to the *Turk* mentioned above, and this pair of figures is well known in Staffordshire salt-glazed stoneware.[6] A figure of *Winter* (Schr. No. 437) similarly occurs in both materials,[7] as well as in Chelsea. The whole family of figures thus holds together in a remarkable way.

In their painting, most of the figures show a distinctive manner of outlining the eyelashes, often in red, and costumes are commonly not flowered as in the productions of other factories, but decorated with star- or formal diaper-patterns, like the costume of the important little figure on the large prickly vase previously mentioned (Schr. No. 445). The harsh, thick, paint-like

1 Lane, op. cit., Plate 84.

2 Simeon Shaw, op. cit., p. 198.

3 Compare Berling, *Meissner Porzellan*, fig. 82.

4 Compare Berling, op. cit., fig. 97.

5 After the sculptor Fanelli. Lane, op. cit., Plate 81B.

6 Both are represented in the Schreiber Collection, No. 858. See Watney, op. cit., Plates 31B, 42 and 45.

7 A specimen is in the British Museum. See R. L. Hobson in *The Burlington Magazine*, vol. XXXVII (Aug. 1920), Plate facing p. 84.

red already noted frequently appears; also a strong dry crimson, much used to outline the scroll-work of the often rather clumsy bases.

Gilding is rare on the most common type of Longton Hall figures; but on one class, apparently inspired by gold-anchor Chelsea, it is more freely used. These are apparently the latest Longton Hall figures, perhaps made in or soon after 1758, when a change of direction is implied in the advertisements, and the firm opened a warehouse in St. Paul's Churchyard in London. The big *America* in the Schreiber Collection (No. 86: Plate 71), formerly called Bow, a small figure of a *Boy as Winter* (Schr. No. 695, marked with a 'K' impressed and formerly called Plymouth),[1] and above all the equestrian figure of *Ferdinand, Duke of Brunswick*,[2] are typical specimens of these late Longton Hall figures, which show on analysis that a small percentage of soapstone was used in their paste. This has suggested that the figures are part of the unidentified Worcester output of figures, but the quantity of soapstone used is too small.

It is noteworthy that the models of the *Boys with a Goat*, the *Boys as Seasons*, a *Seated Man and Woman* appear also in Plymouth porcelain.[3] It has been suggested that the sale at Salisbury may well have come to the notice of William Cookworthy in the course of a journey from Plymouth to London, when he would have passed through Salisbury, and that the use of the same models for both Longton Hall and Plymouth figures could be explained by his purchase of a part of the Longton stock, although this seems unlikely.

A recent discovery has shown that a pottery site near Longton, well-known for its manufacture of redwares and other earthenware, was also manufacturing a soft-paste porcelain at about the same time as the Longton Hall factory. Excavations on this site, situated in Lower Street, Newcastle-under-Lyme, brought to light a quantity of sherds including a bowl, decorated in underglaze

1 Watney, op. cit., Plate 75.
2 Lane, op. cit., Plate 80B, and Watney, op. cit., Colour Plate A.
3 See p. 342.

blue, and inscribed on the base '25th July 1746'. This bowl is the earliest dated example of blue-and-white porcelain so far discovered, pre-dating the Longton Hall factory by three or four years. The names of William Steers and Joseph Wilson have been proposed as successive proprietors, both from London. The latter was perhaps the Limehouse potter seen by Dr. Pococke when visiting the town in 1750.[1]

---

[1] Paul Bemrose, 'The Pomona Potworks, Newcastle, Staffs.', *Transactions E.C.C.*, vol. 9, part I (1973), pp. 1–18. Also Watney, *English Blue and White Porcelain*, pp. 28–9, where a Joseph Wilson is shown to have occupied premises at Duke Shore, Limehouse, at some time between 1744 and 1748; a potter of the same name was at Newcastle-under-Lyme some time between 1746 and 1751.

Chapter 6

Lowestoft

The fame enjoyed by the modest china-works at Lowestoft, in Suffolk, is scarcely due to the intrinsic merit of its actual productions. By a notorious mistake the early editions of Chaffers ascribed to the factory a great deal of hard-paste that could only have been made in China.[1] The name 'Lowestoft', however, still clings to the class of Chinese porcelain painted with bouquets of pink roses, armorial and other European subjects, in a style, it is true, not unlike that of the Suffolk factory. And it is a curious fact that some at least of this 'Chinese Lowestoft' seems to have been copied at Canton from specimens of Lowestoft china shipped to the East by the East India Company. The so-called Redgrave pattern of peonies and rocks, and the familiar 'Chinese' figures in red, pink and green, as well as the shaded pink roses, are not at all uncommon in collections of Chinese porcelain; there are specimens in both the national museums in London. So popular is the type painted with roses that it has been faked in Paris in fairly recent times, a remarkable instance of the copying of copies, three times removed from the original.[2]

It is now perhaps superfluous to state that not only was no hard-paste ever made at Lowestoft, but that there exists no satisfactory evidence that Chinese porcelain was decorated at the factory; a

1 For an account of this mistake, see W. B. Honey, 'Historic Fallacies . . .' in *Transactions E.C.C.*, vol. 2, No. 10, p. 241.

2 These fakes (which are hard-paste) are excellent imitations: they often bear, however, a red mark perhaps intended for a seal character, but showing a quite un-Chinese cursive twist.

teapot in the Schreiber Collection with the name 'Allen Lowestoft' painted on it has as its main subject the Crucifixion copied from a European print by an undoubted *Chinese* hand (in the manner of other so-called 'Jesuit China'). The flower painting on the lid of the teapot (which does not belong to the teapot), together with the name, can alone have been Allen's work. But Robert Allen, besides being a painter at Lowestoft for many years from the factory's beginning, and subsequently its manager (from about 1780), also had his own enamelling kiln and China Shop in the town, where he could have painted ware such as the teapot in question.

The Lowestoft factory was in Bell Lane (now Crown Street) and was founded in 1757, after an unsuccessful attempt at china-making by Hewling Luson at Gunton in the previous year. The first partners were Messrs. Walker, Browne, Aldred and Richman.[1] Robert Browne evidently took a leading part in the manufacture, and probably learned the secret of the Bow porcelain from workmen formerly employed at that factory. The fact that the Lowestoft body contains bone-ash and is chemically the same as that of Bow supports this supposition. By 1770 the firm was Robert Browne and Company, and had a warehouse in Queen Street, Cheapside, London. The factory was closed about 1802. The manufacture was not a very large one, and never employed more than seventy hands at most. Its comparatively long life accounts for the relative abundance of the surviving specimens.

Much Lowestoft china is readily recognized, but its kinship with Bow sometimes leaves room for doubt, particularly in the case of the blue-and-white. The documentary pieces, however, are numerous and serve to establish a few fairly well-marked types. It was the practice of the factory to mark certain pieces—tea-caddies, inkstands and the like, doubtless made for visitors to the town—

1 Gillingwater, *An Historical Account of the Ancient Town of Lowestoft* (1790), p. 112. An insurance policy dated 25 June 1765 named the Proprietors as 'Robert Browne, Obed. Aldred, Robert Williams and Philip Walker': Elizabeth Adams, 'The Bow Insurances etc.', *Transactions E.C.C.*, vol. 9, part 1, p. 74.

with the words 'A Trifle from Lowestoft' (Plate 74C).[1] A dish with powdered blue ground in the British Museum (No. XI. 1) is painted with a view of Lowestoft Church. Dated and inscribed pieces, evidently made to order, are not uncommon, and enable us to fix the sequence of the Lowestoft types. A list of dated pieces is given by Church,[2] and there are several in the British Museum, with dates ranging from 1765 to 1795. Moulds and wasters were found on the factory site in 1902, and casts from some of these are also in the British Museum (Nos. XI. 22 to 51).

The moulds and wasters found on the factory site in 1902 and 1967 confirm the attribution of many pieces decorated in relief. A typical example shows slight blue-painted decoration in panels reserved on a moulded surface, as on the tea-caddy (Plate 77E), which, together with other surviving items of table-ware, has the initial 'I.H.' and the date 1761, or, in a few instances, 1764, moulded in relief. Other examples, similarly moulded, are without initials and date. The initials are (doubtfully) said to commemorate the birth of James Hughes, grandson of Robert Browne, founder of the factory. A half-mould of a teapot excavated on the site has the moulded date '1761', and a teapot from this mould is in the Castle Museum, Norwich (Plate 74A). Other similarly moulded wares bear neither initials nor date, and may be earlier or later than the 'I.H.' examples.

Other of the earliest Lowestoft productions include a wide variety of plain (unmoulded) table-wares, coffee or chocolate pots with handle and spout at right-angles to one another, inkpots, jugs, mugs, sauce-boats, besides *rococo*-moulded wall-vases, ribbed or fluted wares and large jugs with relief-moulded patterns. All are painted in underglaze blue, chiefly in the oriental style, but some have flower motifs, and are often reminiscent of delftware, from which much of the decoration may have derived. Blue and white ware continued to be produced throughout the life of the factory, much of it of mediocre quality, particularly that copied from Worcester after about 1775. An even-toned rather dark blue is

1 Compare, for instance, British Museum, XI. 6 and 17, and Schreiber Collection, No. 455. 'A Trifle from Yarmouth' is also found.
2 Op. cit., p. 87. See also the admirably full account of these by A. J. B. Kiddell, 'Inscribed and dated Lowestoft porcelain', in *Transactions E.P.C.*, III (1931), p. 7.

A. TEAPOT Ht. 5in (12.7cm). Painted in underglaze-blue. Inscribed 'I.H. 1761' (incorporated in the moulding decoration) painter's mark '5' inside footring. *Castle Museum Norwich (80-1928)*

B. TEA CADDY Ht. 4in (10.1cm). 'Redgrave' pattern. About 1775. No mark. *Victoria and Albert Museum (210-1924)*

C. 'TRIFLE' MUG Ht. 4in (10.1cm). About 1795. No mark. *Castle Museum Norwich (36.31.948)*

D. BIRTH TABLET Dia. 4½in (12.4cm). Dated 1795. No mark. *Castle Museum Norwich (28.31.948)*

See pages 200, 204, 208

Plate 74 LOWESTOFT

characteristic, but on the best pieces (such as the wonderful bowl figured in Plate 78), the blue is remarkably pure and luminous.[1]

The mask jug figured in Plate 78C is of a typical Lowestoft form, differing from the Worcester, and was doubtless made for the landlord of a Stag Inn or White Hart. The familiar flower-bud knob on tea-pot lids is on Lowestoft usually closed, but on Worcester half-open, though this rule is of course not infallible. That a powdered blue ground was made at Lowestoft is proved by the dish in the British Museum, painted with Lowestoft Church, noteworthy for an indefinite and wavy outlining of the panels (compare Plate 78A); a similar saucer-dish at South Kensington has a trace of a numeral within the foot-ring. Shape, character of glaze and stronger tone of blue all point to a Bow origin for the well-known powdered-blue plates and dishes with circular and fan-shaped reserves, marked with four or six imitation Chinese characters.[2] In general, the Lowestoft decoration is more meagre and less fantastic than the Bow, though not without a touch of imagination in the variations played upon the borrowed themes. For the rest, the blue-and-white designs (Plate 77) are of great variety, copied from many sources: Chinese scenes, *chinoiseries* in the Pillement manner, copies of the 'pine-cone' pattern and other Worcester transfers, as well as much unpretentious slight flower-painting and feathery scrolls. The transferred engravings show a certain artless incompetence with broken lines and crude hatching, and were sometimes awkwardly cut to fit small spaces.

No recognized mark was used, but those of other factories were imitated as freely as their designs were copied. The Worcester crescent[3] and the Meissen crossed-swords are not only found on pieces attributable by style to Lowestoft, but they were found also

1 The bowl is inscribed 'Success to the Frances' and 'Captain Osborn from Colchester'. Painting in blue by the same hand appears inside a wedding-bowl figured by Spelman (Plate 90), made for 'Mr. and Mrs. Dance'; this is painted on the outside in colours. Mr. Herbert Read suggested that this style, with figures and sometimes ships, and rich scroll-work borders, was probably copied from Bristol delft, in which such designs are not uncommon. The fact that both Bristol and Lowestoft are seaports makes this not unlikely; specimens would be brought by seamen.

2 Often claimed for Lowestoft, see p. 122 others are from Worcester and Caughley.

3 The crescent in the sky in some Lowestoft designs is of course not a mark, but copied from a Chinese design.

A B C

A. Vase and Cover Ht. 6¼in (15.8cm). About 1770–1800. No mark. *Victoria and Albert Museum (C.227-1924)*

B. Cream Jug Ht. 3½in (8.9cm). About 1770–1800. No mark. *Victoria and Albert Museum (C.193-1924)*

C. Mug Ht. 4⅜in (11.1cm). About 1770–1800. No mark. *Victoria and Albert Museum (C.223-1924)*

D. Teapot Ht. 5½in (14cm). About 1770–1800. No mark. *Victoria and Albert Museum (C.266-1924)*

See page 206   Plate 75 LOWESTOFT

on fragments discovered by Mr. Spelman on the factory site. More significant than any other marks are the numerals and letters written in blue on the inner side of the foot-ring. The placing of these workmen's marks is almost peculiar to Lowestoft, and pieces so marked were again found on the site.[1] The numeral most often met with is '5', and this is traditionally said to be the mark of Robert Allen. The foot-ring itself is also peculiar, an inverted broad-based triangle, not at all undercut, well seen in Plate 78B. Blue strokes beside the handle are also characteristic, though not confined to this factory. The paste is naturally very like that of Bow, but the glaze is generally thinner and not so liable to the iridescence and slight discoloration at the foot which marks the Bow porcelain, though this is sometimes present. On the other hand, the glaze seems to have been especially absorbent; discoloration in patches to a pale brown is frequently seen in the tea-cups. A certain peculiar soft lightness is noticeable in many Lowestoft bowls and cups. This quality is quite distinct from the hard crisp thinness of early Worcester, and may be described as a toy-like quality, not altogether unexpected in a factory so much concerned with dated and inscribed 'Trifles' and mementoes. Toy tea-services do in fact figure in the Lowestoft productions.

Coloured wares were not, it seems, produced before 1770, the earliest reliable dated example being of 1774. A well-known pattern consists of conventional rocks and flowering peonies, in red and underglaze blue.[2] Adapted from a Chinese original, this is known as the 'Redgrave Pattern' after one of the family of that name, several of whom worked at the factory at various times (Plate 74B). Mr. Spelman gave a list of the painters, and Mr. Kiddell has given an account of the career of one Richard Powles, a painter at the factory;[3] but apart from this and the tradition relating to Redgrave none of their work has ever been identified. Other Chinese red-and-blue designs (which include also the

---

[1] The mark of a cross scratched in the paste should be mentioned as having been found on a waster from the site (see Spelman, *Lowestoft China*, Plate 58, fig. 1); but see p. 224.

[2] There is an example at South Kensington in green, red and blue. Two cups and saucers figured in Plate 77 are of course versions of the same theme.

[3] A. J. B. Kiddell, 'Richard Powles: Lowestoft Painter', in *Transactions E.C.C.*, VII (1939), p. 112.

A   B

C   D   E

A. CUP AND SAUCER Cup ht. 1⅝in (4.1cm); Saucer dia. 4¾in (12cm). About 1770–1800. No mark. *Victoria and Albert Museum (C.690-1917)*

B. CUP AND SAUCER Cup ht. 1¾in (4.4cm); Saucer dia. 4¾in (12cm). About 1770–1800. No mark. *Victoria and Albert Museum (C.339-1924)*

C. CREAM JUG Ht. 3½in (8.9cm). About 1770–1800. No mark. *Victoria and Albert Museum (496-1899)*

D. TEAPOT Ht. 5⅞in (14.9cm). About 1770–1800. No mark. *Victoria and Albert Museum (C.188-1924)*

E. CREAM JUG Ht. 3¼in (8.2cm). About 1770–1800. No mark. *Victoria and Albert Museum (C.196-1924)*

See pages 206, 208   Plate 76 LOWESTOFT (*Painted in colours*)

Worcester 'whorl pattern')[1] can only be distinguished from Bow by the general characteristics already described. Quite typical of Lowestoft are some designs of Chinese figures (Plate 76E); the light red in these tends to brown and has juxtaposed to it a rather strong pink and a bright turquoise blue and green, giving an attractive discord. The collector will quickly learn to recognize this colouring, as well as the red-brown horizontal dashes on which the sketchily-drawn Chinese ladies and children stand. These were freely copied, by way of Worcester, from examples of the so-called Mandarin porcelain so largely exported from China in the second half of the eighteenth century, and these same Lowestoft designs were themselves copied in China. The favourite globular shape of Lowestoft teapots (Plates 75, 76, 78) was also a close copy of Chinese 'export porcelain' and this may perhaps help to account for the error of 'Chinese Lowestoft'. This Lowestoft teapot was more nearly spherical as a rule, and had a higher foot, than the similar copies made at Worcester and Bristol. The Lowestoft jugs and coffee-pots are usually of an easily recognisable form, with a handle that returns outwards with a knobbed 'kick' at its lower end and is usually provided with a thumb-rest above. Small cylindrical mugs were made, with flat glazed bases.

The bouquets of pink roses and other flowers by one prolific hand are marked by a stiff shading of the petals sometimes in nearly parallel lines (Plates 75 and 76). The mug and small vase in Plate 75 show some rarer Lowestoft painting with a more sensitive touch than is usual. Certain diapers, mainly a sort of trellis-pattern in red or pink regularly dappled with darker spots, also help to identify the Lowestoft types. Hexagonal and other cell-diapers, sometimes in blue alone but occasionally in red and blue, were favourite Lowestoft borders. All these diapers were of course suggested by Chinese porcelain. On the more ambitious pieces, the spaces between the panels are filled with close gilt scroll-work in another Chinese style, also adopted at Worcester. Coloured grounds were seldom if ever used, and the yellow, and perhaps the date also, on the teapot in Plate 75D are later additions.

Among the most charming of all Lowestoft porcelain are the

1 Sometimes known as 'Queen's pattern': copied also at Derby. See pp. 117 and 177.

C

E

F

A

B

C. DISH OF BOW PORCELAIN L. 9¾in (24.1cm). About 1756–60. Mark 'IA' in blue. *Victoria and Albert Museum* (*C.403-1924*)

D. CUP AND SAUCER Cup ht. 1¾in (4.4cm); Saucer dia. 4⅞in (12.4cm). About 1760–70. Painted in underglaze-blue. *Victoria and Albert Museum* (*C.830-1925*)

E. TEA CADDY Ht. 4¾in (12cm). Inscribed 'Hyson Tia' and 'H.T.'. Dated 1761. '1.H.1761' incorporated in the moulding. Mark '5' in blue. *Schreiber Collection* (*448*)

F. CUP AND SAUCER Cup ht. 1½in (3.8cm); Saucer dia. 4⅝in (11.7cm). About 1760–70. Painted in blue and red. *Victoria and Albert Museum* (*C.346-1924*)

A. CUP AND SAUCER Cup ht. 1¾in (4.4cm); Saucer dia. 4⅛in (10.5cm). About 1760–70. Painted in underglaze-blue. *Victoria and Albert Museum* (*C.852-1924*)

B. CUP AND SAUCER Cup ht. 1⅝in (4.1cm); Saucer dia. 4⅛in (10.5cm). About 1760–70. Mark Painter's No. '3' on saucer. Painted in underglaze-blue. *Victoria and Albert Museum* (*C.901-1924*)

ee pages 200, 202, 204

Plate 77 LOWESTOFT AND BOW

bowls, represented here by the fine specimen from Mr. Wallace Elliot's collection already mentioned (Plate 78), made to order for farmers' celebrations, elections, weddings and the like. They are sometimes painted in blue inside and in colours without, and bear such inscriptions as 'John and Eliza Remnant'; 'Success to the Jolly Farmer 1774'. Commemorative pieces, in fact, formed a considerable part of the Lowestoft china. 'Birthday plaques'— small china discs with a name and date (Plate 74D)—and inscribed mugs are not uncommon.[1] Some thirty or forty Birth or Memorial tablets have been recorded, the great majority after 1770, some in underglaze blue and others enamelled. The well-known 'Trifles'— tea-caddies, inkstands, mugs, teapots and so on—all came late in the factory's history, doubtless made for visitors to the towns or villages whose names they bear (Plate 74C).

The *rococo* and Chinese styles persisted at Lowestoft long after they had given place to Neo-classicism elsewhere. During the last ten or fifteen years of the factory, the 'Angoulême'[2] and other 'sprig' patterns such as were fashionable on Paris porcelain began to be used; a piece dated 1795 in the British Museum is typical. Some slight designs of sprigs and garlands and much simplified Chinese motives, sometimes in black and gold (Plate 76B), are pretty in a cottage-china way, and in general this later porcelain is unpretentious and but for the paste and characteristic foot-ring, would be hard to distinguish from New Hall and Liverpool.

A class of figures has been ascribed to Lowestoft on the evidence of fragmentary moulds found on the factory site.[3] One familiar type, however, claimed for the factory, is on the one hand totally unlike the normal Lowestoft porcelain, and on the other quite indistinguishable from that made in Staffordshire.[4] But some small *Cats*, a *Swan*, and some *putti* are with good reason attributed to Lowestoft.[5] Also a figure of a female lute player has been found to match a plaster mould of the torso found on the factory site,

1 See F. A. Crisp, *Catalogue of a Collection of Lowestoft China*, London (privately printed), 1907.
2 See p. 161.
3 Spelman, op. cit., p. 61.
4 See p. 357.
5 See A. J. B. Kiddell, on Lowestoft china in the collection of Mrs. Colman, in *The Connoisseur*, September and October, 1937.

C. Jug with Mask Lip Painted in blue. Inscribed 'John Cable'. About 1760–70. No mark. *British Museum*

A. Teapot Ht. 5¼in (13.3cm). Powdered-blue ground. Blue painting. About 1760–70. No mark. *Schreiber Collection (451)*

B. Bowl Dia. 8¾in (22.2cm). Inscribed 'Success to the Frances' and 'Captain Osborne from Colchester'. About 1760–70. No mark. *Victoria and Albert Museum (C.72-1938)*

See pages 202, 204, 206, 208

Plate 78 LOWESTOFT

together with a biscuit fragment of an arm and hand. Several examples of this figure (and of her companion) are recorded, with various bases and bocages, while other similar figures (some of which have been claimed for Longton Hall) may also be from Lowestoft.[1]

---

1 The arguments for and against these, and other possible Lowestoft figures, are set out by Geoffrey Godden, *An Illustrated Guide to Lowestoft Porcelain*, pp. 28–31. Examples can be seen in the fine collection of Lowestoft porcelain at the Castle Museum, Norwich.

Chapter 7

Lund's Bristol and Early Worcester

Bristol is a town with an honourable place in the history of English earthenware and glass, and both manufactures are likely to have led to early experiments in porcelain-making. Porcelain of some kind was evidently made there as early as 1750, when Dr. Pococke in a record of his travels[1] mentioned a manufacture 'lately established' at 'Lowd'ns Glass House' 'by one of the principal manufacturors at Limehouse which failed'. Dr. Pococke had previously seen at the Lizard a vein of soapstone which he had described as an ingredient of the porcelain made at this Bristol factory. The 'manufacturor at Limehouse' may perhaps have been associated with the Bow factory,[2] where an attempt had been made in 1744 to use under patent a china-clay imported from America,

---

1 Letters, published by the Camden Society in 1888 under the title of *Travels through England of Dr. Richard Pococke*, Oct. 1750: 'We went nine miles to the south near as far as Lizard Point to see the soapy rock which is a little opening in the cliff, where a rivulet runs over a vein of soapy rock into the sea, the lode or vein running along the bottom of the valley . . . there are white patches in it, which is mostly valued for making porcelane, . . . and they get five pounds a ton for the manufacture of porcelane now carrying on at Bristol . . .'. The transcription of the letter as published by the Camden Society contained alterations to the original letter (made subsequently) which caused the name to read 'Lowris China House', whereas the original wording was as above. *Transactions E.C.C.*, vol. 3, part 3, p. 130; Plate 57.

2 Both Bow and Limehouse are in the east of London, not far distant from each other. See p. 81. Limehouse porcelain has not been identified: compare an article by Wallace Elliot, 'Soft paste Bristol porcelain . . .', in *Transactions E.P.C.*, II (1929), p. 6. For the site, see A. J. Toppin, 'A note on the Limehouse china-factory', in *Transactions E.P.C.*, III (1931), p. 70, and F. H. Garner, in *Transactions E.C.C.*, IX (1946), p. 182. See also p. 197.

doubtless the same material as that mentioned in a letter from William Cookworthy in 1745.[1] Cookworthy was a Quaker apothecary with near relatives at Bristol,[2] and Edward Heylyn, who had been named in the Bow patent, was a merchant of Bristol and London, and seemed quite likely to have been the 'Limehouse manufacturor' mentioned by Dr. Pococke. An advertisement of the Bristol china in 1750[3] mentioned a Mr. Lund, who was Benjamin Lund, a brass-founder and subsequently the patentee of a process of copper manufacture. Lund was a Quaker whose wedding was witnessed by Champions of the generation before that of Richard, Cookworthy's successor in the hard-paste manufacture later established at Bristol. A connection may thus be reasonably conjectured between Cookworthy, Heylyn and Lund. As early as 1764, Sarah Champion[4] referred to Cookworthy as 'the first inventor of the Bristol china works' and at this time both he and Champion were certainly experimenting in porcelain manufacture (see pp. 214, 332). A soaprock licence was granted to Benjamin Lund on 7 March 1748/9,[5] and this may indicate the date of foundation of the factory mentioned by Pococke.

The factory to which Pococke referred is now presumed to have been that conducted at a glass-house formerly owned by William Lowdin[6] and situated at Redcliff Backs, Bristol. The names of the proprietors of this early Bristol factory had been the subject of much speculation over the years before the puzzle was finally solved by the late Mr. Aubrey Toppin's discovery and examination of the bankruptcy papers of Richard Holdship,[7] one of the Worcester partners, who failed in 1760. In these documents the Bristol partners were named, William Miller, a grocer and banker,

1 See p. 82.
2 See p. 333.
3 Pountney, pp. 192 and 193. The advertisement announced the extension of the works and offered to engage apprentices 'of either sex . . . to be learned to draw and paint . . . the said Ware, either in the *India* or *Roman* taste, whereby they may acquire a genteel subsistence'.
4 Owen, p. 15.
5 E. Morton Nance in *Transactions E.C.C.*, III (1935), p. 76.
6 'Lowris' in the published letters of Dr. Pococke is a copyist's error for 'Lowdin's'. An advertisement in a newspaper of 1745 (Pountney, p. 187) mentioned 'the glass house, consisting of several tenements lately in possession of William Lowdin'.
7 Public Record Office, Bankruptcy Order Book, No. 40, pp. 19–99.

A. CREAM JUG Ht. 3in (7.6cm). *Longton Hall porcelain.* About 1750–5. No mark. *Victoria and Albert Museum (C.817-1924)*
B. SAUCEBOAT L. 6⅛in (15.5cm). About 1750. Mark 'Bristoll' in relief. *Victoria and Albert Museum (3151-1901)*
C. BUTTERBOAT Ht. 2½in (6.3cm). About 1750–5. No mark. *Victoria and Albert Museum (C.787-1924)*
D. SAUCEBOAT L. 8in (20.3cm). About 1755. Mark Painter's mark in blue. *Victoria and Albert Museum (C.776-1924)*
E. MUG Ht. 2⅝in (6.6cm). About 1755–60. 'Scratched-cross' type. Mark a cross incised and painted over in blue to form a six-pointed star. *Victoria and Albert Museum (C.868-1924)*
F. MUG Ht. 3½in (8.9cm). 'Scratched-cross' type. About 1755–60. Mark a cross incised and a simulated Chinese character in blue. *Victoria and Albert Museum (C.801-1924)*
G. MUG Ht. 2½in (6.3cm). About 1755–60. Mark a cross incised in the base, 'Scratched-cross' type. *Victoria and Albert Museum (C.869-1924)*

pages 216, 218, 220, 224, 226

Plate 79 BRISTOL OR EARLY WORCESTER (*Painted in underglaze-blue*)

and Benjamin Lund of the 1750 advertisement, to whom the soaprock licence had been granted two years previously. Lund was a bankrupt at the time and, no doubt, Miller financed the venture when it was initiated in 1748 or 1749.[1] The factory was short-lived, for an advertisement of 1752[2] announced that this Bristol china manufactory was then to be 'united with the Worcester Porcelain Company'. As late as 1755, however, some of the productions remained unsold at the firm's warehouse in Castle Green, which also continued in use until 1757 as an agency for Worcester porcelain.

A factory in which materials obtained from Cornwall were said to be used is mentioned in a letter from Richard Champion dated from Bristol in February 1766[3] as 'set up here some time ago'. Mr. and Mrs. J. V. G. Mallet's researches have shown this to have been a 'hard paste' factory in which William Cookworthy was himself concerned.[4] A plate dated 1753 with initials said to be those of John Brittan, afterwards foreman at Champion's Bristol factory, was described by Nightingale.[5] A bowl traditionally believed to have been made by Brittan for a relative, dated 1762,[6] was destroyed in the fire at the British Section of the Brussels Exhibition of 1910. Brittan had been apprenticed to Cantle, the Bristol delftware potter, in 1749, and in his evidence before the Committee of the House of Commons in 1775[7] claimed to have had 'great Experience of several China Manufactures'. But a great part of the porcelain which twenty years ago was claimed as Lund's is now recognized as early Worcester. There is too much of it for a factory of such short duration, and the links with Worcester are unmistakable.

We are fortunately on firm ground in identifying some of the

---

1 *Transactions E.C.C.*, vol. 3, part 5, pp. 129–40.
2 *Bristol Intelligencer*, 24 July 1752.
3 Owen, p. 11.
4 Quoted *in extenso* by Watney, *English Blue and White Porcelain*, 2nd edition, p. 127.
5 pp. lxxiv and lxxxv.
6 The inscription 'F.B.' (for Francis Brittan) and date are figured in Owen, p. 14. The plate and bowl may even have been of Bristol delftware.
7 In support of Champion's patent. See p. 335.

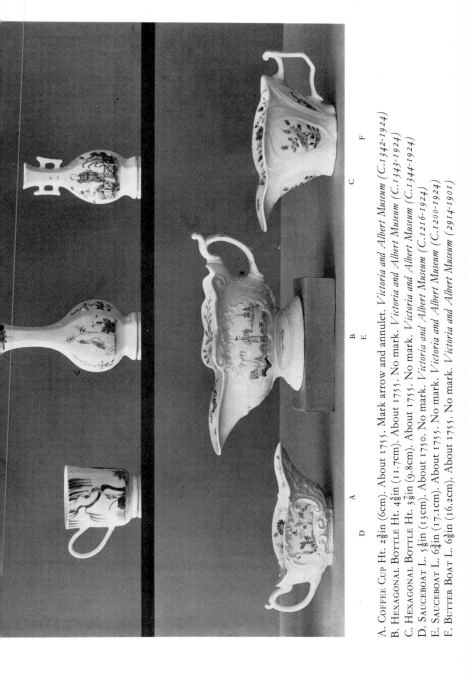

A. COFFEE CUP Ht. 2⅜in (6cm). About 1755. Mark arrow and annulet. *Victoria and Albert Museum (C.1342-1924)*
B. HEXAGONAL BOTTLE Ht. 4⅝in (11.7cm). About 1755. No mark. *Victoria and Albert Museum (C.1343-1924)*
C. HEXAGONAL BOTTLE Ht. 3⅞in (9.8cm). About 1755. No mark. *Victoria and Albert Museum (C.1344-1924)*
D. SAUCEBOAT L. 5⅛in (13cm). About 1750. No mark. *Victoria and Albert Museum (C.1216-1924)*
E. SAUCEBOAT L. 6¾in (17.1cm). About 1755. No mark. *Victoria and Albert Museum (C.1200-1924)*
F. BUTTER BOAT L. 6⅜in (16.2cm). About 1755. No mark. *Victoria and Albert Museum (2914-1901)*

See pages 218, 220, 224

Plate 80 BRISTOL OR EARLY WORCESTER (*Painted in colours*)

earliest of Lund and Miller's china. There exist a number of copies of a figure of a *Chinaman*, moulded from a Chinese specimen, with the word 'Bristoll' in raised letters and the date 1750 on the back near the base (Plate 84A). Three of these are in the Victoria and Albert Museum.[1] It was evidently no accident that Dr. Pococke selected for remark the 'beautiful white sauceboats adorned with reliefs of festoons which sell for sixteen shillings a pair'; one white sauce-boat[2] and several in which the festoons are picked out in colour, together with a number of blue-and-white examples are known bearing the same mark as the *Chinaman*. Three of these marked sauce-boats are in the Victoria and Albert Museum (Plate 79B), and two are in the British Museum (Nos. VIII. 1 and 52).[3] They are moulded in relief from a silver model, as are two others with the same mark—butter-boats rather than sauce-boats—lately in Mr. C. H. B. Caldwell's collection.[4] Though all these are obviously earlier in date than many other moulded sauce-boats, the latter are no less certainly attributable to Lund's factory or its continuation at Worcester.

All these specimens show a decidedly hard-looking paste, and some of them have indeed been erroneously described as hard-paste porcelain. They are, however, essentially soft-paste, and are actually no harder than the normal Worcester porcelain of the next thirty or forty years, of which they were in fact the forerunners. The minutely pitted, and in the earlier specimens very bubbly, glaze shows in most of the marked pieces a strong tinge of blue or a greyish tone. This is due either to a deliberate blueing of the glaze with cobalt or to the conditions of firing. The enamel-painted specimens shows on the contrary that warm ivory tone in the glaze (probably due to the lead in it) which is so pleasant to modern eyes, but which seems to have been regarded as a shortcoming in the

<hr />

1 Others are in the British Museum; the Dyson Perrins Museum, Worcester; and the Katz Collection in America. One of the Victoria and Albert Museum specimens (which are of two sizes) has the base streaked with underglaze manganese-brown. Two *unmarked* figures were formerly in the Glendenning Collection.

2 In the Dyson Perrins Museum, Worcester.

3 An analysed specimen shows 13 per cent of magnesia, equal to 40 per cent of soapstone. See *Analysed Specimens*, No. 24. All are undated.

4 Illustrated in Pountney, Plate 48.

A. TANKARD Ht. 5⅝in (14.7cm). About 1755. No
mark. *British Museum*

B. HEXAGONAL BOTTLE Ht.
4⅝in (11.7cm). About 1755.
No mark. *Schreiber Collection
(459)*

C. MUG Ht. 3½in (8.9cm). About 1755. No
mark. *Victoria and Albert Museum (C.637-
1925)*

See page 220

Plate 81 EARLY WORCESTER (*Painting similar to that on Bristol white
glass*)

eighteenth century.[1] The ideal of the English potter was evidently the Chinese 'export porcelain', which constantly shows a tendency to a cold greenish or bluish tone, especially in the blue-and-white.

The forms were to a remarkable extent moulded from silver.[2] Distinctive features are the wavy rim of a sauce-boat (Plates 79 and 80), and three peculiar handles—one angular (Plate 86A), another with a rosette at the junction with the body and a third which is high and looped (Plate 84B). Moulding with foliate scrolls in relief leaving panels reserved for painting is also a very distinctive feature commonly found. And pickle-trays in the form of scallop-shells were made in quantity as well. A specimen of this shape in the Victoria and Albert Museum is painted in underglaze manganese-brown, a rare colour found also on the marked specimen of the *Chinaman* in the Victoria and Albert Museum (Plate 84A) (see p. 216), a further piece of evidence regarding the origin of the class.

The painting in underglaze blue (Plate 79) is commonly blurred and sometimes almost indecipherable. An artless version of a Chinese landscape, with palm-like plants and horizontally shaded water, is constantly seen; a structure resembling a mast with yards is also characteristic. A feature distinguishing this china from all others is the manner of painting the inside of the rim of the sauce-boats with festoons of flowers or Chinese 'emblems', with a shell commonly painted inside the lip. This feature is found on both blue-and-white and coloured porcelain of Bristol/Worcester origin and seldom found elsewhere.[3]

If the decoration in blue is sometimes without much merit, the painting in colours is often of the greatest charm (Plate 80). One painter in particular used a very fine brush with remarkable skill, and his Chinese figures amid furniture and trellises, and very distinctive birds and flowers (Plates 82B and 83) include some of the most delightful brushwork seen on English porcelain. More rarely European figures were painted, with the utmost delicacy and

1 Dr. Pococke described the porcelain as having a 'yellow cast, both in the ware and the glazing'.

2 To a much greater extent than at the Bow factory, to which many of the pieces here called Bristol or Worcester were formerly ascribed.

3 In Bow examples (such as that in Plate 42B) the effect is quite different, the Lund shell being absent.

A. TEAPOT Ht. 4½in (11.4cm). About 1750–5. No mark. *Victoria and Albert Museum (C.333-1940)*

B. TEAPOT Ht. 5in (12.7cm). About 1750–5. No mark. *Victoria and Albert Museum (C.60-1938)*

See pages 218, 220   Plate 82 BRISTOL OR EARLY WORCESTER

charm (Plate 82A). There is a good group of these pieces in Mr. Broderip's gift in the Victoria and Albert Museum, from which the specimens figured on Plate 80 are drawn. The blue painting on the *Bristoll*-marked sauce-boat figured in Plate 79B may perhaps be recognized as the work of this artist; if it is, we have a further piece of evidence regarding the origin of the whole class with fine-brush painting. Sauce-boat-forms similar to but not absolutely identical with the marked specimens are of course very common (compare Plates 79B and 80D). Some charming flower-painting is seen on a *Bristoll*-marked sauce-boat in Mr. Wallace Elliot's collection.[1] Two other sauce-boats are decorated with festoons in relief from the same mould as this, at South Kensington (Plate 84B) and at the British Museum (Nos. VIII. 1 and 52),[2] and have the *Bristoll* mark painted over with a green leaf, perhaps, as Mr. Elliot suggests, because they were not made there, but at Worcester, though the mould automatically reproduced the mark.[3] A little bulbous-shaped hexagonal bottle in the Schreiber Collection (Plate 81B) is painted in colours with a subject of acrobats and tumblers, a subject found also on 'Bristol' opaque white glass. The birds on a mug in Plate 81 are also a common subject on 'Bristol' white glass.[4] This glass painter has been claimed to be one Michael Edkins (who is known to have painted 'Bristol' glass), but the only documents, if such they can be called, for Edkins' work are a delft plate with the initial 'MBE',[5] said to be those of Michael Edkins and Betty, his wife, but not necessarily painted by him, and a white tea-canister figured in woodcut in Owen (p. 379), 'authenticated' by William Edkins, his grandson.[6] One cannot accept that these pieces are painted by the same hand as the porcelain figured in Plates 81 and 85. Any resemblance is that of a common subject only.

Transfer-printing in black is seen on sauce-boats of forms

---

1 *The Connoisseur*, vol. LXXIX (October 1927).

2 Described as hard-paste in the *Catalogue*.

3 A similar mark in relief, 'Wigornia' (for Worcester), is recorded, on a cream-boat like that in Plate 79; see *Transactions E.C.C.*, III (1935), p. 97. Now in the Dyson Perrins Museum, Worcester.

4 Compare a vase (No. C670—1921) in the Victoria and Albert Museum.

5 In the Victoria and Albert Museum, No. 3125—1901. Figured in an article by Brig. Genl. Sir Gilbert Mellor in *The Connoisseur*, vol. LXX, 1924, p. 76.

6 The Bristol origin of this glass and the authorship of Edkins have been thrown in doubt by recent research.

Vase Ht. 10¾in (27.3cm). About 1750–5. No mark. *Victoria and Albert Museum (C.39-1938)*

See page 218   Plate 83 BRISTOL OR EARLY WORCESTER

obviously akin to those described above. At their best, the impressions are clean and of warm satisfying colour, though the enamel tends to rest on the surface with a very slightly sticky appearance, unlike the impressions on Worcester china of rather later date, where the colour is perfectly incorporated with the glaze. The printing has a certain 'primitive' charm. The dish, butter-boat, and little pickle-tray in the Victoria and Albert Museum, figured in Plate 86, may be considered typical. A mysterious signature, *Rhodes pinxit*, *painted* on the print on a dish (No. 466) in the Schreiber Collection, should be mentioned here. In addition to the printed decoration the dish has a painted green edge, and the name is presumably that of the workman who added this. It can hardly be connected, as was formerly believed, with David Rhodes, the enameller, of Leeds and London. Watney has suggested that the smoky appearance of these prints may have been due to a method of printing in which an impression in 'sticky' oil on the surface was dusted with powdered colour, a method analagous to that of 'bat printing' (see p. 7). The view that these 'smoky primitives' represent the first work done by Robert Hancock after his arrival at Worcester in 1756–7[1] may need revision. While in general effect it is very different from his signed work on Worcester porcelain, in line and handling it is not unlike it, yet it appears these rather sooty and over-inked little landscapes, squirrels and shields, of which there are several examples in Mr. Broderip's gift at South Kensington, could well have been done elsewhere than at the factory and not necessarily by Hancock.[2] The charming little print (Plate 86C) of a boy teaching a girl to play the flute (which we find also on later quite certain Worcester pieces) is of a somewhat different character. Its sensitive line long ago recalled to the writer of the Jermyn Street Museum Catalogue those etchings actually cut with a diamond on porcelain and coloured black by Canon Busch of Hildesheim, which are among the most charming examples of the German 'outside decoration' of the eighteenth century, or *Hausmalerei*, as it is usually called.

1 Compare pp. 116, 118 and 120. Hancock's early work at Worcester is discussed in the paper by H. W. Hughes there cited. Also Cyril Cook, *The Life and Work of Robert Hancock*.

2 Bernard Watney in 'Petitions for Patents concerning Porcelain etc.', *Transactions E.C.C.*, vol. 6, part 2 (1966) (joint paper with R. J. Charleston).

A. CHINAMAN Ht. 6¾in (17.1cm). White
splashed with manganese. Dated 1750.
Mark '*Bristoll 1750*' in relief. *Victoria and
Albert Museum (C.1300-1924)*

B. SAUCEBOAT L. 7½in (19cm). About 1750. Mark '*Bristoll*' in relief. *Victoria and
Albert Museum (C.57-1938)*

See pages 216, 218, 220   Plate 84 LUND'S BRISTOL

Presumably Hancock's first task at Worcester was to discover the composition and exact quantity of black enamel required to produce a clean result. The beautiful prints on the specimens figured in Plates 86A and B show this problem virtually solved. Like much of his work on 'Battersea' and other enamels, these prints of Hancock's were copied from paintings and engravings by L. P. Boitard.[1]

As stated above, it is unlikely that a small factory could have produced in the space of little more than three years[2] so large a quantity of porcelain as the number of these printed and other pieces implies; and it is important to remember that the continuity between Lund's and Worcester would in any case make a sharp division impossible. Many specimens, plainly of either Lund's or Worcester china, must necessarily remain as of uncertain origin, not to be definitely attributed to either factory. The moulds of the presumed Lund's pieces (such as the butter-boat moulded with landscapes in Plate 79C) evidently continued in use at Worcester for a long time, whilst the Lund's blue very closely resembles the distinctive Worcester colour to be described in the next chapter. The workmen's marks found on Lund's pieces further include several (such as the arrow with a ring on the shaft on the coffee-cup figured in Plate 80A) which are common on undisputed Worcester specimens of later date.

Another class of pieces of long-disputed origin is also by body and glaze obviously related to Worcester. These specimens usually bear certain incised marks—a cross[3] or one or two short strokes, or

---

1 Boitard's name, in association with that of Hancock, occurs on some engravings in an album in the British Museum. Perhaps even more important is the occurrence on a Worcester bowl of a print (Cyril Cook, Item 4) actually bearing Boitard's signature. Dr. Watney, *Burlington Magazine*, December 1972, p. 825.

2 The factory was said by Dr. Pococke in 1750 to have been 'lately established'.

3 An incised cross is of course a natural and common mark on porcelain of all kinds and not by itself evidence of origin. A waster with this mark was found at Lowestoft (see p. 204).

A. PLATE Dia. 9in (22·8cm). Painted with the fable of the Fox, the Dog and
the Cock. About 1755. No mark. *Schreiber Collection (170)*
(*See p. 42*)

B. PAIR OF COOKS   Ht. 6½in (16·5cm) and 7in (17·7cm). About 1756. Mark on male figure 'B' impressed. *Schreiber Collection (46)*

(*See p. 106*)

A. VASE Ht. 10½in (26.7cm). Painted in colours. About 1752. No mark. *Victoria and Albert Museum*

B. PAIR OF VASES Ht. 6½in (16.5cm). Painted in colours. About 1750. No mark. *Trustees of the Dyson Perrins Museum Worcester*

See page 220   Plate 85 BRISTOL OR EARLY WORCESTER

a short cut made with a sharp blade on the inner side of the foot-ring. In addition, a number of marks of uncertain significance were painted in blue or colours. A few forms were constantly repeated: a nearly cylindrical mug with spreading base (Plate 79E and G), the handle of which often shows signs of parting from the body, leaving incipient fissures within; another mug, of the form shown in Plate 79F; a pear-shaped jug with lip and scroll handle; and a sauce-boat in the form of folded leaves, copied from Meissen.[1] The painting is often decidedly amateurish, with 'fine-brush' work which is however distinct from that seen on Lund's Bristol or early Worcester. An analysed specimen shows 10 per cent of magnesia, equal to 30 per cent of soapstone.[2] It has been conjectured by Mr. Bernard Rackham[3] that these pieces were perhaps made at Worcester after the transfer of Lund's works, from a special composition indicated by the incised marks, but more probably they are workmen's identification or tally marks.

Several other links with Worcester are noteworthy, particularly the blue-painters' marks[4] which occur on both 'scratched cross' and undoubted Worcester pieces. A pear-shaped jug in the Schreiber Collection (No. 461), in addition to the usual incised marks, has also a script capital '*L*' (or a small '*h*') incised under the base, and is painted with figures and flowers apparently by the same hand as those on the early Worcester jug in the Schreiber Collection (No. 490), here figured in Plate 87A. A jug in the Frank Lloyd Collection (No. 386), quite certainly Worcester, with the arms of Chalmers and the date 1759, is of the typical 'scratched cross' pear-shape. The Worcester design afterwards known as the 'Reynolds' pattern[5] also appears on mugs of this class (such as Schr. No. 460). A mug in the Schreiber Collection (No. 471) has a print generally attributed to Hancock, and several other links with Worcester have been pointed out.[6]

---

1 These sauce-boats are fairly common: there are three pairs in Mr. Herbert Allen's collection, Nos. 30, 31 and 32.

2 Normal Worcester porcelain shows 11 to 13 per cent of magnesia; a *Bristoll*-marked sauce-boat, 13 per cent. See *Analysed Specimens*, Nos. 24–36.

3 *Herbert Allen Catalogue*, p. 55.

4 See Appendix A, p. 391.

5 See p. 258.

6 Barrett *Lund's Bristol and Worcester Porcelain*, pp. 20–2.

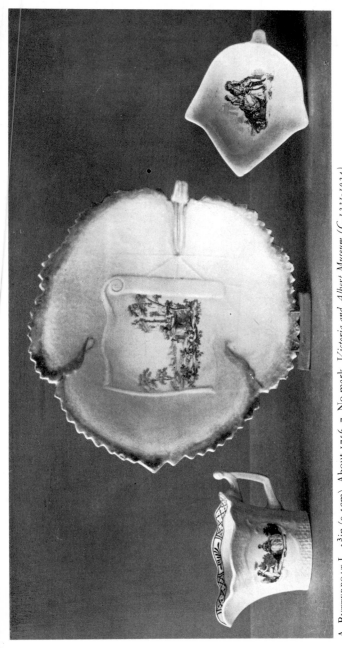

A. BUTTERBOAT L. 3¾in (9.5cm). About 1756–7. No mark. *Victoria and Albert Museum (C.123-1924)*

B. DISH Dia. 7½in (19cm). About 1756–7. No mark. *Victoria and Albert Museum (C.1305-1924)*

C. PICKLE DISH L. 3¾in (9.5cm). About 1756–7. No mark. *Schreiber Collection (468)*

See pages 218, 222, 224   Plate 86 WORCESTER (*Transfer-printed in black*)

Links with Bristol, on the other hand, are not lacking: a *Bristoll*-marked sauce-boat at South Kensington has the additional mark of an incised stroke. A peculiar blue-painted scroll on the handles of jugs is to be found on fairly certain Lund's pieces as well as on the 'scratched cross' family. Painting in blue is in general similar. Marks under the handles[1] are a singular feature of both. The incised marks of the 'scratched cross' family, besides occurring on pieces attributed to Lund's factory and Worcester, are found on some Liverpool wares from Richard Chaffer's factory. The practice of using such tally marks may have been taken there by Robert Podmore who seceded from Worcester in 1755.[2]

The marks most common in this class, as well as on Lund's and early Worcester, resemble alchemist's signs, and may perhaps suggest the mind or habit of Cookworthy, whose leaning in this direction is shown by the mark unquestionably used at Plymouth on his hard-paste china. It is probable that the use of Cornish soapstone in English porcelain was due to Cookworthy's researches and inquiries. He was thoroughly familiar with the *Lettres édifiantes et curieuses* written by the Jesuit missionary Père d'Entrecolles from the Chinese porcelain town of Ching-tê Chên, where an ingredient formerly believed to be soapstone (*hua shih*, slippery stone) is described as an ingredient sometimes substituted for *kaolin* in the Chinese manufacture.

1 See Appendix, p. 391. These marks should be distinguished from those on certain Bow mugs painted in red and blue which have the sign for the planet Mercury painted under the handle.
2 See p. 294.

Chapter 8

Worcester

The Worcester china manufacture stands apart in several respects from the other English ventures of the eighteenth century. Alone of all these it has survived with a record of continuous activity down to the present day. It largely created its own fashions, and the usual criteria for dating do not apply to its earlier work as surely as elsewhere. Its *rococo* was never as wild or its Neo-Classical as severe as at other factories. It was, it must be confessed, a little provincial in its belated adoption of the fashionable metropolitan styles. But it was perhaps more typically English than Chelsea or even Bow.

The origins of Worcester china have been discussed in the previous chapter. It seems highly probable that the use of soapstone was learnt from the Bristol proprietors, though the transfer to Worcester was not advertised until 1752. On the closure of the Bristol factory, one of the arrangements was that Richard Holdship should acquire from Benjamin Lund the soapstone rights under which the Bristol concern had obtained its supplies of 'soapy-rock', and that he would supply this material to the Worcester factory. He was also enabled, under certain circumstances, to supply soapstone to other persons, and when he moved to Derby in 1764 he offered to William Duesbury the recipes for making porcelain containing this ingredient. The 'Worcester Tonquin Manufacture', as it styled itself,[1] was established at

---

1 Somewhat strangely, in view of the statement in the bankruptcy papers of Richard Holdship (see p. 212) that the factory was set up to make porcelain 'in imitation of Dresden Ware'.

Warmstry House[1] in 1751. In June of that year articles were signed by fifteen gentlemen 'to discover for the benefit of themselves and the other subscribers the real true and full art mistery and secret [of porcelain making] by them hitherto invented and found out'. One of these subscribers, Dr. John Wall (*b.* 1708, *d.* 1776), has generally been given credit for the initiative, and his name has become attached to the first and by far the most important period of the factory. But it is more probable that the leading part was played by William Davis, 'apothecary', the first manager and a large subscriber. It may be conjectured that Davis was the chief 'arcanist', whilst Robert Podmore and John Lyes also shared the secret, and special payments were to be made to them.[2] In the list of subscribers should be remarked the name of Edward Cave, founder of *The Gentleman's Magazine*. Several laudatory references to the Worcester china are to be found in the magazine, and though London advertisements were rare in the earlier period it is unlikely that any opportunities for publicity were lost. An article on the porcelain in *The Annual Register* for 1763, quoted by Mr. Hobson,[3] has all the air of an inspired puff, with its concluding remark commending the factory to the attention of the 'Society for Encouraging Arts and Manufactures'.

Its history has been comparatively uneventful.[4] The original company was reconstituted in 1772; shares were held in the new concern by Robert Hancock the engraver,[5] but he was bought out two years later. Dr. Wall died in 1776, though by a convenient fiction the 'Wall period' is extended to 1783, when on the death of William Davis the concern was bought by Thomas Flight, the firm's London agent, for his sons Joseph and John.[6] About 1786

1 A view of Warmstry House and a description appear in *The Gentleman's Magazine* for August 1752. The factory was again described by Valentine Green in his *Survey of the City of Worcester* (1764). See *Transactions E.C.C.*, VIII (1942), p. 121.

2 '. . . the better to engage their fidelity to keep such part of the secret as may be entrusted to them.'

3 *Worcester Porcelain*, p. 26. Also see Barrett, op. cit., p. 14.

4 Binns, with Victorian optimism and complacency, was gratified 'to find the finest productions and the most prosperous results in perfect accord'.

5 Other shareholders were John Wall senr., Rev. T. Vernon, W. Davis senr., W. Davis junr., and Richard Cook, chinaman, of Fleet Street, London.

6 Geoffrey Wills, 'John Flight of Worcester', in *The Connoisseur*, CXIX (1947), p. 87. It has recently been tentatively suggested, following excavations carried out on the Warmstry site in 1969 which yielded much evidence in the shape of

A. Milk Jug Ht. 7⅜in (18.7cm). Painted in colours. About 1760. No mark. *Schreiber Collection (490)*

B. Plate Dia. 7¼in (18.4cm). Painted in colours. About 1755–60. No mark. *Schreiber Collection (491)*

See pages 226, 238   Plate 87 WORCESTER

Robert Chamberlain seceded and founded a rival factory in Worcester.

John Flight died in 1791, and in the next year Martin Barr was taken into partnership. *Flight and Barr* became *Barr Flight and Barr* (1807) and *Flight Barr and Barr* (1813) on the admission of younger members of the Barr family. In 1840 Chamberlain's factory, which had at first only decorated[1] but afterwards actually made porcelain, was amalgamated with the older company. In 1847 the original premises at Warmstry House were abandoned in favour of Chamberlain's works. Walter Chamberlain and John Lilly were the proprietors in 1848, and in 1850 W. H. Kerr joined the firm, which became *Kerr and Binns* in 1852, and the still-existing Royal Worcester Porcelain Company in 1862.

The factory for a long time adopted no regular mark, though a script '*W*' was occasionally used. A crescent, stated by Binns to have been taken from the Warmstry arms, is common enough on Worcester china to be regarded as a factory mark, but it has been so often imitated elsewhere[2] that it is of little use by itself as proof of origin. The 'fretted square', an invention in the manner of a Chinese seal character somewhat resembling the Union Jack, is not uncommon and is fairly trustworthy.[3] These marks were as a rule painted in blue under the glaze. The crescent, however, was printed in blue on blue-printed wares, when it was commonly shaded, and occasionally towards the end of the Wall period and in the subsequent Flight period it was painted in enamel or gold. The series of marks in the form of disguised numerals, one to nine, formerly regarded as denoting a Salopian (Caughley) origin, is now proved a Worcester feature by the occurrence of these marks on unglazed wasters found on the Warmstry House site during the 1968 excavations.[4] As at other English factories, the Meissen and

wasters, that the period from 1776 to 1793 should be segregated, when it appears the factory largely concentrated on the manufacture of the cheaper wares, mainly blue and white. Henry Sandon, *Worcester Porcelain*, p. 13.

1 Usually Caughley (Salopian), but sometimes also New Hall porcelain.

2 Particularly at Caughley, Bow and Lowestoft.

3 It is copied, though rarely, in blue enamel on Salopian imitations of Worcester types; compare a cup and saucer at South Kensington, No. C1051—1924, and also on Bow copies of scale-blue (see p. 124), and by nineteenth-century copyists.

4 See Geoffrey Godden, *Caughley and Worcester Porcelain, 1775–1800* for the argument in favour of a Caughley attribution, subsequently confirmed by the

A. LEAF MOULDED CUP Dia. 3½in (8.9cm). About 1755–60. Crescent mark in blue. *Victoria and Albert Museum (3254-1901)*

B. SAUCEBOAT L. 6¾in (17.1cm). About 1765. Crescent mark in blue. *Schreiber Collection (482)*

C. TEA BOWL Ht. 2in (5.1cm). About 1760. No mark. *Schreiber Collection (475)*

D. TEAPOT Ht. 3¾in (9.5cm). About 1760. No mark. *Victoria and Albert Museum (3242-1901)*

E. BALUSTER VASE Ht. 7⅞in (20cm). About 1765–70. No mark. *Victoria and Albert Museum (721-1907)*

F. CUP AND SAUCER Cup ht. 2¼in (5.7cm); Saucer dia. 4¾in (12cm). Powdered-blue. About 1760–5. Square and Crescent marks. *Victoria and Albert Museum (3271-1901)*

G. BALUSTER VASE Ht. 7⅞in (20cm). About 1765–70. No mark. *Victoria and Albert Museum (721-1907)*

See pages 238, 240   Plate 88 WORCESTER (*Painted in underglaze-blue*)

Sèvres marks as well as Chinese characters were commonly imitated. Forgeries of the Chelsea mark are not unknown.[1]

But early Worcester china itself is perhaps the most distinctive of all eighteenth-century English porcelains. With the exception of Lund's and Caughley, and to a slight extent Chaffers' Liverpool porcelain, which were virtually offshoots of Worcester, it is unlike any other. It is hard-looking though actually fired at a fairly low temperature; the lead glaze is not easily scratched and is invariably even the smooth ('close-fitting' is Mr. Rackham's happy word) and inclined to be thin, seldom collecting in pools or masses at the foot, save in the earliest pieces. It is rare to find a Worcester piece that has needed to be ground level at the foot, as was so often the case with Chelsea and early Derby. Some collectors are in the habit of regarding as an infallible sign of Worcester origin the dryness of the edges and the thinness of the obviously brushed-on glaze on the base of a piece; but these are characteristics occasionally found on other porcelain though rarely absent in genuine Worcester.[2] It may however be asserted that the Worcester body and glaze were so well suited that the latter never 'crazed'.[3] The glaze often has a decidedly greyish or bluish tone, due to a minute quantity of cobalt used to counteract the yellow tinge given by the lead. The greenish colour by transmitted light of early Worcester china is due rather to this 'blueing' of the paste and glaze than to the soapstone used in the body.[4] Iron present as an impurity in one of the materials would also produce a greenish tone. Salopian porcelain also contained soapstone, but is commonly cream-coloured and gives a yellowish tone to transmitted light.[5] Kiln losses were evidently less

excavation. The latter described by Henry Sandon, op. cit., ch. II and pp. 59 to 65.

1 These and other imitations are reproduced in Appendix A.

2 The so-called 'shrinkage' of the glaze from the foot-rim on the base of tablewares was actually due to the removal of the glaze material from this place before firing. Worcester *before about 1760* does *not* possess this feature. Caughley also possesses this characteristic.

3 'Crazing' and 'crackle' are the names respectively used for the accidental and intentional production of a network of lines due to a splitting up of the glaze. The effect is due to a difference in the amount of contraction of body and glaze.

4 A typical Worcester analysis shows about 13 per cent of magnesia due to soapstone. See *Analysed Specimens*, Nos. 26–36.

5 Worcester china made during the Flight period, particularly certain blue-printed wares to be mentioned below, are virtually identical with Caughley by transmitted light. See p. 280.

HEXAGONAL VASE Ht. 15⅜in (39cm). Painted in blue. About 1760.
Painter's mark 'TF'. *Schreiber Collection (478)*

than in most soft-paste manufactures, and the proprietors constantly laid stress on the cheapness of their wares. The material was indeed very practical, withstanding hot water much better than most other artificial porcelains.[1] And this practical quality was characteristic of the ware in other ways. The amusing extravagances of Chelsea and Bow were for the greater part carefully avoided, and neatness and 'English good sense' prevailed in the shapes of the useful wares to which the factory largely confined its attention for the first fifteen or twenty years. The well-proportioned forms and careful finish are quickly recognised by the collector. 'Not good enough for Worcester' (and therefore Liverpool) is often the deciding comment on a doubtful piece of the middle period.[2] But early specimens are sometimes more roughly finished. The decoration commonly strikes the same note, but a certain *naïveté* in the rendering and combination of Meissen, Chinese and Japanese motives gives the early ware a very distinct charm.

The firm usually disposed of its wares to retailers, and until 1769 held no public auction-sales with catalogues such as assist us in identifying the productions of other factories. The first exhibition of the china was announced for 20 September 1752, 'with a great variety of ware, and at a reasonable price'. London advertisements of 1756[3] merely make known to us the existence of the firm's warehouse in Aldersgate Street in the City of London. A sufficient number of dated pieces have survived, however, to enable the sequence of styles to be inferred.

The earliest Worcester style was naturally a continuation of that of Lund's factory, with a considerable Meissen influence also. The moulded early-Bristol sauce-boats have their counterpart in such

---

1 In the *Handmaid to the Arts* (1758) it was stated that 'a manufactory at Worcester has lately produced, even at very cheap prices, pieces that not only work very light, but which have great tenacity, and bear hot water without more hazard than the true China ware'.

2 Perhaps unfair to Liverpool, where some excellent ware was made.

3 *The Public Advertiser*, 20 March 1756; also *Aris's Birmingham Gazette*, 27 February 1758.

A. VASE AND COVER Ht. 8in (20.3cm). Perhaps painted by James Roberts. About 1760. No mark. *Schreiber Collection (496)*

B. VASE Ht. 6¼in (15.8cm). About 1760. No mark. *Victoria and Albert Museum (C.1151-1924)*

C. TEAPOT Ht. 5⅝in (14.3cm). About 1760. No mark. *Schreiber Collection (501)*

See pages 242, 244   Plate 90 WORCESTER (*Painted in colours*)

silver forms as that of a charming jug in the Schreiber Collection
(No. 490: Plate 87A). This is painted with rather artless landscapes
in colours (faintly recalling those of Meissen) which may well be by
the same hand as those on the 'L'-marked jug described in the last
chapter.[1] A more definitely German style of painting is seen on
some of the elaborately moulded pieces that date from this early
period. A plate in the Schreiber Collection (No. 491: Plate 87B) has
a little group of figures and sprays of flowers in colours evidently
copied from a Meissen model. But the well-known figure-subject
depicting sportsmen with queer-looking dogs[2] is quite likely to
have been copied through the medium of a Chinese version of a
Meissen design. Such Chinese copies are not uncommon[3] and
show precisely the same shading and dotting.

The Lund's tradition of forms moulded from silver was perhaps
continued through the influence of Samuel Bradley, a silversmith,
who was one of the original subscribers. An important document
for the earliest styles is provided by a white tureen formerly in the
possession of Mrs. George Barr,[4] dated 1751 in blue. This is
moulded in relief and another in the Dyson Perrins Museum[5]
exactly corresponds with it in this respect but is painted in blue and
has proved on analysis to contain soapstone.[6] Many early
specimens are in the public collections (Plate 88A–D)—some
moulded with *rococo* scrolls, others with ribbed patterns in-
terrupted by flowers. Little cups were formed of overlapping
leaves, again in silver style. These and the horn-shaped flower-
holders and sauce-boats moulded with landscapes, the large dishes
with shells and scrolls on the rims, and many others, all speak of
silver originals.[7]

The analysed tureen in Mr. Dyson Perrins' collection is
additionally important since it proves the Worcester origin of
much blue-and-white formerly ascribed to Bow. The painting on

1 p. 226.

2 Frank Lloyd, No. 133, a sugar-bowl, and a tray, Schr. No. 495, are examples.
The same design was used at Liverpool.

3 There is a specimen at South Kensington (No. C1062—1924).

4 Illustrated by Binns, p. 43.

5 Hobson, *Worcester Porcelain*, Plate 16.

6 Another is illustrated in Barrett, op. cit., Plate 43A.

7 Compare also dish and pierced basket in the Schreiber Collection (Nos. 633
and 480).

Jug with Mask Lip Ht. 10½in (26.7cm). Painted in colours and bearing the Arms of Broadribb with Barrow. About 1760. No mark. *Victoria and Albert Museum (C.104-1932)*

See page 242

Plate 91 WORCESTER

this tureen is unmistakably like that on many pieces bearing a mark resembling the letters 'T' and 'F' conjoined which was at one time believed to be the monogram of Thomas Frye of Bow. The mark is probably no more than a copy of a Chinese character—'a maimed version', as Mr. Hobson calls it, of that for *yü* (jade), a very common mark on Chinese porcelain. The Worcester underglaze blue even at this time already shows its characteristic tendency towards a dark indigo tone, a feature noticeable in the abundant blue-and-white of the next twenty years (Plate 88E–G). Valentine Green, writing in 1795, declared that the early Worcester was chiefly blue-and-white; and it was certainly much made, probably supplying a large provincial market. There is usually little difficulty in distinguishing it. The hexagonal vase in the Schreiber Collection (Plate 89) is typical of the better kind of Worcester blue-and-white and is finely painted: it bears the 'TF' mark, and it seems astonishing now that the distinctive paste and glaze and tone of blue of these pieces should not have prevented their ascription to Bow. On the other hand, much of the abundant Bow blue-and-white ware with powdered-blue ground was wrongly ascribed to Worcester. Powdered blue certainly was made at Worcester, but the soft glaze and rich blue, the shapes, and the characteristic imitation Chinese characters of the marks on the Bow pieces[1] clearly distinguish them from the Worcester, which have the usual qualities I have already described. A cup and saucer at South Kensington (Plate 88F) is a typical piece of Worcester with powdered-blue ground, marked with both crescent and fretted square. The powdered blue made at Caughley is naturally harder to distinguish, but the ground is inclined to be paler and of a coarser grain and, as Mr. Rackham has pointed out, the form of foot-ring is different.[2]

The decade beginning about 1755 shows a fully-developed Worcester style in being. Documentary pieces for this period are

1 See p. 124 and Appendix, p. 386 No. 6. Lowestoft, of course, comes into question as well; see p. 202.
2 See p. 290.

C. VASE   Ht. 16in (40·6cm). About 1770. Square mark. *Schreiber Collection* (554)
(*See p. 264*)

D. GROUP OF VENUS AND ADONIS   Ht. 10¼in (26cm). About 1770. No mark.
Schreiber Collection (731)

(See p. 347)

A. 'GRUBBE' PLATE Dia. 8⅞in (22.5cm). Painted in green and black. About 1765–70. No mark. *Victoria and Albert Museum (C.877-1935)*

B. 'GRUBBE' PLATE Dia. 9in (22.8cm). Painted in carmine monochrome. About 1765–70. No mark. *Victoria and Albert Museum (C.879-1935)*

Plate 92 WORCESTER

fairly numerous. Two large jugs dated 1757 are in the Corporation Museum at Worcester.[1] They are moulded in relief with overlapping 'cabbage' leaves in a style afterwards very familiar in Caughley and Lowestoft as well as in Worcester china. It should be noted that the mask-lip-spout, a common feature of the later jugs in this form, is absent. The painting includes the arms of the city of Worcester, with figures emblematical of Commerce and Justice, and borders of feathery crimson scroll-work. The latter were probably suggested by Meissen but are very characteristic also of Worcester and help us to identify and date many pieces belonging to this period.

The date 1759 is inscribed on an important mug in the British Museum (Frank Lloyd Collection), which bears also the name of Lord Sandys, Dr. Wall's guardian. This mug is of a characteristic Worcester shape, somewhat resembling a bell, and is painted by one of the most accomplished of the artists whose work gives such distinction to this period of Worcester. The rare figure-subjects, as on this piece and on the great jug figured in Plate 91,[2] with the landscapes, birds and flowers also by his hand, are the Worcester counterparts of the Chelsea fable-painter's work. One of this artist's favourite subjects shows an owl on a branch mobbed by other birds, with a characteristic distant landscape in which three or four Lombardy poplar trees are a common feature. His work may be well studied in the Schreiber Collection at South Kensington, as on the typical pear-shaped Worcester vases (such as No. 496: Plate 90A) with domed lids having the half-open flower-bud knob which is characteristic of early Worcester.[3] The hand of this 'painter of the Lord Sandys mug' is sometimes recognisable in the shields of arms surrounded by the deliciously treated *rococo* scroll-work which is one of the most attractive features of this early Worcester porcelain (Plate 93). A beautiful mug of this kind in the Schreiber Collection (No. 500: Plate 93G) is painted with a crest and flowers in lilac, grey and crimson monochromes. A jug in the

1 Hobson, *Worcester Porcelain*, Plate C.

2 The arms of Broadribb with Barrow painted on this jug enabled the late Aubrey Toppin to date the piece with certainty as 1760.

3 Other distinctive Worcester forms of this period are a globular teapot usually not so high in the foot as Lowestoft, and a pear-shaped coffee-pot.

C. TANKARD Ht. 5⅝in (14.3cm). About 1760.
No mark. *Schreiber Collection (500)*

B. TANKARD Ht. 4⁷⁄₁₀in (11.9cm).
About 1760. No mark. *British Museum*
(*Frank Lloyd Collection 388*)

A. TANKARD Ht. 4½in (11.4cm). Painted in
lilac. About 1760. No mark. *British Museum*
(*Frank Lloyd Collection 385*)

See page 242   Plate 93 WORCESTER (*Armorial wares*)

Frank Lloyd Collection (No. 386), with the arms of Chalmers,[1] has a beautiful little landscape in lilac and the date 1759.[2] Scroll-work even more beautiful is seen on the little cups and saucer painted with no less charming flowers (Plate 94A). Worcester flowers in this period are obviously inspired by Meissen, but quite fresh and individual in treatment. Two other styles of flower-painting are shown in Plate 90: that on the vase seems to be by the hand of the 'painter of the Lord Sandys mug'. These flowers are sometimes seen rather arbitrarily painted over the vine- and lettuce-leaf dishes and the plates moulded in relief with rose leaves and flower-buds, all of them adaptations of Meissen forms. The last-named relief pattern is commonly associated with the 'blind Earl' of Coventry, who, however, did not lose his sight until 1780, long after the earliest date of this pattern. Plate 94B shows a specimen of about 1765, painted in colours.[3] This relief pattern certainly remained in use over a long period and it seems to have been the Worcester practice to name designs, years after their introduction, after distinguished patrons who happened to favour them.[4]

The work of another talented painter may best be studied in the charming 'Chinese' landscapes in crimson monochrome, naïvely set in a yellow ground with borders and scattered flowers in the Kakiemon style (Plate 95A). The hand of this 'painter of the Chinese landscapes' may often be recognised in the blue-and-white.

1 Some of the best Worcester porcelain of the Wall Period is painted with armorial bearings; a survey and list of these by H. R. Marshall ('Armorial Worcester Porcelain') is in the *Transactions E.C.C.*, IX (1946), pp. 188–218.

2 The 'painter of the Lord Sandys mug' has been associated with one James Rogers, who in 1757 signed and dated a small Worcester mug painted with 'birds', now in the British Museum. *The Connoisseur*, vol. CXLIX, No. 602 (April 1962), Hugh Tait, 'James Rogers—A Leading Porcelain Painter at Worcester'. See also Barrett, op. cit., pp. 17–18.

3 The large moths on this and other Worcester pieces of this time should be carefully distinguished from the somewhat similar insects which appear on a class of early Derby porcelain. See p. 140.

4 A list of named patterns of this kind is given in Hobson, *Worcester Porcelain*, p. 129. The name was occasionally much too *early* for the porcelain, as in the case of the service in the style of the 1770s named after Lady Mary Wortley Montagu, who died in 1762.

B. PLATE Dia. 7⅝in (19.4cm). Moulded with the 'Blind Earl' Pattern. About 1765. No mark. *British Museum (Frank Lloyd Collection 120)*

A. CUPS AND SAUCER Cups ht. 1¾in (4.4cm) and 2⅝in (6.6cm); Saucer dia. 5⅛in (13cm). About 1760. Meissen Crossed Swords mark. *Victoria and Albert Museum (3210 and 3331-1901)*

See page 244

Plate 94 WORCESTER

The practical and at times distinctly commercial bent of the Worcester proprietors is made plain by their quick adoption on a large scale of transfer-printing. We have no record of the date at which the process was first introduced at Worcester, and portraits of Frederick the Great dated 1757 are the earliest unquestionably Worcester prints. These are the work of Robert Hancock (*b.* 1730, *d.* 1817),[1] round whose name controversy has long raged, and whose early problematical work has been discussed on previous pages.[2] We know that he was at Worcester or working for the factory at the latest by the date of these portraits. He may have been there in the previous year. It was conjectured in the last chapter that his first task at Worcester was to master use of black enamel, the 'jet enamel' of which the factory was afterwards so proud.

Most of Hancock's prints for porcelain were versions of work by others. Many of the prints used by him in this way cannot now be found, but one may conjecture that a collection of work by F. Vivares furnished him with much material for his Worcester work. No original engraving of the famous *Tea-Party* has ever been found, but the design has a decidedly French air and the comparable *L'Amour* is known to be after a French print.[3] Many engravings signed by Hancock were included in the popular collections published by Robert Sayer in the 1760s and 1770s under such titles as *The Ladies' Amusement* and *The Artist's Vade-Mecum*, though it by no means follows (as is often supposed) that their dates of publication in this form give the earliest dates for the porcelain on which they appear. The prints may well have been in use for porcelain decoration for many years previously. Indeed, Binns long ago suggested that their appearance in Sayer's publications was due to their sale to him by Hancock, who evidently owned some of the plates, since he took them with him to Caughley and Staffordshire; and a curious Staffordshire enamel (Schr. Collection No. 406) bears an engraving of the King of

1 Biographical details and a catalogue of his work as a mezzotint engraver and painter are given in A. Randall Ballantyne, *Robert Hancock and his Works*, London, 1885. Also, Cyril Cook, op. cit.

2 See pp. 118–20.

3 See Ballantyne, op. cit., p. 5. Other sources are shown by Dr. Watney, *Burlington Magazine*, December 1972, pp. 818–28.

A. TANKARD Ht. 4⅝in (11.7cm).
Painted in crimson on a yellow ground.
About 1760. No mark. *Victoria and
Albert Museum (C.366-1940)*

B. SAUCER Dia. 2¾in (7cm). Painted in lilac. About 1760. No mark. *Victoria and Albert Museum (3991-1901)*

C. TEAPOT Ht. 5¼in (13.3cm). Painted in black. About 1760. No mark. *Victoria and Albert Museum (C.1185 and a-1924)*

See pages 244, 258

Plate 95 WORCESTER

Prussia signed 'R H *Worcester*', though the signature is concealed by herbage painted over it in dark brown.[1]

Some of the prints, in addition to the signatures 'R. *Hancock fecit*', 'R. *H. fecit*' and '*Hancock fecit*', bear a monogram of 'R' and 'H' with an anchor. The last is by general consent the rebus device of one or other of the brothers Holdship, who were apparently in charge of the printing department of the factory: a printed basket at South Kensington bears a device of two crossed anchors, possibly with reference to the two brothers. Richard Holdship, a glover, was a large subscriber to the original company, and his brother Josiah also held shares. The former left Worcester in 1759, and in 1764 offered his 'process of Printing enamell and Blew' to the Derby proprietors.[2] The significance of the monogram has been the subject of much discussion. For long believed to be Holdship's mark, it was declared by Mr. Hobson[3] (who had at one time held the other view) to be no more than another form of Hancock's signature. But its presence on a piece signed by Hancock in full, as for example on the well-known mugs with portraits of Frederick the Great,[4] is strong evidence in favour of the older view. There is little likelihood that a print would bear two signatures of one engraver, though it has been suggested that the full signature was added by Hancock when he found that his initials were being mistaken for those of Richard Holdship.[5]

Some verses which appeared in *The Gentleman's Magazine* of 20 December 1757, 'Inscribed to Mr. Josiah Holdship' and referring to the portrait of Frederick the Great, included the lines:

1 An enlarged photograph of this concealed signature is reproduced in Mr. Bernard Rackham's article on Hancock in *The Burlington Magazine*, vol. XXVI (1915), p. 155. A mug with the 'Parrot and Fruit' print in the Dyson Perrins Museum has the signature hidden on a tree branch.

2 See p. 155 and Jewitt, vol. I, p. 233, and vol. II, p. 89. Holdship is also said to have offered the Worcester recipes for porcelain, indicating the use of frit and glass and two sorts of 'soapy rock' ('the process of making porcelain ware delivered by Richard Holdship to John Heath and William Duesbury, Dec. 31st 1764'). According to Holdship, tin-ashes were used in the Worcester glaze. The Derby proprietors do not seem to have used the recipes to any considerable extent; but see pp. 136 and 137.

3 *Worcester Porcelain*, p. 74.

4 Such as Schr. No. 622.

5 A mug with the print of the *King of Prussia*, after Pesne, has the rebus of a gamecock on an outstretched hand, a perfect rebus for Hancock, besides the signature 'R. H. Worcester'. Cook, op. cit., Item 56.

A. CREAM JUG Ht. 3⅝in (9.2cm). Printed with 'L'Amour'. About 1765–70. No mark. *Schreiber Collection (649)*

B. SAUCER DISH Dia. 7in (17.7cm). About 1760. No mark. *Schreiber Collection (623)*

C. CUP AND SAUCER Cup ht. 1⅝in (4.1cm); Saucer dia. 4¾in (12cm). Printed with 'The Milkmaids'. About 1765. No mark. *Schreiber Collection (653)*

See pages 246, 250   Plate 96 WORCESTER (*Transfer-printed*)

What praise is thine, ingenious Holdship, who
On the fair porcelain the Portrait drew.

This couplet was reprinted in the *Worcester Journal* in January 1758 with this addition:

Hancock, my friend, don't grieve tho' Holdship has the praise,
'Tis yours to execute, 'tis his to wear the bays.

Such comments could have had little point had not the manager of the printing-shop taken advantage of his position to add his mark to that of the engraver; but there seems to have been some confusion between Josiah and Richard. The interpretation of the monogram as Holdship's implies the corollary that plates which bear it cannot have been engraved after 1759, when Holdship left Worcester, though they may perhaps have remained in use for some years longer, if we may assume that he did not take them all away with him.

The best qualities of 'Worcester transfer' are here illustrated by typical versions of *L'Amour* and of 'the two milkmaids', with a charming specimen of a less familiar subject (Plate 96). The touches of brushwork in delicate scrolls of black or crimson, which often frame the subjects, occur only on the earlier prints of the Hancock period, which ended with his departure in 1774. On the whole, early Worcester printed china is the best of its class ever made in England. Technical excellence is allied to fine taste in the placing of the transfers, and the modest wares deserve a place beside the best achievements in domestic pottery of Josiah Wedgwood, of which they are in a sense the counterpart.[1]

The prints were executed in lilac and (more rarely) in red, as well as in the usual brown or black. The last were referred to in the

1 An artistically unimportant small class of Worcester porcelain, which may be mentioned here, takes the form of tokens printed in black with a 'promise to pay bearer' one or two shillings, signed by W. Davis; on the reverse are the initial 'W.P.C.' (for Worcester Porcelain Company). They were evidently made on account of the prevalent baseness of the currency at the time. As pointed out by Mr. Hobson (*Worcester Porcelain*, p. 126), Binns was in error in supposing that these porcelain discs all date from 1763. They may have been made at any time after the introduction of printing until the death of Davis in 1783. There are specimens in the British Museum (Nos. V. 87 and 87A), and an illustration is in Hobson, loc. cit. Similar tokens were made at Pinxton.

D. CUP AND SAUCER Cup ht. $1\frac{7}{16}$in (4.3cm); Saucer dia. $4\frac{3}{4}$in (12.2cm). About 1760–5. Crescent marks. *British Museum (Frank Lloyd Collection 11)*

B. CREAM JUG Ht. $3\frac{3}{8}$in (8.5cm). About 1760–5. No mark. *Victoria and Albert Museum (83-1909)*

C. SAUCEBOAT L. $3\frac{7}{8}$in (9.8cm). About 1760–5. No mark. *Victoria and Albert Museum (C.631-1925)*

A. CUP AND SAUCER Cup ht. $1\frac{3}{4}$in (4.4cm); Saucer dia. $4\frac{3}{4}$in (12cm). About 1760–5. No mark. *Victoria and Albert Museum (C.1075-1924)*

See page 256

Plate 97 WORCESTER (*Earlier 'Japan' patterns*)

catalogues of 1769 as 'jet-enamelled' suggesting a special pride in that colour.[1] In an important section of the class the prints are further decorated with washes of colour, with a pleasantly soft effect, and such pieces for some reasons are often marked with crossed swords in blue. It is possible that some of this colouring-over was the work of the 'outside enameller' J. Giles, whose name appears as the purchaser at the Worcester sale of 1769 of three lots of 'jet-enamelled' porcelain.[2] Giles had in the previous year advertised as 'China and Enamel Painter' and 'Proprietor of the Worcester Porcelaine Warehouse' that he had a 'great Variety of white Goods by him', and that customers could have pieces 'painted to any pattern they shall chuse'. The Worcester factory proprietors responded to this advertisement a little later, describing their own goods and referring to 'some of their Ware . . . advertised at another Room, painted in London'. Giles's advertisement was then repeated, but with the omission of the words 'Proprietor of the Worcester Porcelain Warehouse'. To judge by the wording of his advertisements it seems certain that Giles decorated Worcester china in other ways besides colouring transfer-prints, and this work will be discussed on a later page, with other painting of the period.

A small class, usually ascribed to Worcester (but also to Liverpool), to be associated with the transfers, has Chinese figures and commonly a red ox, printed in brown outline filled in with washes of colour. A sauce-boat with this decoration at South Kensington[3] is marked with an incised cross, but differs in other respects from the 'scratched cross group' of the last chapter.

When Hancock left Worcester in 1774 he took some at least of his plates with him; in that year the Caughley factory announced that they had secured his services.[4] The Worcester printing then declined in importance, though Hancock's pupil[5] James Ross

1 See pp. 222, 224 and 246.

2 Nightingale, p. 95. The attribution to Giles of this 'colouring over' remains doubtful. Its quality is variable; the best appears over prints in light purple, perhaps intended for such addition.

3 No. C1199—1924.

4 Jewitt (vol. I, Plate 3) illustrates some of Hancock's engravings, printed from Caughley plates which have on them the 'C' and 'S' marks of that factory. See also Barrett, *Caughley and Coalport Porcelain*.

5 An earlier assistant, who left when Ross came in 1765, was Valentine Green, mezzotinter and historian of Worcester. His work on porcelain was never signed.

A. Tea Caddy Ht. 4⅔in (11.2cm). 'Queen's pattern'. About 1765–70.
Square mark. *British Museum (Frank Lloyd Collection 9)*

B. Cream Jug and Cover Ht. 5⅜in (13.6cm). 'Star' pattern. About
1765–75. Imitation Chinese character mark. *Schreiber Collection (530)*

C. Plate Dia. 7½in (19cm). 'Old Japan fan pattern'.
About 1765–75. Imitation Chinese character mark. *British
Museum (Frank Lloyd Collection 58)*

See pages 258, 272   Plate 98 WORCESTER (*Later 'Japan' patterns*)

produced some good plates. A feature of the printed wares of this later period is the gold line encircling the edges, never seen on pieces of Hancock's time.[1] Towards the close of the eighteenth century prints after Angelica Kauffmann and Bartolozzi were made by the newly introduced process of glue-bat printing.[2] These were usually in the fashionable stipple, but line-engravings continued to be used occasionally as late as 1809, the probable date of a flower-pot in the Schreiber Collection (No. 678). Groups of shells and bunches of flowers were virtually novelties in this later printing.

It was at one time believed that printing in under-glaze blue was not in use at Worcester until 1770, when a strike of blue-painters is alleged to have taken place,[3] and printing in blue that can be ascribed to an earlier date is certainly rare; but the process was presumably known at Worcester in 1759, when Holdship left, since he was able to offer it to the Derby people, though this was not till five years later. Worcester blue-printing has all the neatness characteristic of the other Worcester decoration, but is otherwise undistinguished. Designs persisted over a long period. One pattern in particular—a group of conventionalized fruit,[4] including an object resembling a pine-cone but perhaps meant for a strawberry—enjoyed the distinction of being copied, not only in printing on Caughley[5] and Lowestoft china, but in laborious brushwork on Chinese porcelain.[6] Dates are rarely found on this class, and a mug at South Kensington (Schr. No. 489) printed with flowers and a butterfly, is incised '*July 31, 1773*', and is therefore important as a document. The yellow ground on an often-mentioned blue-printed dish at South Kensington (No. 3230—1901) is most probably a later addition, like some other yellow grounds on specimens of early English porcelain.[7]

---

1 Except in the case of the overpainted transfers—perhaps further evidence of outside decoration.

2 See p. 7.

3 Binns (1st edition), p. 87. The statement was, however, omitted without explanation from the second edition.

4 Schr. Nos. 487 and 488.

5 The suggestion that Worcester china was printed in blue at Caughley is discussed on p. 292.

6 A specimen of this kind (No. C594—1924) may be seen at South Kensington with the other Chinese porcelain copied from European models.

7 Compare p. 206.

HEXAGONAL VASE Ht. 11½in (28.4cm). 'Old Dragon Japan' pattern. About 1770. No mark. *British Museum (Frank Lloyd Collection 76)*

See pages 262, 272   Plate 99 WORCESTER

Among the most characteristic of all Worcester inventions were the so-called Japan patterns, which continued to be made from the earliest days until well into the nineteenth century. The favourite Kakiemon 'partridge' and other designs, also found on Bow and Chelsea, were perhaps taken at second-hand from Meissen versions, but are fairly close copies as a rule. They long remained in use. Most of the versions of Oriental designs, however, deserve to rank as creations of the English painters. It is unnecessary to enumerate here the very many designs freely adapted from both Chinese and Japanese sources: they are particularly well represented in the Frank Lloyd Collection at the British Museum. Three typical designs in use at an early period may be selected for mention. A figure-subject evidently adapted from the so-called 'Mandarin porcelain' shows ladies at a table or otherwise employed, in panels set in a ground often diapered in red or gold.[1] A rich clear turquoise adds greatly to the charm of these pieces. Plate 97 shows two of these subjects. A pattern adapted from the *famille verte*, with a kylin in the middle, and border panels containing rocks, flowering plants and mythical animals,[2] is often known as the 'Bishop Sumner pattern', but the only bishops of that name living in the second half of the eighteenth century were born as late as 1780 and 1790. This and kindred designs continued to be made until the end of the century and even later, in coarsened quality with rougher drawing. A simpler and very charming type, only faintly recalling the Chinese style and virtually a Worcester invention, is marked by panels of springing foliage stylised with much grace and vivacity. A tea-service in the Lloyd Collection (No. 11: Plate 97D) is of this kind, and the same qualities are seen in many red-and-green Japan patterns, such as that on a cup and saucer with powdered-blue ground in the Schreiber Collection (No. 518). We may ascribe these pieces chiefly to the second decade of the factory: the simple decoration on a coffee-cup in the Frank Lloyd Collection (No. 73), which is related to these, includes the inscription '*Nancy Squier 1764*'. The cup and saucer figured in Plate 97A, with a Chinese lady surrounded by feathery scrolls, was

1 Nos. 24 to 26 in the Lloyd Collection.
2 No. 2 in the Lloyd Collection.

A. PLATE Dia. 8⅞in (22.5cm). Pink scale border. Giles
decoration. About 1770. No mark. *Schreiber Collection (541)*

B. PLATE Dia. 9in (22.8cm). 'Lady Mary Wortley Montague' Service.
Giles decoration. About 1770. Square mark. *British Museum (Frank
Lloyd Collection 268)*

See pages 244, 262, 264

Plate 100 WORCESTER

perhaps copied from a Chinese version of a Meissen decoration, and is typical in its naïve combination of Eastern and Western motives.

Of Chinese derivation again is a singular type found only at Worcester amongst the English factories, with Chinese and other subjects 'pencilled' in black (Plate 95C). These pieces were doubtless inspired by the Chinese porcelain 'painted in ink', as a Chinese list describes it,[1] often with copies of European prints. A whole series of Chinese pieces painted in this way with the goddess Juno is in the Victoria and Albert Museum. The familiar subject of a Chinaman riding on an ox is often copied on Worcester (Schr. No. 511); and a tray in the Museum collection at South Kensington shows a European floral design rendered at second-hand through the medium of a Chinese imitation. Mr. Hobson has pointed out a saucer in the Dyson Perrins Museum, with a gentleman and a lady fishing, which was certainly copied in this way from a Chinese version of a European print. A saucer at South Kensington (Plate 95B) is painted in lilac with Chinese figures in the same style.

A design in oriental style long popular at Worcester and found also on Lowestoft and Derby consists of vertical or spirally curved panels alternately red on white and white on blue, with gilding (Plate 98A). This is stated by Mr. Hobson to be derived from a Chinese design, but the only Chinese examples met with appear to be themselves copies of this pattern. It was variously known as the 'whorl', 'spiral', 'catherine-wheel' and 'Queen's pattern'.[2] The so-called 'Sir Joshua Reynolds' pattern'[3] with a pheasant on a turquoise-blue rock is another free adaptation of a Japanese design.

---

1 Compare the *List of Decorations used on Imperial porcelain in the reign of Yung Chêng*, No. 40.

2 It is so named in the Sale Catalogue of 1769. This 'Queen's Pattern' should be clearly distinguished from the 'Queen Charlotte's Pattern' or 'Royal Lily', chosen in 1788 at a visit to the factory by George III and his Queen. This later pattern, also of Chinese derivation, is in blue with gilding, with radial panels of conventional floral designs in outline. Herbert Allen No. 323 is an example. It was also used at Caughley and is still made at Worcester.

3 No. 96 in the Frank Lloyd Collection; No. 537 in the Schreiber Collection is an especially charming plate.

Many of these inventions, however, did not reach their fullest splendour until the next period, which may be said to begin with the arrival of hands from Chelsea about 1768. It is likely enough that workmen may have migrated during one of the earlier periods of inactivity at Chelsea, and the 'painter of the Lord Sandys mug' has even been claimed as a Chelsea man on account of the similarity between his flowers and those on some 'raised-anchor' dishes. This resemblance seems rather to be due to their common Meissen model. As evidence of the later migration, however, we have not only Worcester tradition (Binns mentions the names of Willmann, Dontil,[1] Duvivier, Mills and Dyer[2]), but the style of at least one Chelsea painter can be recognised on the actual porcelain. Moreover, the advertisement of 1768, already mentioned in connection with Giles, stated that the proprietors had 'engaged the best painters from Chelsea, etc.', adding that 'any orders will be executed in the highest taste and much cheaper than can be afforded by any painters in London'.

Two public auction sales were held in 1769, following the Chelsea fashion. Of the first, held by Burnsall, no catalogue has survived, but the announcement in *The Public Advertiser*[3] makes clear the ambitious nature of the china offered: 'Table and Desert Services, Leaves, Compotiers, Tea and Coffee Equipages, Baskets, Vases, Perfume Pots, Jars, Beakers, Cisterns, Tureens, Porringers, Bowls, &c., in the beautiful colours of Mazarine Blue and Gold, Sky-blue, Pea-green, French-green, Sea-green, Purple, Scarlet and other Variety of Colours, richly decorated with chased and burnished Gold; and many other Articles both useful and ornamental. The whole enamelled in the highest Taste, and curiously painted in Figures, Birds, Landscapes, Flowers, Fruits, &c.' Seven months later another sale, apparently of less pretentious wares, was held by Christie; extracts from the Catalogue of this with prices and purchasers were published by

---

1 The suggestion recently put forward that this painter gave his name to the 'dontil' or scalloped gilt border on porcelain can scarcely be accepted. The French *dentelle* is more probably the source of the word.

2 Compare p. 86.

3 5 May 1769. Nightingale, p. lxxviii.

Nightingale.[1] Many items may be recognised amongst the porcelain surviving.

The coloured grounds perfected at Worcester at this time rank among the best ever made.[2] The Chelsea dark blue was never equalled, it is true, and the evenness and richness of the Sèvres grounds were in most cases beyond the reach of the English factory. The Chelsea claret-colour was sometimes obtained successfully, and the probability that the workman responsible for this colour at Chelsea migrated to Worcester and not to Derby on the closing of Sprimont's factory has already been mentioned.[3] It was not very much used, however, and was probably uncertain and costly. But the Worcester turquoise and lavender and above all the pea-green (the 'apple green' of the trade) were thoroughly mastered. Moreover, the Worcester method of breaking up the ground-colour by reticulation, fishscale pattern and diapers, such as the tiny circles resembling shagreen and called by the Chinese 'fish-roe', may almost be regarded as an invention, though it was probably suggested by the *Mosaïk* patterns of Meissen and Berlin, where they were especially popular in the 1760s. That pink-scale was used as early as 1761 is shown by a dated specimen in the Dyson Perrins Collection,[4] and it is stated on the authority of a family tradition that a tea-caddy[5] with scale-blue dates from 1763. The earlier specimens of this last and most famous ground show a bold pattern, outlined with a brush on the powdered (underglaze) colour, which was of the usual dark indigo tone. Later a smaller, less definite and obtrusive scale was produced by wiping away the lights. Yellow[6] and brick-red-scale[7] were used in the same way. Worcester gilding admirably continued the Chelsea tradition, and has never been surpassed. The slightly dull gold was applied with

1 p. 94.
2 It should be remembered that at Meissen every ground colour subsequently used in the course of the century was employed, at least tentatively, before 1750, and many were perfected by 1727. Even the pink of the *famille rose* was used by Böttger *before* it appeared on Chinese porcelain. But soft-paste was capable of giving greater depth and richness to the colours.
3 p. 148.
4 Hobson, *Worcester Porcelain*, Plate 59, fig. 2.
5 Hobson, op. cit., p. 114.
6 Frank Lloyd No. 148, and Victoria and Albert Museum C1268—1919. Also Barrett, op. cit., Plate 52A.
7 Frank Lloyd No. 29.

A. TANKARD Ht. 6in (15.2cm). Pea-green ground. About 1770. No mark. *British Museum (Frank Lloyd Collection 231)*

B. TANKARD Ht. 3⅓in (8.5cm). Pink scale border. Giles decoration. About 1770. No mark. *British Museum (Frank Lloyd Collection 342)*

C. PLATE Dia. 8⅞in (22.5cm). Giles decoration. About 1770. No mark. *Schreiber Collection (542)*

See pages 262, 264, 266

Plate 101 WORCESTER

the greatest delicacy in scrolls, foliage and lace-work in *rococo* style, whilst bolder masses were chased with a metal point in the Sèvres and Chelsea manner. Plates 99, 102 and 105 show some excellent specimens.

The most famous and costly of all Worcester china is that painted in panels set in the coloured grounds with the so-called exotic birds, fantastically coloured, and originally an invention of the Meissen factory (Colour Plate C). The classification of the several painters' work in this style is one of the most interesting studies open to the lover of Worcester china.

One of the most distinctive of these styles of bird-painting is that associated with an artist who came from Plymouth and Bristol, the 'Mons. Soqui' of Cookworthy's biographer Harrison, described by Prideaux as an 'excellent painter and enameller ... from Sèvres'.[1] His manner is in some respects an imitation of that of the Sèvres bird-painter Evans, and is usually marked by rather strong colour in thickly stippled brushwork, and by the introduction of a faintly coloured distant landscape with shadowy trees. Many Worcester pieces by him are in the British Museum and at South Kensington,[2] though the Schreiber Collection includes none. The plate from Mr. Allen's collection (Plate 103A) is a typical example.

Another style (Plate 101A)[3] shows a special fondness for rendering the plumage of his birds by dots, and their eyes by well-defined circles. The manner suggests facility, and is not free from hardness. The stiff S-shaped curves of the outlines of the birds and a frequent use of red foliage make the style easy to recognise. Quite distinct again are the birds (Plate 102A) painted by an artist using a smudgy brush-stroke, largely avoiding the dots of most of the painters. His foliage usually has a blunt spikiness, easily recognised.[4] Still another hand was, perhaps, responsible for the

1 The name is also given as Saqui and Lequoi. His style was first identified by Mr. Bernard Rackham. See *The Burlington Magazine*, vol. XXV (1914), p. 104. For his work at Plymouth and Bristol, see p. 346 below.

2 Such as a plate at South Kensington and No. 233 (a vase) in the Frank Lloyd Collection.

3 See also Schr. Nos. 552 and 554, and Frank Lloyd No. 252. This painter's style was closely copied at Liverpool (see p. 298), and the birds on Longton Hall porcelain (Plate 72) were perhaps painted at an earlier date from the same engraved copies.

4 See also Schr. No. 550 and Frank Lloyd No. 265. Also a teapot at Luton Hoo (Barrett, op. cit., Plate 52A).

A. Cup and Saucer Cup ht. $1\frac{9}{10}$in (4.8cm); Saucer dia. $4\frac{1}{2}$in (11.4cm).
'Duchess of Kent' Service. 'Gros-bleu' ground. About 1770–5. No mark.
British Museum (Frank Lloyd Collection 295)

B. Plate Dia. $8\frac{1}{10}$in (20.5cm). Moulded border. About 1775. No mark. *British Museum (Frank Lloyd Collection 113)*

See pages 262, 264   Plate 102 WORCESTER

slender-legged, plump birds often confused with those of the supposed Soqui, but depicted in landscapes more clearly indicated, with trees like billowy clouds (Plate 102B). The differences between the styles will be made clear by a comparison of the two specimens illustrated here in Plates 102B and 103A, both probably painted from the same copy. The practice by which several painters freely copied the same subject seriously complicates the problem of identification.

Reference has already been several times made to the advertisements and work of James Giles, the independent enameller of Soho and Kentish Town.[1] Since the first edition of this book was published it has become clear[2] that Giles's work was not at all the unskilled clobbering it was formerly supposed to be, but included painting equal to the best factory work. Some plates given to the Victoria and Albert Museum by Mrs. Dora Grubbe, a descendant of Giles, have confirmed as the productions of Giles's workshop a number of familiar types of Worcester and other porcelain. Besides the coloured-over transfers and the Bow painting marked with the anchor and dagger, several classes of work may now be ascribed to Giles, who evidently employed several artists and may not have been himself a painter at all (Plate 92).

The first and most prolific of these was the artist often known to collectors of Worcester as 'the Chelsea painter'. His style is marked by bold, fluent brush-strokes. He painted birds, fruit, and flowers and occasionally figures (Plates 100 and 101). One of the Grubbe plates is practically identical with that here figured in Plate 100A. His work on Chelsea, Worcester and imported Chinese porcelain may well be studied in the Schreiber Collection at South Kensington. His birds are always drawn with a peculiar freedom and verve. The heart-shaped dishes, No. 183 (Chelsea) and No. 540 (Worcester), are comparable pieces, though the former is more carefully finished.[3] The differences in colouring might of course be

1 pp. 66, 124.
2 W. B. Honey, 'The work of James Giles', in *Transactions E.C.C.*, V (1937), p. 7. Also H. Rissik Marshall, 'James Giles, Enameller', in *Transactions E.C.C.*, vol. 3, part I, pp. 1–9.
3 Some Chelsea dishes with mazarine ground in the Emily Thomson Bequest show birds which come near to his Worcester work. For his Chelsea work, see p. 70.

B. TEAPOT Ht. 5¼in (13.3cm). Powdered Blue ground. About 1770–5. No mark. *Schreiber Collection (547)*

A. PLATE Dia. 7¾in (19.7cm). 'Gros-bleu' ground. About 1770–5. Crescent mark. *Victoria and Albert Museum (C.426-1935)*

See pages 262, 264, 268   Plate 103 WORCESTER

accounted for by the differences of glaze and the local sources of the enamel colours. The cut fruits and fig with calyx in this painter's work have been noted by Mr. Hobson, but as these were doubtless copied from a pattern-piece (perhaps of Meissen porcelain) they would not be his special property. On the two heart-shaped dishes (Schr. No. 540) they are combined with birds, and again on No. 543 and other plates in the Schreiber Collection they are seen in company with his characteristic flowers. It was evidently his practice to draw with a full brush, and a peculiar 'wetness' is always noticeable in his work. His flowers are seen especially often on services of the *feuille de choux* and 'hop-trellis' patterns copied from Sèvres.[1] This 'Chelsea painter's' figures appear on a curious pattern-plate in the Frank Lloyd Collection (No. 340), painted with specimens of three designs. One of the Grubbe plates (Plate 92B) is painted with an unusual figure-subject in crimson monochrome but is obviously by the same hand. Five other figure-pieces in the Lloyd Collection (Nos. 341 to 345) are by this artist and show his free and attractive style. One of these, a mug (No. 341: Plate 101B), is also an example of 'peacock-scale' in pink; it is clear that Giles had a considerable mastery of coloured grounds and in 1770 advertised wares in 'Mazarine and Sky-blue and Gold curiously enamelled in Figures, Birds, Flowers, etc.' One of the other patterns on the specimen plate is a gadroon- or petal-design in plain gold lines which is virtually a Worcester invention, though perhaps ultimately of Japanese derivation, as has been asserted.

The 'painter of the dishevelled birds' has already been mentioned in connection with Bow and Longton Hall porcelain.[2] The fact that the style is found also on Plymouth and Worcester china as well has suggested that the work may have been that of painters at Giles's work-shop in London decorating porcelain of different makes bought in the white.[3] Against this view is the unlikelihood of white Plymouth porcelain being available in this

[1] Frank Lloyd No. 183 (a deep plate) and Schreiber No. 544 (a plate) are examples.

[2] pp. 124 and 342.

[3] Mr. Honey first made this suggestion in an article in *The Morning Post* and found that Mr. Wallace Elliot had independently come to the same conclusion.

C. Figure of a Gardener Ht. 10½in (26.7cm). About 1770–5. No mark. *Trustees of the Dyson Perrins Museum, Worcester*

B. Hexagonal Vase Ht. 16½in (41.9cm). About 1770–5. Mark 'To' impressed. *Schreiber Collection (571)*

A. Figure of a Turk Ht. 5in (12.7cm). About 1770. No mark. *Trustees of the Dyson Perrins Museum, Worcester*

See pages 274, 276

Plate 104 WORCESTER

way, to any extent, though white Plymouth shell-salts, such as are also found decorated by him, have survived (see Plate 125). It is noteworthy that the gilding on some pieces with his painting (such as the teapot figured in Plate 103B) is rather crude, and the finish of some of them (such as a basket-work dish, Schr. No. 546) often markedly inferior to the usual Worcester work of the period. A plate by him in the Herbert Allen Collection (No. 262) is on the other hand beautifully finished. Good gilding in the Worcester factory style is also seen on some pieces he painted marked with the gold anchor and usually regarded as Chelsea. There is a cup and saucer of this kind in the British Museum (others are in the London Museum) with a pale pinkish 'claret' ground of very poor quality: it is of unmistakable Worcester paste. A pair of crocus-pots (Frank Lloyd No. 250) painted by him has a rough scale-blue ground. On the whole, therefore, the evidence seems to point to the 'painter of the dishevelled birds' as a Giles' man. His hand has also been recognised in much of the characteristic painting in black washed over in clear green on Chelsea[1] as well as Worcester porcelain; one of the Grubbe plates (Plate 92A, by the hand of the 'Chelsea painter') was decorated in this style. It is found also on Chinese porcelain which was more probably decorated in an independent enameller's workshop than in a factory.

Also seen on anchor-and-dagger marked Bow[2] is the work of the painter Jeffrey Hamet O'Neale, who occasionally signed his work on Worcester porcelain. O'Neale's address in an exhibition catalogue of 1765 was 'at the China shop, in Oxford Road', but it is uncertain how much of his work was done independently. The gilt borders on much of his work resemble those on pieces we have attributed to Giles. O'Neale's work may be crude, but its *naïveté* gives it a certain charm. The Frank Lloyd Collection includes a set of three vases (Nos. 347 and 348) as well as an important unsigned vase (No. 349). O'Neale's favourite subjects on Worcester were hunting-scenes in the style of Wouwermans (with delightful impossible horses) (Plate 107B), unconsciously humorous Classical scenes, fables (Plate 107C) and landscapes, identifiable by a red-

---

1 p. 66 and Plate 31B, which is by the 'dishevelled bird painter' and not by the 'Chelsea painter'.

2 See pp. 42 and 125.

C. Cup and Saucer Cup ht. 2¾in (7cm); Saucer dia. 5¾in (14.6cm). Yellow ground. About 1775. No mark. *Schreiber Collection* (563)

B, Vase Ht. 6in (15.2cm). 'Gros-bleu' ground. About 1775. Script 'W' mark. *Schreiber Collection* (561)

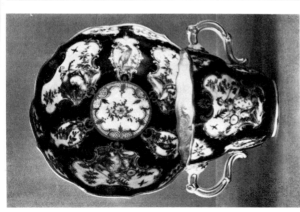

A. Cup and Saucer Cup ht. 2¾in (7cm); Saucer dia. 5⅜in (13.6cm). Blue-scale ground. About 1775. Square mark. *Schreiber Collection* (538)

brown rock in the foreground first pointed out by Mr. Hobson.

Another figure-painter thought to have come from Chelsea is represented in the Lloyd Collection by a coffee-pot (No. 354) with a Pillement Chinaman amid *rococo* scrolls, and a cup and saucer (No. 355), the former with a bold scale-blue ground of the early type. Another cup and saucer is in the Schreiber Collection (No. 538: Plate 105 A). It is tempting to see in this work the hand of the painter who decorated the Thomson tea-service at South Kensington (Plate 29A), though slight differences make the identification not quite certain. As has been said in the chapter on Chelsea, this painting has been wrongly ascribed to the miniaturist John Donaldson, whose style on Worcester china is known from signed pieces (Plate 108).[1] Redgrave[2] stated that he 'painted some vases sent to him in London from the Worcester china-works', and the more elaborate figure-pieces, such as that on a large hexagonal vase in the Lloyd Collection (No. 353), are perhaps his. Mr. Hobson has pointed out a similarity in the features to those in an engraving by J. Finlayson entitled 'The Newsmongers after Donaldson'. The fact that the birds and flowers on this vase are not by the same hand as the figures, also supports this attribution, since vases with blank panels are known,[3] and we may conjecture that these were sent from the factory to London for the addition of figure-painting that was never done.[4]

The hand of a Bow (and perhaps also Chelsea) painter is suggested by some Worcester versions of the Kakiemon 'partridge pattern'. Several specimens with this design brought together by the late Robert Drane[5] included an oviform Worcester vase and an octagonal plate described as Chelsea, on both of which a partridge is rendered with a peculiar humped back, probably indicating the same hand. But the possibility of a common Meissen example

---

1 Signed specimens are illustrated in Hobson, *Worcester Porcelain*, Plate 80. Also in Barrett, op. cit., Plates 77 and 78. Several unsigned examples are in the Marshall Collection at the Ashmolean Museum.

2 *Dictionary of Artists of the English School.*

3 See R. L. Hobson, *Worcester Porcelain*, p. 20. The attribution to Donaldson is not universally accepted.

4 For a supposed painter named Fogo, see W. B. Honey, 'Historic fallacies', in *Transactions E.C.C.*, X (1947).

5 Hobson, *Worcester Porcelain*, Plate 30 and p. 60, where the Worcester specimen is erroneously described as Bow.

A. TEAPOT AND STAND Ht. 4⅞in (12.4cm). Stand moulded with
'Blind Earl' Pattern. About 1775. No mark. *Schreiber Collection*
(582)

EAPOT Ht. 5⅞in (14.9cm). About 1775–80. Square mark. *Schreiber Collection (604)*

REAM JUG Ht. 5¼in (13.3cm). Gold decoration. In Sèvres style. About 1775–80.
sen Crossed swords mark. *Victoria and Albert Museum (3268-1901)*

See page 278   Plate 106 WORCESTER

should be borne in mind. The same feature is seen on Bow versions in Mr. Broderip's gift at South Kensington.

Amongst the painters of the beautiful and unmistakable[1] 'Worcester Japan' patterns of this period should be noted the master of the fretful-looking birds who appear in the midst of tufty red and green willows and scattered strange rocks and 'jewels'. These patterns—the 'wheat-sheaf', 'crab', 'pheasant' and the rest, painted chiefly in red, green and gold, and full of the most fanciful detail—are actually far removed in both spirit and design from their Japanese examples. The 'old mosaick Japan' and 'fine old Japan fan pattern' (all these names are from the Sale Catalogue of 1769) are, on the contrary, fairly exact renderings of the 'brocaded Imari'. The 'Japan star-pattern' is more likely to be the chrysanthemum design (such as Frank Lloyd No. 60 or Plate 98B) than that with slight conventional stars, much less Japanese, to which the name is attached by Mr. Hobson. The 'fan pattern' was probably that with radiating panels (Plate 98C). Of the more elaborate of these inventions, is illustrated (Plate 99) a superb hexagonal vase from the Frank Lloyd Collection (No. 76). This shows an S-shaped object suspended from a scintillating tree, which may be presumed to be the 'fine old rich dragon pattern' of a specimen in the Catalogue, where it is described as having a 'bleu Celeste' border (doubtless the clear turquoise often found with these designs). Such hexagonal vases are among the most highly prized specimens dating from this period. They seem to have given trouble in the making and it is not unusual to find them collapsed at the shoulder or otherwise misshapen.[2] It has often been remarked that some lack of plastic quality in the Worcester paste forbade the more elaborately modelled pieces, figures and the like, such as were made elsewhere, though the practical bent of the Worcester management alone would perhaps account for the abstention. The mishaps of the hexagonal vases, however, suggest that the view approaches the truth. The wandering repairer 'Tebo'[3] was at

1 But exact copies of some were made at Derby, though rarely. See p. 152. The soft glaze of the copies and the thicker gilding reveal their Derby origin.

2 An example of the kind, printed and coloured over, is in the Schreiber Collection (No. 668).

3 See pp. 104 and 340 for a discussion of his identity and of his work at Bow, Plymouth and Bristol.

C. PLATE Dia. 7¼in (19cm). Painted by O'Neale with the fable of 'The Fox and the Goat'. About 1770. Square mark. *Victoria and Albert Museum (C.19-1966)*

B. VASE Ht. 12¾in (32.4cm). Painted by Jefferies Hamet O'Neale. About 1770. Square mark. *British Museum*

A. SPORTSMAN AND COMPANION Ht. 7in (17.7cm). About 1770. No mark. *Ashmolean Museum, Oxford (H. R. Marshall Collection)*

See pages 268, 276

Plate 107 WORCESTER

Worcester at some time in the 1770s, and the *rococo* 'frill vases' which are the most fancifully modelled of any Worcester products were apparently made on his initiative; there are specimens with his mark in the Schreiber (No. 571: Plate 104B) and Frank Lloyd Collections (No. 125). They are very similar to those in Bristol china, presumably also by 'Mr. Tebo'. One may guess, too, that the sweetmeat stands in the form of shells and rocks were his work, and perhaps the basket-work dishes with vine-leaves in relief,[1] again identical with Bristol specimens. More classical in feeling and perhaps rather later in date are the baluster- and urn-shaped vases with festoons of applied white flowers, such as Frank Lloyd No. 126 and A: they were perhaps copies of Meissen pieces.[2] Those just cited are painted with flowers *en camaieu* in the 'dry' blue quite peculiar to Worcester, a very brilliant colour with a curiously matt surface.

In spite of the presumed technical difficulties, a few figures were undoubtedly made at Worcester, and their identity was finally established by an analysis by Mr. Herbert Eccles which proved the presence of magnesia from soapstone in quantity consistent with Worcester.[3] It had long been known from an advertisement of December 1769,[4] and from the diary for August 1771 of Mrs. Lybbe Powys, that figures were actually made at Worcester.[5] The crescent-marked figures, of which a large number exist, were held to be Worcester productions in spite of their obvious resemblance to late Bow specimens.[6] Another diarist, Captain Joseph Roche, R.N., recorded his visit to Worcester on 21 August 1771, and noted 'they make very fine figures or ornamental china, it being done much better and also cheaper at Derby: here they are obliged to mould it, but there it is cast, which is ten times as expedicious'.

1 Frank Lloyd No. 137 and Schreiber No. 570.

2 Also Barrett, op. cit., Plate 84.

3 See an article by Mr. William King in *The Connoisseur*, June 1923; also Wallace Elliot, in *Transactions E.C.C.*, II (1934), p. 29.

4 In *The Public Advertiser*, December 1769, 'Jars, and Beakers, Figures ... Bowls, Basins and other articles'.

5 Though not before 1766. A letter of 30 August in that year, discovered by the late Mr. Dyson Perrins, contains the following passage: 'The great improvement made in the Worcester manufactory of china would have afforded you great pleasure ... They have not yet debased it by making vile attempts at human figures, but stick to the useful.'

6 Analysis had also proved them phosphatic; compare p. 125.

SET OF VASES Ht. of Centre Vase 18½in (47cm); Side Vases 13in (32cm); Right-hand Vase signed 'J.D.' for the painter *John Donaldson*. About 1770. Square mark. *Trustees of the Dyson Perrins Museum, Worcester*

See page 270

Plate 108 WORCESTER

Analysis has provided only the last piece of evidence to a case which might well have been considered proved on style alone; the characteristic Worcester dry blue, the close-fitting glaze and the unmistakable gilding are all present on the identified (coloured) specimens.

Up to the present the Worcester figures which have been recognised are a *Gardener* (Plate 104C) and his companion, two *Turks* (Plate 104A), a *Sportsman and his Companion* (both white and coloured examples exist) (Plate 107A), and a white figure of a *Nurse and Child*, similar to, but smaller than, the well-known Chelsea figure.[1] Additionally, there are a pair of Kingfishers,[2] a candelabra with two Canaries in the Dyson Perrins Museum, some *Pigeon Tureens*, and a *Double-dove Tureen*. Other tureens were made in the form of *Cauliflowers*, some of which bear black prints of moths.[3] Figures were presumably made during the whole period between at least the two dates quoted, so that others may yet remain unidentified in English cabinets. A class of what are believed to be late Longton Hall figures[4] has been found on analysis to contain soapstone and has been on that account claimed as Worcester; but the quantity of magnesia present is so much less than in normal Worcester (about 2 per cent instead of 13 per cent) that the Longton Hall attribution is now generally accepted. Mrs. Powys gave a description of the modelling of the 'little roses, handles, twists and flowers' which were used on the china baskets she saw made at Worcester. 'Pierced baskets with green handles' are also mentioned in the Catalogue of 1769: a specimen in the Schreiber Collection (No. 545) is painted inside with fruit by the 'Chelsea painter'. Three different types of these baskets are in the Frank Lloyd Collection (Nos. 122 to 124): all have applied flowers of precisely the same character as those on the figures—a final proof of the origin of the latter, if one were needed.

1 See p. 26. It has recently (1970) been suggested that this figure might be a Liverpool production.
2 Marshall, *Coloured Worcester Porcelain of the 18th Century*, Plate 20, Item 384.
3 Barrett, op. cit., Plates 86A and 87A.
4 See p. 196.

A. COFFEE CAN Ht. 3½in (8.9cm).
About 1780. No mark. *Schreiber
Collection (592)*

B. COFFEE CAN Ht. 3¼in (8.2cm).
About 1780. No mark. *Victoria and
Albert Museum (C.456-1935)*

C. PLATE Dia. 9in (22.8cm). Probably Giles' decoration. About 1770–5. *Ex.
Alfred E. Hutton Collection*

See page 279　　　　　　　　　　Plate 109 WORCESTER

Though Worcester was to some extent independent of the changes in metropolitan fashions, the Meissen and Chinese styles of its first twenty-five years gradually gave place to the Neo-Classical and a modified and much anglicised *Louis Seize*. Towards 1780 we find the Sèvres green-and-gold 'mignonette' (Plate 106A), hop-standard and trellis styles becoming popular, and shapes tending towards fluting and severity. The fluted egg-shaped vase with small stopper is a characteristic Worcester shape exemplifying the change of taste. The gold-striped ground in Chelsea-Derby style was another rather belated manifestation. A rather dry manner of flower-painting, imitated from Sèvres, with festoons and clusters commonly without the usual bunch of stems of the older style, now began to be preferred. The hand responsible for some of the best 'French flowers' (Plate 105B and C) was also the painter of the monochrome sprays in 'dry blue', as on an unusual teapot in the Schreiber Collection (No. 606). A brilliant *bleu-de-roi* enamel, rather similar to the contemporary 'Smith's blue' of Derby, appeared at this time. It is perhaps best displayed in the teapot in the Schreiber Collection figured in Plate 106B, embellished with fine gilding, and perhaps Giles's decoration. Pieces decorated in gilding alone are not uncommon (Plate 106C) and are also possibly Giles. The familiar turquoise husk-pattern is distinctly of this later style, though we find it on pieces with blue grounds and painting of birds suggesting a continuance of the earlier manner.

To this last phase of the Wall period belong the numerous patterns with urns in monochrome, groups of fruit, and landscapes with hard bright clouds.[1] The fruits and landscapes are very distinctive, but so common that it is scarcely possible that they are the work of a single hand, though the style and certain patterns are alike in all. The often-remarked spotting on the fruits is a feature, but two varieties may be distinguished: the pale summarily rendered specimens, as on a teapot in the Schreiber Collection (No. 590), and the rather unpleasant objects in over-strong colouring on a moulded jug in the same collection (No. 598). The commoner landscapes in spite of their rather harsh colours are often charming, though not to be compared with the earlier Worcester work in the

1 The Lord Henry Thynne Service (Frank Lloyd No. 203) and a tea-service in the Allen Collection (No. 218) are typical.

same field. But the hand of an exceptionally gifted painter may be detected in a mug (Plate 109A) in the Schreiber Collection (No. 592), at a glance seeming like many others, but with a decidedly more sensitive touch. Mr. Alfred Hutton had a set of rare and charming plates (Plate 109C), which are unusual at this date in the scale of the landscapes. The mug with a delicately painted figure-subject, also shown in Plate 109, is of about the same date as these. A strange-looking pattern apparently of this period is a naturalistic representation of festooned blue drapery with a gilt fringe. A sugar-basin in Mr. Allen's collection (No. 222) has this decoration.

After the change of management on the death of William Davis in 1783,[1] the good taste which had governed the work began to give place to pretentiousness and an elaborate pomposity. It may fairly be said that for the next quarter of a century Worcester fell definitely behind the Derby factory, which was then creating a distinctive style in the decoration of table-wares. Doubtless the stock patterns were repeated as long as the older painters continued at work and the demand lasted,[2] but by the end of the century dull Classical forms were the rule, and naturalistic flower-painting followed the fashion set by the Derby factory. The less pretentious of Flight's productions, however, shared much of the charm of the contemporary Derby, in spite of a less attractive material. Simple sprigs in colours or in blue and gold were characteristic. Pearled and beaded borders, gadrooned edges and lavish gilding were characteristic of the 'dress-services' ordered by distinguish patrons in the early nineteenth century and detailed with such pride by Binns. A Derby influence may also be detected in the gilt palmette and formal patterns which at the beginning of the nineteenth century were fashionable borders for the minutely rendered landscapes and figure-pieces.

1 The marks of the Flight and later periods are given on pp. 394–5.
2 The lowest stage of the Kakiemon partridge pattern is seen in certain specimens marked with the incised 'B' of Barr. In these roughly painted pieces the gilding is replaced by a greenish-brown enamel. A somewhat similar colour was, however, occasionally used in the same way in the earlier period.

To this period must also be allocated those table-wares printed in a strong violet-blue and marked with either a shaded crescent or disguised numeral mark.[1] These late, blue-printed wares possess a strong physical resemblance to Caughley. They are printed with subjects some of which appear also on porcelain from the Salopian factory, the best-known being the so-called *Fisherman* pattern, though there are several others,[2] some of which have added brushwork in a lighter underglaze blue.

James Pennington was a figure-painter who worked at Worcester for a long period at the end of the eighteenth and beginning of the nineteenth centuries. A beaker painted with a boy holding a mug of beer, in Mr. Herbert Allen's collection (No. 317), has been attributed to Pennington, but the figure of Hope on the service made for the Duke of Clarence in 1792 is better authenticated: specimens are at South Kensington[3] and in the British Museum (No. V. 84). The portraits of George III and Queen Charlotte on a service in the Worcester Corporation Museum are also said to be his work,[4] as well as that of George III on a jug embellished with oak sprays and roses (Plate 111A).

The most celebrated of these later figure-painters was Thomas Baxter (*b.* 1782, *d.* 1821), the son of a china-decorator who had a workshop at No. 1 Goldsmith Street, Gough Square, Fleet Street.[5] Baxter is known to have worked for Flight and Barr between 1814 and 1816; he then moved to Swansea;[6] returning to Worcester in 1819, and working for both factories until his death in 1821. Baxter was very versatile, and his work may be admired for its skilful technique. Three very important signed works by him[7] at South Kensington are dated 1802, 1808 and 1809. None is

1 See mark, No. 4, p. 394.

2 For other examples see Godden, *Caughley and Worcester Porcelain 1775–1800*, and Sandon, op. cit., pp. 59–65.

3 Barrett, op. cit., Plate 94.

4 Hobson, *Worcester Porcelain*, Plate 103.

5 A water-colour of his father's china-decorating studio, painted by Baxter in 1810, is in the Victoria and Albert Museum (Room 140); it is reproduced in Dillon, *Porcelain*, Plate 47, and in *Apollo*, XXV (1937), p. 92; and Barrett, *Caughley and Coalport Porcelain*, 1951, fig. 81. See also p. 326.

6 See p. 318 for his work at Swansea.

7 These are part of an important gift by Mr. Herbert Eccles, which includes a number of very good Baxters, 'authenticated' by a nephew of Humphrey Chamberlain. Some work of his pupils also included is interesting for comparison.

A. Jug Ht. 5½in (14cm). Painted by Humphrey Chamberlain. About 1810. Mark '59' and 'Chamberlains Worcester' in red, 'Setter and Black Grouse' in red. *Victoria and Albert Museum (C.534-1935)*

B. Beaker Ht. 4¼in (10.8cm). Painted by Thomas Baxter. About 1820. Mark 'Chamberlains Worcester' in gold. Inscribed 'Beauty', 'Sappho and Europa'. *Victoria and Albert Museum (C.539-1935)*

C. Jug Ht. 5in (12.7cm). Painted with a view of *Worcester Cathedral*. About 1810. Inscribed 'Worcester' in red. *Victoria and Albert Museum (C.533-1935)*

See pages 282, 284   Plate 110 WORCESTER (*Chamberlain's Porcelain*)

marked, but all seem to be of Chamberlain's or Caughley porcelain, and were probably decorated in London. The earliest, a vase and cover, is painted in brownish monochrome with a scene from *Hamlet*,[1] and provides a document for the identification of many pieces of his earlier figure work. The other dated specimens are plates painted with apple-blossom and with shells. His work is always distinctly stippled or in short curved brush-strokes; the earlier specimens are more strongly coloured than the elegant later pieces, generally of figures, which are in fact sometimes in grey monochrome, like the beaker illustrated in Plate 110B. Baxter's stippled background seems to distinguish his shell-pieces from those usually attributed to John Barker. The evidence for this artist is of the slightest (amounting to a few words of Binns'),[2] and we do not know whether he worked for Flight and Barr, or for Chamberlain's, or for both. The better work in this style is on Chamberlain's porcelain, and shows feathers and shells painted with minute fidelity to nature upon a white ground (Plate 111C). A set of vases in Mr. Herbert Allen's collection (No. 349) and a plate in the Museum collection show this style at its best. Inferior painting, marked by feeble streamers of seaweed and a background stippled rather in Baxter's manner but distinct from his, appears on Flight and Barr porcelain of rather earlier date. It is perhaps earlier work of Barker's. A pair of plates in Mr. Allen's collection (No. 335) and some little vases (Nos. 301 and 302) are examples. Birds were sometimes copied from text-books of natural history, but about 1800 one Davis imitated the earlier style of the supposed 'Soqui' (Plate 111B), and exotic birds continued to be painted occasionally for a long time.[3] The painting of porcelain to imitate marble was in keeping with the Classical tendencies of the period. Gilt 'seaweed' patterns distinct from those of Derby and of an all-over character, and grounds striped or vermiculated in gold (Plate

1 Barrett, op. cit., Plate 90.
2 It has even been suggested that his existence is a myth, springing from a misspelling of Baxter's name.
3 A plate, Herbert Allen No. 326 is probably by Davis. These 'exotic bird' pieces are not likely to be mistaken for the earlier work. Imitations (virtually forgeries) of this class of Worcester were made at Tournay and in Paris in the nineteenth century. The copies made by Booth of Tunstall and still sold by them are of course earthenware; the scale-blue grounds are transfer-printed.

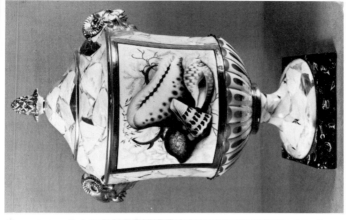

A. JUG Ht. 7in (17.7cm). Painted in sepia with a portrait of George III. About 1792 Mark 'Flight and Barr' in gold script beneath a crown. *The late Mrs. Dorothy Howell's Collection*

B. VASE Ht. 9⅛in (23.2cm). Green ground. Birds perhaps by Davis. About 1815. Mark 'F.B.B.' impressed and printed mark. *Victoria and Albert Museum (C.459-1935)*

C. VASE Ht. 10½in (26.7cm). Perhaps painted by Thomas Baxter. About 1820. Mark 'Chamberlains Worcester'. *Victoria and Albert Museum (C.511-1931)*

See pages 280, 282

Plate 111 WORCESTER

110C), were favourites at Worcester; but by about 1790 the fine dull gold of the earlier time had given place to the hard and brassy mercury-gilding. Black stipple-prints associated with gilt vermiculation were a characteristic decoration of about 1810. The short period of employment of Billingsley and Walker between 1808 and 1811 had no influence on the Flight and Barr style.[1] The first reverberating kiln used at Worcester was, however, installed by Walker during their stay.

The taste in decoration shown at CHAMBERLAIN's was on the whole worse than at Flight and Barr's. The earliest work of the factory is probably often mistaken for Salopian;[2] a marked plate at South Kensington is a rare example of Chamberlain's work of a date apparently before the end of the eighteenth century. Baxter's and Barker's styles I have spoken of; those of Humphrey Chamberlain, junior, and his brother Walter[3] are perhaps worth mention. A laborious minuteness was the most famous quality of Humphrey's work: it was proudly said that the brush-strokes could not be discerned, even with a glass. His sporting subjects were probably his best. In the Allen and Schreiber Collections (Nos. 372: Plate 110A, and 612) are a jug and a plate with copies by Humphrey Chamberlain of engravings by J. Scott after W. B. Daniell in *Rural Sports*, published in 1801–2. A plate in the British Museum (No. V. 88) is inscribed on the back '*Beating for a Hare*'. Perhaps the worst of all Chamberlain's productions were the gaudy 'Japan' vases of about 1810–20, though passable versions of the old 'Worcester Japans'[4] had been made at a rather earlier date. Brilliant gilding was applied in profusion, and a salmon-coloured ground was particularly favoured.

The identification of FLIGHT AND BARR and CHAMBERLAIN's Worcester china is generally made easy by the marks, but in their absence the hard-looking and slightly grey paste and glaze are

---

1 But see p. 285.

2 It should be remembered that Chamberlain (who commenced *c.* 1783) at first only decorated white porcelain from other places, including Caughley and New Hall. A marked specimen, with decoration in the Chinese *famille verte* style of the 'Bishop Sumner' service of Dr. Wall's time, has proved on analysis to be true hard-paste, obtained most probably from the New Hall factory.

3 A panel painted with flowers in the Allen Collection (No. 358) is reputed to be his work.

4 Compare Allen Nos. 367 and 378.

sufficiently distinctive to be recognized. Notes upon its dating will be found in the Appendix dealing with the marks. The incised 'B' is said to indicate a paste improved by Martin Barr, doubtless by the addition of bone-ash, and though by the early-nineteenth century both factories had adopted a porcelain formula approximating to that of the modern Staffordshire body, analysis of a dated piece[1] has proved that soapstone continued to be used at least occasionally as late as 1823.

The later productions of the combined factories (amalgamated in 1840) are beyond the scope of this book. A full and nearly contemporary account of their work and that of the later Royal Worcester Porcelain Company will be found in Binns and in Jewitt,[2] as well as in Mr. R. L. Hobson's monumental *Worcester Porcelain* (1910), where all the later work of the factories is described.[3]

A third Worcester factory of no great importance was founded in 1801 by Thomas GRAINGER, a nephew of Humphrey Chamberlain, with whom he had served an apprenticeship as a painter. He did not make porcelain at first, but decorated wares brought from elsewhere. About 1812 he took his brother-in-law into partnership, and a plate at South Kensington marked 'New China Works, Worcester', in red, is shown to be the work of their factory by other marked pieces decorated with similar motives. It is of fine translucent porcelain resembling Billingsley's and it is tempting to conjecture some connection with his stay at Worcester between 1808 and 1813. Their later productions, marked '*Grainger Lee and Co.*,' resemble those of Chamberlain's factory. This and other marks of the firm are given in the Appendix. Two mugs of Grainger's porcelain at South Kensington are datable by the painting of the Worcester Regatta of 1846 upon one of them.

---

1 *Analysed Specimens*, pp. 17 and 38.
2 Vol. I, pp. 240–54, where their 'wondrous state of perfection' is fully described. 'Neither in ancient nor in modern specimens', writes Jewitt, 'have such exquisitely beautiful works been produced.'
3 Also Henry Sandon, *Royal Worcester Porcelain from 1862 to the Present Day*.

Chapter 9

Caughley

A pottery was in existence at Caughley (pronounced 'Calfley') near Broseley, about one mile from the right bank of the Severn, soon after 1750. In 1754 the works were leased to a Mr. Gallimore, whose daughter in 1783 married Thomas Turner (*b.* 1749, *d.* 1809), who had been in the service of the Worcester china-factory.[1] Turner became a partner with Gallimore in the Caughley works and new premises are said to have been built in 1772.[2] Porcelain began to be made there soon after this date.[3] A 'Salopian china warehouse' was opened in Portugal Street, Lincoln's Inn Fields, London, about 1783 or a little earlier.[4] In 1799 the works were purchased by John Rose (a former apprentice of Turner's), Edward Blakeway and Richard Rose, proprietors of the successfully competing factory at Coalport on the left bank of the Severn. The Caughley factory, much diminished, continued to be used for making biscuit porcelain, which was glazed and decorated at Coalport, to which materials and plant were finally transferred in 1814.[5]

1 Jewitt, vol. 1, p. 264.

2 Chaffers, op. cit., 3rd edition, p. 559. A rare mark 'Gallimore Turner' in a circle with the word 'Salopian', links the two names together. See p. 398.

3 Jewitt, vol. I, p. 267, quotes an advertisement of 1775, stating that 'the porcelain manufactory erected near Bridgnorth . . . is now quite completed'.

4 Hobson, *Catalogue*, p. 103.

5 The extent to which the manufacture was continued at Caughley after 1799 remains conjectural. Wasters found on the site include a minority of biscuit sherds of hard non-steatitic porcelain, probably made after John Rose's acquisition of the factory, and possibly at Coalport (see p. 326), rather than Caughley.

The chief marks used at Caughley were the initials 'C' and 'S', printed or painted in underglaze blue. The former sometimes resembles the crescent of Worcester (which was also freely copied in its various forms); the latter stands for 'Salopian', the name by which the porcelain was generally known.[1] The word 'Salopian' was itself sometimes used impressed in full, in capitals or small letters. Imitation Chinese characters, similar to Worcester, are also found, particularly on 'powder-blue' pieces. An impressed star is proved as a Caughley mark by its occurrence with the blue 'C', but is so rare as scarcely to be regarded as a factory mark.

An impressed circle, found also on other wares, is so common on Salopian porcelain as to be almost an indication of Caughley manufacture.[2]

Salopian china is well represented at the Victoria and Albert Museum, particularly in Mr. Alfred Darby's large gift of upwards of a hundred and fifty pieces.

The earliest porcelain made at Caughley naturally resembled that of Worcester, from which it is sometimes not easily distinguished, being of similar composition, that is, containing soapstone as one of the ingredients. Salopian porcelain, particularly that painted in colours, often (but not invariably) shows a yellowish or brownish tone by transmitted light, in contrast to the usually greenish tone of most Worcester. This is evidently due to the absence of the 'blueing' used at Worcester, and from the same cause the earlier Salopian is usually whiter or of creamy colour in contrast to the greyish hue of Worcester. Later Salopian and the earlier Coalport are, however, grey and hard-looking, due to a change from the soapstone body to one of hard-paste, as evidenced by sherds from the Caughley factory site; many of fluted form akin to New Hall.[3]

Turner is said to have been an engraver under Hancock at Worcester, as well as a pottery-chemist, and much of the earlier ware is printed in blue. A pale and misty tone is quite distinctive and appears on many pieces. Amongst the printed designs the so-called 'willow pattern' and the 'Broseley Dragon' are both

1 Contemporary advertisements refer to 'The Salopian China Manufactory'.
2 Apparently from the 'turning' operation and not an intentional factory mark.
3 David Holgate, *New Hall and its Imitators*, Plates 205 and 206.

supposed to have been invented and engraved by Thomas Minton, working as Turner's pupil,[1] but existing examples of the latter pattern appear to post-date Turner's proprietorship. The Caughley 'willow pattern' is a 'Chinese' design in the manner of the nineteenth-century print called by the name, but is not identical with it. Numerous patterns of this type were used at Caughley; one of these 'Temple' designs is illustrated (Plate 112D). Printing over the glaze is not so much in evidence, though it was advertised in 1775[2] that Robert Hancock was then associated with the factory. And in that year Hancock himself announced that, having disposed of his share in the Worcester China Factory, he was now engaged in the Salopian China Manufactory at the China Warehouse in Bridgnorth, where he was sole agent for Thomas Turner, except for the London trade. Hancock claimed already to have 'an ample assortment' of blue and white china and would 'with all expedition proceed in the enamelled or burnt-in china'. In the same notice he advertised for a man 'used to china printing', which may indicate that Hancock proposed to undertake overglaze printing on Caughley china at his Bridgnorth premises. Jewitt published[3] impressions of some Caughley engraved plates, one of them bearing both a 'C' and an 'S' and unmistakably in Hancock's style. A blue-printed jug in Mr. Darby's gift at South Kensington is dated 1776. A jug, of grey, hard porcelain, in the Schreiber Collection (No. 682) with an inscription referring to the '*Brimstree Loyal Legion*' may reasonably be dated between 1794, when the Volunteer movement began, and 1802, when the Royal Arms (which are printed on the jug) were altered after the Peace of Amiens. The original copper-plate in Mr. Clifton Roberts' collection from which the inscription was printed bears also the words '*Wenlock Loyal Volunteers*' and is initialled 'T T', for Thomas Turner.[4]

A documentary piece for the earlier painting in underglaze blue

1 See p. 360 for his factory at Stoke-on-Trent.
2 *Aris's Birmingham Gazette*, 3 July 1775.
3 Vol. I, Plates III and IV.
4 This, together with other copper plates from the Clifton Roberts collection, is in the British Museum. Other impressions from Caughley copper plates are reproduced in Barrett, *Caughley and Coalport Porcelain*, figs. 3, 5, 6, 23, 24, 32, 34–41. Others may be seen at Clive House Museum, Shrewsbury.

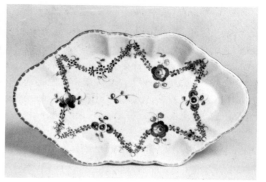

A. Jug Ht. 7⅛in (18.1cm). Painted in blue, inscribed *James Kennedy*. Dated 1778. Mark 'C' in blue. *Victoria and Albert Museum (3147-1852)*

B. Spoon Tray L. 6⅝in (16.8cm). Painted in colours. About 1785. Mark *'Salopian'* impressed. *Victoria and Albert Museum (C.1046-1924)*

C. Dish L. 10½in (26.7cm). Painted in blue and gold. About 1790. Mark *'Salopian'* impressed. *Victoria and Albert Museum (C.136-1921)*

D. Plate Dia. 6⅞in (17.4cm). Printed in blue. About 1785. Mark 'S' in blue. *Victoria and Albert Museum (1100-1869)*

E. Plate Dia. 8¾in (22.2cm). Powdered-blue decoration. About 1775–80. Mark *'Salopian'* impressed. *Victoria and Albert Museum (C.156-1921)*

See pages 288, 290

Plate 112 CAUGHLEY

is a jug at South Kensington painted with a bouquet of flowers and inscribed '*James Kennedy 1778*' (Plate 112A). Powdered-blue grounds with painting in blue in reserved panels were done at Caughley (Plate 112E), as at Bow and Worcester. An unquestionable Salopian specimen at South Kensington shows the impressed mark and three simulated Chinese characters which are quite different from those of the other factories.[1] The tone of blue resembles Worcester, but is paler, and the foot-ring, as is usual in Salopian, is roughly rectangular in section in contrast to the triangular foot-ring usual in Worcester. In the later productions the slight 'Salopian sprig' patterns imitating those of Chantilly[2] in strong violet blue are noteworthy (Plate 112B). Towards the end of the century a dark underglaze blue, as well as a blue enamel, was much used in combination with the distinctive Salopian bright thin gilding (Plate 113A),[3] again in the Worcester manner: striped patterns and wavy lines, and spirally fluted forms in the Flight and Barr style, were popular.[4] A favourite gilt border consisted of interlacing ovals, or beading in Classical style. Some finely pencilled slight floral patterns in black or brown, in combination with gilding, are peculiar to the factory. An important instance of a Worcester pattern exactly copied is the 'Royal lily' chosen by Queen Charlotte in 1788.[5] The Salopian versions are distinguishable by the tone of blue. To the same period belong some unusual landscapes in underglaze blue, with an architectural flavour, such as that on a dish in Mr. Darby's gift at South Kensington (Plate 112C).[6]

Painting in colours is sometimes very ambitious. The Worcester dry blue enamel appears, and also some exotic birds, on some moulded cabbage-leaf jugs with mask-lip, but their colour is

1 See Appendix, pp. 386, 392 and 398.

2 The Chantilly mark is actually copied on a bowl at the Victoria and Albert Museum (see Appendix, p. 398). But this is painted in red and gilt as well as with blue sprigs.

3 Some of this gilding was, however, probably done in London at the workshop of Baxter, Snr. See p. 326.

4 Some oval and fluted teapots, etc. of New Hall type are among these later Caughley productions.

5 See p. 258 (footnote).

6 For these see *Transactions E.C.C.* Vol. 10, part I, pp. 59–68. Miss Gaye Blake-Roberts, 'Sources of decoration on an unrecorded Caughley dessert Service'.

A. COVERED CUP AND SAUCER Cup ht. 5¾in
(14.6cm); Saucer dia. 5⅜in (13.6cm). Blue and gold
decoration. About 1790. Mark 'S' in blue. *Victoria
and Albert Museum (3346-1901)*

B. JUG Ht. 8½in (21.6cm). Perhaps painted at
Chamberlain's Worcester Factory. About 1790.
Mark 'S' in blue barred over in gold. *Schreiber
Collection (679)*

See pages 290, 292   Plate 113 CAUGHLEY

inclined to be hot and sticky-looking, and the execution laborious. The fruits and flowers are sometimes better, and distinct from the early Worcester examples that inspired them. The mannerism of crowding the flowers into a tight mass is a noteworthy feature of this painting, most of which seems likely to have been executed at Chamberlain's factory rather than at Caughley itself[1] (Plate 113B). Simpler decoration of flowers in colour recalls similar work at Lowestoft or New Hall, though it is unlikely that either was conscious of the other.[2]

It is often asserted that the Worcester factory sent its wares by river to Caughley to be printed in blue,[3] but there is no proof of the existence of such friendly relations. On the contrary, the secession of Turner from Worcester is more likely to have been a cause of hostility. But the relations between the factories remain obscure. It is certain, however, that much Salopian porcelain was decorated outside the factory. Its use in this way by both Chamberlain and Grainger at Worcester[4] and even by Flight, should again be mentioned, and John Rose (from 1799 onwards) evidently sold much of his 'Caughley-Coalport' porcelain to the London dealers for decoration in the enamelling studios of such independents as Baxter, Robins and Randall, Simms and Muss.[5]

1 The Chamberlain Account Books at the Worcester Royal Porcelain Company record many purchases from the Salopian factory, both white and with underglaze blue decoration, also charges for gilding and enamel decoration. Many examples are reproduced in Godden, op. cit., ch. V.

2 David Holgate, op. cit., Plates 207 and 208.

3 Jewitt, 2nd edition, 1883, vol. I, p. 162, stated that 'it is well known' that this took place, but gives no evidence in support of the statement.

4 pp. 232, 284 and 285.

5 pp. 326, 382 and 383; compare also pp. 318 and 328.

Chapter 10

Liverpool

Amongst the potteries active at Liverpool in the eighteenth century, several appear from advertisements to have made porcelain as well as earthenware. Further evidence of this was provided by the wasters and other material found by Mr. Peter Entwistle in 1921 in excavations on pottery sites in the city, and by the chance discovery in 1966 of a large number of wasters during an excavation in William Brown Street, formerly the site of premises on Shaw's Brow, where both Richard Chaffers and Samuel Gilbody were china manufacturers. There are also many traditions embodied in attributions at the Liverpool Museum and in collections in the neighbourhood, and recent researches by Dr. Knowles Boney, Dr. Bernard Watney and Mr. Alan Smith, have enabled progress to be made towards a more satisfactory classification of a body of material which has hitherto stood in much confusion.[1]

An advertisement of 1756[2] proves Richard Chaffers to have been making porcelain at that date, at a pottery at Shaw's Brow. Samuel Gilbody, William Reid,[3] William Ball, Seth, James and John

---

1 Bernard Watney's monograph dealing with this porcelain will, when published, be definitive. See also Knowles Boney, *Liverpool Porcelain*; Watney, *English Blue and White Porcelain*; *Transactions E.C.C.*, vol. 4, part 5, pp. 13–25, part 1, pp. 42–52 and vol. 7, part 2, pp. 100–2; Alan Smith, *Transactions E.C.C.*, vol. 7, part 2, pp. 102–7.

2 Jewitt, vol. II, p. 37.

3 Jewitt, vol. II, p. 38, gives an advertisement dated 1756.

Pennington,[1] Zachariah Barnes[2] and Thomas Wolfe appear from advertisements, or are said by tradition, to have made porcelain at Liverpool in the second half of the eighteenth century.

RICHARD CHAFFERS (d. 1765)[3] was in 1756 the licensee of a soapstone mine in Cornwall, and the use of this ingredient in porcelain was probably suggested to him by a workman of his named Podmore,[4] previously employed by Worcester and most likely the Robert Podmore to whom special payments were made for his services as 'arcanist' to the Worcester factory in 1751.[5] This Liverpool factory may thus be regarded as an offshoot of Worcester, though it now seems that some early Chaffers' porcelain is, in fact, phosphatic.[6] The only 'documentary' piece of Chaffers' porcelain is a mug formerly in the Liverpool Museum, acquired from one John Rosson, a descendant of Richard Chaffers.[7] It is painted by the same hand as others in the Victoria and Albert Museum and another in Mr. Wallace Elliot's collection (Plates 116A and C). Others of similar material and decoration, such as a mug at South Kensington (Plate 116B) may be confidently assigned to this factory. The free and charming brushwork seen in the decoration of this little group suggests the hand of a delft painter,[8] disciplined by the use of the brush on the absorbent surface of unfired tin-enamel. The clean and hard-looking but rather grey porcelain of the earliest wares is in appearance not unlike the soapstone porcelain of Worcester. It is noteworthy that Chaffers in his advertisement declared that every piece 'had been tested with hot water' for this also points to the use of soapstone.[9] Chaffers' mugs are of a distinctive form, a barrel-

1 Jewitt, vol. II, p. 38.

2 Jewitt, vol. II, p. 24.

3 The date of birth appears uncertain. Watney gives it as '?1722' and he was married in 1744 (Watney, op. cit., p. 63).

4 Jewitt, vol. II, p. 35.

5 See p. 230.

6 Watney, op. cit., pp. 69–70.

7 It is erroneously stated in Mrs. Willoughby Hodgson, *Old English China* (Plate 3), to be signed by Richard Chaffers. This piece appears to have been destroyed in the Second World War.

8 Liverpool had a flourishing delftware industry.

9 Chaffers' soapstone mine was eventually sold to the Worcester firm in 1776, and it is likely that at about this time, or a little before, the prevalent bone-ash body began to be used by Christian's successors, Pennington and Part.

shape with a grooved foot, formerly believed to be peculiar to Liverpool, but, as has been shown,[1] probably used also at Longton Hall. Some mugs of this shape having black transfer prints with the signature 'Sadler, Liverpool'—the name of a very active pottery-decorator with a 'Printed Ware Manufactory' in Harrington Street—may be of Chaffers' porcelain, or from the neighbouring factory of Samuel Gilbody (see below). In a document[2] signed by Thomas Shaw and Samuel Gilbody and dated 1756, it was declared that as many as twelve hundred tiles had been printed in six hours by a process which John Sadler (*d.* 1789) and Guy Green were said to have invented. They seem to have contemplated patenting their process, but did not do so, probably because they had not invented it and it was in use elsewhere. The document speaks of trials made 'in the past seven years', and, on the strength of this, priority has been claimed for Liverpool transfer-printing,[3] but no actual pieces can be ascribed to a date before about 1756, when the 'King of Prussia' prints were probably made.[4] The statement in *Moss's Liverpool Guide* of 1790[5] that 'copper-plate printing . . . originated here in 1752 and remained some time a secret with the inventors Messrs. Sadler and Green' is similarly discounted by the absence of pieces to which so early a date could be assigned. The claim that the process was first used in 1753 at the Battersea enamel-factory is superseded by the discovery of John Brooks' printing activities in Birmingham in 1751–2;[6] and the relations between Worcester and Liverpool suggest that it was through someone from the former factory that Sadler gained knowledge of the process.

The Sadler prints were taken from the usual sources, and are, it must be confessed, often poor, compared with the best Worcester

1 p. 190.

2 Published by Jewitt, vol. II, p. 29.

3 J. E. Hodgkin in *The Burlington Magazine*, vol. VI (1904–5), pp. 232 and 315. An advertisement of 1757 in the *Liverpool Advertiser* of a pamphlet on printing, does not mention Liverpool among the places at which the method was practised, and we may infer that it had not then been long in use in the city or it would have been better known there.

4 The enamel 'dated' 1756 mentioned by Jewitt (vol. II, p. 27) is apparently one exhibited at Liverpool in 1907 (Catalogue No. 115), which is signed '*J. Sadler Liverp*[l]. *Enam*[l]' and inscribed 'Done from an Original painted at Berlin in 1756'.

5 Quoted in Jewitt, vol. II, p. 27.

6 R. J. Charleston and B. Watney, 'Petitions for Patents concerning Porcelain etc.', *Transactions E.C.C.*, vol. 6, part 2.

work. A distinctive quality of line may be recognised in such prints as the version of *La Cascade* on the saucer figured in Plate 118A (Schreiber Collection No. 787). Such pieces as these are probably of Liverpool manufacture, and the coarse, often blurred line indicates a special quality in this Liverpool glaze. *Frederick the Great*, *The Tea-Party*, *L'Amour* and other Worcester subjects are often repeated. A print inscribed 'Frederick III King of Prussia' (based on a portrait of Frederick the Great) on a cylindrical mug in the Liverpool Museum is signed '*Gilbody Maker*' and '*Evans Sct.*'.[1] Another print, of William Pitt, is signed '*T. Billinge*'. A print used only by Sadler was the 'arms' of the Society of Bucks (Plate 118B), a body which was at first a convivial order, but from 1756 a charitable organisation. It should be mentioned again here that some of the mugs with Sadler's printing were undoubtedly made at Longton Hall and sent to Liverpool to be printed.[2] Worcester ware was similarly decorated by Sadler and Green.

PHILIP CHRISTIAN, one of Chaffers' partners, continued the manufacture of soapstone porcelain after Chaffers' death in 1765, under the name 'Philip Christian and Son', from 1769[3] to 1776, when Christian sold the remaining term of his soapstone licence to the Worcester factory. Wares ascribed to Philip Christian include pieces with blue borders crudely marbled in gold, represented by a set of five vases of soapstone porcelain in the Clough Collection in Lancashire,[4] and by two important large jugs in the Schreiber Collection (No. 783). The flower-painting on these is characteristic, which, with its hard black outlines, is often seen on pieces attributed to Liverpool on other grounds. A bottle at South Kensington (Plate 115) shows these flowers and the marbling very well. The rather laborious style of figure-painting on some pieces of this class is seen again on a bowl (also with gilt-marbled blue border) and was formerly believed to be the work of Dr. Wall of

1 A recent analysis of this 'Gilbody' mug, together with its general physical characteristics, seems to point to its being of Worcester origin. Watney, *Transactions E.C.C.*, vol. 7, part 2, p. 101; also Watney, *English Blue and White Porcelain of the 18th Century*, p. 77.

2 p. 190.

3 Watney, op. cit., p. 73.

4 Perhaps the garniture now in the Liverpool Museum. *Transactions E.C.C.*, vol. 5, part 5, Plate 255a.

A. SHIP BOWL Dia. 9½in (24.1cm).
Inscribed 'Success to the WILL R. BIBBY
1783). Dated 1783. No mark. *City of
Liverpool Museums* Pennington's factory

B. BOWL Dia 10¼in (26cm). Painted in colours.
About 1765. No mark. *Victoria and Albert
Museum (C.232-1921)* ?Christian's factory

C. MUG Ht. 4⅞in (12.4cm). Painted
in blue. About 1755–60. No mark.
*Victoria and Albert Museum (C.63-
1967)*
?Reid's factory

D. TUREEN AND COVER Ht. 8½in
(21.6cm). Painted in blue. About
1770. No mark. *Victoria and Albert
Museum (C.327-1940)*
Philip Christian's factory

See pages 298, 300, 304   Plate 114 LIVERPOOL

Worcester (Plate 114B). The hunting-scene on one of the Schreiber jugs is identical with that in a probably Liverpool print on cream-coloured ware, and it is noteworthy that these two jugs were called Liverpool by Lady Charlotte Schreiber at a time when such an attribution would not have suggested itself without some further information as to the provenance of the pieces, evidence now unfortunately lost. The same gilt-marbled blue also occurs on a teapot at South Kensington, moulded with leaves at the foot and with a pattern of palm-tree columns forming compartments in which are painted flowers and exotic birds in Worcester style. There are other specimens of the family in Mr. Herbert Allen's collection (Nos. 497 and 498: Plate 117C). Fragments moulded with the same pattern were found at Liverpool and help to confirm the attribution of this little class, which was often erroneously called Longton Hall[1] on the showing of the rather Staffordshire-like moulded patterns.

Two other small classes may be assigned to the Chaffers-Christian factory on the ground of paste and glaze and form of foot-ring. The first of these bears a decoration of peonies in Chinese style by a painter with a very decided manner and a fondness for clusters of dots.[2] A bowl at South Kensington with cut fruit in panels in a gilt-diapered blue ground of a type long attributed to Worcester, must be regarded as a Liverpool imitation, showing a kinship with the pieces with gilt-marbled ground described above.

SAMUEL GILBODY, mentioned above in connection with Sadler's printing on porcelain, was making porcelain at a pottery adjacent to, or near to, that of Chaffers on Shaw's Brow between 1754 and 1760, when he became bankrupt. Much of Gilbody's porcelain appears to have been printed by Sadler and Green, but among wasters found on the factory site were some painted in underglaze blue. Of greater significance, however, is the discovery in the same excavation of biscuit fragments of a porcelain figure which have been found to correspond with the white figure of a *Shepherd* in Mr.

---

1 As in an article in *The Connoisseur*, vol. XXXVI (1913), p. 2, where a similar specimen in the Stoke-on-Trent Museum is illustrated. Liverpool porcelain has been frequently classified wrongly as Longton Hall and as Worcester.

2 The hand is also recognisable on delftware.

BOTTLE Ht. 11½in (28.6cm). Painted in colours. About 1770. No mark. *Victoria and Albert Museum (C.73-1925)*

See page 296   Plate 115 LIVERPOOL (*Perhaps Christian's factory*)

Dudley Delevingne's collection (Plate 119C). The figure is of a model known also from the Derby factory, but the Gilbody example is press-moulded, not slip-cast as were the Derby figures.[1] A coloured figure of *Minerva* (Plate 119D) has also been attributed to Gilbody's factory on grounds of its decoration corresponding with that on a spoon tray. The *Minerva* (Plate 119D), however, has a clear glaze, not blued as in the case of Mr. Delevingne's *Shepherd*.[2]

Tin-glazed porcelain was evidently made at Liverpool, and fragments found there have been proved to contain this ingredient. A mug at South Kensington, painted in blue and manganese (again in delft style), corresponds exactly with one of these fragments and has just such a glaze; its form—a tall and only slightly waisted 'bell-shape'—is also found in Liverpool delft. This tin-glazed porcelain has been associated with the short-lived factory of WILLIAM REID,[3] commenced, on the evidence of insurance policies, in 1755 and ending with Reid's bankruptcy in 1761. Among Reid's partners was John Baddeley, who had a pottery at Shelton (Staffordshire) in which Reid also had an interest.[4] William Reid's factory was situated in Brownlow Hill Lane and included a windmill for grinding colours.[5] Most of the presumed productions (Plate 114C) of Reid's factory bear-a striking resemblance to those of Benjamin Lund's Bristol Factory, as Dr. Watney has observed. Several curious examples have been linked with William Reid, notably some tea-caddies in the shape of boys' heads,[6] though it must be noted that wasters similar to these were excavated recently at Newcastle-under-Lyme in the Potteries.[7]

After Reid's bankruptcy the factory appears to have been in the proprietorship of WILLIAM BALL,[8] who may have been Reid's

---

1 *The Connoisseur*, December 1970: Patrick Synge Hutchinson, 'The First Recorded Liverpool Porcelain Figure'. Also *Transactions E.C.C.*, vol. 8, part I, p. 79.

2 *Transactions E.C.C.*, vol. 8, part 2, p. 229.

3 *Transactions E.C.C.*, vol. 4, part 5, pp. 13–20.

4 Elizabeth Adams, 'Towards a More Complete History of the Liverpool China', *Northern Ceramic Society Journal*, vol. 1, pp. 6–7.

5 Elizabeth Adams, loc. cit.

6 Watney, op. cit., Colour Plate E.

7 See p. 196.

8 Formerly believed to have had his factory at a 'Pot House' in Ranelagh Street, but it now seems likely that this was his private address: Elizabeth Adams, loc. cit., p. 8.

C. TANKARD Ht. 5in (12.7cm). About 1760. No mark. *Victoria and Albert Museum (C.938-1924)*

B. MUG Ht. 2⅝in (6.6cm). About 1760. No mark. *Victoria and Albert Museum (C.1040-1929)*

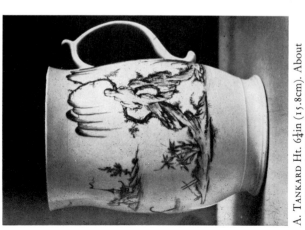

A. TANKARD Ht. 6¼in (15.8cm). About 1760. No mark. *Victoria and Albert Museum (C.68-1938)*

See page 294

Plate 116 LIVERPOOL (*Richard Chaffers' factory: wares painted in colours*)

manager at the Brownlow Hill Lane pottery. In 1763 the owners were described in an insurance policy as 'James Pennington and Company', William Ball not being specifically mentioned.[1]

To William Ball has been ascribed a rare type of transfer-printing in several colours from one plate. First identified by Dr. Newman Neild,[2] the process is described in John Sadler's *Book of Recipes*.[3] Two printed plates in the Schreiber Collection (No. 469), one of them marked with an incised stroke and formerly ascribed to 'Lund's—Worcester', are evidently of the same origin though printed in brown only, coloured over with the brush. Other examples are in the Liverpool Museum (Plates 119A and B). Fine blue painting, often in delft-painters' style, and blue and red painted porcelain, are characteristic of William Ball's factory.

JAMES PENNINGTON commenced his career as a porcelain manufacturer with Chaffers and Christian at Shaw's Brow (see above) about 1755, and we have seen that he was named as a proprietor of the Brownlow Hill Lane pottery in 1763. About 1769, under the firm name of 'Pennington and Part' he was making a bone-ash porcelain at Shaw's Brow or elsewhere, the evidence is not clear precisely where, but there is a reference in John Sadler's Notebook, under date 1st. March 1769, to 'Pennington's body', a main ingredient being bone-ash. The sequence of events in the history of the Pennington venture needs clarification as do the parts played by the three brothers, Seth, James and John. An admired blue is attributed to Seth Pennington, and the blue decoration on a jug, once in the Liverpool Museum, painted with classical figures from horticultural allegory, is of an unusual tone, rather bright with a peculiar 'sticky' appearance. Records show that this 'Horticulture Jug' was acquired from a descendant of the Penningtons.[4] Punch-bowls painted with ships, such as were popular in Pennington's delftware (there are examples at the Liverpool Museum), were made also by Pennington and Part in

1 Elizabeth Adams, loc. cit., p. 8.
2 Compare Dr. Newman Neild, 'Early Polychrome transfer on porcelain', in *Transactions E.C.C.*, III (1935), p. 71.
3 E. Stanley Price, *John Sadler—A Liverpool Pottery Printer*, p. 71.
4 The jug appears to have been one of the items destroyed by enemy action in 1941, but a photograph survives at the Liverpool Museum.

C. TEAPOT Ht. 6½in (16.5cm). Painted in colours. About 1775. No mark. *Victoria and Albert Museum (C.662-1938)* (Christian's or Pennington's factory)

B. TANKARD Ht. 5⅞in (14.9cm). Painted in blue. About 1775. No mark. *Schreiber Collection (781)*

A. JUG Ht. 9½in (24.1cm). Painted in blue. Dated 1773. No mark. *British Museum*

See pages 298, 304   Plate 117 LIVERPOOL (*Pennington's factory*)

their bone-ash porcelain (Plate 114A), and Mr. Wallace Elliot had a porcelain bowl with this decoration, depicting the ship *Swallow*,[1] evidently a Liverpool production and presumably Pennington's. The 'sticky blue' may be seen in many specimens at South Kensington, and one of the best examples is a fine cylindrical mug in the Schreiber Collection (No. 781: Plate 117B) painted with a subject from *The Ladies' Amusement*, its free style of painting suggesting the hand of a delft-painter. It is interesting to recall that the mug was formerly considered to be an early Bristol piece[2] decorated by John Bowen, who also painted delft. But a Liverpool origin is suggested by the tone of blue, and especially by the form of the base, which shows the flat bottom common in Liverpool porcelain. Many other 'sticky blue' pieces show the free style of the delft-painters.[3] Numerous specimens were evidently moulded after silver originals, such as the very ugly sauce-boats and a large jug in Mr. Wallace Elliot's collection with the additional interest of a date (1773) (Plate 117A).

A group of pieces, all crudely painted by the same hand with Chinese figures copied probably from a Worcester model, is represented at Liverpool by a tea-caddy with a printed border of the same pattern as that on the 'Heinzelman' jug in the British Museum (see below). A number of pieces by the same painter are at South Kensington; of these a bowl and a jug are marked with the monogram 'HP' in underglaze blue. The bright red on these is distinctive. Painting in underglaze blue by the same hand is also seen, distinguished by the curiously lax cluster of circles that represents a tree in his Chinese landscape. These, again, are all of a type provisionally regarded as Pennington's.

Fragments found on the pottery site seem to prove the origin of two other patterns which occur on porcelain otherwise resembling that thought to be Liverpool: a pattern including a stiff spray of red star-shaped flowers; and a heavily printed design in blue painted over in red with touches of yellow.

1 Figured in *The Connoisseur*, vol. LXXIX (October 1927). A particularly fine example is that in the Liverpool Museum, inscribed 'Success to the Issabella 1779'. Watney, op. cit., Plate 60.

2 It was also called Bow by Lady Charlotte Schreiber.

3 Watney, *Transactions E.C.C.*, vol. 5, part 1, pp. 42–7, suggests that such pieces may have emanated from William Ball's factory (see p. 302).

B. MUG Ht. 3¾in (9.5cm). Printed in black by Sadler and Green with the Arms of the Society of Bucks. About 1765. No mark. *Victoria and Albert Museum* (*C.658-1931*) Probably Chaffers' factory

A. SAUCER Dia. 4¾in (12cm). Printed in black by Sadler and Green. About 1790. No mark. *Schreiber Collection* (*787*) Probably Thomas Wolfe's factory

A small class with Chinese figures printed in outline and filled in with colours closely resembles Worcester porcelain,[1] but the borders of blue *lambrequins* have sometimes suggested a Liverpool origin for this disputed group of pieces.

Another small class of cold-white, hard-looking porcelain, painted usually with Chinese figure subjects in which a strong pink is prominent, includes a tea-caddy in the Hanley Museum with traditional ascription to Longton Hall, but is now accepted as of Liverpool origin. Dr. Watney has adduced arguments in favour of Thomas Wolfe as the maker of this porcelain.[2]

Printing in underglaze blue was practised at Liverpool, and a document for this is a jug in the British Museum (No. X.12) inscribed '*Frederick Heinzelman Liverpool*', dated 1779. The rough printing in blue, chiefly of scroll-work and flowers, includes two birds of the kind called 'livers', holding sprigs of liverwort in their beaks (they are taken from the arms of the City of Liverpool). There is also a border of hexagonal cell-diaper rendered in a peculiar way that helps to identify other Liverpool china.[3] Much of this ware roughly and thickly printed in heavy dark blue is traditionally ascribed to ZACHARIAH BARNES, but it seems doubtful if Barnes was, in fact, himself a potter.[4]

The porcelain thus ascribed to Liverpool is of widely varying quality, with a general tendency to a rather heavy coarse paste having only slight translucency. A blued glaze is prevalent, much disfigured by bubbles which are especially noticeable under the base, where the glaze commonly shows a dark bluish grey ('thundercloud' or 'starch blue') tone in the pools near the foot-ring. Among the characteristics of form are foot-rings undercut rather than bluntly triangular in section as at Lowestoft, the mug-shape with flat unglazed base, handles like Worcester but thin and 'skimpy', and the tall bell-shape already mentioned. A tall octagonal coffee-pot is also characteristic.

1 See p. 252.

2 Thomas Wolfe had a factory at Folly Lane, Liverpool *c.*1790–1800. He also had potteries in Staffordshire and was associated at both places with Miles Mason of Lane Delph between 1796 and 1800.

3 The cell-diaper motif is also sometimes found on Lowestoft and other English porcelain, and was of course derived from Chinese export wares.

4 Knowles Boney, op. cit., pp. 143–7.

A. PLATE Dia. 9⅛in (23.2cm).
Polychrome printed and coloured.
About 1760. No mark. *City of
Liverpool Museums*
Attributed to William Ball's factory

B. PLATE Dia. 9¼in (23.5cm).
Polychrome printed and coloured.
About 1760. No mark. *City of
Liverpool Museums*
Attributed to William Ball's factory

C. FIGURE OR A SHEPHERD Ht. 8¾in
(22.1cm). About 1760. No mark.
Collection of Dudley Delevingne Esq.
? Gilbody's factory

D. FIGURE OR MINERVA Ht. 5⅝in
(14.5cm). About 1760. No mark.
Private Collection, London
? Gilbody's factory

See pages 300, 302   Plate 119 LIVERPOOL

THE HERCULANEUM POTTERY[1] at Liverpool, established in 1796 on the right bank of the Mersey, made porcelain from 1801 until its closing in 1841. The productions are usually indistinguishable in style from contemporary Staffordshire wares. They are generally marked with the name of the pottery and a 'liver-bird'. There are examples at South Kensington (with the 'Miscellaneous porcelain' and in Mr. Herbert Allen's collection, No. 496).[2]

[1] So named in emulation of the Etruria of Josiah Wedgwood.

[2] A very full account of this factory, which also had a great output of earthenware of Staffordshire type, is given by Mr. Alan Smith in *Transactions E.C.C.*, vol. 7, part 1, pp. 16–38, and in his monograph *The Illustrated Guide to the Herculaneum Pottery*.

Chapter 11

Pinxton

A short-lived porcelain-factory was set up in 1796 at Pinxton in Derbyshire, about six miles from Mansfield, by John Coke (1775–1841) of Brookhill Hall, afterwards of Debdale Hall, with the help and at the instance of William Billingsley of Derby, who had invented a soft porcelain of high translucency. Billingsley left Pinxton in 1799, taking his recipes with him.[1] Coke sold the works

---

1 Billingsley went first to Mansfield, where he decorated porcelain bought from Staffordshire and elsewhere. A covered cup with undistinguished decoration of gilt diaper, and a large jug with monochrome views of Nottingham Castle and Sherwood Forest, in the Cardiff Museum, are signed '*Billingsley Mansfield*'. He is said to have manufactured china about 1802 or 1803 at Torksey in Lincolnshire, and this is confirmed by wasters found there. A cup and saucer of heavy paste and childishly crude decoration, in the Museum collection at South Kensington (No. C437 and A—1920), are traditionally said to have been made there by him or under his direction, though they bear no resemblance to his known work at Derby, Pinxton or elsewhere. Billingsley's name is also linked with a pottery at the neighbouring hamlet of Brampton, but it is likely that he was chiefly occupied with the decoration of porcelain made elsewhere: a plate in the Victoria and Albert Museum, of Paris (La Courtille) hard paste, bears a view of Hardwick Hall, so described on the back, and a sugar-basin in a similar service in private possession is painted with a view described as 'A North East View of the intended manufactory Brampton Lincolnshire'. The Brampton partnership was dissolved in 1807, when Billingsley left the place. Billingsley is also said to have attempted the manufacture of porcelain at Wirksworth in Derbyshire between 1804 and 1808, but this too has never been established or the production identified. In 1808 he took his recipes to Worcester. In conjunction with Samuel Walker, who had married his daughter Sarah, he is said to have installed at Worcester a reverberating enamel kiln in place of the box kilns until then in use. He left for Nantgarw five years later. Messrs. Flight, Barr and Barr had paid him a sum of money for the right to use his recipe, and a letter from them dated 12 November 1814, protesting against Billingsley's partnership with Dillwyn of Swansea, is reprinted in *Analysed Specimens*, p. 51. Billingsley had changed his

to John Cutts in 1805 or 1806;[1] in 1808 the staff was reduced, but a coarse and relatively opaque china of Staffordshire type continued to be made until the closing of the factory about 1813, when Cutts went to Staffordshire.

No mark was regularly used on Pinxton porcelain. The name of the factory, in script characters in gold, occurs on a mug in the British Museum (XII. 1).[2] A script 'P' in red or black with or without a pattern number is sometimes seen. A crescent alone or with a sun with rays resembling a star (from the arms of Coke), and a bow and arrow, in purple or red, occur on unquestionable specimens of Pinxton china in the small collection at the Victoria and Albert Museum. Various impressed capital letters were found on unglazed fragments discovered on the site of the works, and a specimen marked with an impressed 'B', companion to a cup with a script 'P' in red, was analysed by Mr. Herbert Eccles, and proved to contain much bone-ash as well as a high percentage of lead oxide due to the use of flint-glass in the frit.[3] A script 'B' and '26' occur on a yellow-ground cream-jug painted with Pinxton Church, so named. As the only other *script* letter found is 'P' (presumably for Pinxton), one may fairly regard this as the initial of Billingsley, especially as the teapot to this service (which appears to be of Pinxton porcelain), painted with similar landscapes, is inscribed 'Billingsley Mansfield', where, evidently, it was decorated.[4]

Billingsley's very translucent milk-white porcelain was here, as, at Nantgarw later on, very liable to collapse in the kiln, and Pinxton pieces of this material are often out of shape. A slightly wavy surface is often to be observed and this will sometimes help

name to 'Beeley', apparently after leaving Torksey, though in the letter from Messrs. Flight and Barr he is still referred to by his full name. For details of his career at Nantgarw and later, see p. 314.

1 Exley, *The Pinxton China Factory*, pp. 20–8. In 1801 John Coke took into partnership a Lincoln attorney, Henry Bankes, who brought new finance to the concern but 'took no part in the potting', and the partnership was dissolved on 1 January 1803.

2 The name written in full was however declared by Haslem (*Old Derby China Factory*, p. 227) to be a sign of forgery. A saucer formerly in the Exley collection has the gold mark and Jewitt, op. cit., vol. 4, p. 140, refers to a teapot so marked inside the lid. See also Exley, op. cit., p. 32.

3 See *Analysed Specimens*, No. 19.

4 See Exley, op. cit., Plate 14(b).

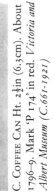

C. COFFEE CAN Ht. 2½in (6.3cm). About 1796-9. Mark 'P 174' in red. *Victoria and Albert Museum* (C.661-1921)

B. CUP AND SAUCER Cup ht. 2⅞in (7.3cm); Saucer dia. 5¼in (13.3cm). About 1796-9. No mark. *Victoria and Albert Museum* (3083-1901)

A. BEAKER Ht. 4⅛in (10.5cm). About 1796-9. No mark. *Victoria and Albert Museum* (C.361-1935)

See pages 312, 313

Plate 120 PINXTON

the collector to recognise Billingsley's Pinxton china; another paste, akin to that of Derby, is greenish by transmitted light. The shapes were the simpler of the Neo-Classical forms popular at the time. Egg-cups, and vases of similar form are for some reason often met with. The styles of painting naturally resembled those current at Derby, whence most of the workmen came. Amongst the latter were W. Coffee, the Derby modeller, and several landscape-painters, including James Hadfield and Edward Rowland. A Richard Robins from London was the subsequent partner of T. M. Randall at Spa Fields.[1] Cutts, afterwards the proprietor, was a landscape-painter who subsequently decorated Wedgwood's porcelain.[2] He is said to have been famous for his rapid execution, and freely drawn but summary views of local scenery, often in Boreman's Derby style, are common on Pinxton porcelain (Plate 120A). The vignetted landscape, i.e. without defined margins, was especially favoured. A pale red and a yellowish green are distinctive features of the colouring. Coloured grounds—yellow, green and pinkish fawn, never very good technically—were frequently applied, again in the Derby fashion. Gilding, contrary to Haslem's assertion that such form of decoration was used but sparingly, was added to all the more important productions, at least in Billingsley's time, though the productions of the later years were generally of cottage type and ungilded. The factory Account Book records numerous purchases of gold, and also mercury, during Billingsley's time at the factory, the gilding being of the bright mercury gilding first used on English porcelain about this time. The popular sprig patterns, particularly the so-called 'Tournay sprig' in underglaze blue[3] and the 'Paris cornflower' in blue, green and pink,[4] edged with a blue or brown line, are characteristic, and such specimens may safely be ascribed to Pinxton. Genuine pieces more elaborately decorated are rarer.

Billingsley's own flower-painting is not often recognisable;

1 For fuller particulars of the workmen, see Jewitt, vol. II, p. 140, and Haslem, pp. 239–46. Also Exley, op. cit., pp. 48–57.

2 See p. 370.

3 Victoria and Albert Museum, No. 1627—1871 (a large cup and saucer).

4 Victoria and Albert Museum, No. 3081—1901 (a plate); a characteristic goblet also has this decoration.

however, the painting on two goblet-shaped vases in the Schreiber Collection (No. 796) is probably his, and a rich floral border on a big ice-pail with a yellow ground at South Kensington is traditionally said to be his work.[1] Though the painting on this pail is different from Billingsley's work at Derby, the piece has a good pedigree and the tradition cannot be disregarded. Acquired in 1869, it was stated to have been given by John Coke to his father, the Rev. D'Ewes Coke of Brookhill Hall, where it remained for many years. An uneven yellow ground with scroll-work in brownish black similar to that on the ice-pail occurs on some cups and saucers at South Kensington formerly in the Jermyn Street Museum, where they were 'authenticated' as Pinxton by John Haslem; Plate 120B shows one of these with a little landscape in early Pinxton style. The coffee-cup in Plate 120C bears another typical landscape and is marked 'P174' in red. A beaker in Mr. Herbert Allen's collection, Plate 120A, shows another style, and a cup and saucer in Mr. Wallace Elliot's collection[2] bearing a tiny landscape with sheep has the date 1796: a peculiar bright yellowish green is noticeable in the work of this hand, and a fragment found on the factory site, painted with deer, contains the same colour.

The later Pinxton porcelain may be well studied in Mr. Herbert Allen's collection. Some vases (Nos. 197 to 199) are typical, and may be compared with the beaker of the earlier, more translucent paste of Billingsley's making,[4] the later ware having a yellow or light orange tone by transmitted light.

1 Exley, op. cit., frontispiece.
2 Figured in *The Connoisseur*, vol. LXXIX (Sept. 1927).
3 Figured in *Apollo*, XXV (1937), p. 91. Compare also p. 257.
4 China money-tokens similar to those made at Worcester are said to have been made and issued by John Coke, and a specimen dated 1801 is described by Haslem, p. 243, and illustrated by Jewitt, vol. II, p. 141.

Chapter 12

Nantgarw and Swansea

A porcelain-factory at Nantgarw, in the county of Glamorgan, between Cardiff and Pontypridd, was started in 1813 by William Billingsley of Derby and Pinxton, and his son-in-law Samuel Walker,[1] with the help of William Weston Young. The famous porcelain made from Billingsley's recipe was a glassy soft-paste containing a considerable proportion of bone-ash.[2] It was highly translucent and of beautiful whiteness, but very liable to melt out of shape in the kiln, and therefore costly to produce. Financial difficulties led Billingsley to appeal for Government help, claiming that his porcelain was equal to the best soft-paste of Sèvres, and Lewis Weston Dillwyn, a Swansea potter, was asked by the Board of Trade to report upon the matter. Impressed by the fine quality of Billingsley's china, Dillwyn arranged for the manufacture to be transferred to his Cambrian Pottery at Swansea, in 1814.[3] Porcelain made from Billingsley's recipe, both at Nantgarw and Swansea, was as a rule marked with the name of the former place and the initials 'C.W.' (for China Works'[4]) impressed in the paste. It is thus

1 For the earlier history of Billingsley and Walker, see pp. 164 and 309.

2 See *Analysed Specimens*, No. 21.

3 Porcelain had not previously been made at Swansea. The 'opaque china' made rather before this at the rival Glamorgan Pottery in the town was a fine earthenware.

4 Formerly read as 'G. W.' for 'George' Walker. The potter's name, however, was Samuel. Solon's suggestion that 'CW' stands for 'Cambrian Works' cannot be accepted, as the mark was used *before* the transfer to Swansea, as is shown by the discovery of fragments so marked on the Nantgarw site. Moreover, the mark with the initials is much the more frequently found; though the recipe was comparatively little used at Swansea.

impossible to decide at which of the two places a particular piece was made, unless it is painted by a hand known to have been employed only at one or other of them.

Dillwyn found Billingsley's recipe too costly and unpractical, and by the introduction of a larger proportion of china-clay endeavoured to make a porcelain body which would be more stable in the kiln.[1] A porcelain in which ground flint was also substituted for the Lynn sand was first produced; this is known to collectors as the 'duck's egg' body from its greenish translucency, and was usually marked with the word 'SWANSEA', impressed or printed in capitals or written in script letters, in red or occasionally in gold. Written capital letters were rarely used. About 1817 a new glassy body containing soapstone was introduced. This was markedly inferior to 'Nantgarw' and 'duck's egg'; it has a hard-looking, minutely pitted surface somewhat resembling pig-skin, with a smoky yellow translucency. Porcelain of this composition was usually marked with a trident, impressed, in addition to the name 'SWANSEA'. A rare variety of the same body, without the soapstone, is very glassy with a dull white surface and a colourless translucency which Mr. Eccles has likened to 'sodden snow'. Of the porcelain with these bodies, collectors will value most highly the 'Nantgarw', but the 'duck's egg' also is a beautiful material.

By 1817 Billingsley and Walker had finally left Swansea and returned to Nantgarw.[2] Of the former's two daughters (who are said to have helped in the painting of his porcelain) the elder, Sarah, had died at Swansea in 1817; the younger, Lavinia, died shortly after his return to Nantgarw. In 1820 Billingsley took his recipes to Coalport[3] at the invitation of John Rose, who had previously bought up the works at Caughley.[4] It is probable that Rose was aware of the high repute of the Welsh china and wished to limit its production to his own manufacture. Moreover, the

1 See *Analysed Specimens* (pp. 47–50), in which extracts from Dillwyn's note-books are reprinted, recording his experiments towards a more workable formula.

2 Messrs. Flight and Barr of Worcester had previously (in 1814) protested against the use of Billingsley's recipe at Swansea. They did not, apparently, object to his manufacture of porcelain on his own account.

3 See p. 326 for certain pieces apparently made from the Nantgarw formula at Coalport.

4 See p. 286.

London dealers had previously taken much Coalport china in the white, to be decorated to their order, but were now preferring the Nantgarw and Swansea, thus injuring Rose's business. Billingsley continued to work at Coalport until his death in 1828.[1]

After Billingsley's departure porcelain is said to have been made, and was certainly decorated, at Nantgarw until 1822 by William Weston Young (b. 1776, d. 1847), who had previously worked as a flower-painter at Swansea, with the assistance of another painter from Bristol, Thomas Pardoe, whose work will be described presently. Young's porcelain (if it was ever made) is not easily identified, but from entries in his diary[2] it is supposed to have been of the Swansea 'trident' type. In or about 1822, the Nantgarw moulds and stock were bought by John Rose, who a year or so later acquired the moulds, etc., from Swansea.

Long after this, in 1838, Young suggested to Pellatt, the London dealer, that he should supply him with the Nantgarw paste in casks, but nothing came of the proposal; and there is apparently no ground for the statement that Young supplied Daniel, a Staffordshire potter, with mixed Nantgarw ingredients in this way.

In 1817 Dillwyn leased his Swansea pottery to Bevington and Company, whose names from this time occasionally appear as a mark on Swansea porcelain, which finally ceased to be made about 1822 at latest. After Dillwyn's retirement an action (Roby[3] v. Dillwyn, 1821) was brought against him, it being alleged that the recipes for the finer porcelain had been withheld, whilst the quality of the stock transferred with the factory was of inferior quality— apparently for the greater part of the 'trident' body. A Swansea plate at South Kensington, painted by Baxter (see page 320 below) and given to the Jermyn Street Collection by Mrs. Dillwyn, is said to have been produced at the trial of the case. Little if any porcelain was made by the Bevingtons, who were content to decorate the porcelain in stock. They were, in any case, in possession of the recipes for the 'duck's egg' and 'trident' bodies, not of the Nantgarw, which Dillwyn had not possessed.

---

1 He is buried in Kemberton churchyard, near Shifnal, Shropshire.

2 See *Analysed Specimens*, pp. 20, 21.

3 Roby, with Timothy and John Bevington and George Haynes, senior and junior, had purchased Dillwyn's share in the Cambrian Works.

Simple forms inclining to the Classical style were the rule at both factories, and shapes for table-ware were largely imitated from the Paris hard-paste, which was very fashionable at the time. Plates moulded on the rims with flowers in low relief were popular. Flowers modelled in white biscuit and applied to decorative vases (there are two specimens in Mr. Herbert Allen's collection, Nos. 425 and 426) are said to have been the work of Goodsby (or Goadsby), a modeller who came to Swansea from Derby. The impressed initials '*I.W.*' which occur on a biscuit figure of a ram also marked 'swansea' and '*Bevington & Co.*' impressed, are those of a modeller named Isaac Wood, who was also manager and may have made these and other similarly marked pieces by way of experiment.

Most of the painting was of flowers in the naturalistic style of the time, in many cases obviously done in imitation of Billingsley's manner. The peculiar dark green enamel imitated from some Paris porcelain is almost peculiar to Swansea. Gilding of excellent quality, but rather liable to tarnishing, was done at both factories.

For the identification of the painting on Nantgarw and Swansea porcelain, the reader must be referred to Mr. E. Morton Nance's book, where the matter is discussed at very great length (pages 286 to 350).[1]

Billingsley's own painting is not often seen on Nantgarw and Swansea china, though the roses on the sides of a sugar-bowl in Mr. Herbert Allen's collection (No. 430) are decidedly in his manner. Two plates exhibited at Swansea in 1914[2] are, however, almost certainly by his hand. It should be mentioned

1 Also W. D. John, *Nantgarw Porcelain*, and the same author's *Swansea Porcelain*.
2 Reproduced in the *Catalogue of a Loan Exhibition* held in 1914 at the Glynn Vivian Art Gallery, Swansea, pp. 10 and 11, and in Turner, Plate XXX. Much of the clean white china painted with rather large and blurred pink roses commonly attributed to him is not only not his work, but is not even Swansea china, but Coalport or Staffordshire porcelain of 1820–30. The romance associated with Billingsley and his porcelain has led to the attribution to Swansea of much porcelain made elsewhere.

that much of the discussion of the painters' mannerisms by the late Robert Drane in Turner's book on the factories is invalidated by an initial confusion between the work of Billingsley and Pardoe.

For the greater part of the duration of the two factories, Thomas Pardoe (*b.* 1770, *d.* 1823)[1] was living at or near Bristol, decorating porcelain and earthenware sent to him 'in the white' from various places, chiefly from Worcester and Caughley-Coalport. His painting may be studied in a very important signed plate at South Kensington of unmarked china very like Caughley or early Coalport.[2] Pardoe's rather 'wet' style of flower-painting as well as more elaborate and naturalistic painting of landscapes, birds and animals, is recognisable on Nantgarw porcelain, painted during the last three years of his life.

The well-known studies of plants copied from the *Botanical Magazine*,[3] with names written on the backs of the pieces, which were formerly believed to be the work of William Weston Young, are now recognised as early work of Thomas Pardoe (Plate 123A); they are usually on Swansea earthenware. Young illustrated a work on natural history written by Dillwyn, and this circumstance has led to the attribution to him of all the plant-subjects, birds and butterflies painted on pottery with the names written on the backs of the pieces. But several styles are distinguishable on these. The handwriting of the names is a clue to the authorship of the painting, and Pardoe's trick of writing each letter separately helps us to recognize as his the hand commonly seen on services painted with 'botanical' flowers. Young's more laborious style is seldom seen on porcelain, but is not uncommon on pottery.[4]

Thomas Baxter (*b.* 1782, *d.* 1821) was a highly skilled and versatile painter who came to Swansea from Worcester in 1816,[5] and returned thither in 1819 having been latterly an independent artist. At Swansea he excelled in botanical studies of plants, as well

1 For details of his life, see W. J. Pountney, op. cit., pp. 115, 116, and Turner, op. cit., p. 179. Also W. D. John, op. cit.

2 Figured in *Apollo*, XXV (1937), p. 90.

3 Dillwyn was a devoted botanist and friend of Sir Joseph Banks, and favoured this kind of decoration.

4 The butterflies are often his: the handwriting of the Latin names provides a clue, as in the case of Pardoe.

5 For his Worcester work, see p. 280.

B. PLATE Dia. 8¼in (20.9cm). About 1815. *Victoria and Albert Museum (Illidge Loan No. 7)*

A. PLATE Dia. 10in (25.4cm). About 1815. Mark 'Nantgarw C.W.' impressed. *Victoria and Albert Museum (C.585-1935)*

See pages 322, 323   Plate 121 NANTGARW

as in landscapes and figure-subjects in Sèvres style.[1] His work at Swansea may be studied at South Kensington on a well-authenticated plate (No. 3491 — 1901). His flower- and plant-pieces generally have a landscape or painted-over background of a quite peculiar kind.

Matthew Colclough, a bird-painter (to judge by the examples traditionally ascribed to him) worked in a simple but naturalistic style, which should be distinguished from the more elaborate painting of birds done on Swansea china in London. Plates in the Schreiber (No. 801) and Victoria and Albert Museum Collections are in the style said to be his, whilst the birds on one (No. 419) in Mr. Herbert Allen's collection, formerly in the J. G. Mortlock Collection, were probably done in London for the dealer of that name. But the attribution of Turner's example (Plate XV in his book) may be questioned. His authority is even more grotesquely untrustworthy than most of its kind. It seems that the specimen was 'identified by Mr. Blank who knows the mannerism of this artist, who was a personal friend of his grandfather'! It has been suggested that the supposed Colclough is the work of Baxter. The touch is similar, but not conclusively so, and it is difficult to explain why Baxter for all his versatility should have been engaged on bird-painting at Swansea, though never practising it at Worcester, early or late. In favour of an attribution to Baxter, perhaps, is the simple gilt border which is the same on the authenticated Baxter plate and on those with the birds supposed to be by Colclough.

Mention may be made of a few other artists whose work has been identified. A well-authenticated specimen of the work of William Pollard (b. 1803, d. 1854), who worked chiefly for Bevingtons, is a mug at South Kensington acquired from one of his descendants. His flowers are as a rule loosely bunched; his mannerism of filling the spaces between the flowers with an indefinite purple-black may be observed on a large service and on other pieces in the collection at South Kensington. The Swansea plate figured in Plate 122B is in his style. His work is hard to distinguish from that attributed to David Evans, who may have taught him. Evans was apparently a painter of wild flowers with

1 But the vase figured in the *Swansea Exhibition Catalogue* (p. 6) is apparently a forgery.

A. VASE Ht. 6½in (16.5cm). Probably painted by Henry
Morris. About 1815. No mark. *Victoria and Albert Museum*
(C.598-1935)

B. PLATE Dia. 8¼in (20.9cm). Probably painted by William Pollard.
About 1815. Mark 'SWANSEA' in red. *Victoria and Albert Museum*
(C.604a-1935)

See page 320   Plate 122 SWANSEA

slender stems. A distinct and mannered style seen on both Nantgarw and Swansea-marked pieces is that of a painter generally known among collectors as 'the Frenchman', whose hand has been recognized on Paris porcelain made by Nast. A stiff spiky spray and an auricula or similar flower with the dark centre indicated by a hard broken ring, are peculiarities of his style. He is supposed to have been the 'de Junic' recorded as employed at Swansea. The painting on a pot-pourri vase in Mr. Allen's collection (No. 428: Plate 122A) closely resembles that on a plate signed by Henry Morris (b. 1799, d. 1880).[1]

Transfer-printed designs and patterns printed in outline and filled in with washes of colour are also found on Swansea as well as on Coalport porcelain.

Much plain white Nantgarw and Swansea china was sent to London to be decorated by independent enamellers or to the order of the dealers John Mortlock, Pellatt and Green, and others[2] whose names were sometimes added to the marks. Of the numerous pieces of this class some are believed to have been decorated by Moses Webster, a painter from Derby employed by Robins and Randall of Spa Fields, Islington, London. A group of 'outside enamelled' pieces at South Kensington includes a plate in his style (Plate 121B), which has already been described.[3] An especially elaborate specimen of the London-decorated class is a plate in Mr. Herbert Allen's collection (No. 438), minutely painted with views of English mansions copied from engravings issued in the *Copper Plate Magazine* between 1792 and 1802. The figure-subject on another plate in Mr. Allen's collection was probably done by a painter named Plant (d. about 1850) who was employed by Sims, another 'outside enameller' with an establishment in London. The basket of roses on a Nantgarw plate at South Kensington was declared by Haslem to have been painted by

---

1 Turner, op. cit., Plate IV.
2 Such as J. Bradley & Co., Neal and Bayley, Boucher and Guy, 'Powell, 91 Wimpole Street' (Herbert Allen Collection, No. 434).
3 See p. 170.

James Turner of Derby, working for Sims, who was himself an old Derby hand. Much of the Swansea and Nantgarw china smothered with soft indefinite roses may be put down to Sims and his painters. But by no means all the London-painted Nantgarw china was decorated in costly fashion. For example, a plate with the impressed mark, painted with a few slight sprays of flowers not unlike those on the specimen figured in Plate 121A, is inscribed underneath, '*Mortlock*', in gold.[1]

It should be added that no make of English porcelain has been so extensively copied and supplied with forged marks as Nantgarw and Swansea.

---

[1] Rollo Charles (*English Porcelain*, ed. R. J. Charleston, p. 133) draws attention to the feature of a 'narrow halo of iridescence' occurring on London-decorated Nantgarw in the area of the decoration.

Chapter 13

Coalport

The Coalport factory was founded by John Rose (*b.* 1772), who is believed to have been an apprentice of Turner at Caughley. He joined Edward Blakeway[1] in a pottery at Jackfield in Shropshire about 1793, and, together with Blakeway, moved in 1795 or 1796 to Coalport, a township on the Severn bank nearly opposite Jackfield. There is evidence in the shape of bills for china supplied to Richard Egan, China Dealer of Bath,[2] some 1796 Election jugs, and an account of a visit in August 1796 by the Prince and Princess of Orange, when 'His Highness bought some pieces of Mr. Rose',[3] that a china factory was in existence at Coalport as early as that year. In 1793 Richard Egan also had dealings with Blakeway as shown by correspondence between Egan and Joseph Lygo, London Agent for Duesbury of Derby, but at what location is not disclosed. The original partners in the John Rose factory were John Rose, Richard Rose and Edward Blakeway.

Two important documentary pieces are a two-handled cup and cover, and a beaker, in the Shropshire Yeomanry Museum, Shrewsbury, the former inscribed on the base in puce 'This CUP was made at the COAL-PORT MANUFACTORY a.d. 1799 for Thos. N. Parker Major Commandant of the Brimstree Loyal Legion'.[4] The

1 Edward Blakeway was a Shrewsbury draper with interests in the ironworks of the Severn Valley (he was a brother-in-law of the ironmaster, John Wilkinson), and acquired the Jackfield pottery in 1783. Barrie Trinder, *The Industrial Revolution in Shropshire.*

2 The Duesbury papers in the Derby Public Library.

3 *Shropshire Journal,* 24 August 1796.

4 A Caughley Jug in the Victoria and Albert Museum also has an inscription to the Brimstree Loyal Legion. See p. 288.

beaker, which commemorates the presentation of colours to the Pim Hill Light Horse Volunteers, has inscribed on the base the name 'Lord Pultney Bath', the names of the officers of the unit, and the date of the presentation, 4 June 1799.

A second china factory was set up at Coalport about 1800,[1] the original partners being William Reynolds, a prominent industrialist, Robert Horton and Thomas Rose, the latter being brother to John. Robert Anstice, William Reynolds' cousin, became a partner on Reynolds' death in 1803.[2] The Anstice, Horton and Rose works were situated close to those of John Rose, with the canal between them, the River Severn being at the other side of the Anstice buildings. Anstice, Horton and Rose were acquired by John Rose and Company in 1814, in which year, also, John Rose closed down the Caughley factory which he had acquired from Thomas Turner in 1799.

The Productions of the Anstice factory, in so far as they have been identified, were similar to the early productions of John Rose and Co.[3]

Porcelain was made at both Caughley and Coalport under Rose's management until the closure of the older factory. The Nantgarw and Swansea moulds and stock were also acquired in 1822–3[4] by Rose, who died in 1841 and was succeeded by his nephew William. The firm was until lately still in existence, though the factory had been removed to Stoke-on-Trent.[5]

John Rose's manufacture was a very large one, and all grades of china were made. Only a small proportion of the pieces was ever marked; and of these many made towards the middle of the nineteenth century were close copies of Meissen, Sèvres and Chelsea models and bore the marks of those factories. These copies

1 Evidence of a partnership agreement of that date exists, though the commencement of manufacture may have preceded it. (William Reynolds Exors.' Accounts in Staffordshire Records Office, ref. D876/155, p. 36.) Information kindly supplied by Mr. Barrie Trinder, Salop Education Department.

2 B. Trinder, op. cit., p. 218. The works are now a Museum under the care of the Ironbridge Gorge Museum Trust.

3 Geoffrey Godden, in *Coalport and Coalbrookdale Porcelain*, has identified some of these wares. The Anstice productions were not marked except for pattern numbers, some of which are referred to in the existing Coalport Pattern Books in association with the corresponding pattern at John Rose's factory.

4 See pp. 315 and 316 for an account of Rose's relations with these factories.

5 Now absorbed by the Wedgwood group.

are quite likely to deceive the inexperienced collector, though their true origin may always be detected merely by an examination of the gilding, which is usually thin and highly burnished, and always quite unlike the dull soft-looking gold of the earlier work; and there is naturally a quite different touch in the painting.

The earliest Coalport cannot be separated from Caughley,[1] and the 'C' and 'S' of Salopian were probably also used as marks. The soapstone body may have been continued for a while at Caughley, but a harder body and glaze were early used, wasters of which have been found at the sites of both factories.

Underglaze blue decoration was continued and much Coalport porcelain was decorated outside the factory. The objects shown on the work-table in Thomas Baxter's water-colour of his father's studio[2] in London include not only a plate with a figure-subject of the kind done by Baxter himself, but also a number of pieces with decoration in underglaze blue, such as must have been added in a factory. Mr. Bernard Rackham suggested that these pieces may have been sent only to be gilded in Baxter's workshop. They include spirally fluted cups and other pieces with simple conventional floral borders of a type common enough on both Worcester and Salopian china in the early nineteenth century. Strangely enough, among them are a blue-and-white teapot and vase which could not have been painted anywhere but at a factory with glaze-firing kilns, since the decoration is under the glaze. A notice shown on the wall of the studio is headed '*Coalport White China*', pointing to the probability that the porcelain made at Caughley after the purchase of the works in 1799 by John Rose of Coalport, as well as that made at Coalport in its earliest days, may have been sent for gilding (and perhaps sometimes painting) to Baxter in London.

When Billingsley came from Nantgarw to Coalport in 1820 his recipe was undoubtedly tried experimentally by Rose, and it is possible that the 'NANTGARW' stamp was used at Coalport as it had been at Swansea, and the productions are thus likely to be mistaken. A red mark 'NANTGARW' also appears on porcelain thought to be Coalport. But pieces so marked in a style later than that of about 1820 are rarely seen. In Mr. Allen's collection,

1 See p. 286. 2 See p. 280.

A. DISH. Painted by Thomas Pardoe. About 1815. Swansea porcelain. *Victoria and Albert Museum (C.13-1939)*

B. PLATE Dia. 9⅛in (23.2cm). About 1815. Mark 'COALBROOKDALE' in red. *Victoria and Albert Museum (C.1025-1929)*

C. DISH OF FRUIT Dia. 10½in (26.7cm). About 1820–30. Mark 'C.D.' in blue enamel. Coalport porcelain. *Victoria and Albert Museum*

See pages 318, 328, 330   Plate 123 SWANSEA AND COALPORT

however, there is a little group of unmarked pieces (Nos. 414–16) that may well have been made at Coalport from the Nantgarw formula. The not uncommon wide-mouth jugs, often dated and inscribed under the lip, painted with large indefinite pink roses and by custom miscalled Swansea, are almost certainly Coalport productions of about 1830, as is much else besides that goes by the name of Swansea. Some Coalport painting is even claimed as Billingsley's, but the only convincing example, a plate at South Kensington (Plate 123B), seems to date from the period *before* his Nantgarw venture. It is of the greyish 'Caughley-Coalport' paste[1] and bears the very unusual mark 'COALBROOKDALE' in red written in a circle; this suggests that it was perhaps a piece sent to be painted by him outside the factory, or it may have been painted at the time of Billingsley's visit to Coalport in 1811 when he installed a new kiln there.[2] The best Coalport porcelain from 1825 onwards was certainly of fine quality and highly translucent, and perhaps made from a modified Nantgarw formula. Some of the finest Coalport of the middle of the century was declared by Jewitt to be indistinguishable from Nantgarw. Some of this porcelain is marked with what looks like an impressed figure '2' (mark No. 3, p. 401).

Rose was awarded in 1820 the 'Isis' Gold Medal of the Society of Arts for a leadless feldspathic glaze, and one of the factory marks[3] commemorates this. The characteristic Coalport 'useful china' of the period 1820 to 1850 is mainly distinguished by its comparatively sparing decoration, in which the mannered flower-painting already mentioned in connection with Derby plays a leading part. Moulded patterns are much in evidence and gilding was lavish, but the white porcelain surface was not so completely smothered in decoration as at other factories. The rich dessert-services which competed with those of Spode and Rockingham may sometimes be identified only by this characteristic, which is one of the few merits of early Coalport. The practice of using outlines for flower-painting printed in pink or purple is a distinguishing mark of some Coalport table-ware of this and later times. The Coalport paste was

1 Compare p. 287.
2 Haslem, p. 56.
3 Appendix, p. 401.

A. Inkstand with Raised Flowers L. 12½in (31.7cm). About 1830.
Victoria and Albert Museum (C.555-1935)

B. Pair of Vases Ht. 13in (33cm).
Rose-Pompadour ground. Perhaps
painted by James Rouse. About
1850. Mark 'CBD' monogram in
blue. *Victoria and Albert Museum*

C. Vase Ht. 28in (71.1cm). Painted and
signed by John Randall. About 1865.
*Shrewsbury Museum and Art Gallery (Clive
House Museum)*

See page 330   Plate 124 COALPORT

especially translucent and the gilding was usually light in colour, in contrast to that on Rockingham.

The vases and decorative pieces were too often overloaded with moulded decoration; flowers and fruit modelled in the round were applied in profusion (Plates 123C and 124A) and the 'Revived Rococo' of the period 1820 to 1830 was especially distressing. In the crude colouring a strong pink and a particularly unpleasant bright, rather yellowish green were prominent. The inkstand figured in Plate 124A is a characteristic specimen.

Towards 1845 not only were Sèvres models closely copied, but the Sèvres style was attempted in more or less original work. About the period of the Great Exhibition of 1851 the most 'exquisite' of all the English painting in this manner was done by William Cook (see below), who specialised in groups of trophies as well as in flowers and fruit. The cup and saucer numbered 3370—1901 at South Kensington and the plates in Mr. Allen's collection (Nos. 409 and 410) are good examples of a somewhat deceptive class which commonly bears the Sèvres mark. The imitation of Chelsea gold-anchor vases inspired the production of large pieces with figure-subjects in the manner of Boucher (Plate 124B). A *rose Pompadour* ground (always miscalled at the time *rose du Barry*) was one of the proudest achievements of the factory, though poor enough in our eyes beside the Sèvres colour. A maroon-coloured ground is said to have been introduced by Samuel Walker, who had come to Coalport with his father-in-law. The egg-shell porcelain of almost paper-like thinness made in this period was according to Jewitt, 'a pure porcelain; one stone and one clay alone, without bone-ash'. Figures and other decorative objects in parian porcelain[1] were made from about 1850 and were a feature of the Great Exhibition of 1851.

The later painters at Coalport, whose work can be identified, include John Randall, nephew of Thomas Martin Randall,[2] famed for his painting of birds (Plate 124C) (1835–81) and William Cook, painter of flowers and fruit, also in the manner of Sèvres (*c.* 1840–70). James Rouse, apprenticed at Derby, painted figure

---

1 Invented at Copelands, see pp. 5 and 369.
2 See p. 383.

subjects and flowers at Coalport for about thirty-five years before returning to Derby about 1865, and T. J. Bott imitated Limoges enamels as his father had done at Worcester for Kerr and Binns.[1]

A class of work practised at Coalport and elsewhere, much esteemed about the middle of the century, took the form of paintings in enamel on flat plaques of porcelain; highly finished naturalistic groups of flowers and fruit were especially favoured. Some work in this style was done by Jabez Aston and R. Eaton; examples are in Mr. Herbert Allen's collection (Nos. 403 and 626). The Coalport productions of the later nineteenth century lie outside the scope of this book.

1 See p. 232.

Chapter 14

Plymouth and Bristol

────────────

We have seen that, as early as 1745,[1] William Cookworthy (*b.* 1705, *d.* 1780), a Quaker chemist of Plymouth, was acquainted with the nature of the clay used by the Chinese in the manufacture of true porcelain. Moreover, it is certain that his search for it in Cornwall was rewarded at the latest by 1758,[2] when Tregonning Hill, the place of his discovery, was mentioned in Borlase's *Natural History of Cornwall* as the source of a fine white clay. In the meantime the use of Cornish soapstone as an ingredient of soft-paste may well have been due to Cookworthy's researches.[3]

In 1765 a further consignment of china-clay from America was sent to Richard Champion by his brother-in-law, Caleb Lloyd of Charleston, South Carolina. This was the same 'unaker' that had been sent twenty years earlier and used at Bow, and we find the young Champion, a member of a Bristol family of merchants and then twenty-two years of age, already interested in the manufacture of china. Champion wrote in reply in the same year of a 'new work just established' attempting to make porcelain with Cornish materials; 'the body is perfectly white within,' he wrote, 'but not without, which is always smoky'.[4] Champion promised to try the

1 See p. 82.

2 In an undated memorandum, probably written in 1765, he speaks of having found the china-clay and stone 'nearly twenty years ago'. For evidence of dating the memorandum see J. V. G. Mallet, 'Cookworthy's First Bristol Factory of 1765', *Transactions E.C.C.*, vol. 9, part 2.

3 See pp. 212 and 214.

4 Regarding this Bristol hard-paste concern, see Watney, *English Blue and White Porcelain*, p. 127, where he refers to Cookworthy's association with the enterprise,

American clay, but pointed out that it was useless without the fusible china-stone. This last, a variety of granite or feldspar known in Cornwall as 'moor-stone' or 'growan-stone', was found by Cookworthy at a slightly later date in the tower of St. Columb Church,[1] though the first specimens proved impure, and the desired whiteness on melting was not obtained, the presence of iron causing reddish stains. A suitable variety, which showed greenish spots comparable to the green tone described by Père d'Entrecolles, was eventually found near St. Austell, and a patent for porcelain manufacture with these materials was taken out by Cookworthy in 1768.[2] A note-book written by one John Allen of Liskeard, quoted by Lady Radford,[3] states that the factory was started by a company subscribing 'fourteen shares of £15 or £20 each . . . held . . . three by William Cookworthy and one by each of the other partners, viz. Philip Cookworthy, Richard Champion, John and Joseph Harford, William Phillips, T. Were and Sons, John Bulteel, William Wolcott, Joseph Fry, and Thomas Franks [*sic*]. Some of these afterwards advanced further sums and the undertaking seems to have been attended with loss.' Thomas Frank was a son of a Bristol potter; the others were prominent Bristol men or relatives of Cookworthy. Before 1767, a brother-in-law, Thomas Were, had advanced money on account of 'William Cookworthy on the china affair or the Plymouth Porcelain Company: To Bill remitted on China affair at Bristol £30.'[4]

Cookworthy's account of his discovery[5] is worth reading for its demonstration of his scientific method, as well as for its connection

brought to notice by Mr. and Mrs. J. V. G. Mallet. Also Mallet, loc. cit., pp. 212–20.

1 There is a legend to the effect that Cookworthy observed some stones which had fused at a bell-casting, and so obtained a clue for the discovery of *petuntse* (quoted from a manuscript diary of 1797 by Rev. John Skinner, in a well-documented article by Lady Radford in the *Devonian Year Book*, 1920, p. 31). Nevertheless it seems that Cookworthy knew of Cornish China Stone at a much earlier date (see above).

2 Specification No. 898, 17 March 1768.

3 Loc. cit., p. 36.

4 Quoted by Lady Radford, loc. cit., p. 34.

5 Quoted from G. Harrison's *Memoir of William Cookworthy*, pp. 199–207, in Hugh Owen's great work, *Two Centuries of Ceramic Art in Bristol*, pp. xv–xxii. Owen's book is not free from errors, but these and its typographical eccentricities do not seriously affect its importance as a contribution to the history of English pottery.

with a landmark in the history of English china manufacture. The letters of Père d'Entrecolles,[1] diligently studied, were evidently the inspiration of his researches; the lime and plant-ash used in his glaze were in fact prepared in precisely the same manner as at Ching-tê Chên.

The factory was at first conducted at Coxside, Plymouth,[2] with the assistance of Thomas Pitt, afterwards Lord Camelford.[3] The close association of Plymouth and Bristol parties in the concern from its beginning makes it difficult to decide the exact date of the transfer of the manufacture to Bristol, but the last firing took place, it appears, on 27 November 1770. Some decoration, at all events, seems to have been carried out at Bristol from this date, since an advertisement in a Worcester newspaper of 1770 invited painters desiring work at the 'Plymouth New Invented Patent Porcelain Manufactory' to apply to Thomas Frank at Castle Street, *Bristol*.[4] In this year, too, Thomas Were and Sons sold their share 'to the proprietors of the New China Manufacture at Bristol—where the work is intended to be carried on'.[5] A drawing by Champion of a kiln, dated 1770, was published by Owen,[6] and the removal from Plymouth may well have been on Champion's insistence. The latter in his evidence given before Parliament a few years later claimed that he had been connected with Cookworthy's manufacture 'nearly since the time of the patent'; and we have seen that his

1 See p. 228.

2 It was contended by R. N. Worth (*Transactions of the Devonshire Association for the Advancement of Science, Literature and Art*, 1876, p. 480) that it was conducted at a bakery near Cookworthy's house in High Street, Plymouth, but it is more likely that early experiments only were made there. A former employee asserted that the works were at Coxside: see a letter quoted by Lady Radford, loc. cit., p. 37.

3 Interesting details about the discovery are given in a letter from Lord Camelford quoted in Polwhele's *History of Cornwall*. He refers to the discovery on an estate of his of a 'certain white saponaceous clay, and close by it a species of granite or moorstone, white with greenish spots, which he (Cookworthy) immediately perceived to be the two materials described by the missionary Père d'Entrecolles'. The use of the first person plural elsewhere in this letter proves Lord Camelford's connection with the manufacture.

4 R. W. Binns, *A Century of Potting in the City of Worcester*, p. 87. Frank was, as I have mentioned, a partner in the Plymouth company, but even so, it is unlikely that application to Bristol would have been invited for a Plymouth factory.

5 Lady Radford, loc. cit., p. 40.

6 p. 18. The words written on the drawing, 'The Last Burning of Enamel Nov. 27 1770', may refer to the impending removal. Several pieces marked with the same date may also have been inscribed with the event in view.

interest in the subject dated from 1765 at the latest. The dissolution of a partnership between 'Joseph Harford and R. C.' is mentioned in 1769 in the diary of his sister, Sarah Champion. A later entry, of 1771, speaks of the 'china work' carried on at Castle Green; and premises there were in the rate-book for that year with William Cookworthy as occupier. Cookworthy was then an old man, and in 1773 the patent rights and business were finally purchased by Champion, who renamed the works the Bristol China Manufactory. John Brittan was his foreman.

The patent expired in 1782, and in 1775 Champion's application for an extension had been opposed by Wedgwood and other Staffordshire potters, whose natural self-interest was cloaked in pretensions of zeal for the public welfare. Champion was granted certain rights over the sale of the Cornish minerals and their sole use in translucent porcelain for fourteen years, but others were allowed the free use of the clay and stone in opaque pottery. This set-back and the ambitious nature of much of the Bristol china prevented it attaining any commercial success. Champion, too, was an ardent Whig politician, and his divided attention probably handicapped his work as a potter. In any case, such a manufacture could scarcely have been successful without royal or princely patronage or a Government subsidy, such as were enjoyed by the Continental factories of the same order. Financial difficulties obliged Champion to sell the patent rights in 1781 to a company of Staffordshire potters, who continued the manufacture of the more simply decorated wares at a factory opened in the following year, called the New Hall, at Shelton.[1]

For a short time after this date Champion was Deputy Paymaster-General to the Forces under his friend Edmund Burke, but a change of Government deprived him of the post and finally led to his emigration in 1784 to a farm in South Carolina, where he died on 7 October 1791, aged 48.

---

1 See p. 357. It is sometimes said on the authority of the inaccurate Simeon Shaw that the sale took place in 1777; but Owen pointed out that this is disproved by Champion's figure made in memory of his daughter, who died in 1779. Shaw, it may be noted, attributed the failure of the Plymouth and Bristol manufacture to ignorance of the 'principles of combinative potency'!

Marks were by no means always used at Plymouth and Bristol, though the sign for tin (which is also that for the planet Jupiter), resembling the numerals 2 and 4 conjoined, in underglaze blue, gilt or enamel, occurs fairly often on the earlier pieces. It referred, no doubt, to the ancient tin-mining industry of Cornwall, and reveals the chemist in Cookworthy. But it was evidently used by him also at Bristol. There are a number of pieces in existence bearing this mark together with that commonly employed later at Bristol, a cross painted in enamel or gold.[1] An early vase in a set in the Schreiber Collection (No. 710) has a cross incised in the glaze, whilst the others have the tin-mark. A capital 'B' in blue enamel was also used at Bristol, occasionally in combination with the cross.[2] This and the crossed swords in underglaze blue in imitation of Meissen were often accompanied by numerals, commonly believed to be painters' marks. These will be discussed presently in connection with the painting on Bristol china. It is noteworthy that the porcelain figures seldom if ever bear a factory mark: of the thirty examples in the Schreiber Collection, not one has the mark.

To distinguish Plymouth china from Bristol is not always easy, and the hard porcelain made at the two places would be more conveniently classified, as it may be by style, into Cookworthy's and Champion's, representing the earlier and later productions.

The identification of the unmarked china attributable to one or other of the two factories is of course simplified by the fact that it is hard-paste. Some training of the collector's eye is required before the distinctive quality of this true porcelain can be surely recognised. Whilst the glaze is often pitted and milky with numerous minute bubbles[3] and quite unlike the glassy covering of soft-paste, the body with its compact texture is not unlike a kind of very hard glass. In colour, both Plymouth and Bristol show a

1 A milk-jug in the British Museum (No. VIII. 50) and a basin painted in blue in the Schreiber Collection (No. 692) are examples.

2 A coffee-pot formerly in the Trapnell Collection bears both marks.

3 According to the patent quoted by Jewitt, vol. I, p. 376, and Owen, p. 392, the Bristol glaze contained tin-ashes, which would give it opacity.

constant tendency to a brownish smoke-staining, never quite overcome, and when this is absent in the Bristol the glaze is cold and glittering. Technical short-comings mark much of the work, both early and late. Grit has often adhered to the foot-ring. The presence of slight spiral ridges in 'thrown' pieces is a common defect (known as wreathing), due to unskilful work: a vase or cup evenly wetted or compressed by the thrower's fingers has shrunk unequally in the kiln. Handles are often askew from the same cause. A rib, or ring in relief, under the base of the plates and dishes was a device used to support them in the kiln and to prevent warping. Plates were a weak point in the Bristol manufacture, and are consequently rare.[1] Warping and fire-cracks are in fact common; figures lean forward quite literally overcome by the heat of their firing. Analysis has shown[2] that the fluxing material in Bristol china is even less than in the Chinese or Meissen, and the very high temperature required for its firing was obviously hard to obtain and control. Lord Camelford, writing in 1790 of the former Plymouth factory, spoke of the difficulty that had been experienced in apportioning the ingredients; Champion, speaking of a later time, declared that no two specimens of the Cornish china-stone behaved alike. To the relative infusibility of glaze is due the fact that the enamels, baked on at a second firing, are seldom perfectly incorporated but tend to stand out as a superficial incrustation. An obviously *fused* appearance, due to the imperfect control of the firing of the ware, is seen in the details of many figures, and this, with the common smokiness, distinguishes the pieces usually regarded as Plymouth. But Bristol was also liable to the same faults, though to a slighter extent. The same shortcomings are commonly seen in the hard-paste porcelain of the small German factories in Thuringia, where figures were made in the same period. These are often erroneously classified as English.[3]

---

1 Wedgwood was aware of this weakness, and pressed the point in his case against the Bristol patent. His own 'Queen's ware' plates could be made perfectly true.

2 Church, p. 81.

3 As are several items in the *Catalogue of the Trapnell Collection* and in Owen. The collector should compare the exhaustive and fully illustrated *Alt-Thüringer Porzellan* (Kloster-Veilsdorf, Ilmenau, Limbach, etc.) of R. Graul and A. Kurzwelly (Leipzig, 1909).

One of Cookworthy's earliest productions, a mug in the British Museum (No. VII. 9), is painted in underglaze blue with the Plymouth arms and has the inscription '*March 14 1768 C.F.*', the initials presumably standing for '*Cookworthy fecit*'.[1] A tradition in the Cookworthy family insists that the earliest blue-painting was done by the inventor himself. If this is true, the British Museum mug is a most likely specimen, perhaps done as an exhibit, since it bears a date before that of the patent. Prideaux[2] repeated a legend, apparently the creation of Simeon Shaw, to the effect that Cookworthy had invented a new process of making cobalt-blue direct from the ore. However this may be, the underglaze colour on Plymouth china is commonly of blackish or greyish tone. Notwithstanding this shortcoming the Plymouth blue-and-white is often decidedly attractive in an unpretentious way, and shows an individual treatment of the Chinese motives, as in the mugs figured in Plate 125. Classical style borders were, for some reason, a feature of this blue-and-white; those on two cups and saucers in the Schreiber Collection (No. 693) include the Classical ox-skull. Painting in red-and-blue in Japanese style was also practised at Plymouth; a jug and a mug at South Kensington are examples. Another blue-and-white mug, inscribed '*Josiah and Catharine Greethead March 13 1769*' and important for its date, is in the Schreiber Collection (No. 694), where the collector may see what is undoubtedly the finest existing assemblage of Cookworthy's porcelain.

Lady Charlotte Schreiber had the good fortune to purchase many fine pieces which had been preserved by members of Cookworthy's family.[3] Many of these, like most of the figures, were unquestionably presentation pieces, and do not at all represent the average quality of the Plymouth and Bristol work. The enormous tea- and coffee-pots (Schr. Nos. 735 and 736), $9\frac{3}{4}$ in. and $11\frac{1}{8}$ in. high, bearing the Plymouth mark in gold, were evidently show-pieces of this kind; ambitiously but unskilfully gilded on a marbled blue ground they are apparently imitated from

1 The date is three days before that of the patent.
2 *Relics of William Cookworthy*, p. 7.
3 The collections of John Prideaux, Miss Fox and Miss Tregellis were all inherited in this way.

A. Puttio Representing *SUMMER* Ht. 5⅝in (14.3cm). Coloured. About 1770. No mark. *Schreiber Collection (699)*

B. Pheasant Ht. 8in (20.3cm). White. About 1770. No mark. *Schreiber Collection (688)*

C. Puttio Representing *WINTER* Ht. 5½in (14cm). Coloured. About 1770. No mark. *Schreiber Collection (699)*

D. A Musician Ht. 6¼in (15.8cm). White. About 1770. No mark. *Schreiber Collection (683)*

E. A Musician Ht. 5⅞in (14.9cm). White. About 1770. No mark. *Schreiber Collection (683)*

F. Mug Ht. 3¾in (9.5cm). Painted in blue. About 1770. Mark Sign for tin in blue. *Schreiber Collection (690)*

G. Salt Cellar W. 5in (12.7cm). White. About 1770. No mark. *Schreiber Collection (689)*

H. Mug Ht. 4⅞in (12.4cm). Painted in blue. About 1770. *Victoria and Albert Museum (C.797-1924)*

See pages 268, 338, 340, 342   Plate 125 PLYMOUTH

Worcester. They are often held to be work of the Bristol period,[1] though their flower-painting links them with certain early vases, and like them they were evidently made by way of displaying the new porcelain to Cookworthy's friends. The sets of vases (or *garnitures*[2]) of which there are two in the Schreiber Collection (Nos. 710 and 711), show very well the difficulty with which the porcelain was made. The pieces which purport to be uniform vary in size and are sometimes distorted in shape; one of the pieces was chipped before it was painted (but nevertheless was considered worth decorating, a leaf having been painted over the chip). To the same class of show-pieces belongs a claret-ground teapot in the same collection (No. 737), also marked in gold. The ground-colour is mottled and scarcely successful.

Of the less pretentious pieces, a noteworthy document, given by Mr. Sydney Whiteford to the Plymouth Museum, is a small sauce-boat inscribed '*Mr. Wm. Cookworthy's Factory Plym.º 1770*'. Sauce-boats from the same mould are at South Kensington, in the Schreiber and Museum Collections; two of these are painted in colours on either side with a cock, presumably from the crest of the Cookworthy family—a cock gules.

These earlier things are not only marked by imperfections in the paste, but a muddy tone is also characteristic of certain of the enamel colours. A brownish-crimson appears very often, particularly on the slight *rococo* scroll-work for which the elderly Cookworthy evidently retained a liking. Chinese subjects and patterns, as a rule decidedly crude, were apparently copied from Worcester porcelain.

The 'Tº' mark, ascribed to 'Mr. Tebo', to which such frequent reference has already been made in this book,[3] reappears on porcelain which must be ascribed to the Cookworthy period. Shell-salts were evidently a favourite invention of this 'repairer', for we find them again in Plymouth porcelain: Plate 125 includes an unusually effective example with the shells and coral arranged

---

1 Compare Owen, p. 79, and Church, p. 79.

2 Two beakers and three covered vases after the fashion of the so-called *garnitures de cheminée* made in China for export to Europe.

3 p. 104, where is explained the improbability of his having modelled the Bristol *Seasons*, and pp. 106 and 108.

FIGURE OF 'ASIA' FROM A SET OF 'CONTINENTS'. Ht. 12½in (31.7cm).
About 1770. No mark. *Schreiber Collection (697)*

See page 342   Plate 126 PLYMOUTH

with some approach to rhythm. The reappearance on these salts[1] of the familiar 'dishevelled birds' of Bow and Worcester has already been discussed.[2] Painting perhaps by the same hand is seen on a Bristol plate in the Schreiber Collection (No. 755), though this may have been done, as asserted by Owen, as a careful copy to match a Bow service.[3] Though white Plymouth porcelain can never have been available in London for this purpose to any considerable extent, the survival of undecorated pieces shows that it was not impossible for Giles to have obtained them.

It is remarkable that Longton Hall models were sometimes used for Plymouth figures. The latter may, of course, have been moulded from actual Longton specimens, but the coincidence (or partiality) has never been satisfactorily explained. Another suggested explanation is that Cookworthy purchased the Longton moulds at a sale at Salisbury in 1760.[4] Instances of this identity of moulds are the *Boys with a Goat* (Schr. No. 702), and the *Seated Musicians* (Schr. No. 683: Plate 125D and E), though these are unlikely to be the work of the same 'repairer' as the Longton figures[5] since the flowers and accessories are quite different. Some of the Plymouth and Bristol figures, however, seem to be original compositions, and in spite of all shortcomings rank with the best ever made in England. Among these are the *Continents*, of which a complete set with a good pedigree is in the Victoria and Albert Museum. Further examples of the splendid *Asia* and *America* are in the Schreiber Collection (Nos. 697: Plate 126, and 696). The grave *Shepherdess* (Plate 127A) is a well-known 'Plymouth model, and the little naked boys as *Seasons* (Schr. No. 699: Plate 125A and C) are very delightful things, obviously of the earlier period. There are also the figures of birds and beasts (Plate 125B).

These earlier figures may readily be distinguished from the others by their scrolled *rococo* bases, often picked out in the

1 As on the specimens at South Kensington (Nos. 210, 211 and 212—1864).
2 See pp. 124 and 266.
3 A Bow plate in the Schreiber Collection (No. 107) is similar.
4 See pp. 178 and 196.
5 Such as C707 and 708—1925 at South Kensington.

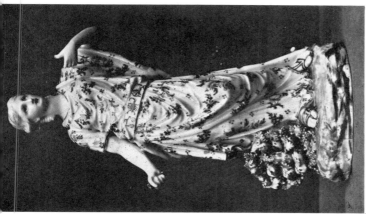

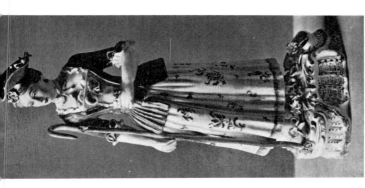

A. SHEPHERDESS Ht. 12¼in (31.1cm). About 1770. *Victoria and Albert Museum (C.609-1935)*

B. AUTUMN FROM A SET OF 'SEASONS' Ht. 10½in (26.7cm). About 1775. Mark 'To' impressed. *Schreiber Collection (745)*

C. AUTUMN FROM THE 'CLASSICAL SEASONS' Ht. 9⅞in (25cm). About 1775. No mark. *Schreiber Collection (742)*

See pages 344, 345   Plate 127   PLYMOUTH AND BRISTOL

distinctive 'Plymouth' brown-crimson; the later 'Bristol' bases are, by a curious anomaly, of the indefinite *rockwork* favoured at Sèvres and elsewhere in the *Louis Seize* period. We have a rare piece of evidence of the conceiving of some of the most ambitious Bristol figures in Champion's instructions to the (unfortunately anonymous) modeller of the *Elements* and *Seasons*, published by Owen,[1] and reprinted by Mr. Rackham in the Schreiber Catalogue. Writing of the *Elements*, Champion says: 'As I have an inclination to fancys of this kind, I chose to write to you as wish to have some elegant Designs. I have seen the four Elements which are made at Derby they are very Beautifull the Dress easy, the forms fine, two in particular Air and Water are the charming figures. I apprehend that you made the models & therefore hope that from your execution the following fancies will not look amiss.' Then follows a description of the figures as he wished them made. This connection between Derby and Bristol seems to have been generally overlooked. A set of Derby *Elements* appears in the extant price-list as the work of Stephan, who was modelling for Duesbury from 1770 onwards. There is no record, however, that Stephan ever went to Bristol, though there is a legend that another workman, described as 'Thomas Briand of Derby', was responsible for the biscuit plaques to be mentioned presently. A connection with Derby is suggested by the very marked similarity of the figures of children made at both factories. With their large heads, smirking expressions and affected attitudes[2] they are all clearly of the same family. But as many of the English figures seem to be original models, and the style is so distinctive, a single modeller is suggested for both factories. The Bristol children as *Seasons* (Schr. No. 745 : Plate 127B) show the style very well, whilst the *Boy and Girl carrying dogs* closely follow a Derby model.[3] The grown-up *Seasons* and *Elements* for which Champion's instructions have been preserved show much less of the contemporary Derby

---

1 Facsimile (of Champion's manuscript) No. 4. Complete sets of the figures are in the Schreiber Collection (Nos. 742 and 743).

2 'Smirking, hydrocephalic children . . . all of them real horrors', is a description of these by Dr. F. Severne Mackenna in a paper entitled 'The Artistic Content of Cookworthy's and Champion's Porcelain', in *Transactions E.C.C.*, IX (1946), p. 219.

3 Compare the Chelsea-Derby pair, Schr. No. 349.

style, and do not seem in the least like Stephan's work. Mr. Rackham has suggested that the Derby *Elements* referred to were perhaps the earlier figures of which the white *Pluto* ascribed to the factory on p. 133 was the *Earth*; the Bristol *Elements* show the same excellent lively movement. The *Seasons*, of which is illustrated the stately *Autumn* (Plate 127C), are clearly the work of the same hand. The *Shepherds* and *Shepherdesses*, *Children with Dogs* and the fine *Venus and Adonis* (Colour Plate D), may all be seen in unequalled specimens in the Schreiber Collection. Many of the best have the 'T^o' mark. More recently two pairs of Sphinxes, once regarded as Fulda, have been recognised as Bristol; these also have the 'T^o' mark impressed as well as a cross in blue enamel. One pair is coloured, the other white and gold, and are supposed to be portraits of the actresses Kitty Clive and Peg Woffington. Similar Sphinxes were made at the Bow factory.[1]

A form evidently favoured by 'Mr. Tebo' was the large 'frill vase' with applied masks, acanthus foliage and festoons of flowers. Bow specimens of the type sometimes bear his mark, as do certain Worcester vases[2] almost identical in form with two Bristol specimens in Mr. Herbert Allen's collection (Nos. 444 and 446). One may assume that the 'repairer' would take from factory to factory the simple moulds for masks and flowers required for the applied decoration on such vases. It was formerly believed that 'Tebo' modelled most of the Bristol figures, but the coincidence of the mask on a Bristol jug with the head of *Winter* in the *Seasons*, remarked upon by Mr. Rackham, does not imply that the 'repairer' (who might mould a jug) was also the modeller of the figure. It may well be that the mask was cribbed by the 'repairer', who moulded the figure from a model made by another. Another Bristol type found at Worcester, and perhaps due to 'Mr. Tebo', is the basketwork dish moulded with vine leaves in relief. An ambitious type, eloquent of Champion's determination but scarcely successful, is represented by two large vases painted with birds in panels

1 *Transactions E.C.C.*, vol. 8, part 2, pp. 228–9, Plates 184 and 185. Also Lane, op. cit., pp. 123–8.
2 No. 125 in the Frank Lloyd Collection and No. 571 in the Schreiber Collection (here figured in Plate 104B), are examples.

reserved on a light scale-blue ground, and mounted in ormolu, in Mr. Allen's collection (No. 447).

Much more successful than these are the large hexagonal vases with painting on a white ground, of which there are fine examples both at South Kensington (Schr. No. 750: Plate 128) and at the British Museum (VIII. 18), painted with birds in distant landscapes in a very personal manner. These show strong Sèvres influence and are by the same hand as some well-known painting on Worcester porcelain.[1] Their painter was almost certainly the 'Mons. Soqui' mentioned by Harrison in his *Memoirs of Cookworthy*, and the 'excellent painter and enameller from Sèvres' referred to by Prideaux.[2] Landscapes, without birds, by the same hand are sometimes seen. Some smaller and very charming examples often bear the 'Plymouth' mark: one such—a coffee-cup in the Schreiber Collection (No. 723)—is painted *en camaieu* in a very pleasant blue and crimson. Other specimens bearing his painting in the same collection are two coffee-cups (No. 722), and an early vase (No. 712) showing his undeveloped style. The painting on the great hexagonal vases is perhaps the best of his work at either Bristol or Worcester.

The interest of much of the Plymouth and Bristol painting goes far to compensate for the imperfections of the china itself. Owen gives a list of workmen[3] and the names of some other painters have been preserved in the apprentice-lists.[4] There were doubtless several skilled painters found amongst the 'lads of genius' who were offered 'encouragement' in an advertisement of 1775. As usual in English porcelain, one can do little more than bring together the work of certain hands; to ascertain their names is unfortunately beyond hope.

The most celebrated of all the painters was Henry Bone (*b.* 1755, *d.* 1834), the son of a Plymouth cabinet-maker and afterwards a fashionable miniaturist. He is sometimes said to have been apprenticed at Plymouth, though he was only fifteen years of age

---

1 See p. 262.

2 *Relics of William Cookworthy*, p. 5.

3 William Fifield, a well-known painter of Bristol pottery, is sometimes said to have worked for Champion, but he was not born until 1777.

4 Owen, pp. 289 and 299; Jewitt, vol. I, p. 397, and Pountney, p. 224.

HEXAGONAL VASE Ht. 15⅜in (39cm). Painted in colours. About 1775. No mark. *Schreiber Collection (750)*

See page 346   Plate 128 BRISTOL

when the works were transferred to Bristol, and Owen asserts that he was apprenticed to Champion in 1772 for a period of seven years. The monochrome bird-painting just mentioned has been attributed to him, but, as Mr. Rackham has shown,[1] the 'tin' mark on some of these indicates a date before 1773, when Bone was only eighteen years old, and such accomplished painting could scarcely be the work of so young a man. Moreover, there is good reason to regard this as the work of the Frenchman already discussed. Owen asserted that all the pieces decorated by William Stephens were marked with the numeral '2',[2] and since the several pieces of one service were sometimes marked with different numerals, he inferred that these could not be pattern numbers, but must be the marks of Champion's apprentices, of whom William Stephens was believed to be the second. Owen thence conjectured that the mark of Henry Bone, the first, would be '1'. There is good reason to abandon this theory. It is likely that numbers indicating seniority, if ever used at all, would vary with changes in the staff. And the numeral '1' appears on the plate painted with 'dishevelled birds' mentioned above.[3] Moreover, the numeral '2' occurs on a saucer and a plate at South Kensington, handled in very different styles. Further, the painter of the plate just mentioned was evidently also the painter of the very beautiful monochrome flowers in pale-blue enamel on a cup and saucer, but this is marked '6'. Again, a cup and saucer in the Herbert Allen Collection (No. 470) are both painted with the same pattern and evidently by the same hand, but the cup bears the numeral '3' and the saucer '1'. Numerals in gold are also likely to be gilders' numbers rather than enamellers'.[4] In view of his subsequent career and the statement of his biographer that he painted landscapes and flowers on china, it is more likely that Bone's work is to be found in such things as the charming crimson landscapes which decorate a tea-pot at South Kensington, with the initials 'HMB'; or perhaps the little oriental sea-shore scene on a

1 *The Burlington Magazine*, XXV (1914), p. 104.

2 F. Severne Mackenna agrees, *Transactions E.C.C.*, vol. 4, part 1 (1957), p. 42, where a full account of William Stephens is given.

3 Other examples marked with the numeral '1' are a tureen and cover at South Kensington (No. 3116—1901) and a tea-cup and saucer (VIII. 26) at the British Museum.

4 Mackenna, loc. cit., adduces arguments in favour of the same artists being employed on both painting *and* gilding.

A. CUP AND SAUCER Cup ht. 1⅞in (4.7cm); Saucer dia. 5⅛in (13cm). About 1775–80. Mark Meissen crossed swords in blue, and '3' in gold. *Schreiber Collection (762)*

B. CUP AND SAUCER Cup ht. 2¾in (7cm); Saucer dia. 5¼in (13.3cm). About 1775–80. Mark a cross in blue enamel, and '1' in gold. *Schreiber Collection (774)*

C. DISH L. 11⅞in (30.1cm). About 1775–80. Mark An arrow-head in blue. *Victoria and Albert Museum (3107-1901)*

See pages 352, 353   Plate 129 BRISTOL

cup and saucer in Mr. Allen's collection (Plate 130C).

Champion made a number of handsome china services for his friends.[1] The wife of Edmund Burke was the recipient of one of these, on his election as Member for Parliament for Bristol, largely with Champion's assistance, in 1774. A cup and saucer from the service is in the British Museum (No. VIII. 20), painted with figures and the arms of Burke impaling Nugent. A Bristol china service decorated with the favourite green festoons and a monogram of two S's was also made for presentation by Burke to Mrs. Smith, the wife of one of his supporters. Specimens are at South Kensington and the British Museum (No. VIII. 25). The 'Robert Smyth service', made for the wedding in 1776 of the fifth baronet of that name, of Colchester, has the monogram 'R S' composed of tiny flowers in the contemporary German style: an example is in Mr. Allen's collection (No. 464), which also includes a cup and saucer with the initial 'C', below a ring, composed of forget-me-nots. The 'Mark Harford service'[2] was made for a member of a Bristol family associated with Champion's factory from the first. The earliest-dated Bristol-marked pieces are two coffee-cups in the Schreiber Collection (No. 763) with the initials 'I.H.' and the date 1774.[3] The service from which these came was traditionally believed to have been made for Joseph Harford, whose partnership with Champion was mentioned above, but Owen pointed out that the initials are more likely to be those of Joseph Hickey, a friend of Edmund Burke and London agent for the factory. A service made for William Cowles, a merchant of Castle Green, Bristol, is represented in the Schreiber Collection by a group of pieces, some of which bear the Bristol cross and the date 1776.[4]

For the rest, the 'useful ware' made at Bristol during Champion's proprietorship varied from elaborate things like these

---

1 A full list of these services is given in the *Catalogue of the Alfred Trapnell Collection*, pp. xxii–xxvii.

2 Illustrated in Pountney, Plate L.

3 These have the curious feature of the Bristol cross-mark *inside* the cups.

4 Apart from these services, a rather crude pattern with festoons of flowers in green and black in 'cottage style' (such as the cup and saucer, Schr. No. 770) has become known for some unexplained reasons as the 'Horace Walpole pattern'.

A. Teapot Ht. 6⅜in (16.2cm). About 1775–80. No mark. *Schreiber Collection (757)*

B. Covered Cup and Saucer Cup ht. 3¾in (9.5cm); Saucer dia. 6in (15.2cm). About 1775–80. Mark A cross in blue and '2' in gold. *Victoria and Albert Museum (814-1892)*

C. Cup and Saucer Cup ht. 2in (5.1cm); Saucer dia. 5in (12.7cm). About 1775–80. No mark. *Victoria and Albert Museum (C.636-1935)*

See pages 350, 352, 353

Plate 130 BRISTOL

services [1] to the simple 'cottage china' for which Champion, with more foresight, could undoubtedly have secured a large market. For his porcelain was genuinely 'useful', as his advertisements claimed,[2] capable of good service, and standing sudden changes of temperature as well as the fine earthenwares of Staffordshire. Wedgwood and his fellows were well aware of this and doubtless feared its competition. In the British Museum are two tumbler-shaped cups (No. VIII. 39), produced as evidence in Champion's case before the House of Commons in 1775, and it is noteworthy that these are marked with the Meissen crossed swords. Champion constantly insisted on the kinship between his china and the 'Dresden', and the mark was perhaps innocently meant to show that the specimens were indistinguishable from the German. In a surviving catalogue of an auction-sale of Bristol china held by Christie in 1780,[3] there are repeated references to 'Dresden' and 'French' patterns. Champion's models are clearly avowed in a letter of 1776, where he claims that his china equalled 'the Dresden in strength', 'in elegance perfectly resembling the beautiful manufacture of Sèvres'. The ribbon and festoon patterns of the latter were a principal decoration (Plates 129 and 130); the laurel and husk (the so-called mignonette) pattern was especially in favour, as was the grey *camaieu* painting of the same factory (Plate 130). These are combined on a cup and saucer in the British Museum (No. VIII. 21), also said to have been shown in the House of Commons. Much of the flower-painting is the work of two hands. One of these, with a fluent style of brush-work, was the painter of the pale-blue monochrome flowers on a cup and saucer already mentioned and of the dish figured in Plate 129. The second arranged his flowers in tighter bunches, with less emphasis on the

1 The beautiful 'cabaret' sets are among the most sought after of Champion's wares.

2 A Bristol advertisement of 1776 included the following: 'The Bristol china is superior to any other English Manufactory [*sic*]. Its texture is fine, exceeding the East India and its strength so great that water may be boiled in it. It is . . distinguished from every other English China which being composed of a Number of Ingredients mix'd together the principal part being glass occasions it soon to get dirty in the wear, renders it continually liable to Accidents and in every respect only an Imitation and therefore is stiled by Chemists, a false Porcelain.'

3 Reprinted in Nightingale, p. 101.

slender curving stems which are characteristic of the other style; a teapot (Plate 130A) shows the general effect of his painting. The severely 'Classical' cups of cylindrical form are worthy of comparison with the best contemporary work of Sèvres and Derby; the small cup with gilt 'S'-shaped scrolls (Plate 129A) is typical of many pretty things in the same style.

The 'cottage china', which is particularly well represented in Mr. Herbert Allen's collection, was slightly decorated with festoons and sprigs, without gilding. It is often unmarked and at times scarcely distinguishable from the New Hall porcelain that succeeded it. In general, however, the Bristol colouring is distinctive. Pinks tended, as at Plymouth, to be brownish; a clear yellow, an uncommonly wet and juicy red and a bright translucent leaf-green are characteristic of this as of other Bristol (and Plymouth) china. Bristol shapes are subtly different from others. The globular teapot copied from the Chinese and adopted also at Lowestoft, Liverpool and Worcester, tended at Bristol to have straighter sides, sometimes even slightly incurved (Plate 130A). Jugs and even cups have the same outline, and a double curve in the handles, not seen elsewhere, is also common. A twig handle with tiny buds is peculiar to Bristol, as is the double-twig of a kind most often associated with Leeds and Staffordshire earthenware; longitudinally ribbed and simple loop handles flattened only on the inner side are also characteristic.

Transfer-printing was rarely used, but a few poorish things are met with, the prints roughly coloured over. A teapot of characteristic shape in the Victoria and Albert Museum is crudely painted in colours over a design of Chinese figures printed in outline. A print of birds washed over in colours is sometimes seen (specimens are at South Kensington and the British Museum). All these seem to be of the 'Plymouth' period. A rare jug with a decidedly Salopian-like black print of a Chinese lady and boy, in the Schreiber Collection (No. 779), was for long regarded as Chinese porcelain printed at Caughley, but has the Bristol 'wreathing' and smokiness. The crude, skimpy handle suggests an imperfect piece on which a trial of transfer-printing has been made. It is not impossible that such pieces as this were done at the instance of Robert Hancock, after he had left Worcester in 1774.

The glaze of hard-paste is not fusible enough for printing on it to be readily successful. Some specimens printed in underglaze blue with flowers (such as the mug in the Schreiber Collection, No. 730) have a decidedly Worcesterish look. Underglaze-blue painting is seen on a pair of strainers in the Schreiber Collection (No. 729).

Standing apart from the other Bristol productions are the biscuit plaques with modelled and applied flowers and portrait busts, shields of arms and the like in relief, which Champion delighted to make for presentation to his friends. It was stated by Owen[1] that a plaque inscribed 'G G' and said to have been made for Gabriel Goldney[2] bore a pasted-on label inscribed in his handwriting, 'Specimen of Bristol china modeled by Thomas Briand of Derby 1777', to whom, in the absence of other evidence, this class of work has been consequently ascribed.[3] The British Museum is especially rich in these plaques, many of which have the interest of quite certain documentation.[4] One of the specimens in the British Museum (No. VIII. 3) survived with little damage a fire at the Alexandra Palace which reduced many valuable specimens of soft-paste china to shapeless lumps.

At a much later date, about 1845–50, somewhat similar panels were made by Edward Raby for the Water Lane Pottery at Bristol, then under the management of J. D. Pountney, who died in 1852. These are sometimes mistaken for early specimens, but they were of a softer paste, with the ground occasionally stained blue on the surface. In the rare instances of a blue ground in Champion's plaques the paste was stained throughout before firing. The latter, moreover, usually have a very slight but perceptible gloss or

1 p. 87.

2 It is not quite certain, however, that the 'G G' of the plaque is the Gabriel Goldney of the label, who may well have been a nineteenth-century Bristol citizen of the same name, partner in Pountney and Allies' Bristol pottery in 1836. In this case, the attribution may be no more than a surmise, made long after the event, though possibly recording a tradition not to be disregarded. There is no certainty that the label is contemporary with the plaque.

3 Perhaps a son of the Thomas Briand mentioned on p. 19 as a possible Chelsea arcanist. A paper, read by Mr. Arnold Mountford to the English Ceramic Circle on 18 November 1967, indicates that a Mr. Thomas Briand, likely to be the 'Chelsea arcanist', died in February 1747: 'Thomas Briand, a Stranger', *Transactions E.C.C.*, vol. 7, part 2, pp. 87–99.

4 A full account and classification of the plaques is given in an article by Philip Nelson in *The Connoisseur*, vol. VI (1903), p. 139; see also Wallace Elliot, in *Transactions E.C.C.*, I (1933), p. 23.

'smear' due to vapourised glaze in the kiln. Champion used a similar biscuit to make models of birds' nests with eggs: specimens of these are in the British Museum (No. VIII. 9) and in Mr. Herbert Allen's collection (No. 485), which also includes some of Raby's work.

Chapter 15

Staffordshire

_____

NOTE Although porcelain was made in Staffordshire at Longton Hall between 1750 and 1760[1], and even earlier at the short-lived 'Pomona Potworks' at Newcastle-under-Lyme[2] and, towards the end of the eighteenth century, at New Hall on transfer of Richard Champion's hard-paste patent, it now appears that the establishment of china manufacture in the Staffordshire Potteries was essentially a nineteenth-century development following the introduction of the English bone-china body. Interest in the products of this period has greatly increased in recent years and this chapter includes a general account of the main factories concerned and of their products. For a more detailed study the reader's attention is recommended to the numerous works listed in the Bibliography. F.A.B.

It is a matter for wonder that among Staffordshire potters for nearly twenty years after William Littler, none ever attempted the making of china figures. Perhaps the hazards of soft-paste forbade them, but the commercial success of the Cannock-born Duesbury should have made the attempt seem worth while.

We have at all events no porcelain figures that can reasonably be considered of Staffordshire origin until about 1790, a date we may

1 See p. 174.
2 See p. 196.

assign to those rather rustic but attractive pieces in the style of the Ralph Woods, which some have wished to claim for Lowestoft on the evidence of some fragmentary moulds found on the site. Modelling and colour make it highly improbable that these were made anywhere but in Staffordshire; they are in fact the porcelain counterparts of the Wood figures in earthenware. A pair of figures of this kind in a private collection in the Isle of Wight[1] bears a mark 'W(***)', stated by Chaffers without any reason given to be that of Aaron Wood, but there is no positive evidence that any of the Woods ever made porcelain. The 'W(***)' mark is found also on some bulb-pots of hard-looking porcelain of cold and greyish tone, painted with landscapes in Pinxton style and apparently dating from about 1800. It appears as well on a plate of cream-coloured earthenware in Leeds style in the Victoria and Albert Museum. These widely differing pieces suggest the work of a 'general potter' such as Enoch Wood, rather than Aaron Wood, who indeed could not have made pieces in so late a style. Further evidence that they were made at the Wood factory is provided by a specimen in the Victoria and Albert Museum bearing an impressed mould-number corresponding to one in the list of moulds published by Frank Falkner in his book *The Wood Family of Burslem*. Mr. Broderip's gift to the Victoria and Albert Museum includes a fine little group of these Staffordshire figures, which are for the greater part of decidedly soft paste; Plate 131 shows some of these. Figures of a harder material are sometimes encountered, rather later in date and usually of the insipid Classical models which by the end of the century had largely replaced the more vigorous rustic subjects. Figures in porcelain of *c.* 1800 of the 'flat back' type are occasionally seen marked' *Neale & Co.*'[2]

The patent held by Richard Champion for the manufacture of hard-paste porcelain was purchased in 1781 by a company of six Staffordshire potters: Samuel Hollins, John Turner, Jacob Warburton,[3] William Clowes, Charles Bagnall and Anthony Keeling, who began operations at the pottery of the last-named at

1 The collection has not been identified.
2 See also *English Porcelain* (ed. Charleston), p. 166.
3 Jacob Warburton is said by Simeon Shaw to have been 'distinguished for his moral and convivial habits of mind'.

Tunstall. In 1782 the works were transferred, after a disagreement amongst the partners, to an establishment at Shelton, near Hanley, called the NEW HALL.[1] The company (which styled itself the 'New Hall China Manufactory') was as much interested in the sale of the materials over which it held patent rights as in the manufacture of china from them, and by about 1812 hard-paste had lapsed in favour of a glassy-looking dull white porcelain. A specimen of this has been analysed[2] and proved to be essentially a bone-porcelain of the modern Staffordshire type. Wares of this period were usually marked with the name of the factory in a double circle, printed in red or brown. The earlier porcelain had seldom been marked, except occasionally with pattern-numbers preceded by 'N' or 'No.' in script characters. Manufacture ceased c. 1830 and the stock etc was finally sold in 1835.

The hard-paste of New Hall is sometimes not easily distinguishable from the Bristol 'cottage china'. It seems certain, too, that it was sometimes marked with the Bristol cross.[3] The slight patterns are often very charming, though the material itself was seldom free from imperfections and was often cold or grey in tone. A straight-sided silver-shape teapot (Plate 132A) was very popular at the New Hall factory[4] which also made round and boat-shaped teapots some with a raised collar. Sprigs and festoons were much in favour as before at Bristol; black, red and pink enamels predominate in contrast with the green, red and yellow of Bristol. But the style of the patterns was adopted also by several other Staffordshire factories; the impressed mark of Miles Mason occurs on pieces in the New Hall style, while Minton's earliest pattern-books include much that is very similar.[5] Similar patterns too are found on the

1 For a full account, see David Holgate, *New Hall and Its Imitators*.

2 *Analysed Specimens*, No. 43.

3 Mr. G. E. A. Grey (*English Porcelain*, ed. Charleston, p. 154) finds the New Hall glaze to be softer than Bristol and suggests that it was not fired together with the raw body. David Holgate, op. cit., believes the Bristol cross in enamel on New Hall to be in most cases, faked. He also finds lead in the New Hall glaze which is absent in Bristol glazes.

4 There is one at South Kensington signed '*Ralph Clowes New Hall fecit*'.

5 Some characteristic New Hall patterns have also been ascribed, probably in error, to a factory at Wirksworth in Derbyshire. See p. 380. For an account of Miles Mason's porcelain, see Reginald Haggar, 'Miles Mason', *Transactions E.C.C.* vol. 8, part 2, p. 183ff., and (with Elizabeth Adams) *Mason Porcelain and Ironstone* 1977.

FIGURES IN THE STYLE OF THE WOOD FAMILY Ht. 5⅝in (14.3cm) and 8in (20.3cm). About 1790. No marks. Victoria and Albert Museum (246-1924; C.311-1924 and C.245-1924)

very different paste of late Lowestoft. Somewhat crude but bold designs, by no means without character, are seen on the later New Hall; birds and landscapes in which pink and silver lustre[1] were used have a rustic quality that is decidedly refreshing in contrast with the pretentious work done at Worcester and other contemporary china-factories. Simple formal patterns in lustre, with white lines taken out with a point, are equally satisfying. Peter Warburton, a son of the patent-holder, in 1810 patented a process of printing in metallic gold.[2] Other patterns are decidedly modern in their feeling for the stylisation of floral motives and are very attractive; black monochrome was sometimes used. The colour of the paste and its peculiar glassy translucency serve to identify this later porcelain when it is unmarked. There is a very full representation of New Hall, both early and late, at South Kensington (Plate 132).[3]

Of all the Staffordshire factories New Hall alone inherited any part of the eighteenth-century tradition. Little can be said in praise of the other Staffordshire productions of the early-nineteenth century. Though we are beginning to respect some of the moral qualities of the Victorians, having been too long overshadowed by their defects, those qualities were scarcely synonymous with artistic expression in porcelain. It is astonishing now to read the complacent eulogies of contemporary productions pronounced by that painstaking antiquary, Llewellynn Jewitt.

The present-day existence of the firm founded in 1796 at Stoke-on-Trent by Thomas MINTON (1765–1836) may indicate an honourable record in the nineteenth century, not least in porcelain manufacture. Minton was a pupil of Turner of Caughley and, as a free-lance, later engraved copper plates for pottery-printing. In 1796 he set up his own factory with William Pownall and Joseph Poulson as partners. He died in 1836, and for five years his son

1 From gold and platinum.
2 Hobson, *Catalogue*, p. 145; a dish so decorated and marked 'Warburton's Patent' is in the Victoria and Albert Museum. Also Holgate, op. cit., fig. 150.
3 See also *English Porcelain* (ed. Charleston), pp. 154–60. T. A. Sprague, 'Hard Paste New Hall Porcelain' (*Apollo* XLIX, July 1949, pp. 16–18) provides a detailed description of these wares; also David Holgate's *New Hall and its Imitators*. Also Geoffrey Grey, 'New Hall Hard Paste Porcelain', *Transactions E.C.C.*, vol. 8, part 1, pp. 1–15.

A. TEAPOT Ht. 6in (15.2cm). About 1790–1805. No mark. Hard paste. *Victoria and Albert Museum (C.717-1921)*

B. CUP AND SAUCER Cup ht. 2¼in (5.7cm); Saucer dia. 5⅝in (14.3cm). About 1820–30. Mark 'New Hall' within a double circle and No. '88'. Bone china. *Victoria and Albert Museum (C.676-1935)*

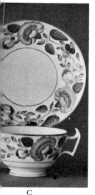

C. CUP AND SAUCER Cup ht. 2¼in (5.7cm); Saucer dia. 5⅝in (14.3cm). About 1800–20. No mark. Factory of origin doubtful. *Victoria and Albert Museum (C.1503-1924)*

D. CUP AND SAUCER Cup ht. 2in (5.7cm); Saucer dia. 5½in (14cm). About 1795–1810. No mark. Hard paste. *Victoria and Albert Museum (C.474-1920)*

E. CUP AND SAUCER Cup ht. 1⅝in (4.1cm); Saucer dia. 4½in (11.4cm). About 1795–1810. No mark. Hard paste. *Victoria and Albert Museum (C.266-1918)*

See pages 358, 360   Plate 132 STAFFORDSHIRE (*New Hall*)

Herbert carried on the business in partnership with John Boyle, under the style of 'Minton and Boyle'. From 1845 the firm was Minton and Hollins. Herbert Minton died in 1858, but Colin Minton Campbell continued the factory in partnership with Michael Hollins, and later with the grandsons of Thomas Minton. In 1883 the present company was formed. The marks used were numerous; some of them are reproduced in the Appendix to this book.

Porcelain of normal Staffordshire body was made from about 1798. Most of the current styles were adopted in the usually unmarked productions of the first twenty years; in particular, simple and effective designs of the types in use at New Hall figure largely in the firm's pattern-books of this period. The only mark used in this early period was a monogram of two 'S's' (not unlike the Sèvres mark) with 'M' below them, in blue enamel. Minton's Japan patterns were perhaps cleaner and generally in better taste than those of his rivals at Derby, Worcester and Spode's. Good stipple-printing was done; and the excellent slight landscapes in monochrome are again in later New Hall style. The only distinctive early Minton style is one represented at South Kensington by a bowl with bold gilding on a strong blue ground and panels of rather crude flowers in hot colouring. Mr. Allen's collection includes three vases (No. 517) in the same style (Plate 134). The 'Minton and Boyle' period was one of prosperity, and to this belong the numerous services marked with the name and number of the pattern in a scrolled cartouche, sometimes with the initials 'M & B'. The well-known 'Amherst Japan' pattern, first made for Lord Amherst, Governor-General of India (1823), occurs on Minton's 'stone-china'.

From 1841 begins the modern period. If the standard of invention seldom rose above the academically respectable, the work was always finely finished and sometimes beautiful. The numerous imitations of Sèvres[1] were at least as good as those of Coalport and Copeland's. Geoffrey Godden has identified with drawings in the Minton pattern books a number of figures,

---

1 The earlier work in Sèvres style, with turquoise ground, is not easily recognised. Robins and Randall (see p. 383) did similar work, and sometimes used Minton's porcelain. Compare Herbert Allen Collection, No. 523, etc.

B. Dish Dia. 8⅛in (20.6cm). Painted by Thomas Steele. About 1815. Mark 'Davenport Longport' in red. *Victoria and Albert Museum (2550-1901)* Davenport's porcelain

A. Set of Vases Ht. 4¾in (12cm); 5¼in (13.3cm); and 4½in (11.4cm). Painted by Edwin Steele. About 1830. *Victoria and Albert Museum (C.701-1935)* Spode's porcelain

See pages 368, 370   Plate 133 STAFFORDSHIRE (*Spode and Davenport*)

candelabra, etc., among them some hitherto regarded as of Coalport manufacture. The figures, in general, are stiffly posed and meticulously decorated in enamels and gilding.[1] A number of French artists joined the staff, amongst them Léon Arnoux (d. 1902), who came in 1848 and was a leading figure in the direction of the work. Turquoise grounds were constantly made with success, and the 'parian' biscuit invented by Copeland was used to great advantage;[2] such figures as those by Carrier (afterwards Carrier-Belleuse) on the service made for the wedding of King Edward VII in 1863 are undeniably accomplished. The accomplished work of Marc-Louis Solon in *pâte sur pâte* is too well known and too recent to need more than mention.

The SPODE factory at Stoke-on-Trent was founded by Josiah of that name, who was born in 1733 and in 1749 was an apprentice of Thomas Whieldon. At first earthenware only was made; the factory rapidly became prosperous, and a London warehouse in Fore Street, Cripplegate, proving too small to deal with the firm's business, large premises were taken in 1796 at the Theatre Royal, in Lincoln's Inn Fields and Portugal Street. A second Josiah Spode (*b.* 1754, *d.* 1827) succeeded to the management on his father's death in 1797; about 1813[3] he took into partnership the firm's London representative, William Copeland, and in 1833 the factory passed into the hands of the latter's son, William Taylor Copeland. The third Josiah Spode (d. 1829) seems to have taken little active part in the management. The firm was Copeland and Garrett from 1833 to 1847; then 'W. T. Copeland, late Spode'. Several marks are given in the Appendix.

Porcelain does not seem to have been made until the time of the second Josiah Spode. It has been contended on the evidence of the water-marks on certain pattern-books that porcelain was made at

---

1 G. A. Godden, *Minton Pottery and Porcelain of the First Period 1793–1850*, provides a full account of this factory.

2 Though George Cocker of Derby was allowed to repeat his popular successes. *Glazed* 'Parian' (compare the dessert dishes and cruet-stand in Mr. Allen's collection, Nos. 529 and 530) has a distinctive silky appearance.

3 An inscription on a bowl in the British Museum (XIV. 8) reads '*Spode & Copeland Manufacturers Feby. 1813*'. Hugh Tait (*Connoisseur*, May 1970) describes in detail this bowl with its inscriptions, which were part of a 'publicity campaign' to revive the china clay industry.

SET OF VASES Ht. 6½in (16.5cm) and 6 in (15.2cm). About 1820. Mark Interlaced double 'S' over 'M/780' in blue enamel. *Victoria and Albert Museum (C.683-1931)*

an earlier date,[1] but from the style of the surviving specimens none can be dated much before the beginning of the nineteenth century. The younger Spode is generally believed to have discovered the most satisfactory formula for bone-china, using a proportion of bone-ash in place of some of the china-clay in a formula otherwise similar to that for hard-paste.[2] Spode's formula seems to have enabled him to abandon the former preliminary 'fritting' of some of the ingredients. The Spode body has remained the English standard to the present day. Natural feldspar, distinct from the partly feldspathic china-stone, was used also in porcelain which from its style dates from about 1820–1; this bears the distinctive 'Feldspar' mark. A third type of body, intermediate between porcelain and earthenware and introduced in 1813, was named 'stone china'. The last-named type also bore a distinctive mark, but much of Spode's china had only a pattern number, though '*Spode*' in red or gold is not uncommon.

Practically nothing is known of the workmen responsible for Spode's designs or their execution, and the few names that have been recorded cannot be associated with particular specimens. This is hardly to be regretted, as no English porcelain is more clearly the product of the bad taste of the early years of the nineteenth century, particularly of the period following the Napoleonic wars, and of the commercialism that pandered to it. It is scarcely conceivable that a sensibility capable of appreciating the delicate art of eighteenth-century china could fail to be repelled by the vulgarity of most of Spode's wares. His commercial success was evidently enormous; Simeon Shaw naïvely remarked that 'Mr. S. was well capacitated, by the extensive knowledge he possessed relative to those subjects apparently best adapted for public demand, and which seem calculated to secure quick and profitable returns'. According to the same authority, in one year 'the clear profits of the London business alone exceeded £13000'.

1 Water-marks naturally give only the *earliest* possible date for the designs upon them, which may be many years later.

2 It should be mentioned, however, that so great an authority on the chemistry of pottery as Professor Church declared that Spode's formula was a matter of common knowledge in Staffordshire long before his time, and Martin Barr of Worcester undoubtedly experimented in the same direction not much later than 1795.

A. VASE Ht. 4¼in (10.8cm). (One of a set of three.) About 1810–20. Mark 'SPODE 1166' in red. *Victoria and Albert Museum (C.702-1935)*

B. CUP AND SAUCER Cup ht. 2¼in (5.7cm); Saucer dia. 5½in (14cm). About 1810–20. No mark. *Victoria and Albert Museum (C.975-1922)*

C. SPILL VASE Ht. 4¾in (12cm). About 1810–20. Mark 'SPODE 711' in red. *Victoria and Albert Museum (C.703-1935)*
Spode's porcelain

D. BOTTLE Ht. 6¼in (15.8cm). About 1835.
Griffin mark in puce. *Victoria and Albert Museum (3177-1901)*
Rockingham porcelain

See pages 368, 369

Plate 135 STAFFORDSHIRE (*Spode*) AND SWINTON (*Rockingham*)

The great house built by Spode at Penkhull Mount is depicted on a characteristic vase at South Kensington, with a dull claret-coloured ground, white flowers in applied relief and the heavy raised gilding said to have been the invention of his chief enameller, Henry Daniel. Later (after 1822) Daniel had his own china factory at Stoke-on-Trent at which were produced table wares in bone china that, whilst of good quality, are virtually indistinguishable from those of other contemporary factories.[1]

A large collection which had been preserved in the Spode family was presented to the South Kensington Museum in 1899 and 1902 by Miss. H. M. Gulson, niece of a fourth Josiah Spode. This and Mr. Herbert Allen's collection illustrate most of the types made at the factory. These were very numerous; but in fact most other factories' styles were adopted and no well-marked Spode style can be said to have emerged. Paste and glaze were technically excellent, but not as a rule distinguishable from other Staffordshire or from Rockingham china. The mannered flower-painting associated with the Steeles (Plate 133) and the later Derby porcelain (but perhaps not invented there), the designs wholly in gilt, again like Derby, and some very weak figure-painting are also found. Modelled and applied flowers like those of Coalport and Derby were occasionally used, and imitations of the Meissen '*Schneeballenvasen*' were made in this way. Some carefully finished naturalistic birds and landscapes were evidently reserved for the most costly pieces. The Japan patterns in red, blue and gold were among the earliest productions; at their best and least pretentious they were neat (Plate 135), but the more showy kinds were as hideous as Bloor's later 'Derby Japans', which are closely similar. Black stipple-prints of very good quality included the usual landscapes, and printed flowers were occasionally done with pleasant effect.

Spode's 'stone china' was obviously for the greater part intended as common useful ware; much was in fact made to match the heavy dishes of blue-and-white still being imported in quantity from China. But the very free adaptations of Chinese designs, with simple washes of colour over printed outlines, often have

---

1 1822 to 1845. Daniel also had an independent decorating shop within the Spode Works until 1822. For an account of his china, see G. A. Godden, *Daniel's Fine China* in *Antique Dealer and Collectors Guide*, September 1969, pp. 73–6.

originality and force as well as sincerity which is entirely lacking in the more pretentious pieces. Some very exact copies of Chinese *famille rose* were also made on Spode's 'stone china'; a Chinese plate and a Spode copy are shown side by side in Mr. Herbert Allen's collection (No. 640) at South Kensington.

The best Spode's later porcelain, made towards 1830 (and often bearing the 'Feldspar' mark), and the earlier Copeland tend towards the revived Sèvres style, affected also at Coalport and Rockingham. The rich dessert services of this period are at least handsome. Several of the coloured grounds were distinct from those of the rival factories: a soft greenish or pinkish grey, a pale green, a canary yellow, a deep rich fawn, and a very pale biscuit-colour were of shades peculiar to Spode's. Flowers painted in reserve on a gilt or dark-blue ground were much done at Spode's (Plate 135A). Other and less attractive coloured grounds used in this and earlier periods included a hideous matt blue (usually decorated with gilding), a dull pink and a heavy lifeless claret colour.

Messrs. Copelands' productions are beyond the scope of this book, but it is perhaps worth noting that Jewitt, writing of some of them in 1878, declared that 'in this ware it is a literal truism to say, Perfection can no farther go . . . the vases and other decorative articles . . . take rank with the finest productions of any age or any country'. 'Parian porcelain' was produced about 1845 after an attempt to find the secret of the earlier Derby biscuit.[1] It was largely used to imitate marble sculpture on a small scale. Some very carefully painted pieces made by Copeland about the time of the Great Exhibition of 1851 show that the firm shared in the general wish to outdo Sèvres in exquisiteness. A cup and saucer at South Kensington marked '*Copeland and Garrett*', is a creditable production of this kind.

A large pottery was conducted by the firm of DAVENPORT, at Longport, near Burslem, from 1793 until 1882,[2] and some surviving porcelain dating from the first half of the nineteenth

1 But the Parian body was of a quite different, harder, material than the biscuit porcelain of Derby.

2 For an account of this factory see T. Lockett, *Davenport Pottery and Porcelain*, Newton Abbot, 1972.

century bears their mark. It is without much character, though usually good, technically. The styles adopted were various, and the material, whilst sometimes as grey as late Worcester, is occasionally almost as white and translucent as Nantgarw. The Derby styles especially were favoured, however, and richly gilt borders of formal patterns and naturalistic flower and fruit painting in Derby style were characteristic. The famous Derby painter of fruit, Thomas Steele, seems actually to have worked at Davenport's, and two plates at South Kensington are unmistakably by his hand (Plate 133B). Edwin Steele's Rockingham-style flowers are also sometimes seen on Davenport porcelain. Figure-subjects on two plates in Mr. Herbert Allen's collection (Nos. 515 and 516), in the style of Chamberlain's Worcester, but attributable to Davenport's on the showing of their borders, are signed 'W. Fletcher', an artist otherwise unknown. Jesse Mountford, the Derby landscape-painter, is recorded to have moved to Longport, and Joshua Cristall, the water-colourist, is stated by Jewitt to have served an apprenticeship to John Davenport.

The firm of WEDGWOOD made porcelain for a short time, according to some recent authorities only between 1812 and 1816.[1] Useful ware was chiefly made, and it is without much distinction. The careless landscapes which appear on much of it are obviously by the hand of John Cutts of Pinxton, who is known to have worked for Wedgwood's.[2] Aaron Steel has been credited with some good bird paintings.

From about 1820 porcelain was produced as an article of commerce at very many other Staffordshire factories, among them Ridgways of Shelton, Miles Mason of Lane Delph, and Shorthose and Co. of Shelton. The latter made chiefly printed wares. Samuel Alcock and Co., of Cobridge and Burslem, made a variety of wares including biscuit china and encrusted vases in the Coalport and Minton manner. Few of these wares were marked.

Among the many other Staffordshire firms who also made

1 Porcelain manufacture was of course revived at Wedgwood's in more recent years, c. 1878.
2 Mr. John Cook of the Works Museum at Etruria kindly supplied a copy of a letter addressed by Cutts to Wedgwood and dated from Pinxton in 1813.

'stone china' (which was usually decorated with Japan patterns), C. J. Mason took out a patent in 1813 for an 'ironstone china' which was especially hard and was alleged to contain slag or ironstone. The Masons' business was later acquired by Ashworth's. Jewitt says of Ashworth's 'ironstone' wares that they 'include priceless Art treasures . . . deserving to be in every home of taste'. 'Turner's patent stone china' is sometimes met with. Ridgway's of Cauldon Place made excellent porcelain as well as stone china. Jewitt's comment on the 'toilettes Victoria' 'used by the Imperial Family', and other of Ridgway's productions, is that they 'achieved results never before attempted or attained as to magnitude and finish of goods'. Staffordshire 'stone china' was both cheap and durable, and quickly secured a very large market at home and abroad.[1]

1 For a comprehensive account of these porcelains see Godden, *Ridgway Porcelains*; the same author's *Mason's Patent Ironstone China*; Reginald Haggar, *The Masons of Lane Delph*; and R. Haggar, 'Miles Mason', *Transactions E.C.C.*, vol. 8, part 2, p. 183, and (with Elizabeth Adams) *Mason Porcelain and Ironstone*, 1977.

Chapter 16

Swinton (Rockingham)

Porcelain was successfully made between 1826 and 1842 at Brameld's Pottery on the estate of the Marquis of Rockingham, at Swinton near Rotherham, Yorkshire, when the factory was in the hands of the three sons of William Brameld, who died in 1813. The eldest, Thomas, was according to Jewitt 'a man of exquisite taste . . . intent on making Art-advances in his manufactory'. Pottery of all kinds had been and continued to be made. The brown-glazed 'Rockingham china' was, of course, not porcelain but earthenware; the so-called Cadogan tea- or hot-water pots of this material, in the form of the Chinese peach-shaped wine-pot, were a celebrated Rockingham production.

Experiments were made in the manufacture of porcelain from about 1820. These were evidently not altogether unsuccessful, though financial difficulties led the proprietors to appeal in 1826 to Earl Fitzwilliam, who granted them a subsidy. From that date the factory took the name 'Rockingham Works', with the right to use the Earl's crest (a griffin passant) as a mark. The production in that year of so difficult a piece of porcelain as the enormous 'rhinoceros vase', made for the Earl and now in the Rotherham Museum, shows that the potters were by no means without experience in porcelain manufacture. Reproduced here (Plate 136) is the companion vase in the Victoria and Albert Museum[1] as an

---

1 No. 47—1869. The Wentworth House specimen was painted by J. W. Brameld, one of the three partners of the firm.

'THE RHINOCEROS VASE' Ht. 38½in (97.8cm). Painted by Edwin Steele. About 1826. No mark. *Victoria and Albert Museum (47-1869)*

See page 372   Plate 136 SWINTON (*Rockingham*)

excellent illustration of the taste of the period. It is recorded to have been painted by Edwin Steele, son of Thomas Steele of Derby,[1] himself employed at Swinton for a short time. Other examples of Edwin Steele's work at Swinton are in Mr. Allen's collection (Nos. 596, 598 and 601). Amongst the other painters were William Corden, also of Derby; George Speight, who sometimes signed his work; Thomas Brentnall, Collinson and Llandig were fruit-and-flower-painters; and one William W. Bailey is named by Jewitt as 'principal butterfly painter'. Their styles, however, are seldom distinguishable, as few documentary pieces seem to have been preserved. But, as A. A. Eaglestone and T. A. Lockett have pointed out,[2] such pieces as the Rhinoceros Vases, though showing great technical skill, should not be regarded as typical of the factory, the great majority of the ornamental wares being more tasteful in design and decoration.

In 1830 the factory received an order from William IV for a large dessert-service,[3] now in Buckingham Palace, and from this date until the end of the reign styled itself 'Royal' and 'Manufacturer to the King'.

The 'Rockingham' porcelain was of good quality and its decoration no more florid than was usual in the period (Plate 135D). Painters listed by Dr. Rice[4] are Isaac Baguley, John Cresswell, Haigh Hirstwood, William Leyland, John Lucas (son of Daniel Lucas of Derby), John Randall and Benjamin Wolfe. Some of these were employed at the factory for a brief period only. The factory produced a great range of decorative wares in addition to large and elaborate services. Among those listed by Dr. Rice are vases of various shapes, baskets, scent bottles, pastille burners, inkstands, trays, trinket boxes, and toys. The Derby style was followed rather than that of Coalport, but unmarked pieces are often not easy to identify. A certain light feathery touch in the details of painted decoration often distinguishes Rockingham dessert-services from those made by Spode and at Coalport. The

1 See p. 130.
2 *English Porcelain* (ed. Charleston), pp. 136–42.
3 Numbering 200 pieces, said to have cost £5,000. Several sample plates are illustrated in colour by D. G. Rice, *The Illustrated Guide to Rockingham Pottery and Porcelain*.
4 D. G. Rice, op. cit.

lavish gilding sometimes includes delicate lace-patterns of a kind not found elsewhere: the gilding itself is generally darker than on Coalport, inclining to a coppery tone. The coloured grounds were not very distinctive; a deep *gros bleu* inclining to violet, and a thick smooth opaque green, however, were peculiar to the factory, as was the so-called 'Rockingham glaze' of manganese brown, used on the tea-pots already mentioned. A large cup and saucer with this glaze is in the collection at South Kensington. A neutral grey ground was also much favoured.

Rockingham coloured figures were often on a larger scale than those of other factories, and coarsely enamelled with broad half-translucent washes. Certain smaller shepherdesses and the like and some seated figures in a rather chalky biscuit are easily mistaken for Derby. Toy houses in porcelain with encrusted vegetation have a North of England 'peasant' flavour that is charming by contrast with the more ostentatious work done at the factory.[1]

It should be mentioned that undecorated Rockingham china was bought and painted by Allen of Lowestoft.[2]

1 The fact that none have yet been found with the factory mark requires caution in the acceptance of such as Rockingham. D. G. Rice, op. cit., pp. 63–4.
2 Jewitt, vol. I, p. 502. See p. 199.

Chapter 17

Miscellaneous Factories, Legends and Decorators

The obscure beginnings of English porcelain have naturally permitted the wildest conjectures regarding supposed early specimens. The originally vague significance of the word 'china', which we now take to mean porcelain only, is doubtless responsible for some of the myths. It was current in the seventeenth and eighteenth centuries for several sorts of ware, particularly blue-and-white earthenware, and its use does not necessarily imply porcelain as we now understand it. It has been explained how JOHN DWIGHT and FRANCIS PLACE came, partly in this way, to be credited with the making of some unquestionably Chinese porcelain.[1]

An often-quoted early report of porcelain-manufacture appeared in a publication of 1716[2] and spoke of 'a try'd and infallible method' by which ground-up oriental china was mixed with gum-water and burnt oyster-shells. Mr. Hobson described this as Gilbertian, but admitted that Dossie's *Handmaid to the Arts* (1764) indicated that powdered Chinese porcelain was actually an ingredient in some of the earlier soft-pastes. And Mr. William Burton[3] thought the recipe not so absurd as it seems. Dossie said he

---

1 See p. 3.
2 Quoted in Hobson, *Catalogue*, p. xvi, from *Essays for the Month of December 1716*, by a *Society of Gentlemen* (said to be the work of Aaron Hill).
3 *English Porcelain*, p. 8. Burnt oyster-shells have of course been used as a source of lime, and gum-water was apparently used in early porcelain manufactures to remedy a lack of plasticity in a paste containing little clay.

had seen 'near London' eleven mills at work, grinding eastern china for this purpose, but the porcelain made was 'grey, full of flaws and bubbles'. We cannot of course recognise the productions from this, and the description may not be altogether accurate, but it is interesting to recall that casks of 'broken India china' were sent from Chelsea to Derby in 1790.[1] 'Grog' or ground-up potsherds is a common ingredient in pottery bodies, and perhaps some of the alumina in the analyses of English soft-paste is due to this ingredient. But we may be certain that artificial porcelain was not made in any quantity by the 'try'd and infallible method' of 1716, or at all events not at that date.

Another mystery has been made round the efforts in England of the Duc de BRANCAS, Comte de LAURAGUAIS, who in 1766 took the first step towards an English patent for hard-paste, but never entered his specification.[2] He discovered *kaolin* at Alençon in 1758, and is believed to have found it also in Cornwall about the time of his application for a patent. His supposed productions in France, of dates between 1764 and 1768, bear a monogram 'L.B.' or 'L.R.'[3] and include a plate painted in *famille rose* style,[4] as well as busts and reliefs, all said to be greyish and full of imperfections. A breakfast-cup and saucer and a plate in Mr. Allen's collection (No. 624), painted with flowers in natural colours, has the mark 'L.P.' in monogram in blue and has been claimed as Brancas-Lauraguais porcelain. But it is of nineteenth-century date and probably Continental, and the mark decidedly suspect as a later addition. Brancas-Lauraguais's English porcelain is, one fears, a myth.

An imperfect knowledge of London topography may well have assisted in the creation of some of the legendary factories. The eastern suburbs and outskirts of London were perhaps as little known to the citizens in the eighteenth century as they are today. The exact site of the Bow factory may not have been described or

1 '. . . in 1790 and previous thereto.' W. Bemrose, *Bow, Chelsea and Derby Porcelain*, p. 37.

2 Jewitt, vol. I, p. 114.

3 A list of his productions is given in Comte Xavier de Chavagnac and A. de Grollier, *Histoire des manufactures françaises de porcelaine*, pp. 403–5. Owen, p. xxiii, described a tea-bottle declared to be of Brancas-Lauraguais porcelain, 'marked in red . . . B.L.,' which has since been lost sight of.

4 Illustrated in E. Hannover, *Pottery and Porcelain*, vol. III, fig. 478.

understood by the gossips of the time, and Jonas Hanway[1] may have heard of the Bow factory from two different sources and not realised that the STEPNEY of one informant was perhaps the same as the Bow of another. A confusion between the locality of the factory and of the City church of St. Mary-le-Bow familiarly called Bow Church,[2] would facilitate the mistake. A similar error would account for the reference to different factories at STRATFORD and Bow, in an account in the *London Chronicle*, 1755, of the departure of some china-makers for Scotland.[3] LAMBETH,[4] LIMEHOUSE[4] (for which advertisements of 1747 and 1748 exist) and KENTISH TOWN,[6] on the other hand, seem well-documented, though none of their productions has yet been identified. The latter factory was commenced in 1755 by John Bolton from the Lambeth manufactory for one William Kempson, who was bankrupt in the following year.

Dr. Pococke[7] spoke of the 'china and enamel manufactory' at York House at BATTERSEA. Rouquet,[8] after describing the Chelsea works, referred to a neighbouring 'manufacture de porcelaine' where certain pieces were printed ('en camayeux par une espèce d'impression'). Elsewhere[9] is mentioned the resemblance of certain Bow prints to those of Ravenet and the young Hancock, and the possibility that both Chelsea and Bow porcelain may have been occasionally decorated at Battersea. On the other hand the 'porcelaine' may have been white-enamelled copper! Similarly we may explain the BIRMINGHAM china of an advertisement of 1757 quoted by Nightingale[10] as a mistaken reference to South

1 He wrote in his *Travels* (1753), vol. IV, p. 228, after visiting Meissen in 1750, 'It is with great satisfaction that I observe the manufactures of Bow, Chelsea and Stepney so improved.'

2 See p. 88 for a reference to 'Bow Churchyard'. Frank Hurlbutt, *Bow Porcelain*, p. 138, spoke of Bow 'with its well-known bells'. See p. 81 for reference to Stratford-le-Bow and Stratford Langhorne (where the Bow factory was actually sited), and the possibility of early 'Bow' experiments at Stepney.

3 Quoted in Hobson, *Catalogue*, p. xviii.

4 p. 86.

5 p. 211.

6 A. J. Toppin, 'The Kentish Town China Factory' in *Transactions E.C.C.*, I (1933), p. 30.

7 Op. cit., vol. II, p. 69.

8 Op. cit., p. 143.

9 p. 118.

10 p. lxv.

Staffordshire and Birmingham enamels. Dr. Pococke's presumed confusion of the two materials at Battersea will perhaps justify us in disregarding his report[1] of a former china-manufacture at the 'Sturbridge' (STOURBRIDGE) glass-works, which had been discontinued, however, at the time of his visit in 1751. Opaque white glass, often confused with porcelain, had perhaps been made.

More persistently and ardently supported by local patriots are the supposed porcelain-factories at ISLEWORTH, WIRKSWORTH and CHURCH GRESLEY. For the first of these we have no written evidence relating to porcelain[2] until 1795, when Lysons spoke of a 'china manufactory' there; but that author was probably not concerned to distinguish porcelain from white earthenware. The traditional ascription to Isleworth of two pieces formerly in the Jermyn Street Collection with a mark resembling an 'I'[3] and now at South Kensington is quite certainly mistaken: they are both of Lund's Bristol or Worcester china. A saucer, also at South Kensington, painted in blue with the initials 'CHS' surmounted by a crest of a portcullis, is of different character. A similar plate once in the possession of the Earl of Jersey at Osterley Park (near Isleworth) has the monogram of Sarah Child (b. 1764, d. 1793), heiress of Robert Child of Osterley and mother of Sarah, Countess of Jersey. The traditional ascription of these pieces to Iselworth is more respectable, but they may equally well be Worcester or Salopian porcelain made to order.

Of an attempted manufacture at CHURCH GRESLEY near Burton-on-Trent there is some circumstantial evidence, but of its productions in porcelain little indeed. It is said to have been established in 1794 by Sir Nigel Bowyer Gresley, who engaged amongst others William Coffee, the Derby modeller;[4] it was sold to W. Nadin in 1800 and finally closed in 1808. A mug, painted in blue, in the British Museum (XIII. 1),[5] formerly ascribed to

1 Vol. II, p. 223.
2 Pottery was evidently made in some quantity at an earlier date. Black and other ware is supposed to have been made.
3 The little mug figured in Plate 79G (No. 3147—1901), and a bowl (No. 3777—1901) with the same pattern. Two bowls in the British Museum (Nos. XVI. 1 and 2) have been similarly ascribed. Compare Mark No. 5 on p. 391.
4 But by 1795 he had 'finished all there was to do there' (Jewitt, vol. II, p. 98).
5 There are others similar at South Kensington (Nos. C841—1924 and C1307—1924).

Church Gresley on traditional grounds, is almost certainly a Bow piece. A showy service with yellow panels alternating with panels of coloured flowers, also attributed to the factory, is very like Flight and Barr's Worcester[1], and in any case too 'slick' and accomplished to have been made at a factory that is admitted to have been a failure, technically and commercially.[2] That the pattern is known as the 'Church Gresley pattern' would merely imply that it was ordered (of the Worcester firm) by someone from that place: it was a Worcester practice so to name their patterns. A vase claimed as Church Gresley by a descendant of the second proprietor[3] is a Continental production of a well-known type. Its date is shown by its style to be nearer 1820 than the period given for the factory. Church Gresley porcelain must therefore be considered to be another myth.

Similar traditions, partly mistaken,[4] have given some porcelain to a WIRKSWORTH (Derbyshire) factory.[5] Fine white china-clay in the neighbourhood may well have tempted potters to start a pottery in the district, but of porcelain made from it there is no sure record. The Catalogue[6] of a Fine Art and Industrial Exhibition held at Derby in 1870 is full of praise for Wirksworth china, but states that the factory came to an end in 1777. Jewitt[7] quotes a lease dated 6 November 1777 of 'Holland House' in Wirksworth 'heretofore used for the making ... of China Ware',[8] and also mentions the story that William Billingsley started a porcelain-factory at Wirksworth at some time between 1804 and 1808. The

1 The pattern is also on a service at Windsor Castle, made for Edward, Duke of Kent, who visited the Church Gresley works. Hence the mistake?

2 'The china always came out of the ovens cracked and crazed.' See a letter quoted by Jewitt, vol. II, p. 156, and Haslem (*Catalogue*, p. 48) says that it was 'so soft that it came out of the oven every shape but the right'.

3 In *The Expert*, 25 May 1907.

4 Traditions about pottery orally transmitted usually prove to be of very doubtful value.

5 Terence Lockett, quoting from the *Chandos–Pole–Gell Papers* in the Derbyshire County Record Office, gives clear evidence that the building of the factory was in progress in the autumn of 1772. In the *Northern Ceramic Society Journal*, vol. I, pp. 45–57, a valuable survey of this minor factory is made.

6 By W. Bemrose and A. Wallis.

7 Vol. II, pp. 142–4.

8 A notice in the *Derby Mercury* for 23 May 1777 records the sale of moulds etc. as well as wares, by Mrs. Dickens at the 'Three Crowns, Wirksworth'.

discovery of wasters[1] proves, indeed, that porcelain of some sort was made there, but what it was like and whether it was made in any quantity are questions still unanswered. Most of the pieces traditionally said to have been made at the factory appear to be of late eighteenth- or early nineteenth-century date. They are too late in style to have been made before 1777, and do not in the least resemble, either in paste or decoration, the china made by Billingsley, at Pinxton just before the dates given for his supposed Wirksworth factory, or later at Nantgarw. On the other hand, they closely resemble Staffordshire porcelain[2] of New Hall type, and none of them corresponds with the porcelain wasters found on the factory site. Plate 132D shows a cup and saucer of one of these patterns. In fact, it may be said that no Wirksworth china has been authenticated.[3]

Reference has already been made to Billingsley's ventures at Mansfield, Torksey and Brampton (p. 309) but, in spite of the wasters found at Torksey, he seems at this time to have been occupied mainly in the decoration of china obtained from elsewhere.

Some myths (if myths they be) survive by virtue of the quantity of unmarked and, to most people, problematical early china in existence. On the other hand, factories have sometimes been invented to account for marks—actually those of dealers—which occasionally appear on pieces. Several examples of these have been mentioned.[4] A puzzling mark on a Derby coffee-cup in the British Museum collection (No. III. 24) and a Worcester tea-pot in the Frank Lloyd Collection (and many other extant pieces) is that of

1 See articles by T. L. Tudor in the *Transactions of the Derbyshire Archæological and Natural History Society*, 1916, p. 117, and in *The Connoisseur*, vol. LI (1918), p. 25 ; but see also Bernard Rackham in *The Burlington Magazine*, vol. XXIX (1916), p. 339. The wasters are now in the Victoria and Albert Museum.

2 The resemblance said to exist between the supposed Wirksworth and Lowestoft depends only on the use of certain diapers of Chinese origin such as were common also on Staffordshire porcelain well into the nineteenth century. But the paste of genuine Lowestoft is entirely different from that of the supposed Wirksworth specimens.

3 Terence Lockett, loc. cit., quotes from invoices among the *Chandos–Pole–Gell Papers*, apparently emanating from the Wirksworth factory (they are described as 'scraps of paper') which describe useful porcelain 'both printed and painted, and ornamental, including vases and figures—at least of dogs'.

4 pp. 322 and 403.

Coombs, a china-repairer of Queen Street, Bristol, who fixed together broken parts with frit and re-marked the pieces in enamel colour or fired 'ink';[1] he is known to have worked between 1780 and 1805. An associate named Daniel is also recorded with the address 'David Street, near the Broad Main Bristol' with the dates 1789 and 1791. A similar mark records a repairer named 'Strong' but nothing is known of him.

A small group of porcelain, consisting of table-wares and a snuff-box, marked with the letter 'A' in underglaze blue or incised, has been uncertainly ascribed to an unnamed Italian factory, but recently adduced evidence seems in favour of a British, possibly Scottish, origin for the class. In a paper read before the English Ceramic Circle it was suggested that present evidence indicated that Nicholas Crisp of Vauxhall, or a hitherto unknown venture at Gorgie, near Edinburgh, might be responsible,[2] and yet a possible third candidate appears in a soft-paste factory newly discovered during excavations at Newcastle-under-Lyme.[3]

Much has already been said of the 'outside enamellers' who decorated porcelain but did not make it. For those disturbers of the collector's peace—Duesbury and Giles, in particular, as well as the mysterious Richard Dyer—the reader is referred to earlier pages,[4] where are discussed the doubts about some Bow, Chelsea, Derby and Worcester attributions, due to their activities. In the later eighteenth and early part of the nineteenth centuries, London dealers and decorators took much Caughley-Coalport[5] and Nantgarw-Swansea[6] porcelain. The decorators' names seldom appear, but the dealers who employed them sometimes added theirs as marks.[7] Allen[8] of Lowestoft, Duvivier,[9] Thomas Pardoe,[10] Thomas Baxter and his father,[11] and the Donovans of

---

1 For marks in fired ink ('ink residues'), of a pale brownish colour with faint lustre, see 'Invisible marks', *Transactions E.C.C.*, vol. I (1933), pp. 55 and 56.

2 Charleston and Mallet, 'A Problematical Group of Eighteenth Century Porcelain', *Transactions E.C.C.*, vol. 8, part I, pp. 80–177.

3 'Soft Paste at Newcastle-under-Lyme', *Transactions E.C.C.*, vol. 9, part 1, and see p. 196.

4 pp. 86, 96, 102 and 264.

5 pp. 326   6 p. 322

7 pp. 323 and 403.   8 p. 204.

9 p. 313. A large mug of Caughley-Coalport porcelain signed by F. Duvivier is figured in Margaret Vivian, *Antique Collecting*, fig. 38.

10 p. 318.   11 pp. 280, 290 and 318.

Dublin have been spoken of. There are examples of the work of the last-named in Mr. Herbert Allen's collection (No. 588) and in the British Museum (No. XIV. 10); on the latter, Donovan's mark is added to that of Minton's factory. William Absolon, Jnr., of Great Yarmouth, painted earthenware, porcelain and glass from various sources between about 1784 and 1815, signing his name on the reverse.[1] Thomas Martin Randall (*b.* 1786, *d.* 1859) and Richard Robins,[2] of Spa Fields, not only decorated English china for the London dealers, but painted in the most costly Sèvres manner much white Sèvres china bought up in Paris in the early years of the nineteenth century by Baldock and Jarman, when the *pâte tendre* was abandoned at the French national factory. Lightly decorated Sèvres porcelain was even stripped of its painting with acid and re-decorated with more pretentious designs. Much of the supposed Sèvres china in English collections was painted by Robins and Randall, who used also in the same way white china obtained from Minton's.[3] Randall is stated by Jewitt to have himself started a manufacture of soft-paste about 1825, at MADELEY, near Coalport, in Shropshire, and there made imitations of Sèvres, as well as painting actual Sèvres porcelain obtained in the white.[4] A family named Bevington of Hanley is also said to have made imitations of Sèvres in quantity about 1870.[5] Sims was another enameller who took Nantgarw china in the white.[6] Zachariah Boreman, after leaving Derby, is said to have worked for Sims, himself an old Derby hand. Cartwright, Battam,[7] Anderson and Muss are other decorators mentioned by Haslem, who had good opportunities to obtain information about these establishments. Muss employed amongst others the famous John Martin (b. 1789, d. 1854), who painted a very striking picture illustrating *Paradise Lost* on a panel of Flight and Barr porcelain in the Allen Collection (No. 312).

---

1 A. J. B. Kiddell, 'William Absolon, Jnr., of Great Yarmouth', *Transactions E.C.C.*, vol. 5, part I, pp. 53–63.
2 p. 322.
3 A sugar-basin with a Sèvres mark in the Allen Collection (No. 531) is an example of this kind of fake.
4 See Barrett, *Caughley and Coalport Porcelain*, Chapter VI.
5 See G. W. Rhead, *British Pottery Marks*, p. 35.
6 p. 322.
7 Afterwards with Copeland's.

Appendix A

Marks

The following tables include all the well-established factory-marks in their characteristic forms. In all cases where a reasonable doubt exists in the attribution of a mark, attention has been drawn to the fact in the text, which should always be consulted. Workmen's marks, numerals and initial-letters could, of course, be added to indefinitely, but this would not help the collector in identifying his specimens.

'In blue' in every case means in underglaze blue: marks in blue over the glaze are described as 'in blue enamel'.

CHELSEA

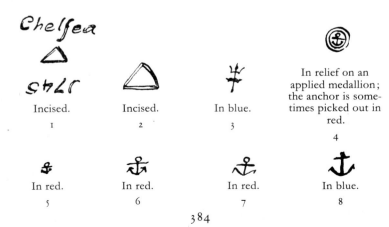

Incised.	Incised.	In blue.	In relief on an applied medallion; the anchor is some-times picked out in red.
1	2	3	4
In red.	In red.	In red.	In blue.
5	6	7	8

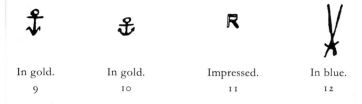

In gold.
9

In gold.
10

Impressed.
11

In blue.
12

(1) 1745.

(2) About 1745 to about 1750.

(3) About 1750 (see page 22).

(4) From about 1749 to 1753.

(5) to (8) About 1753 to 1756 and occasionally later. Imitated also at Derby, Bow and Worcester. A red anchor, as a rule much larger than these, was used at Venice (Cozzi factory); an anchor, usually printed, was also a Davenport mark (see p. 405). A list of factories using an anchor as a mark, on earthenware as well as porcelain, is given in Rhead, *British Pottery Marks*, p. 13.

(9) and (10) From 1758 to 1769. Found also on Derby, and copied on imitations of Chelsea made at Coalport, and on modern French and German copies of Chelsea figures and of the Derby figures of the 1760s, formerly believed to be Chelsea.

1) 'Repairer's mark' (not Roubiliac's, see p. 60). About 1760–5.

2) Imitation Meissen mark on a cup of about 1750 in the Schreiber Collection.

BOW

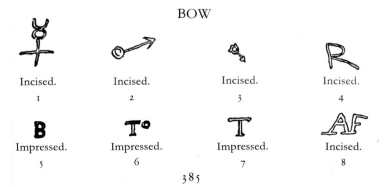

Incised.
1

Incised.
2

Incised.
3

Incised.
4

Impressed.
5

Impressed.
6

Impressed.
7

Incised.
8

Incised.

9

Impressed.

10

In blue.

11

In blue.

12

In blue.

13

In blue.

14

13

In blue.

15

In blue.

16

In blue.

17

In red.

18

2

In red.

19

F

In red.

20

In red.

21

In blue and red.

22

I

In blue.

23

A

In blue.

24

In blue and red.

25

In blue.

26

In blue.

27

In blue.

28

In red.

29

(1) to (3) On early pieces, probably about 1750.

(4) to (10) Presumably 'repairers' marks. About 1750 to 1760.

(11) to (17) On blue-and-white. About 1755 to 1765. For No. 11, see pp. 122 and 240. Compare Nos. 16 and 17 with the Worcester mark No. 7 and the Caughley mark No. 10. Compare No. 15 with Lowestoft numerals and pp. 122 and 204.

(18) to (20) On enamelled useful wares; other numerals and initials also occur.

(21) to (29) On figures and other late pieces. The heavy dagger in (22) and the cursive 'B' in (25) are in underglaze blue. The colour of the anchor and dagger is often decidedly brown rather than red. About 1760 to 1775.

DERBY

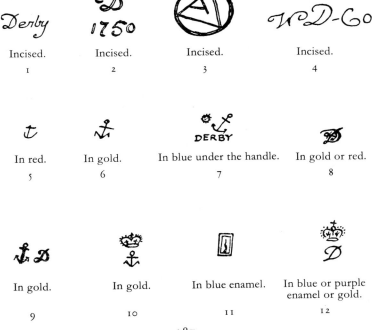

Incised.
1

Incised.
2

Incised.
3

Incised.
4

In red.
5

In gold.
6

In blue under the handle.
7

In gold or red.
8

In gold.
9

In gold.
10

In blue enamel.
11

In blue or purple enamel or gold.
12

Incised.
13

Incised.
14

Incised.
15

Incised.
16

Incised.
17

Incised.
18

Incised.
19

In blue.
20

In blue.
21

In blue, crimson or puce
enamel, or in gold.
22

In purple.
23

In red.
24

In red.
25

Printed in red.
26

Printed in red.
27

Printed in red.
28

In blue enamel.
29

Incised.
30

In red.
31

Printed.
32

388

(1) and (2) On white cream-jugs of about 1750.

(3) About 1750–5. Conjectured to be a Derby mark.

(4) Much reduced. Presumably standing for 'William Duesbury and Company'. About 1760.

(5) Forged Chelsea mark on a plate of about 1760. Also on Chelsea-Derby useful wares occasionally.

(6) Forged Chelsea mark on a figure of Lord Chatham (Schreiber Collection). Also occasionally on Chelsea-Derby useful wares.

(7) Reputed mark of Richard Holdship on a printed mug (but see p. 142).

(8) The normal 'Chelsea-Derby' mark on useful wares. About 1770–84.

(9) Rare Chelsea-Derby mark on a service of the pattern figured in Plate 58A.

(10) About 1770–80.

(11) About 1770–80: on an early 'Japan' pattern (Plate 59I).

(12) For a short time about 1784.

(13) to (19) Marks on figures. The numbers are model-numbers. The symbols are those of 'repairers' (see p. 158). In (19) 'B' may mean 'best' or 'biscuit'. A similar script 'N' occurs on useful wares of about 1780.

(20) Meissen mark on reproductions or 'replacers'.

(21) Frankenthal mark on copies of gold-striped pieces (see p. 148), perhaps replacers.

(22) About 1784 to about 1810.

(23) Duesbury and Kean period (1795–6). One example only is recorded.

(24) and (25) Bloor period (1811–48). Occasionally also in gold or black.

(26) to (28) Later Bloor period, about 1820–48 (according to Haslem these began to be used 'shortly before 1830'), but see note on Locker's mark (see p. 156)—'LOCKER & CO., LATE BLOOR DERBY'—resembles No. 27.

(29) Forged Sèvres mark on late Derby.

(30) George Cocker's mark (see p. 160).

(31) Stevenson and (also Sampson) Hancock's mark: about 1850–70.

(32) Mark of the Royal Crown-Derby Factory, founded in 1876 and still in existence.

LONGTON HALL

On early wares. All in blue.

The last two 'marks' occur in the field of the decoration (see p. 182) and were perhaps imitated from the conventionalised distant mountains of a Chinese landscape. Numerals and letters of the alphabet are found in underglaze blue. Dr. Watney records some alchemical incised marks.[1]

LOWESTOFT

ʒ   ᴣ   ᵴ   z   ℓ   w   ℓ   ⚔   28

All in blue.

The thin crescent with open ends (No. 7 in the line) is printed, on blue-printed pieces; the other marks are painted. The first four are examples of the Lowestoft marks written inside the foot-ring. The crescents and the 'W' are copies of Worcester marks; the crossed swords, a Lowestoft version of the Meissen mark.

LUND'S BRISTOL AND EARLY WORCESTER

Bristoll	Bristol	Bristoll 1750	ℓᵒˣ
Embossed in relief.	Embossed in relief.	Embossed in relief.	In red.
1	2	3	4

1 Watney, *Longton Hall Porcelain*, p. 49.

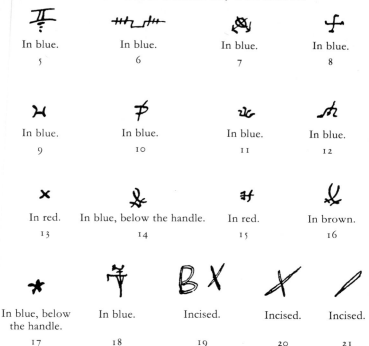

In blue.	In blue.	In blue.	In blue.
5	6	7	8
In blue.	In blue.	In blue.	In blue.
9	10	11	12
In red.	In blue, below the handle.	In red.	In brown.
13	14	15	16
In blue, below the handle.	In blue.	Incised.	Incised.	Incised.
17	18	19	20	21

Nos. 4 to 18 are probably workmen's marks: some of them are found on undoubted Worcester porcelain (see below and p. 226). No. 18 occurs on a mug of the 'scratched cross' family. There are many others. The 'alchemists'' marks (Nos. 4–15, etc.) were formerly ascribed to Bow, and also occur, but much more rarely, on porcelain from that factory; compare p. 122.

Nos. 19 to 21. For the significance of these incised marks, see pp. 224 and 228.

WORCESTER

'DR. WALL' PERIOD (1751–83)

(1) to (6) and (8) Painters' marks: 1751 to about 1770. There are many others; compare also Bristol (Lund's), above. The

In red.

1

In blue.

2

In blue.

3

In blue.

4

In blue.

5

In blue.

6

In blue.

7

In blue.

8

In blue.

9

In red.

10

Printed in blue.

11

In gold, black
or blue enamel.

12

Printed in blue.

13

In blue.

14

In blue.

15

In blue.

16

In blue.

17

Printed in blue.

18

In blue or black.

19

In red.

20

In blue enamel.

21

In blue.

22

In blue.

23

In blue.

24

In blue enamel.	In blue.	In blue.	In blue.
25	26	27	28

R.H.f	RH Worcester	J Ross sculp'		O.N.P
Printed in black.	Printed in black.	Printed in black.		
29	30	31	32	33

Chinese characters (No. 7) should be compared with the Bow (Nos. 16 and 17) and Caughley (No. 10) marks of a similar kind.

(9) In slightly varying forms: in use until about 1795.

(10) On enamelled wares: 1770–90.

(11) On wares printed in underglaze blue.

(12) Chiefly used in the Flight period, but occasionally also (as on the 'Duke of Gloucester's' service) in the earlier period, 1770–80.

(13) On blue-printed wares.

(14) to (17) On all classes of porcelain, 1755–83. There are many other slightly varying forms.

(18) On blue-printed wares only. Also occurs enclosed in a rectangle.

(19) This occurs on black-'pencilled' china (p. 258), and also on pieces of Lund's type painted in colours and in blue.

(20) Seen occasionally on enamelled wares after about 1768, probably added by a Chelsea painter working at Worcester or by Giles. A specimen analysed by Mr. Herbert Eccles has this mark (see *Analysed Specimens*, No. 29). The anchor in *gold* is very rare, but occurs on a pale-claret-ground cup and saucer painted with 'dishevelled birds', in the British Museum (see p. 266).

(21) On transfer-printed wares coloured over, perhaps added by Giles (see p. 252).

(22) Imitation Meissen mark common on many classes of china. The number added between the blades is sometimes '91'. Almost the only mark ever seen on black-printed wares, usually unmarked.

(23) and (24) Imitations of Tournay and Chantilly marks.

(25) and (26) Imitations of the Sèvres and Fürstenberg marks.

(27) and (28) Probably workmen's marks; both occur on an enamelled piece of about 1775.

(29) Initials of Robert Hancock.

(30) Monogram and rebus device of Richard Holdship: but see p. 248.

(31) Signature of James Ross.

(32) Initials of John Donaldson on painted decoration.

(33) Initials of O'Neale (for 'O'Neale pinxit') on painted decoration; the name is sometimes written in full.

'FLIGHT' TO 'FLIGHT, BARR AND BARR' PERIODS (1783–1840)

In blue.	Impressed.	In red or blue.	In blue.
1	2	3	4

Incised.	Incised.	In red.	Impressed.
5	6	7	8

(1) to (4) Marks of the 'Flight' period (1783–92). No. 2 is rare. The crown (No. 3) was added after the granting of a royal patent in 1789. '*Flight*' and a crescent is sometimes found in red, blue or gold. No. 4 is one of the series of disguised numerals (1–9), formerly believed to be Caughley marks.

(5) to (7) are marks of the 'Flight and Barr' period (1792–1807).

(5) and (6) indicate experimental pastes introduced by Martin Barr; stated by Binns not to have been used after 1803, but an incised B occurs on a flower-pot in the Schreiber Collection (No. 678) to be ascribed to the year 1809.

BARR FLIGHT & BARR
Royal Porcelain Works
WORCESTER
London House
Nº 1 Coventry Street

Printed in red
or black.

9

Barr Flight & Barr
Worcester
Flight & Barr
Coventry Street
London
Manufacturers to their
Majesties &
Royal Family

In red or black.

10

FBB

Impressed.

11

Flight Barr & Barr
Worcester.

In red or black.

12

Printed in red or black.

13

(8) to (10) are marks of the 'Barr, Flight and Barr' period (1807–13): the Prince of Wales' feathers were added in 1807 after the royal appointment of that year. The London branch retained the style of 'Flight and Barr'.

(11) to (13) are marks of the 'Flight, Barr and Barr' period (1813–40). Joseph Flight died in 1829, but his name continued to be used in the marks.

CHAMBERLAIN'S

Chamberlains
Wor No276

In red.

1

Chamberlains
Worcester
403

In purple.

2

Chamberlains
Worcester

In gold.

3

Chamberlain's
Worcester
& 63, Piccadilly,
London.

Printed in red.

4

Chamberlain's
Regent China
Worcester
& 155
New Bond Street,
London

Printed in red.

5

Chamberlains

Incised.

6

CHAMBERLAINS

Impressed.

7

Chamberlain
Worcester.

In red.

8

CHAMBERLAIN & Cº
WORCESTER
155 NEW BOND St
& Nº I.
COVENTRY St
LONDON.

Printed in red.

9

(1) Early mark, about 1800.

(2) and (3) About 1810–20: the gold mark was used on the more
ambitious productions.

(4) The Piccadilly premises were in use by Chamberlain's for the
period 1814–16 only.

(5) The crown was used after the beginning of the Regency in
1811, when the 'Regent china' body was introduced by
Chamberlain's for occasional use: this body is very
translucent and somewhat resembles Nantgarw china, but
is harder. No. 5 above was the special mark used upon it. A
plate at South Kensington (No. 3301–1901) is an example.
The Bond Street address dates from 1816, and there are
other marks including it. The words 'Royal Porcelain

Manufacturers' began to be used in 1820 on the accession of George IV.

(6) and (7) Late marks, about 1845–50. (7) occurs on pieces with a very hard paste and thick raised gilding.

(8) About 1845. The smaller and more laboured writing distinguishes this from the earlier mark.

(9) The two addresses indicate the period between 1840 (when the two Worcester firms were amalgamated as 'Chamberlain and Company') and 1845, when the Coventry Street house was given up. Also used in script characters.

MODERN PERIOD

Printed or impressed.

1

Printed.

2

Impressed.

3

Printed.

4

In red.

5

In red.

6

GRAINGER & CO

Printed.

7

Printed or impressed.

8

Printed.

9

(1) and (2) Marks of Kerr and Binns (1852–62). The second of these was used only on pieces of exceptional quality: the date (here '52' for 1852) was added in gold.

(3) and (4) Marks of the Royal Worcester Porcelain Company, founded in 1862 and still in existence. 'WORCESTER'

impressed sometimes appears with these.

(5) to (7) Marks of Grainger's factory, founded in 1801.

(8) Modern 'Grainger's' mark used by the Royal Worcester Porcelain Company.

(9) Mark of James Hadley, a rival modern Worcester firm started in 1896 and absorbed by the older company in 1905.

CAUGHLEY

('SALOPIAN')

S	*S*	*C*	*C*
In blue.	Printed in blue.	In blue or (rarely) in gold.	Printed in blue.
1	2	3	4

S ×	*C*	*C*	*C*
In blue.	In blue.	In blue.	Printed in blue.
5	6	7	8

			SALOPIAN
In blue.	In blue.	In blue.	Impressed.
9	10	11	12

Salopian		*3*	△
Impressed.	Impressed.	In blue.	In gold.
13	14	15	16

Nos. 6 to 8 are of course imitation Worcester marks. The fretted square is rarely seen, and if enamelled is likely to be a later addition.

No. 9 is transfer-printed on a Jug in the Watney collection.

No. 10 occurs on a powdered-blue plate in the Victoria and Albert Museum in combination with the mark '*Salopian*' impressed. Compare Bow (Nos. 16 and 17) and Worcester (No. 7) marks of this character.

No. 11 is an imitation of the Chantilly mark of a hunting horn. Its status as a Caughley mark is open to doubt; pieces so marked are by some thought to be Worcester rather than Caughley.

LIVERPOOL

In blue.	In blue.	Impressed mark.	Printed in red.
1	2	3	4

Nos. 1 and 2 occur on enamelled pieces of about 1765; see p. 304. Nos. 3 and 4 are marks of the Herculaneum Factory (about 1796–1840).

PINXTON

Pinxton.	**T**	**M**	⅄ 190
In gold.	Impressed.	Impressed.	In blue enamel.
1	2	3	4

P

↑

↑

In red or puce. In purple. In black. In red. In red.

5   6   7   8   9

The word '*Pinxton*' in full (No. 1) is rare, but occurs on a mug in the British Museum (No. XII. 1). The impressed capitals are usually early, the arrows late.

NANTGARW AND SWANSEA

NANT - GARW
C. W.

SWANSEA

SWANSEA

SWANSEA

Impressed.   Impressed.   Impressed.   Impressed.

1   2   3   4

SWANSEA

Swansea

DILLWYN & CO.
SWANSEA.

Printed in red or
other colour.

In gold or red,
rarely other colour.

Impressed.

5   6   7

BEVINGTON & CO.

Impressed.   Printed in red.

8   9

(1) Used at both Nantgarw and Swansea, and possibly also at Coalport on Billingsley's paste. The letters 'C.W.' (which are sometimes absent) most probably stand for 'China

400

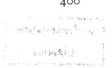

Works' and not for 'Cambrian Works' as asserted by Solon, since the mark was used before the transference of Billingsley's manufacture to Dillwyn's Cambrian Pottery at Swansea (see p. 314). Jewitt and Haslem both erroneously regarded the initials as those of 'George' Walker, but Billingsley's son-in-law was named Samuel. The word '*Nantgarw*' in red script characters is very rare, but is known to occur on old pieces believed to have been made at Coalport from a formula adapted from Billingsley's. Two examples figured by Nance appear to be in Billingsley's own handwriting. Herbert Eccles states that the word written in gold or colour occurs on later forgeries and imitations made at Coalport (*Swansea Exhibition Catalogue*, p. 23).

(2) to (6) Swansea marks, 1814–17: see p. 315.

(7) Two separate stamps. Rarely seen on porcelain but common on earthenware.

(8) Rare mark on Swansea china after 1817: see p. 316.

(9) On earthenware from the Glamorgan Pottery (Baker, Bevan and Irwin).

COALPORT

In blue.	Printed in red.	Impressed.	In blue.
1	2	3	4

GD	*Coalport*	*Coalport*	⊕
In blue.	In blue.	In gold.	In blue or gold.
5	6	7	8

(crossed mark)	(C mark)	⚓	(mark)
In blue enamel.	In blue enamel.	In gold.	In blue.
9	10	11	12

(mark)	(CSN mark)	COALPORT. A.D. 1750	ENGLAND (crown) COALPORT A.D.1750
In blue.	In gold.	Printed or painted.	Printed.
13	14	15	16

(1) *C.* 1800–20 on Willow Pattern Wares printed in pale blue, sometimes with the words 'C. Dale'.

(2) From 1820 onwards several versions occur.

(3) On table wares *c.* 1820–30.

(4) to (7) Second quarter of the nineteenth century.

(8) Middle of nineteenth century.

(9) to (13) Imitations of the Sèvres, Chelsea and Meissen marks. An *impressed* anchor is stated by Jewitt (vol. I, p. 290) to have been used at Coalport.

(14) From 1861 to *c.* 1875. The letters enclosed are the initials of the names of the factories claimed as absorbed—Caughley, Nantgarw and Swansea.

(15) About 1875–81.

(16) modern mark. The year in this, 1750, is the date of foundation claimed for the factory and not the date of the porcelain bearing the mark. Without the word 'ENGLAND', 1881–*c.* 1891.

The very rare early mark '*Coalbrookdale*' has been mentioned in the text (p. 328). Rather later marks include various forms of the abbreviation '*C. Dale*', as well as the names of the London dealers, Daniell and Sparks. A formal rose (for John or W. Rose) is also said to have been used.

Several printed marks incorporating the name of the factory and its proprietors were in use during the mid-nineteenth century.

PLYMOUTH

In blue, blue enamel,
red, or gold.

1

Incised through the glaze.

2

In blue.

3

No. 2 occurs on one of a set of vases and beakers in the Schreiber Collection (No. 710), the others of which are marked with No. 1.

'T' and 'T⁰' impressed (see p. 340) also occur.

BRISTOL

In blue enamel.

1

In blue enamel.

2

In underglaze blue
and blue enamel.

3

In blue
enamel.

4

In blue
enamel.

5

In red or
fired ink.

6

No. 3 has the crossed swords in underglaze blue, and the small cross in blue enamel.

No. 6 is one of the marks of a china-burner and repairer who added his name in enamel or ink to pieces he had mended with fusible vitreous cement. The name was sometimes spelt '*Coombs*', and dates between 1780 and 1805 were often added (see p. 382).

The 'T⁰' mark also occurs.

SWINTON (ROCKINGHAM FACTORY)

Rockingham Works
Brameld.

Printed in red or brown.

The griffin mark was used only after the factory began to be assisted by Earl Fitzwilliam in 1826. The word '*Royal*' prefixed to the name of the factory indicates a date after 1830. The words '*Manufacturer to the King*' naturally occur only up to the date of the death of William IV (1837). The name '*Brameld*' in relief on an applied medallion occurs (but rarely) in conjunction with the printed mark.

STAFFORDSHIRE

Adams: a Tunstall and Stoke family including four members named William Adams, made pottery of many kinds during the eighteenth and nineteenth centuries, notably jasper ware and blue-printed earthenware. About the second quarter of the nineteenth century porcelain made by Adams of Greenfield, Tunstall, was marked.

W A & S

Marks on 'ironstone' and other wares included the name of

the firm (which still exists) in full, sometimes with other matter.

Alcock: S. Alcock of Hill Top, of a firm established about 1830, made biscuit figures and other wares sometimes marked

S A & Co

or with the name in full, sometimes accompanied by devices suggesting the name of the service upon which they appear.

Ashworth, see *Mason.*

Booths, of Tunstall, a still-existing firm, sometimes marked its wares, which included modern copies in earthenware of Worcester china

T B & S

for T. Booth and Sons.

Bourne: The name of Charles Bourne of the Foley pottery is said to appear on porcelain of early nineteenth-century date.

Brownfield: W. Brownfield of Cobridge used the mark of the 'Staffordshire knot' (from the county arms), with the initials 'W B', on porcelain dating from the last third of the nineteenth century. The knot is, of course, common to many modern Staffordshire marks.

Copeland, see *Spode.*

Davenport, of Longport.

  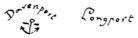

With the exception of No. 4 all are printed, usually in red.

Hilditch and Sons, of Longton, made porcelain about 1825–30 marked

Printed in red.

Mason:

M. MASON   MILES MASON

impressed, appear on porcelain in New Hall style of about
1800–20, and the imitation Chinese seal character given below
was also used on some early pieces.

Printed, usually in blue. Not to be confused with the similar Coalport mark
(see p. 401).

Mayer and Newbold of Lane End used their initials as a mark on
china dating from about 1835.

M & N

In red.

Mintons:

X m 780	M	Devon M&B	✳	MINTON
In blue. enamel.	In blue.	Printed.	Printed or impressed.	Impressed.
1	2	3	4	5

(1) and (2) are early marks, 1800–30.
(3) Minton and Boyle (1836–41).
(4) After 1851.
(5) After 1865.

Since 1842 certain signs have been used to indicate the year of manufacture. A list is given in G. W. Rhead's *British Pottery Marks* (London, 1910), page 181.

Neale: Porcelain figures and useful wares are occasionally found marked with the name of this Hanley firm.

NEALE & CO.

NEALE & WILSON impressed also occurs as a mark on a plate painted with fruit, of about 1790, in the Cardiff Museum.

New Hall:

N421

In red or crimson.   Printed in red.

1   2

(1) 1782 to about 1810.
(2) About 1810 to 1825.

The rampant lion of Frankenthal also occurs on some hard-paste blue-printed wares.

Patent Mark From 1842 to 1883 pottery designs could be registered at the Patent Office. In the following specimen marks, 'X' is a code-letter for the year of registration. A key to these code-letters is given in J. P. Cushion, *Pocket Book of British Ceramic Marks, including Index to Registered Designs 1842–83,* 1976, and G. A. Godden, *The Handbook of British Pottery and Porcelain Marks.* No. 1 was in use from 1842 to 1867, No. 2 from 1868 to 1883, after which the diamond was discontinued and a Registered Number only applied. (See p. 408.)

Ridgway: The firm of Ridgway of Cauldon Place, Stoke-on-Trent, flourished especially during the period of the management of

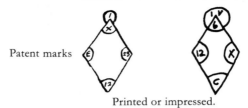

Patent marks

Printed or impressed.

John, a son of Job Ridgway, the founder, from 1814 to 1859. The name of the firm appeared in most of the marks. The following mark is typical of those in which the initials only are used. It dates from the period 1815–30.

India Temple
STONE CHINA
J.W.R

Printed.

Shorthose, of Hanley, a general potter, marked some printed porcelain of about 1800–23 as follows:

Spode and *Copeland*:

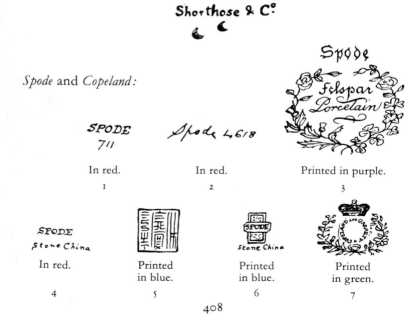

SPODE
711

In red.

1

Spode L.618

In red.

2

Spode
Felspar
Porcelain

Printed in purple.

3

SPODE
Stone China

In red.

4

Printed
in blue.

5

SPODE
Stone China

Printed
in blue.

6

Printed
in green.

7

(1) and (2) On various porcelain *c.* 1800–33; also printed in blue
 or impressed.
(3) Generally late: about 1825.
(4) to (6) First quarter of nineteenth century.
(7) 1833–47.

Turner of Lane End.

Turner's Patent

In red.

The mark above occurs on a crudely decorated stone-china
plate, of early nineteenth-century date, at South Kensington.
A mark on a porcelain bowl in the British Museum, '*Lane End
1787*' is probably Turner's; the mark 'Turner' impressed also
occurs on porcelain of the same period.

Wedgwood, of Etruria. Porcelain was made at Etruria only in the
early nineteenth century (see p. 370), never under the
management of the first Josiah Wedgwood.

WEDGWOOD

Printed, usually in red.

Wood, of Burslem. No mark on porcelain is unquestionably to be
associated with Aaron or Ralph Wood the elder, but the
following may refer to Ralph the younger or Enoch Wood
(see p. 357):

W(✳ ✳ ✳)

Impressed.

Appendix B

English Porcelain Bodies

Table showing the Ultimate Adoption of Bone-ash as an Ingredient in all the English Porcelain Bodies

Glassy porcelain: xxxxxxxxx
Soapstone porcelain: ooooooooo
Hard-paste porcelain: ....
Porcelain containing bone-ash: ———

	1745	1750	1755	1760	1765	1770	1775	1780	1785	1790	1795	1800	1810	1815	1820	1825
CHELSEA	xxxxxxxxxxxxxxxxxxx ———————															
BOW	xxxxx															
DERBY	xxxxxxxxxxxxxxxx ———————															
LONGTON HALL	xxxxxxxxx															
WORCESTER	oooooooooooooooooooooooooooooooooooooooooooooooooo															
LIVERPOOL																
CHAFFERS,	ooooooooooooo															
CHRISTIAN & PENNINGTON				oooooooooo												
GILBODY					———————											
BALL	ooooooooooo															
WOLFE							———————									
REID	oooooooo															
CAUGHLEY							oooooooooooooooooooooooooooooooo									
COALPORT											———————					
PINXTON										———————						
NANTGARW & SWANSEA														———————		
PLYMOUTH & BRISTOL							....									
NEW HALL													....			
SPODE AND LATER STAFFORDSHIRE																———————

410

Notes   (1) The very small percentage of phosphoric acid in the analysis of some Longton Hall specimens may be due to ingredients other than bone-ash, and in any case the paste is essentially glassy rather than of bone-ash type.

(2) The paste used after about 1800 in Staffordshire and elsewhere was a hybrid feldspathic porcelain containing china clay and bone-ash.

(3) Some early Chaffers porcelain seems to have been phosphatic, and the factory reverted to bone-ash shortly before Chaffers' soapstone mine was sold in 1775.

(4) Some wasters found at both Caughley and Coalport, principally of fluted wares, are of a hard body and belong to a period at the turn of the century. This body may have been made for a short time at either or both factories.

Locations of Collections referred to in the Text

Herbert Allen Collection	Victoria and Albert Museum
A. H. S. Bunford Collection	Sold at Sotheby's, 9 November 1934
C. H. B. Caldwell Collection	Part went into the Wallace Elliot Collection (see below). Blue and white sold at Sotheby's, 7 October 1969
Mrs. Dickson's Collection	Mostly, if not entirely, at the Fitzwilliam Museum, Cambridge
F. C. Dykes Collection	Now dispersed
Dyson Perrins Collection	Dyson Perrins Museum, Royal Worcester Porcelain Works, Worcester
Wallace Elliot Collection	Part at the Victoria and Albert Museum; part at the British Museum; remainder sold at Sotheby's, 24–6 May 1938
Lord and Lady Fisher Collection	Fitzwilliam Museum, Cambridge
C. T. Fowler Collection	Now dispersed
Dr. J. W. L. Glaisher	Fitzwilliam Museum, Cambridge

Frank Hurlbutt Collection	Sold at Sotheby's, 9 October 1945
Alfred Hutton Collection	Mostly in the Museum of Fine Arts, Boston, Massachusetts
Jermyn Street Collection	Transferred to the Victoria and Albert Museum
Frank Lloyd Collection	British Museum
Mr. and Mrs. Donald MacAlister's Collection	Part at the British Museum; part at the Victoria and Albert Museum
Mrs. Radford Collection	Sold at Sotheby's, 3–5 November 1943
Schreiber Collection	Victoria and Albert Museum
R. M. W. Walker Collection	Sold at Christie's, 18–19 July 1945

The present locations of the following collections, also mentioned in the text, have not been traced:

The S. W. Woodhouse, Egerton Leigh, Mrs. Esdaile, Leonard Middleditch, E. S. McEuen, and Glendenning collections.

Bibliography

<hr />

Since the appearance in 1948 of the second edition of this book, the literature on English porcelain has greatly grown in volume, reflecting not only the widening interest in antiques generally but also the considerable amount of research that has taken place in the field of ceramics. The situation in this respect is thus much more satisfactory than was the case when Mr. Honey was constrained to lament the lack of trustworthy books on the subject. The works listed in the earlier editions have therefore been supplemented with a number of these more recent publications.

The following list comprises most of the more important and readily accessible books. Some monographs have been included only for the sake of their illustrations; it will be understood, however, that the ascriptions attached to these cannot always be regarded as trustworthy guides to classification. Where an abbreviated title has been used in the course of the book it is added in brackets after the full title.

GENERAL WORKS

SHAW, SIMEON, *History of the Staffordshire Potteries*, 1829. Reprinted Newton Abbot, 1976.

JEWITT, LLEWELLYNN, *The Ceramic Art of Great Britain*, London, 1878. (Jewitt)

NIGHTINGALE, J. E., *Contributions towards the History of Early*

English Porcelain from Contemporary Sources, Salisbury, 1881. (Nightingale)

MUSEUM OF PRACTICAL GEOLOGY (Jermyn Street), *Handbook to the Collection of British Pottery and Porcelain*, London, 1893.

BEMROSE, W., *Bow, Chelsea and Derby Porcelain*, London, 1898.

BURTON, WILLIAM, *A History and Description of English Porcelain*, London, 1902.

CHURCH, SIR ARTHUR H., *English Porcelain*, London, 1904. (Church)

HOBSON, R. L., *Catalogue of the Collection of English Porcelain in the Department of British and Mediæval Antiquities in the British Museum*, London, 1905. (Hobson, *Catalogue*)

RHEAD, G. W., *British Pottery Marks*, London, 1910.

ECCLES, H., and RACKHAM, BERNARD, *Analysed Specimens of English Porcelain*, London, 1922. (*Analysed Specimens*)

RACKHAM, BERNARD, *Catalogue of the Herbert Allen Collection of English Porcelain*, 2nd edition, London, 1923. (*Herbert Allen Catalogue*)

KING, WILLIAM, *English Porcelain Figures of the Eighteenth Century*, London, 1925. (King, *Figures*)

RACKHAM, BERNARD, *Catalogue of the Schreiber Collection of English Porcelain, Earthenware, Enamels, etc.*, vol. I, 'Porcelain', 2nd edition, London, 1928. (*Schreiber Catalogue*)

ENGLISH PORCELAIN CIRCLE (later ENGLISH CERAMIC CIRCLE), TRANSACTIONS, 1928—. (*Transactions E.P.C.* and *Transactions E.C.C.*)

MACALISTER, MRS. DONALD (ed.), *William Duesbury's London Account Book: 1751–53*, London (English Porcelain Circle Monograph), 1931.

RACKHAM, BERNARD, *Catalogue of the Glaisher Collection (Fitzwilliam Museum, Cambridge)*, Cambridge, 1934.

HONEY, W. B., 'English Porcelain: some independent decorators', in *Apollo*, XXV (1937), p. 87.

HONEY, W. B., *English Pottery and Porcelain* (1947), 5th edition, revised by R. J. Charleston, London, 1962.

ENGLISH CERAMIC CIRCLE, *Catalogue of the 1948 Exhibition at the Victoria and Albert Museum*, London, 1949.

BEMROSE, GEOFFREY, *19th Century English Pottery and Porcelain*,

London, 1952.

DIXON, J. L., *English Porcelain of the 18th Century*, London 1952.

SAVAGE, GEORGE, *18th Century English Porcelain*, London 1952.

HACKENBROCH, YVONNE, *Chelsea and Other English Procelain . . . in the Irwin Untermyer Collection*, London, 1957.

CUSHION, J. P., *Pocket Book of British Ceramic Marks, including Index to Registered Designs 1842–83* (1959), 3rd edition, London, 1976

LANE, ARTHUR, *English Porcelain Figures of the 18th Century* London, 1961.

WATNEY, BERNARD, *English Blue and White Porcelain of the 18th Century* (1963), 2nd edition, London, 1973.

CHARLESTON, R. J. (ed.), *English Porcelain, 1745–1850*, London 1965.

GODDEN, G. A., *An Illustrated Encyclopaedia of British Pottery and Porcelain*, London, 1966.

RAY, ANTHONY (ed.), *English Delftware Tiles*, London, 1973.

CHELSEA

READ, RAPHAEL W., *A Reprint of the Original Catalogue of One Year's Curious Production of the Chelsea Porcelain Manufactory*, Salisbury 1880.

KING, WILLIAM, *Chelsea Porcelain*, London, 1922. (King)

BLUNT, REGINALD (ed.), *The Cheyne Book of Chelsea China*, London 1924 (*Cheyne Book*). Reprinted Wakefield, 1973.

BRYANT, G. E., *Chelsea Porcelain Toys*, London, 1925.

MACKENNA, F. S., *Chelsea Porcelain, the Triangle and Raised Anchor Wares*, Leigh-on-Sea, 1948.

MACKENNA, F. S., *Chelsea Porcelain, the Red Anchor Wares*, Leigh-on-Sea, 1951.

MACKENNA, F. S., *Chelsea Porcelain, the Gold Anchor Wares*, Leigh-on-Sea, 1952.

SYNGE-HUTCHINSON, PATRICK, 'G. D. Ehret's Botanical Designs on Chelsea Porcelain', in *The Connoisseur* (October 1958), pp. 88–94.

ᴸᴀɴᴇ, Aʀᴛʜᴜʀ, 'Chelsea Porcelain Figures and the Modeller Joseph Willems', in *The Connoisseur* CXLV (1960), pp. 245–51.

ᴸᴀɴᴇ, Aʀᴛʜᴜʀ, and Cʜᴀʀʟᴇsᴛᴏɴ, R. J., 'Girl-in-a-Swing Porcelain and Chelsea' in *Transactions E.C.C.*, vol. 5, part 3 (1962), pp. 111–44.

Mᴀʟʟᴇᴛ, J. V. G., *Upton House, the Bearsted Collection, Catalogue of Porcelain*, London, The National Trust, 1964.

BOW

Mᴇᴡ, Eɢᴀɴ, *Old Bow China*, London, 1909.

Hᴜʀʟʙᴜᴛᴛ, Fʀᴀɴᴋ, *Bow Porcelain*, London, 1927.

Tᴏᴘᴘɪɴ, Aᴜʙʀᴇʏ J., 'Bow Porcelain: some recent excavations', and 'Some early Bow Muses', in the *Burlington Magazine*, XL (1922), p. 224; and LIV (1928), p. 188.

Tᴀɪᴛ, Hᴜɢʜ, *British Museum Exhibition Catalogue, Bow Porcelain, 1744–1776*, London, 1959.

Tᴀɪᴛ, Hᴜɢʜ, 'Some Consequences of the Bow Porcelain Special Exhibition', in *Apollo*, February, April and June 1960.

Tᴀɪᴛ, Hᴜɢʜ, 'The Bow Factory under Alderman Arnold and Thomas Frye (1747–1759)', in *Transactions E.C.C.*, vol. 5, part 4 (1963), pp. 195–216.

Aᴅᴀᴍs, Eʟɪᴢᴀʙᴇᴛʜ, 'The Bow Insurances and Related Matters' in *Transactions E.C.C.*, vol. 9, part 1 (1970), pp. 67–108.

DERBY

Hᴀsʟᴇᴍ, Jᴏʜɴ, *The Old Derby China Factory*, London, 1876. (Haslem)

Hᴜʀʟʙᴜᴛᴛ, Fʀᴀɴᴋ, *Old Derby Porcelain and its Artist Workmen*, London, 1925.

MᴀᴄAʟɪsᴛᴇʀ, Mʀs. Dᴏɴᴀʟᴅ, 'The early work of Planché and Duesbury', in *Transactions E.P.C.*, vol. II (1929), p. 45.

Wɪʟʟɪᴀᴍsᴏɴ, F., *The Derby Pot Manufactory known as Cockpit Hill*, Derby, 1931.

Gɪʟʜᴇsᴘʏ, F. B., *Crown Derby Porcelain*, Leigh-on-Sea, 1951.

Gɪʟʜᴇsᴘʏ, F. B., *Derby Porcelain*, London, 1961.

BARRETT, F. A., and THORPE, A. L., *Derby Porcelain*, London, 1971

LONGTON HALL

BEMROSE, W., *Longton Hall Porcelain*, London, 1906.
MACALISTER, MRS. DONALD, 'Longton Hall Porcelain', in *Apollo* January 1927, and 'Early Staffordshire China' in *Transactions E.C.C.*, I (1933), p. 44.
WATNEY, BERNARD, *Longton Hall Porcelain*, London, 1957.

LOWESTOFT

SPELMAN, W. W. R., *Lowestoft China*, London and Norwich, 1905 (Spelman)
CRISP, F. A., *Lowestoft China Factory*, London, 1907.
KIDDELL, A. J. B., 'Inscribed and Dated Lowestoft Porcelain', in *Transactions E.P.C.*, vol. III (1931), p. 7.
KIDDELL, A. J. B., 'Richard Powles, Lowestoft Painter', in *Transactions E.C.C.*, vol. II, No. 7 (1939), pp. 112–14.
GODDEN, G. A., *Lowestoft Porcelain* (Illustrated Guide), London, 1969.
SMITH, SHEENAH, *Lowestoft Porcelain in the Norwich Castle Museum, vol. I Blue and White*, Norwich, 1976.

LUND'S BRISTOL FACTORY

POUNTNEY, W. J., *The Old Bristol Potteries*, London and Bristol, 1920. (Pountney)
ELLIOT, WALLACE, 'Soft Paste Bristol Porcelain', in *Transactions E.P.C.*, II (1929), p. 6.
TOPPIN, A. J., 'The Proprietors of the Early Bristol China Factory', in *Transactions E.C.C.*, vol. III, No. 2 (1954), pp. 129–40.
BARRETT, F. A., *Lund's Bristol and Worcester Porcelain*, London, 1966.

SANDON, HENRY, *Worcester Porcelain, 1751–1793* (Illustrated Guide), London, 1969.

WORCESTER

BINNS, R. W., *A Century of Potting in the City of Worcester*, London and Worcester, 1865. (Binns)

HOBSON, R. L., *Worcester Porcelain*, London, 1910.

HOBSON, R. L., *Catalogue of the Frank Lloyd Collection of Worcester Porcelain of the Wall Period*, London, 1923. (*Frank Lloyd Catalogue*)

ELLIOT, WALLACE, 'Worcester Porcelain Figures', in *Transactions E.C.C.*, II (1934), p. 29.

DYSON PERRINS, C. W., 'John Wall and the Worcester Porcelain Company', in *Transactions E.C.C.*, vol. II, No. 8 (1942), pp. 121–31.

MARSHALL, H. R., 'Armorial Worcester of the First Period', in *Transactions E.C.C.*, vol. II, No. 9 (1946), pp. 188–218.

COOK, CYRIL, *The Life and Work of Robert Hancock*, London, 1948; and Supplement, London and Tonbridge, 1955.

MACKENNA, F. S., *Worcester Porcelain*, Leigh-on-Sea, 1950.

MARSHALL, H. R., 'James Giles, Enameller', in *Transactions E.C.C.*, vol. III, No. 1 (1951).

MARSHALL, H. R., *Coloured Worcester Porcelain of the First Period*, Newport, 1954.

MARSHALL, H. R., 'Notes of the Origins of Worcester Decoration', in *Transactions E.C.C.*, vol. 4, No. 3 (1957), pp. 24–44.

TAIT, HUGH, 'James Rogers, a Leading Porcelain Painter at Worcester', in *The Connoisseur*, April 1962.

BARRETT, F. A., *Lund's Bristol and Worcester Porcelain*, London, 1966.

SANDON, HENRY, *Worcester Porcelain, 1751–1793* (Illustrated Guide), London, 1969.

GODDEN, G. A., *Caughley and Worcester Porcelains, 1775–1800*, London, 1969.

LEARY, EMMELINE, and WALTON, PETER, *Transfer-printed Worcester Porcelain at Manchester City Art Gallery*, Manchester, 1976.

CAUGHLEY

CLIFTON ROBERTS, C., in *The Connoisseur*, LIV (1919), p. 187; LV (1919), p. 223; and LVII (1920), p. 143.

HOBSON, R. L., in *Transactions E.P.C.*, III (1931), p. 66.

BARRETT, F. A., *Caughley and Coalport Porcelain*, Leigh-on-Sea, 1951.

GODDEN, G. A., *Caughley and Worcester Porcelain 1775–1800*, London, 1969.

SHREWSBURY ART GALLERY, *Catalogue of the Bi-centenary Exhibition of Caughley Porcelains*, Shrewsbury, 1972.

LIVERPOOL

GATTY, C. T., *The Liverpool Potteries*, Liverpool, 1882.

MAYER, J., *History of the Art of Pottery in Liverpool*, Liverpool, 1885.

ENTWISTLE, P., *Catalogue of Liverpool Pottery and Porcelain*, Liverpool, 1907.

RACKHAM, BERNARD, and HONEY, W. B., 'Liverpool Porcelain', in *Transactions E.P.C.*, vol. II (1929), p. 27.

NEILD, NEWMAN, 'Early Polychrome Transfer Porcelain', in *Transactions E.C.C.*, vol. I, No. 3 (1935).

STANLEY PRICE, E., *John Sadler*, Liverpool, 1948.

BONEY, KNOWLES, *Liverpool Porcelain*, London, 1957.

WATNEY, BERNARD, 'Four Groups of Porcelain, possibly Liverpool', in *Transactions E.C.C.*, vol. IV, part 5 (1959), pp. 13–25; vol. V, part 1 (1960), pp. 42–52.

WATNEY, BERNARD, 'The Porcelain of Chaffers, Christian and Pennington', in *Transactions E.C.C.*, vol. 5, part 5, pp. 269–82.

SMITH, ALAN, 'The Herculaneum China and Earthenware Manufactory Toxteth, Liverpool', in *Transactions E.C.C.*, vol. 7, part 1, pp. 16–38.

SMITH, ALAN, *Liverpool Herculaneum Pottery* (Illustrated Guide), London, 1969.

ADAMS, ELIZABETH, 'Towards a More Complete History of the Liverpool China Manufactory' in *Northern Ceramic Society Journal*, vol. 1 (1972–3), pp. 5–12.

PINXTON

EXLEY, C. L., *The Pinxton China Factory*, Derby, 1963.

NANTGARW AND SWANSEA

TURNER, WILLIAM, *The Ceramics of Swansea and Nantgarw*, London, 1897. (Turner)

SWANSEA, GLYNN VIVIAN ART GALLERY, *Catalogue of a Loan Exhibition, 1914. (Swansea Exhibition Catalogue)*

WILLIAMS, ISAAC J., *A Guide to the Collection of Welsh Porcelain* (National Museum of Wales), Cardiff and London, 1931.

NANCE, E. MORTON, *The Pottery and Porcelain of Swansea and Nantgarw*, London, 1942.

JOHN, W. D., *Nantgarw Porcelain*, Newport, 1948.

JOHN, W. D., *Nantgarw Porcelain* (supplement), Newport, 1956.

JOHN, W. D., *Swansea Porcelain*, Newport, 1958.

MEAGER, K. S., *Catalogue of Welsh Pottery and Porcelain at the Glynn Vivian Art Gallery, Swansea*, Swansea, 1949.

COALPORT

BARRETT, FRANKLIN A., *Caughley and Coalport Porcelain*, Leigh-on-Sea, 1951.

GODDEN, G. A., *Coalport and Coalbrookdale Porcelains*, London, 1970.

TRINDER, BARRIE, *The Industrial Revolution in Shropshire*, London, 1972.

PLYMOUTH AND BRISTOL
(COOKWORTHY AND CHAMPION)

OWEN, HUGH, *Two Centuries of Ceramic Art in Bristol*, London, 1873. (Owen)

POUNTNEY, W. J. (*see p. 418*).

RADFORD, LADY, 'Plymouth China', in *The Devonian Year Book*, 1920, p. 31.

HURLBUTT, F., *Bristol Porcelain*, London, 1928.

ELLIOT, WALLACE, 'Bristol Biscuit Placques' in *Transactions E.C.C.*, vol. I (1933).

MACKENNA, F. S., *Cookworthy's Plymouth and Bristol Porcelain*, Leigh-on-Sea, 1946.

MACKENNA, F. S., *Champion's Bristol Porcelain*, Leigh-on-Sea, 1947.

MACKENNA, F. S., 'William Stephens, Bristol China Painter' in *Transactions E.C.C.*, vol. 4, part 1 (1957).

BRISTOL PORCELAIN BI-CENTENARY CATALOGUE, *City Art Gallery*, Bristol, 1970.

MALLET, J. V. G., 'Cookworthy's First Bristol Factory of 1765' in *Transactions E.C.C.*, vol. 9, part 2 (1974).

SWINTON (ROCKINGHAM)

RICE, DENNIS, *Rockingham Porcelain* (Illustrated Guide), London, 1970.

STAFFORDSHIRE

DAVENPORT

LOCKETT, TERENCE, *Davenport Pottery and Porcelain*, Newton Abbot, 1972.

MASON'S

HAGGAR, REGINALD, *The Masons of Lane Delph*, London, 1952.

GODDEN, G. A., *Mason's Patent Ironstone China* (Illustrated Guide), London, 1971.

HAGGAR, REGINALD, and ADAMS, ELIZABETH, *Mason Porcelain and Ironstone, 1796–1853*, London, 1977.

MINTON

GODDEN, G. A., *Minton Pottery and Porcelain of the First Period, 1793–1850*, London, 1969.

NEW HALL

STRINGER, G. E., *New Hall Porcelain*, London, 1949.

HOLGATE, DAVID, *New Hall and its Imitators*, London, 1971.

HOLGATE, DAVID, 'Further thoughts on New Hall', in the *Northern Ceramic Society Journal*, vol. I (1972–3), pp. 59–62.

RIDGWAY

GODDEN, G. A., *Ridgway Porcelain*, London, 1972.

SPODE

HAYDEN, ARTHUR, *Spode and His Successors*, London, 1925.

WILLIAMS, S. B., *Antique Blue and White Spode*, London, 1949.

TAIT, HUGH, 'Spode and Copeland, a Regency Bowl dated Feby. 13th, 1813', in *The Connoisseur*, May 1970.

WHITER, L., *Spode*, London, 1970.

WIRKSWORTH

LOCKETT, TERENCE, 'The Wirksworth China Factory', in the *Northern Ceramic Society Journal*, vol. I (1972–3), pp. 45–57.

Index

Page references to plates are in italics

144

018 P